CRONYISM

Liberty versus Power in
Early America, 1607–1849

PATRICK NEWMAN

SPECIAL THANKS

This book would not have been possible
without the generous help of the following supporters:

Benefactors
Hunter Lewis and Elizabeth Sidamon-Eristoff
Mr. and Mrs. J. Ryan Alford
Juliana and Hunter Hastings
James Nardulli

Patrons
Steven R. Berger
Mr. and Mrs. Roger H. Box
Remy Demarest
Mr. and Mrs. Jule R. Herbert, Jr.
R. Anderson Hord III
James E. Kluttz
Russell C. Lemley
Jeff Leskovar
Jeffrey S. Skinner

Donors
Jean Angle
Anonymous
Dr. John Bartel
Jon Carnes
Brandon Combs
Kenneth Deitz
Julian Fondren
Explorers Foundation, Inc.
Charles F. Hanes
Sheldon Hayer
Nathan Hines
Rachel Kennerly
Kenneth King
Mr. and Mrs. Nathan J. Kleffman
Jeremy S. Levy, In memory of my grandfather, Peter Surzycia
Dr. Qian Li
Captain M.A. Malagón-Fajar, USN retired, In memory of Manuel Fajar Rodriguez [1904–1974]
Thomas S. Nunn III
John Olsen
Jorge F. Roca Arteta
Dr. and Mrs. Murray Sabrin
Steven M. Sadler
Roy H. Simmen, Jr., Florida Southern College Class of 1989
Carlton M. Smith
Dr. James Speights
Dirck Storm
Emanuel Strategos
Joseph Vierra
Mr. and Mrs. Jonathan J. Wilcox

CRONYISM

Liberty versus Power in
Early America, 1607–1849

PATRICK NEWMAN

MISESINSTITUTE

AUBURN, ALABAMA

Cover design by Dani Wallace.

Mises Institute
518 West Magnolia Ave.
Auburn, Ala. 36832
mises.org
contact@mises.org

ISBN 978-1-61016-738-3

To

Murray N. Rothbard

I cannot accept your canon that we are to judge Pope and King unlike other men, with a favourable presumption that they did no wrong. If there is any presumption it is the other way against holders of power, increasing as the power increases. . . . Power tends to corrupt and absolute power corrupts absolutely.

LORD ACTON, 1887

TABLE OF CONTENTS

ACKNOWLEDGEMENTS

Hunter Lewis of Axios Press inspired me to write *Cronyism*. In the spring of 2019 he generously provided a research grant to write the history of crony capitalism in America. As I started working, I realized that to accurately describe the history of cronyism I needed to spend a significant amount of time on early United States history, when reformers made the greatest strides toward nipping special privileges in the bud. I hope this work is up to his standards.

I would also like to thank Dr. Joseph Salerno, my intellectual mentor and the academic Vice President of the Mises Institute, and Jeff Deist, President of the Mises Institute, for publishing this book. Since my first Mises Summer Fellowship in 2012, Joe has continually inspired me to write in the Austrian tradition. Similarly, Jeff vigorously promotes and encourages my research. The Mises Institute provides a great network for young scholars such as myself, and I immensely enjoyed spending the summers of 2019 and 2020 in Auburn working on *Cronyism*.

Chris Calton, a graduate student in the history PhD program at the University of Florida, played an indispensable role. Chris commented on multiple manuscripts and encouraged me to clarify my ideas, rewrite sections, and improve my narrative. There is no doubt that Chris' editorial suggestions significantly improved the final product. I would also like to thank Timothy Blanton, Robert Bradley, Tate Fegley, Richard Garber, Jeffrey Rogers Hummel, Tyler Kubik, Karras Lambert, Julia Norgaard, and Roy Simmens for commenting on earlier drafts. Lastly, Judy Thommesen and Daniella Bassi corrected typographical errors and prepared the book for publication. All errors, of course, are entirely my own.

Above all, I must give profound thanks to a man I have never met, Murray Rothbard, who provided both my thesis and narrative. I have built my academic career on Rothbard's writings, and this book is no exception. I dedicate it to him, Mr. Austro-Libertarian.

INTRODUCTION

The present book is an economic and political history of early America, describing government policies and their effects on marketplace activity. In particular, it is a history of cronyism: when the government passes policies to benefit special-interest politicians, bureaucrats, businesses, and other groups at the expense of the general public. Examples include a central bank's selective credit expansion, discriminatory taxes and regulations, business subsidies, territorial acquisitions and other foreign policy maneuvers, and new constitutions. The rewards of cronyism take the form of monetary gains, particularly increased incomes and profits for individuals and businesses, or psychic gains from greater power and authority. The government's claim that it passed legislation to enhance the public welfare is only a thin veneer for privileges and redistribution.

Special-interest legislation is inherent in the very nature of government. On the free market, the network of voluntary exchanges, all activity is based on individual liberty and results in mutually beneficial outcomes. The competitive profit and loss mechanism incentivizes individuals to produce goods and services that consumers desire. However, the government, the legitimated monopoly of power, lacks this mechanism and produces outcomes that are harmful to society. The incentive structure is different: unlike the Invisible Hand of the market, individuals that control the coercive Visible Hand are encouraged to pass legislation that benefits them at the expense of others. The stronger the government, the more lucrative the rewards. To control the government machinery is to control the levers of cronyism.

Researchers have analyzed American special privileges before, but their studies focus on individual cases in select time periods that remain unintegrated into an overarching narrative. There is still a need for an overview of cronyism that covers the motivations behind and development of relevant policies, their effects on the economy, and the critical attempts to reform the system. To achieve this goal, I utilize the "Liberty versus Power" theory, developed by Murray

RETALITORY RESTITUTIVE

Rothbard in his five-volume *Conceived in Liberty* series. It contains three core components.[1]

First, history is a clash between the forces of liberty, or those in favor of individual decision-making and the market allocating resources, and the proponents of power, the factions that support coercion and government organization of production. Libertarians want to reduce government power to limit cronyism while statists strive for the opposite. Favoritism is limited when a substantial interest with an ideological and pecuniary incentive to promote freedom exists. Otherwise, only clashing groups that want to control power mitigate special privileges. The liberty and power forces, with a spectrum in between, continually define the evolution of a government's interference with the free society. When liberty triumphs over power, cronyism is reduced; when the opposite occurs, privileges increase.

Second, those who control the government's power are corrupted over time. To quote Lord Acton, "[P]ower tends to corrupt and absolute power corrupts absolutely."[2,3] I define corruption as the willingness of government officials to push for interventions that benefit themselves and other favored interests. Coercion and the use of force increase the ability to dispense favors, which incentivizes corruption. While there is often a strong moral element to corruption, my primary focus is the increased inducement to secure special-interest policies. Lord Acton's famous quote can be modified accordingly: "Power tends to incentivize cronyism and absolute power incentivizes cronyism absolutely." Cronyism is due to the corrupting nature of government power and only by eliminating it can society destroy such favoritism.

Third, reforms that eliminate restrictions and redistributions are difficult to achieve because they require smaller government. This can only be accomplished through an outside amputation of power, particularly secession, or a change in the administrative leadership that internally dismantles the government's power. The problem with

---

[1] Murray N. Rothbard, *Conceived in Liberty*, vols. 1–4 (Auburn, AL: Mises Institute 2019); Murray N. Rothbard, *Conceived in Liberty*, vol. 5, *The New Republic, 1784–1791*, ed. Patrick Newman (Auburn, AL: Mises Institute, 2019).

[2] John Acton, *Essays on Freedom and Power* (New York: A Meridian Book, 1955), p. 335.

[3] Unless otherwise noted, all spelling, punctuation, and italics in quotations are taken from the cited source

reform, internal or external, is that any attempt requires laissez-faire proponents to use the coercive structure to enact their preferred policies. However, power tends to corrupt, which means that the previous advocates of freedom ineluctably start to pass their own special privileges. Radicals lose sight of their original goals, moderates stress the need to compromise with the opposition, and political office increases the incentive to provide favors to supporters. Soon the temptation to grant cronyism becomes irresistible. While in office, the libertarian faction transforms into a new coalition indistinguishable from the former statist party.

My thesis is the following: in early American history, special privileges increased in a staggered fashion and the Liberty versus Power theory explains this evolution. A majority of the population adhered to a basic libertarian ideology while the remainder supported big government. When the interventionist parties, i.e., the Federalists, National Republicans, and Whigs, secured control, cronyism shot upward. When the people elected the reform parties—the Antifederalists, Republicans, and Democrats—cronyism declined before increasing due to the corrupting nature of power. The ultimate driver of privileges on both sides was the insatiable urge to create an empire, a territorially vast and influential country. Statists wanted to replicate the European empires that easily facilitated cronyism. In stark contrast, libertarians envisioned their empire consisting of small independent governments that shared classical liberal values. However, power and the lure of territorial acquisition corrupted the libertarian parties into creating the same belligerent empires they previously weakened. Therefore, cronyism increased in a nonlinear fashion.

To prove my thesis, I describe the history of special-interest legislation over the backdrop of political history. My narrative concentrates on the motivations of the major "players," or America's "Great Men"—the politicians and businessmen involved in the legislative process—and their attempts at reform. As a result, my work is "a throwback to a traditional approach to politics, focusing on elections, parties, and the maneuvering of elite white males in government."[4] By utilizing the Liberty versus Power theory and a political narrative that stresses the Great Man perspective, I have intentionally made

---

[4] Gordon Wood, *Empire of Liberty* (New York: Oxford University Press, 2009), p. 741.

this work "old fashioned," and deservedly so, given that the goal is to accurately study American cronyism.[5]

Cronyism: Liberty versus Power in Early America, 1607–1849 starts with Jamestown in 1607 and finishes with the election of 1848. It is broken down into the following five parts.

"Part I: The Road to Empire, 1607–1790" covers the American colonies to the US Constitution. It intentionally relies on Rothbard's writings, particularly *Conceived in Liberty*. Chapter 1 describes how the Old Order Empire of England failed to impose mercantilism and feudalism over the New World. Consequently, the thirteen colonies imbibed the Enlightenment's radical theories, developing a basic libertarianism that recognized individualism, natural rights, and private property. Classical liberal colonists that supported radical change and decentralization fought reactionary defenders of the status quo and government power, particularly over declaring independence from Great Britain. As chapter 2 explains, during the American Revolutionary War the radicals exercised the preeminently decentralist reform of secession. However, Pennsylvania's merchant prince Robert Morris and other nationalists tried to institute an Old Order American Empire through the formidable Articles of Confederation. The nationalists hoped that their new empire would centralize government power, weaken the independent states, and facilitate special privileges, particularly a central bank and assumption of debts held by speculators.

While the reactionaries narrowly failed during the war, after the conflict ended they engineered a second movement through the Constitution under the guise of Federalism. This is the focus of chapter 3. Virginia's James Madison and Alexander Hamilton of New York led the Federalists. The Antifederalists, commanded by George Clinton of New York and Patrick Henry of Virginia, bitterly opposed the new dispensation, correctly recognizing that the proposed power-aggrandizing polity was antithetical to the ideals they fought for during the Revolution. Despite the Antifederalists' resistance, the Federalists utilized dirty political tactics and imposed their new government on the United States. While the ostensible leader was President George Washington of Virginia, Congressman Madison arranged the major policies behind

---

[5] Joseph T. Salerno, "Introduction," in Murray N. Rothbard, *A History of Money and Banking in the United States*, ed. Joseph T. Salerno (Auburn, AL: Mises Institute, 2002), pp. 7–43.

the scenes. Madison strengthened the new government, particularly with a weak Bill of Rights that imposed few structural limitations upon the Constitution.

"Part II: The Hamiltonian Era, 1790–1801" continues the narrative into the early years of the new republic. As explained in chapter 4, Secretary of the Treasury Hamilton alienated Madison by using the Constitution to push for crony policies that benefitted Morris and other northern Federalist elites, such as assuming public debts, enacting the Bank of the United States, and protecting land speculators. In response to Hamilton's program, Madison opportunistically allied with the radical-moderate Thomas Jefferson of Virginia and disgruntled Antifederalists. Chapter 5 narrates how Hamilton and New England's Essex Junto merchants secured a military program that moved the country towards their cherished goal of an American Empire. The Federalists suppressed resistance to taxes that financed their special-interest policies, expanded the territorial domain, and encouraged the Quasi-War with France to monopolize international commerce. By the end of the decade, Inspector General Hamilton was dangerously close to leading the long-awaited empire.

To defeat the Hamiltonian Federalists' power grab, libertarians formed the Republican Party. This is the subject of chapter 6. The new coalition, composed of former Antifederalists and alienated Federalists, strategically interpreted the Constitution strictly to stop the Federalists' machinations. They enshrined their states' rights philosophy, the compact theory, in the "Spirit of 1798." During the Revolution of 1800, the people rose up, drove the increasingly unpopular Federalists from office, and elected Jefferson president.

However, just when the Republicans thought they could roll back cronyism, power corrupted them and warped Jefferson's dream for an "Empire of Liberty" into an Old Order Empire. "Part III: The Failed Jeffersonian Revolution, 1801–1817" analyzes the presidential administrations of Jefferson and Madison. With the Federalist Party out of the picture, the Jeffersonian Republicans split into two groups: Madison's ex-Federalist moderate Republicans and the Antifederalist Old Republicans led by the Virginian John Randolph. In the middle stood President Jefferson. Chapter 7 documents the ways in which power corrupted the Republicans into moderation during the early years of Jefferson's administration. They secured some notable reforms, such as over the judiciary system and spending, but did not go as far as the

Old Republicans desired because moderates wanted to court the opposition Federalists.

Despite the efforts of Randolph, chapter 8 shows that power soon corrupted the Republicans to pursue outright cronyism. The 1803 Louisiana Purchase and its massive territorial acquisition incentivized the Republicans to compromise on speculative land grants, pursue foreign policy maneuvers in Spanish Florida, support internal improvements to bind the country together, and engage in bellicose trade relations to protect commerce and conquer Canada and Florida. Chapter 9 narrates the final stage of the corruption process: the Madison administration created an Empire of Power by aggressively encouraging conflict against Great Britain. After the War of 1812, the new National Republicans adopted the old Federalist cronyism, including the Second Bank of the United States (SBUS) and protective tariffs. With the National Republicans' embrace of Federalist policies, the Jeffersonian Revolution ended in a resounding failure.

"Part IV: The Era of Corruption, 1817–1829" focuses on the aftermath. It explains the National Republicans' adoption of the "American System" to strengthen the Madisonian empire, which advocated monetary nationalization, manufacturing subsidies, federally funded internal improvements, increased congressional interference with newly formed states, and imperialistic aggression. Major beneficiaries included the Philadelphia financial elite and the commercial Boston Associates. However, as explained in chapter 10, Congressman Henry Clay of Kentucky, Massachusetts' Congressman Daniel Webster, and Secretary of State John Quincy Adams only partially implemented the American System. This setback resulted from the Panic of 1819, caused by the Second Bank of the United States' (SBUS) reckless credit expansion. Chapter 11 documents how the resultant downturn increased opposition to the American System and exposed sectional animosities, interfering with National Republicans' plans to enact protective tariffs and public works. Chapter 12 shows the ways in which the panic bled into disputes over slavery and the National Republicans' foreign policy of imperialism. Despite the Panic of 1819, slowly but surely the National Republicans fastened the American System upon the country.

Consequently, New York's senator Martin Van Buren organized a new libertarian coalition, the Democratic Party, to cripple the American System. This is the subject of chapter 13. The Corrupt Bargain of 1825, when Clay helped Adams win the presidency in an overtime House election, especially motivated Van Buren to create his new party. Andrew Jackson of Tennessee, Van Buren's standard bearer, denied Adams' reelection in the Revolution of 1828.

"Part V: The Failed Jacksonian Revolution, 1829–1849" finishes the narrative. From the presidential administrations of Jackson to James K. Polk of Tennessee, the Democrats strove to destroy the American System despite furious Whig opposition. The Jacksonians succeeded where the Jeffersonians failed because of their radical free market ideology and determination to not work with the opposition. Chapter 14 explains how the Jacksonians transformed the executive branch to eliminate the SBUS and institute the independent Treasury. As described in chapter 15, the Democrats also used presidential power to move the country toward free trade, pay down the national debt, and reduce internal improvements spending, thereby weakening the American Empire.

But power corrupts, and what happened to the Republicans also afflicted the Democrats. This is the subject of chapter 16. The executive branch's burgeoning power incentivized the Jacksonians to belligerently expand the empire to monopolize world commerce, a goal of expansionist southerners and northern businessmen. This portended an explosive situation regarding the growing slavery controversy, an issue largely absent from earlier political debates. Jackson and Van Buren pursued a peaceful foreign policy in the 1830s, but in 1844 they split over Texas annexation and its implications for slavery and war against Mexico. President Polk used annexation as a pretext for conquering California ports during the Mexican War, a goal internationalist merchants and manufacturers had long desired. By the end, the Democratic Party's laissez-faire creed was irrevocably extinguished. The Jacksonian Revolution was another deafening failure for liberty and anti-cronyism.

PART I

THE ROAD TO EMPIRE,
1607–1790

CHAPTER 1

THE PATH TO AMERICAN INDEPENDENCE

England Charters the Colonies

United States history began in the seventeenth century with European colonization, particularly by Old Order England. The Old Order referred to the combination of absolutism, the ideology that the divine monarch could lord over the people; mercantilism, the economic philosophy that advocated special privileges; and feudalism, the system that tied the monarch's subjects to the land. Absolutism ensured mass obedience, while mercantilism and feudalism created important allies and a hierarchical caste system. To strengthen this dispensation, the monarch allied the throne and altar by promoting the established church and mercantilist theorists to court intellectuals. In short, the unrepentant cronyism of the Old Order concentrated power in the monarch, feudal landlords, privileged merchants, the royal bureaucracy, and the church against the laborers, peasants, artisans, and discriminated religious groups.

In the late sixteenth century, Queen Elizabeth controlled England with mercantilist policies. Monopoly grants restricted competition, usually through a corporate charter. In addition to any explicit monopoly granted, the contemporary corporate charter was a license: to use the corporate form and the benefits of limited liability, a company had to acquire a legislative charter. Businessmen bribed the Crown to obtain monopoly charters for goods such as coal, soap, iron, and leather. This resulted in higher prices and a decrease in quality, benefitting only the Crown and privileged company.[1]

---

[1] Brian Murphy, *Building the Empire State* (Philadelphia: University of Pennsylvania Press, 2015), pp. ix–xi; Murray N. Rothbard, *An Austrian Perspective on the History of Economic Thought*, vol. 1, *Economic Thought Before Adam Smith* (Auburn, AL: Mises Institute 2006), pp. 221–26; Murray N. Rothbard, *Conceived in Liberty*, vols. 1–4 (Auburn, AL: Mises Institute 2019), pp. 5–31; Murray N. Rothbard, "Mercantilism," in *Economic Controversies* (Auburn, AL: Mises Institute, 2011), pp. 649–51.

When King James I assumed the throne in 1603, he accentuated the Elizabethan system, envisioning the colonies as appendages and extensions of the Old Order. James expected the colonies to provide living space for recalcitrant subjects to work on feudal estates and produce raw materials under rigid taxes, regulations, and licenses. In other words, James conceived of the colonies as the beginning of a new grandiose empire.

The Crown created the colonies through special privilege, blatantly neglecting the rights of European homesteaders. England also discarded Indian rights. This aggression occurred because the natives, in addition to the land they farmed, claimed ownership of large tracts of unused land they only hunted on.[2]

In 1606 James chartered the North Virginia Company and the South Virginia Company, named after the Virgin Queen. Each corporation possessed separate monopoly grants to unappropriated land. James gifted the North Virginia Company (soon called the Plymouth Company) the area from modern New York to Maine, while he granted the South Virginia Company (soon called the Virginia Company) a tract from modern North Carolina to Virginia. In 1609, James egregiously extended ownership of the latter from "sea to sea"—to the other side of the continent.[3] In addition, he assigned the lands between the companies to the first claimant, but when the Dutch later settled the land, England confiscated it through war.

In 1607, the Virginia Company established Jamestown. However, the colony's success was short lived and James dissolved the Company after it failed during the depression of the 1620s. He made Virginia a royal colony, appointing the governor and upper legislature. In 1632 King Charles I granted part of northern Virginia to *one* individual, Lord Baltimore, who wielded feudalistic control over the residents. It was named Maryland after Charles I's wife. In 1663 King Charles II expanded the southern border, awarding a feudal grant to eight favored supporters. This colony was named Carolina after Charles I.[4]

In the colonies, feudal manors exported agricultural commodities, such as tobacco and later rice, to England. Oligarchical planters

---

[2] Rothbard, *Conceived in Liberty,* 1–4, pp. 31, 36–39, 85, 552; Carl Watner, "Libertarians and Indians," *Journal of Libertarian Studies* (1983): 147–56.

[3] Rothbard, *Conceived in Liberty,* 1–4, p. 48.

[4] Ibid., pp. 29, 31–35, 43–54, 104–15, 156.

received arbitrary land grants and imposed a system of land taxes (quitrents) upon the actual homesteading settlers. Taxes and restrictions heavily regulated agriculture. For a cheap supply of labor the plantations imported indentured slaves from England. Significantly, planters also augmented the business of corrupt African chieftains involved in the slave trade. The labor system required a panoply of subsidies to stop escaping and revolting slaves. Among others, the colonies conscripted patrols to catch runaways and put down rebellions, regulated slave meetings and travels, required the return of fugitive slaves, and restricted voluntary manumissions. England assisted by incorporating the Royal African Company with a monopoly over African land and the slave trade. Colonial feudalism, from the land grants to the coerced workforce, embodied cronyism.[5]

Although the Plymouth Company made little progress in colonization, the Pilgrims established Plymouth in 1620, and Charles I chartered the Massachusetts Bay Company for exiled Puritans in 1629. In the mid-1630s, the settlements acquired self-governance after wealthy colonists bought control from the English owners. However, this hardly meant freedom for the individual settlers, because stock ownership guaranteed arbitrary land grants. A theocratic and oligarchical elite quickly amassed power, fastening domestic mercantilism on hapless settlers. Elites implemented maximum wage controls to ensure cheap labor and limit upward mobility; subsidized and monopolized various industries such as fur, iron, salt, and textiles; and passed debtor laws to benefit wealthy borrowers. The oligarchs also sanctioned slavery, systematically cleared out Indians, and privileged the Puritan church to create a new alliance of throne and altar.[6]

Despite these privileges in Virginia and Massachusetts, England maintained the upper hand. The King and Parliament enacted various navigation acts to benefit English commercial interests, particularly shippers and shipbuilders. The 1650 Navigation Act required a restrictionist license for foreign shippers trading with the colonies, and the 1660 Navigation Act accelerated this with a virtual monopoly to English shippers. The 1663 Navigation Act prohibited colonial

---

[5] Andrew P. Napolitano, *Dred Scott's Revenge* (Nashville, TN: Thomas Nelson, 2009), pp. 1–24; Rothbard, *Conceived in Liberty*, 1–4, pp. 55–103, 516–18, 532–33, 542–44, 584–86, 595–98, 714.

[6] Rothbard, *Conceived in Liberty*, 1–4, pp. 145–71, 217–19, 227–56; Rothbard, "Mercantilism," pp. 651–52.

imports that did not first pass through English ports, and the 1673 Navigation Act instituted a tax on tobacco shipped between colonies. Elites designed these laws to ensure the colonies' commerce worked for their benefit: artificially low prices on exports subsidized English industry at the expense of Dutch competition. English cronyism layered over colonial cronyism.[7]

Despite the feudalism, mercantilism, and pledged loyalty to the Crown, the Old Order never secured absolute hold and the imposed restrictions failed. First, the ruling class failed to enforce colonial feudalism because of the distance and sheer abundance of land, which allowed settlers to avoid paying quitrents on their homesteaded farms. In some cases, colonists created entirely new settlements free from control, such as Rhode Island in the 1630s. Moreover, natural homesteading instilled the colonists with a rudimentary understanding of private property rights, making them averse to government encroachment.[8]

Second, the Old Order failed to enforce the Navigation Acts because of English turmoil culminating in the Glorious Revolution of 1688. In addition, related wars with France, Spain, and the Dutch Republic hampered oversight. Smuggling outside of English jurisdiction became rampant.[9]

Third, whenever the elites managed to enforce cronyism, the settlers rebelled, the most basic form of resistance. Colonists directed the rebellions against both the local state and the Crown. However, while the rebels possessed classical liberal orientations, they failed because the reins of coercion corrupted the leadership into supporting power-aggrandizing policies. Bacon's Rebellion in 1676, named after the Virginian Nathaniel Bacon, was a prominent example. Although the desire to take land the Indians claimed partially motivated the rebels, they also criticized special-interest legislation. After Bacon secured Jamestown, he enacted new democratic reforms to weaken the ruling oligarchy. But, shortly thereafter, Bacon morphed into a despot and alienated his supporters before suddenly dying. Bacon's Rebellion ended in failure.[10]

---

[7] Rothbard, *Conceived in Liberty*, 1–4, pp. 77–79, 763–64.

[8] Ibid., pp. 36–39, 172–207, 497–99.

[9] Ibid., pp. 121–33, 157, 313, 413–27, 704.

[10] Ibid., pp. 85–103, 500–502.

Therefore, by the beginning of the eighteenth century the Old Order maintained control. English mercantilism and feudalism still gripped the colonies.

The Enlightenment and Salutary Neglect

By the mid-eighteenth century, the governing bodies that became the thirteen states had emerged. Colonists established Virginia, Maryland, North and South Carolina, and Georgia in the South; New York, New Jersey, Pennsylvania, and Delaware in the Mid-Atlantic; and Massachusetts, Rhode Island, Connecticut, and New Hampshire in New England. The Old Order of Great Britain (in 1707 England merged with Scotland) had cleaned up its internal affairs to become the rising imperial superpower. Although the Glorious Revolution of 1688 destroyed absolutism, the king still exerted enormous influence over Parliament through patronage. In addition, the clergy and mercantilist theorists spun crucial apologia for British depredations.[11]

Parliament passed new navigation acts, such as the monopolistic 1696 Navigation Act, tightening the enforcement of previous regulations. The 1699 Wool Act prohibited wool exports from one colony to another, ensuring artificially low prices for England's wool manufacturers. The 1705 Naval Stores Act and the 1711 and 1712 White Pine Acts instituted regulations over forests and siphoned lumber to British shipbuilders. The 1732 Hat Act protected British hat makers, the 1733 Molasses Act's taxes protected British West Indies molasses producers at the expense of those in the French West Indies, and the 1750 Iron Act restricted colonial iron production to subsidize British iron manufacturers.

However, rampant smuggling and black market production continued. When the Whig King George I succeeded the Tory Queen Anne in 1714, he appointed Robert Walpole as chief minister of his Privy Council and in effect Britain's first prime minister. Walpole chose the Duke of Newcastle, Thomas Pelham, for the Secretary of State for the Southern Department, which oversaw the colonies. The pro-peace and pro-market Walpole and Newcastle ironically presided over a centrist Whig Party that espoused mercantilist and expansionist policies, a stark contrast to the traditionalist and absolutist Tory Party. Walpole and Newcastle astutely realized that prosperous colonies benefitted

---

[11] R.R. Palmer and Joel Colton, *A History of the Modern World* (New York: McGraw-Hill, 1995), p. 179; Rothbard, *Conceived in Liberty*, 1–4, pp. 501, 605–18, 654–56, 700–01.

England. Contemporaries later described their philosophy of leaving the colonies alone as "salutary neglect."[12] Through political manipulation and patronage, Walpole and Newcastle deliberately refused to enforce the Navigation Acts.[13]

Salutary neglect dovetailed with the burgeoning religious liberalization and libertarian ideology that flourished during the mid-eighteenth century. The Enlightenment that swept the colonies stressed man's inner reason and ability to discover the world's natural laws. This new perspective encouraged individuals to seek out freedom to improve their social standing, radicalizing the colonists against British cronyism.

A prominent Enlightenment thinker was the English theoretician John Locke. Momentously, the natural-rights philosopher argued in his libertarian *Two Treatises of Government* (1689) that the people were not inexorably bound to their rulers. The radical Whigs John Trenchard and Thomas Gordon preached the Lockean creed to the public through *Cato's Letters* (1719–23). Against Old Order propaganda, they forcefully exposed governments as the source of power and privilege in society. Brilliantly describing how power corrupts rulers into expanding their control, Trenchard and Gordon reasoned that only strict laws and constitutions with enumeration can limit such power. For Trenchard and Gordon, the history of mankind was a titanic struggle between the people's liberty and the rulers' power. Their ideological writings infused the colonists with libertarianism, and writers soon praised liberty as the source of human flourishing and castigated power as a cancerous tumor. The solution to their problems, the colonists reasoned, was to embrace freedom and eradicate coercion.

Consequently, *Cato's Letters* aggravated the growing battle between the colonists and their governments. By the mid-eighteenth century, most political structures consisted of a royally appointed governor and his council (the upper legislature) and a democratically elected assembly (the lower legislature). The governor and council represented the reactionary oligarchs in favor of feudalism and mercantilism. The oligarchs wanted policies and officials to be remote from the people, defending the governor's ability to protect cronyism through

---

[12] Rothbard, *Conceived in Liberty*, 1–4, p. 705.

[13] Thomas J. DiLorenzo, *How Capitalism Saved America* (New York: Crown Forum, 2004), pp. 64–69; Rothbard, *Austrian Perspective on the History of Economic Thought*, 1, p. 340; Rothbard, *Conceived in Liberty*, 1–4, pp. 703–12.

his veto power and the bicameral legislature's extra layer of gridlock in the upper chamber. On the other hand, the democratically elected assembly represented the radicals in favor of greater freedom. The radicals supported short terms for elected officials, rotation in office, and the lower chamber to weaken the political oligarchy. The political and ideological landscape had drastically changed from just a few decades prior.[14]

Monetary Mercantilism

This philosophical revolution does not imply that the colonies adhered to pure salutary neglect, or "laissez-faire." The colonists' libertarianism was inchoate and Old Order mercantilism percolated through it. One extremely important example is monetary intervention.

Mercantilists, besides advocating business privileges, argued that a country's wealth is associated with the specie (gold and silver) accumulated through a favorable trade balance. These writers, John Law in particular, advocated increasing (inflating) the money supply to stimulate economic activity. Even classical liberal Enlightenment thinkers, such as David Hume, endorsed similar fallacies. Correspondingly, England forbade colonial mints and the exporting of "hard money" specie to her satellites. The colonists responded by importing foreign coins, particularly the Spanish silver dollar, though they still used England's silver pound for accounting purposes. The colonial governments also printed paper money, or "soft money," to expand their money supplies, beginning with Massachusetts in 1690. The colonies linked their irredeemable money to specie through promises of future redeemability and taxes. In addition, they forced the public to accept the money through legal tender laws. This initiated Gresham's Law—overvalued paper money drove out undervalued hard money from circulation.[15]

---

[14] Bernard Bailyn, *The Ideological Origins of the American Revolution* (Cambridge, MA: Harvard University Press, 2017), pp. 55–59; Ronald Hamowy, "Foreword," in *The English Libertarian Heritage*, ed. David Jacobson (San Francisco: Fox & Wilkes, 1994), pp. vii–ix; Rothbard, *Conceived in Liberty*, 1–4, pp. 654–71, 684–96, 699–702, 1239–43.

[15] Jeffrey Rogers Hummel, "Mises, the Regression Theorem, and Free Banking," *Liberty Matters* (January 2014); Murray N. Rothbard, *An Austrian Perspective of Economic Thought*, vol. 2, *Classical Economics* (Auburn, AL: Mises Institute, 2006), pp. 327–35, 425–31, 437–38, 462–63; Rothbard, *Conceived in Liberty*, 1–4, pp. 621–29.

The colonies also imported mercantilist banking interventions. In 1694, England chartered the Bank of England (BOE). The new corporation was a fractional reserve bank, because redeemable notes and deposits remained greater than specie reserves. The Bank could inflate through loans to businesses and the government, also known as credit expansion. Parliament vested it with immense privileges and King William III and various government officials purchased shares. In addition to the privilege of holding government deposits, Parliament blocked a land bank proposed by the rival Tory party, passed laws prohibiting the chartering of new corporate banks, restricted other banks from issuing notes, and allowed the Bank of England to periodically suspend specie payments. Overall, the monopolistic central bank controlled banking activities and centralized inflation.[16]

Colonists latched on to the banking concept. For example, the wealthy merchant and real estate speculator John Colman founded the Massachusetts Land Bank in 1740. Colman and his supporters desired a bank whose credit expansion (with land as collateral) would finance speculation in government land grants. They also wanted it to subsidize local manufacturers by allowing loans to be repaid in iron and hemp. During this time, competing merchants established a fractional reserve silver bank, issuing notes redeemable in specie after fifteen years. Massachusetts did not incorporate either bank but sanctioned their inflationary emissions.

Various groups clashed over who would get the new money first, and therefore, who would benefit. Great Britain vociferously fought the colonists' paper money inflation, not out of animosity toward paper money but because British merchants and creditors did not want payments in depreciated currency. Thus, in 1741 Parliament outlawed both Massachusetts banks. Mercantilist banking fallacies persisted after the eighteenth century, along with the intense debate over what constituted the government's proper role in banking. It would take a long time for the laissez-faire solution—free banking where unchartered fractional reserve banks competitively issued redeemable notes and deposits—to affect economic theory and politics.[17]

Despite the monetary interventions, salutary neglect, in conjunction with the burgeoning libertarianism, allowed the colonies to move

---

[16] Rothbard, *Austrian Perspective on the History of Economic Thought*, 2, pp. 227–31.

[17] Rothbard, *Conceived in Liberty*, 1–4, pp. 627, 630–38.

in a classical liberal direction, away from the European Old Order. Liberty was on the rise.

The Turn to Rebellion

After salutary neglect ended in the 1760s, colonists embraced increasingly radical measures to fight new British cronyism. By 1775, they had openly revolted.

King George II and the Tory warmongers ousted Walpole and Newcastle to move against their archenemy, France, whose territories Canada and Louisiana spread north and southwest of the British colonies. The French only controlled this vast and mostly unsettled "New France" with scattered forts near Indian fur traders. The British continually argued that New France was the aggressor, despite its population numbering only 75,000 while the British colonies housed nearly 1.5 million. In reality, they coveted French land to benefit favored speculator interests and further British domination.[18]

By this time, Virginia settlers had reached New France's borders near the Appalachian Mountains. Unsurprisingly, Virginia invoked its grandiose ownership claims against the French. In 1749, Virginia granted nearly 1.5 million acres of New France land in the Ohio Valley to land corporations. Similar to the royal land grants, these grants transferred the privileged companies colonial governments' claims to unappropriated land, and they planned to sell at a massive profit. Understandably, the French constructed forts when they heard of the Ohio Company's plans to move in. Consequently, Robert Dinwiddie, the Virginia governor and an Ohio Company shareholder, lobbied for Crown approval to repel the "invasion."[19]

In 1754, matters rapidly escalated into the French and Indian War. Great Britain hastily imposed conscription and the quartering of soldiers upon a reluctant colonial public. By the end of the conflict in 1763, Great Britain, now ruled by King George III, emerged the undisputed European superpower and possessor of New France.[20]

However, the ungrateful colonists avoided paying for the British elites' swollen empire, much less abiding by the Navigation Acts. George III and the Tories now implemented their mercantilist "Grand Design": Great Britain would station peacetime standing armies to stringently

---

[18] Ibid., pp. 713, 721–22, 724–25.
[19] Ibid., pp. 725–29.
[20] Ibid., pp. 729–66.

enforce the Navigation Acts, restrict western settlement, and impose new taxes.[21] The elites cunningly schemed to stifle economic growth and the libertarian ideas that challenged cronyism, such as those in *Cato's Letters.*

The mother country quickly implemented the Grand Design: the 1763 Proclamation Line restricted western settlement and voided all speculative land sales in the area (thus double crossing the land companies); the 1764 Sugar Act imposed taxes on sugar with stringent enforcement; the 1764 Currency Act restricted colonial governments' ability to print paper money; and the 1765 Stamp Act levied taxes on paper products.[22]

The hated Stamp Act produced a storm of protest, particularly by the libertarians Patrick Henry, a Virginia lawyer, and Samuel Adams, a Massachusetts politician and newspaper editor. They respectively wrote the Virginia and Massachusetts Resolves that challenged the Stamp Act. Henry's resolves earned the admiration of the young Virginian Thomas Jefferson, and Sam Adams' resistance group soon expanded into the colony-wide Sons of Liberty.[23]

Virginia and Massachusetts quickly stressed resistance while Pennsylvania and New York, under the influence of corrupt financial and landed interests connected to the British, urged caution. Resistors called the Stamp Act Congress for late 1765 and engaged in mass civil disobedience by not recognizing the taxes. It was a rudimentary but highly effective form of nullification—to declare a law illegal and refuse to obey and enforce it. Great Britain, realizing the imminent rebellion, quickly repealed the measure in 1766.[24]

While this seemingly resolved the crisis, problems remained, particularly in Massachusetts after the 1767 tax-increasing Townshend Acts. British troops soon occupied Boston and the colonies responded with voluntary nonimportation protests that crushed British commercial interests, who consequently pushed for repealing the Townshend Acts in 1770. Despite this uneasy lull, matters reached a fever pitch with the 1773 Tea Act.[25]

---

[21] Ibid., p. 791.

[22] Ibid., pp. 781–97, 805–11, 831, 853–59.

[23] Ibid., pp. 803, 860–73, 893.

[24] Ibid., pp. 889–920.

[25] Ibid., pp. 920–87.

The Tea Act extended the privileged British East India Company's tea monopoly to American shores. Colonists feared that the corporation's monopoly would extend to other imported goods. They responded accordingly with the famous Boston Tea Party of December 1773. To prevent customs officers from seizing and selling cargo on East India tea ships after Bostonians protested paying the required tax, the Sons of Liberty boarded the ships and destroyed the tea. When Great Britain counterattacked with the Coercive Acts of 1774, the colonies formed a congress of representatives to coordinate boycotting and resistance measures. They once again nullified British cronyism.[26]

When the first Continental Congress met in September 1774, it became clear that two distinct factions had coalesced. The Massachusetts and Virginia radicals Sam Adams, his distant younger cousin John Adams, Patrick Henry, and the planter Richard Henry Lee led the first. Pennsylvania and New York reactionaries Joseph Galloway, James Duane, and John Jay led the second. The radicals wanted maximum resistance to uphold the libertarian ideals of Trenchard and Gordon, while the reactionaries, financially ensconced with Great Britain, only wanted more representation in the British Empire and discouraged nullification. Radicals appropriately labeled them Tories.

At the Congress, the Tory Galloway introduced his "Plan of the Proposed Union between Great Britain and the Colonies."[27] In the first of the statists' many attempts, Galloway proposed uniting the independent governments with a central coercer: the colonial assemblies would elect members to a grand council, who would work with a royally appointed president-general to represent the colonies in Great Britain. The American elites hoped that this constitution would grant them their fair share in Britain's mercantilism.

But Henry and Lee would not stand for such moderation, defeating the plan. Congress settled on nullification through a boycott of all British products, causing the British Empire to respond with more soldiers and standing armies. This escalation could lead to only one outcome: a cataclysmic clash between American freedom and British coercion. Henry, understanding the upcoming struggle with crystal clarity, thundered in March 1775:

---

[26] Ibid., pp. 1024–60.
[27] Ibid., p. 1061.

> Let it come. I repeat Sir, let it come! . . . Is life so dear, or
> peace so sweet, as to be purchased at the price of chains
> and slavery? Forbid it, Almighty God! I know not what
> course others may take; but as for me, give me liberty,
> or give me death![28]

In April 1775, British soldiers tried to arrest Massachusetts radicals John Hancock and Sam Adams. Colonial minutemen soon confronted the approaching troops, leading to the famous "shot heard round the world."[29] It was a climactic scene: an open fight erupted at Lexington, causing Adams to proclaim, "Oh! What a glorious morning is this!"[30] The mass-movement American Revolution—the People's War—had begun. The new conflict built on the prior struggles and reform movements against British cronyism. But this time, after radicals committed to the truly revolutionary reform of secession, the American Revolution ushered in a new epoch of resistance.[31]

---

[28] Ibid., p. 1087. See also pp. 899 and 1060–89.
[29] Ibid., p. 1093.
[30] Ibid., p. 1092.
[31] Ibid., pp. 1090–93.

CHAPTER 2

THE AMERICAN REVOLUTIONARY WAR: THE TRIUMPH OF LIBERTY

A Reactionary Military and Financial Strategy

The American Revolutionary War played an indispensable role in the eternal struggle between liberty and power. The colonists unhesitatingly fought the British Empire's cronyism but disagreed over whether they wanted an American Empire's cronyism. Reactionaries created a new Articles of Confederation to facilitate American privileges, but failed to secure total dominance because of the pro-liberty radicals. Their special-interest policies resulted from wartime military, financial, and bureaucratic planning.

When the second Continental Congress met in May 1775, it faced open war in Massachusetts. The appalled Joseph Galloway withdrew from political life and joined the British. John Dickinson of Philadelphia, now leading the reactionary statists, initiated an Olive Branch Petition to plead for immediate negotiation.[1] More ominously, the delegates decided how to conduct the current hostilities: conventional instead of guerrilla warfare.[2]

Conventional military planning referred to the ancient practice of organizing a formally trained conscript army to fight the enemy in pitched battles. This method required a war machine to furnish supplies and invasive financing measures (e.g., taxes, debt, inflation, and outright confiscation of supplies), which lead to cronyism. On the other hand, guerrilla warfare, a new and still developing strategy, advocated for informal militiamen and volunteers to ambush, harass, and disrupt enemy supply lines. This persistent snipping at the opposition

---

[1] Murray N. Rothbard, *Conceived in Liberty*, vols. 1–4 (Auburn, AL: Mises Institute, 2019), p. 1145.

[2] Ibid., pp. 1131–36, 1144–45.

complemented the colonists' comparative advantage since they knew their own terrain, and did not formally train for pitched battles, and could not match Britain's military resources.[3]

However, the Continental Congress chose the first option, appointing the conventional George Washington of Virginia instead of the guerrilla strategist Charles Lee of Great Britain as commander in chief. In addition to sending out Dickinson's Olive Branch Petition, Congress also approved an ill-fated Canadian invasion because of the expectation that its citizens would join in resistance.[4]

While Washington adopted the Prussian method and turned the army into a standard, regimented, and hierarchical system, Congress turned to finance. Recognizing that the colonists would not tolerate taxes, the landed oligarch Gouverneur Morris of New York, a supporter of reconciliation and grandson of a former royal governor, pushed for soft-money financing. As a result, Congress started to issue Continental dollars that it promised to redeem in specie sometime in the future (a promise quickly dropped).[5]

Shortly thereafter, Congress created a nine-man Secret Committee to negotiate foreign munitions purchases and a six-man Committee of Secret Correspondence to communicate with potential allies. One man quickly assumed the committees' leadership: Philadelphia merchant Robert Morris (no relation to Gouverneur Morris), yet another supporter of reconciliation. Out of the Secret Committee's $2 million in lucrative cost-plus contracts from 1775 to 1777, Morris steered $500,000 to his own company, Willing & Morris, and $300,000 to the firms of other committeemen. Unsurprisingly, the corrupt Robert Morris soon tried to consolidate power in the government he largely controlled. By this time, his cadre included Gouverneur Morris; the landed oligarchs Philip Schuyler and Robert Livingston of New York; the theoretician Colonel Alexander Hamilton of New York, aide to Washington and son-in-law of Schuyler; and the lawyer James Wilson of Pennsylvania. These men would contribute significantly to the reactionary cause.[6]

---

[3] Ibid., pp. 1137–39; Joseph R. Stromberg, "Mercenaries, Guerrillas, Militias, and the Defense of Minimal States and Free Societies," in *The Myth of National Defense*, ed. Hans-Hermann Hoppe (Auburn, AL: Mises Institute, 2003), pp. 215–38.

[4] Rothbard, *Conceived in Liberty*, 1–4, pp. 1144–53, 1160–66.

[5] Ibid., pp. 1157–59, 1167–69, 1175, 1338–39; Richard Sylla, "The Transition to a Monetary Union in the United States," *Financial History Review* (April 2006): 77–78.

[6] Philip Burch, *Elites in American History*, vol. 1 (New York: Holmes & Meier Publishers, 1981), p. 61; Rothbard, *Conceived in Liberty*, 1–4, pp. 1161, 1223–30, 1342, 1502.

Secession Declared

These statist machinations mirrored growing splits regarding the particular path of reform. First, the Americans debated whether to secede (the radical position championed by Patrick Henry, Richard Henry Lee, Sam Adams, and John Adams) or instead fight for British representation (the reactionary position supported by Gouverneur Morris and his associates). Second, assuming independence, Americans fought over establishing localist and limited governments (the radical view) or a corrupt empire that would enrich political, landed, military, and commercial elites (the reactionary view). A proper analysis of cronyism requires discussion of the important ideological developments that followed the Enlightenment and *Cato's Letters*, particularly Thomas Jefferson's epochal Declaration of Independence, Adam Smith's influential *Wealth of Nations*, and the new state constitutions.

Colonists largely resolved the first debate with Thomas Paine's explosive *Common Sense* (1776). His popular pamphlet radicalized the colonists, imbuing them with basic Enlightenment principles and how the Old Order infringed on Americans' natural rights. Significantly, Paine's *Common Sense* stole the thunder from the theoretician John Adams, who unfortunately responded by drifting into the reactionary ranks. The return of Richard Henry Lee, the arrival of the merchant Elbridge Gerry, and the crown's punitive response to the Olive Branch Petition also bolstered Congress' independence sentiments.[7]

On July 2, 1776, the most libertarian event in American history occurred: Congress seceded from Great Britain. This formation of thirteen separate states was the most extreme action that could be undertaken to fight cronyism: external amputation from a coercive apparatus. Some holdouts remained: predictably, John Dickinson and Robert Morris opposed the decision and abstained from the final vote so that Pennsylvania could declare independence.[8]

Congress tasked Thomas Jefferson with writing a philosophical justification. The Virginian brilliantly grounded it in a Lockean worldview, appealing to a public that read *Cato's Letters*. Congress approved his amended Declaration of Independence on July 4. In it, Jefferson eloquently stated the colonists' natural rights to "life, liberty and the pursuit of happiness," and

---

[7] Burch, *Elites in American History*, 1, p. 65; Rothbard, *Conceived in Liberty*, 1–4, pp. 1239–64.

[8] Rothbard, *Conceived in Liberty*, 1–4, pp. 1289–91.

> whenever any form of government becomes destructive
> of these ends, it is the right of the people to alter or to
> abolish it, and to institute new government, laying its
> foundation on such principles and organizing its pow-
> ers in such form, as to them shall seem most likely to
> effect their safety and happiness.[9]

This spectacular enunciation of natural rights formed a mighty bulwark against cronyism: the people did not have to idly submit to their overlords but instead possessed the right to fight back.

Jefferson's original draft was far more extreme. For example, he condemned King George III for strengthening the slave trade—the literal antithesis of the secessionists' libertarianism. Jefferson, like many other leading Virginians, was a planter who owned slaves but deeply regretted the institution. However, at the fierce insistence of South Carolina, Georgia, and New England slave transporters, Congress removed Jefferson's remarks from the final draft, leaving the issue of slavery unresolved.[10]

Jefferson also started to envision an American Empire different from the reactionaries' dream. The theoretician did not want an Empire of Power; he desired an Empire of Liberty composed of independent yeomen who would homestead the frontier. He did not care if a loose confederation of states or multiple confederations controlled the continent. Common language, constitutional systems, and market values, *not force*, would link the empire and resist the European Old Orders' corruption.[11]

Americans debated the extent of Jefferson's Empire of Liberty and government intervention in the coming decades. Significantly, the classical liberals already started to answer this question by reading new economic works and securing constitutional reforms.

In the same year as Jefferson's Declaration of Independence, an Enlightenment thinker published an economic treatise in Great Britain that encapsulated the thrust of the seceding American colonies: *An Inquiry into the Nature and Causes of the Wealth of Nations*. Adam

---

[9] Ibid., p. 1292.

[10] Burch, *Elites in American History*, 1, p. 48; Rothbard, *Conceived in Liberty*, 1–4, pp. 1292–94.

[11] Glenn Tucker and David Hendrickson, *Empire of Liberty* (New York: Oxford University Press, 1990), pp. 20–21, 159–63, 312–13; Gordon Wood, *Empire of Liberty* (New York: Oxford University Press, 2009), pp. 357–59, 371.

Smith, like other Enlightenment economists, supported some mercantilist interventions. However, his work spearheaded the laissez-faire assault against Old Order intellectuals such as James Steuart and Jean-Baptiste Colbert. Smith described the "invisible hand": a self-interested individual acting under a framework of private property is incentivized to "promote an end [prosperity] which was no part of his intention."[12] He also criticized Great Britain's mercantilism, from the corporate charters to the Navigation Acts, arguing that "in the mercantile system, the interest of the consumer is almost constantly sacrificed to that of the producer."[13]

Smith's free market economics was heavily influenced the radicals, particularly Jefferson, who by 1790 considered *The Wealth of Nations* the best work in political economy. On the other hand, the preeminent intellectual working on behalf of government power, Alexander Hamilton, sneered at Adam Smith's reasoning and praised the "indefatigable endeavours of the great Colbert."[14] This dividing line over the free market continued in ensuing decades.[15]

Ideological breakthroughs aside, radicals also battled reactionaries and replaced Old Order colonial charters with new state constitutions. The new governments informally united in the Continental Congress to coordinate the war effort. Each sovereign state had to agree to fundamental decisions, and this unanimity significantly limited Congress' privileges. Furthermore, the new constitutions increased representation of the people, instituted rotation of office, and prohibited interventions through bills of rights. Gordon Wood rightly states that "nothing . . . in the years surrounding the Declaration of Independence engaged the interests of Americans more than the framing of these separate governments."[16]

---

[12] Murray N. Rothbard, *An Austrian Perspective on the History of Economic Thought*, vol. 1, *Economic Thought Before Adam Smith* (Auburn, AL: Mises Institute 2006), p. 464.

[13] Murray N. Rothbard, "Mercantilism," in *Economic Controversies* (Auburn, AL: Mises Institute, 2011), p. 644.

[14] Ivan Jankovic, *American Counter-Revolution in Favor of Liberty* (Switzerland: Palgrave Macmillan, 2019), p. 146.

[15] Rothbard, *Austrian Perspective on the History of Economic Thought*, 1, pp. 246–49, 437–38, 463–69; Murray N. Rothbard, *An Austrian Perspective of Economic Thought*, vol. 2, *Classical Economics* (Auburn, AL: Mises Institute, 2006), pp. 7–8.

[16] Gordon Wood, *The Creation of the American Republic* (Chapel Hill: The University of North Carolina Press, 1998), p. 128. See also Rothbard, *Conceived in Liberty*, 1–4, pp. 1244, 1357.

The most prominent example of the new state polities was Pennsylvania, which Murray Rothbard describes as a "beacon and inspiration to libertarians" and a "triumph of the radicals."[17] In the fall of 1776, against the resistance of the entrenched elites, the radicals passed a constitution with a unicameral legislature, an executive consisting of a plural council, and a judiciary with seven-year terms. These reforms weakened the oligarchs and made it harder for them to pass special-interest legislation.[18]

In Virginia, radicals Patrick Henry, Thomas Jefferson, Richard Henry Lee, and the lawyer George Mason battled ultra-reactionaries, creating a constitution in June 1776. Virginians elected Henry to the governorship and the state now supported western settlers' rights. In addition, radicals included Mason's Declaration of Rights in the Constitution, a bill of rights in the tradition of *Cato's Letters* that imposed restraints through enumerations of government power. Mason's work inspired Jefferson's Declaration of Independence. Unfortunately, Virginia reactionaries revised Mason's Declaration to clarify that slaves did not possess a natural right to freedom. Furthermore, Henry and Jefferson later split over the nature of executive power—Jefferson for a weak governor, Henry for a strong—fatefully sundering their relationship.[19]

In 1777, New York's pro-power forces responded to independence with a highly reactionary constitution that restricted suffrage through high property requirements and contained no bill of rights. However, after a tenant uprising against feudalism's remaining vestiges, the radical George Clinton defeated Morris affiliate Philip Schuyler in the state's first gubernatorial race. Once in control, the radicals redistributed crony feudal landholdings, solidifying support among upstate libertarians such as Abraham Yates.[20]

Clearly, 1776 was a high point for liberty. The colonists seceded and Jefferson articulated a libertarian justification for the decision. They were well on their way to answering the second debate with the impact of Smith's laissez-faire treatise and new state constitutions. At

---

[17] Rothbard, *Conceived in Liberty*, 1–4, pp. 1371, 1374.

[18] Murray N. Rothbard, "Bureaucracy and the Civil Service in the United States," *Journal of Libertarian Studies* (Summer 1995): 19–20; Rothbard, *Conceived in Liberty*, 1–4, pp. 1371–76.

[19] Jon Kukla, *Patrick Henry* (New York: Simon & Schuster, 2017), pp. 257–60; Rothbard, *Conceived in Liberty*, 1–4, pp. 1268–74, 1293, 1363–64.

[20] Rothbard, *Conceived in Liberty*, 1–4, pp. 1387–90, 1543–47.

the same time, though, interventionists secretly brainstormed how to undo the radicals' accomplishments.

The Articles of Confederation

Against the libertarian secession, statists planned to consolidate the thirteen independent states, thereby facilitating crony economic and military legislation. These former supporters of the British Empire cunningly shifted tactics, now arguing that only a centralized federal government transcended local interests and represented the will of "The People." Spearheading the charge, Dickinson released a draft for the Articles of Confederation and Perpetual Union in July 1776, which radicals only partially defeated.

Dickinson's draft resembled Galloway's proposal before the war. On top of creating a permanent executive council, the draft established Congress' supreme national sovereignty and made its powers sweeping and vague, particularly a clause that stated Congress possessed "authority for the Defence and the Welfare of the United Colonies and every one of them."[21] This ambiguous "general welfare" clause, unshackled by any real enumeration of powers, made it easier for legislators to pass future special-interest legislation, because opponents could not criticize proposals as unconstitutional. Furthermore, at the behest of large land companies, the draft ordered states to cede western land claims to Congress. The only power not granted was the crucial power to tax—the states provided revenue to Congress voluntarily. However, reactionaries knew that the states would vehemently object to any taxing authority; better to push for it after ratification.

Against this rampant accretion of power, Thomas Burke of North Carolina assumed the radicals' leadership, drastically weakening the plan. Burke recognized power's "irresistible propensity to increase" and how inevitably it "will some time or other be abused unless men are well watched, and checked by something they cannot remove when they please."[22] In other words, to stop corruption, one must reform and shackle government institutions.

In addition to his assistance in removing the executive council, Burke secured a states' rights amendment that drastically weakened the new government. It became Article Two of the completed Articles of Confederation:

---

[21] Jankovic, *American Counter-Revolution*, p. 137.

[22] Rothbard, *Conceived in Liberty*, 1–4, p. 1360.

> Each state retains its sovereignty, freedom and independence, and every power, jurisdiction, and right, which is not by this confederation expressly delegated to the United States, in Congress assembled.[23]

Article Two provided a mighty bulwark for states' rights, because it "expressly delegated" what the central enforcer could do. The people who elected the state legislatures reserved all other governance.[24]

Classical liberals also raised fierce resistance about how the proposed constitution dealt with the western lands problem, particularly the nationalization of Virginia's claims over the Northwest. On the surface, this seemed the right decision given Virginia's past history with land companies. However, Virginia's new constitution reasserted land claims on behalf of the individual settler. Consequently, Lee and Jefferson resisted nationalization. Jefferson in particular believed that speculative land companies could more easily corrupt a centralized Congress instead of the separate states. Confirming his fears, three large land companies led the nationalization drive—the Indiana Company, the Illinois Company, and the Wabash Company. Robert Morris participated in the Indiana Company, which also employed his lawyer, Wilson. The land companies fought bitterly, but ultimately Virginia and the other landed states won: the Articles did not require them to cede territorial claims.[25]

Congress finished revising the Articles of Confederation in November 1777, sending it to the states for unanimous ratification. Only Maryland, whose oligarchs owned the Wabash Company, failed to ratify, wanting Virginia to cede its land claims like the other states, but Virginia refused. Maryland finally ratified in February 1781, believing Congress would press for Virginia's land claims. Even after Maryland ratified, Virginia only relinquished its claims in March 1784, when the Confederation Congress voided the speculative land companies' claims. Afterward, Congress passed Jefferson's Ordinance of 1784, outlining the future policy of creating western states out of self-governing territories. Jefferson's original Ordinance tried to forbid slavery in any western territories after 1800, an immense attack on the

---

[23] Ibid., p. 1367.

[24] Jankovic, *American Counter-Revolution*, pp. 137–38; Rothbard, *Conceived in Liberty*, 1–4, pp. 1357–62, 1364, 1367–68.

[25] Burch, *Elites in American History*, 1, p. 61; Rothbard, *Conceived in Liberty*, 1–4, pp. 1362–66.

institution. However, the South resisted and slavery was fatefully not prohibited, though the Ordinance of 1787 forbade it in the Northwest. Once again, the institution lingered.

In addition to Article Two and allowing states to keep their land claims, the Articles conferred many benefits. Significantly, the state legislatures annually elected the representatives of the unicameral Confederation Congress on a revolving basis, preserving rotation in office. Each state delegation cast one vote, and fundamental policies required a supra-majority of nine states. The Articles also required unanimity of the state legislatures for ratification and amendments. Crucially, and to the statists' chagrin, the revised Articles still did not allow Congress to tax either the states or the public. This important structural feature severely weakened Congress' ability to increase its own power and distribute special privileges.

Despite the revisions, the Articles unfortunately encouraged consolidation, including a perpetual union and two general welfare clauses. Article Three declared that the states enter into a "league of friendship . . . [for] their mutual and general welfare," while Article Eight allowed for "expenses that shall be incurred for the common defense or general welfare."[26] In addition, the Articles weakened state armies, invoked the states to supply Congress with revenues in proportion to land values, and made Congress the final court of appeal for various disputes between states. Significantly, it also assumed all of the old Continental Congress' debts and paper money.[27]

Therefore, the Articles of Confederation were ultimately a defeat for reform, because the new polity centralized governance and provided a springboard for future interventions. The radicals quickly learned that this future was not far off.

The Reactionary Counterrevolution

Statists quickly moved to augment the Confederation's power through executive departments, a national taxing power to benefit debt speculators, and a central bank to channel inflation to privileged borrowers. They succeeded in creating executive departments and a

---

[26] William Watkins, *Crossroads for Liberty* (Oakland, CA: Independent Institute, 2016), pp. 227, 230.

[27] Rothbard, *Conceived in Liberty*, 1–4, pp. 1364, 1367–70, 1483–86, 1527–29; Murray N. Rothbard, *Conceived in Liberty*, vol. 5, *The New Republic, 1784–1791*, ed. Patrick Newman (Auburn, AL: Mises Institute, 2019), pp. 88–89.

central bank but failed at the eleventh hour to equip the Confederation with a taxing power.

The pro-power coalition first built up their political base in the new states. In 1780, the wealthy oligarch James Bowdoin worked with John Adams to devise a reactionary Massachusetts constitution with limited suffrage, a strong executive, and an upper house. They also managed to regain control of Pennsylvania in the 1780 elections.[28]

Reactionaries then turned their eyes to the main prize: money. From 1775 to 1780 the Continental Congress and the states inflated to finance their military operations, causing a fifty-fold increase in the money supply. When they imposed legal tender laws, specie predictably disappeared from circulation. After the institution of controls to combat skyrocketing prices, mass shortages resulted. By early 1781, federal and state paper money started to depreciate out of existence. However, the governments did not repudiate the debt instruments used to purchase supplies. Privilege-seeking speculators bought up these securities, lobbying governments for redemption at face value. They sought windfall profits, courtesy of the taxpayer.[29]

In early 1781, reactionaries in Congress proposed a 5 percent federal tariff to fund debts and expand operations, envisioning it as an entering wedge for higher taxes in the future. Since the tax was an amendment to the Articles, it required the approval of every state. Reactionaries quickly commenced lobbying efforts.

Around the same time, James Duane of New York, inspired by Alexander Hamilton, proposed foreign affairs, war, navy, and finance departments to create a powerful executive branch. The Confederation Congress obliged, choosing Robert Morris for the crucial Department of Finance.[30]

With Hamilton's backing, Morris first pushed for the corporate chartering of the confederation's first central bank. But Congressman James Madison of Virginia, otherwise a proponent of centralization, worried about federal incorporation because such a power did not explicitly exist in the Articles. However, he voted for the motion and did not protest the bank's constitutionality. When Morris asked Congress

---

[28] Rothbard, *Conceived in Liberty*, 1–4, pp. 1498–501.

[29] Ibid., pp. 1487–97, 1508–11; Murray N. Rothbard, "The History of Money and Banking Before the Twentieth Century," in *A History of Money and Banking in the United States*, ed. Joseph T. Salerno (Auburn, AL: Mises Institute, 2002), pp. 59–62.

[30] Rothbard, *Conceived in Liberty*, 1–4, pp. 1502–04, 1514–15.

to grant the charter, the legislature justified it as a wartime emergency. In particular, the constitutionality derived from the general welfare clauses. However, Congress required the bank to get permission from states it wanted to operate in, a move consonant with states' rights. Morris also secured a charter from Pennsylvania, so Congress could not completely dissolve the bank.

Modeled after the Bank of England, Morris envisioned the Bank of North America (BONA) as the Confederation's privileged fractional reserve bank. The central bank wielded a temporary monopoly charter over commercial banking in return for loans to the government, a partial owner of the institution. The BONA inaugurated the cozy partnership between government and banking.

Astoundingly, Morris appropriated money loaned to Congress to meet the Bank's capital requirements, an action Murray Rothbard describes as "virtual embezzlement."[31] He then made his business partner Thomas Willing president and in January 1782 opened up shop in Philadelphia, the confederation's financial capital. The BONA's first directors and shareholders were Morris' wartime chums and Willing's commercial relatives, such as Gouverneur Morris. Robert Morris soon loaned $1.2 million to the government, channeling these loans into lucrative war contracts for his associates.[32]

By the fall of 1782, Morris appeared to have won. The Bank existed, and one by one the dragooned state legislatures ratified the impost. His supporters controlled the federal machinery, and the reactionary New York legislature, led by Hamilton, even issued a call for a constitutional convention to strengthen the Articles. Demoralized radicals, such as Richard Henry Lee, left Congress in 1781, and some, like John Adams, fully transitioned to the reactionary side.

At this crucial moment, though, the reactionaries failed to breach the final bulwark: the Articles' unanimity requirement. Rhode Island had not yet ratified the Articles, and with the indomitable radical Congressman David Howell, it would not. Howell, a classical liberal professor at Brown University, staunchly contrasted with contemporary court intellectuals and refused to ally the throne with the secular altar. The

---

[31] Ibid., p. 1506.

[32] Irving Brant, *Madison, The Nationalist* (New York: Bobbs-Merrill, 1948), pp. 125–30; Merrill Jensen, *The New Nation* (New York: Alfred A. Knopf, 1950), pp. 60–63; Brion McClanahan, *How Alexander Hamilton Screwed Up America* (Washington, DC: Regnery History, 2017), pp. 40–41; Rothbard, *Conceived in Liberty*, 1–4, pp. 1504–07, 1523–24.

Rhode Islander recognized that the power to tax "will be like *Pandora's box*, once opened, never to close," and the federal government would have free reign to tax and intervene as much as it wanted.[33]

Without Rhode Island, the tariff could not go into effect. Recognizing this, Robert Morris and his cadre intimidated Rhode Island into ratifying, and it looked as if the little state would succumb. But suddenly, in December 1782, Virginia libertarians repealed the state's ratification once they realized the war was virtually over. The impost was no more, halting the government's recent expansion and stopping Morris and his crony counterrevolution.[34]

Recognizing imminent defeat in January 1783, Morris raised the stakes and bluffed Congress, promising to resign unless it funded the debt. In March, he worked with Gouverneur Morris, Wilson, and Hamilton to enact their dream national government, this time *by force*. With the war winding down, disgruntled army officers wanted the Confederation Congress to officially restructure the army along European lines. The commanders desired half-pay pensions to officers for life and better pay for their wartime efforts. Rumors circulated that the army in Newburgh, New York, refused to disband, waiting for a powerful general to take charge. Naturally, the reactionaries looked to George Washington. However, unlike numerous commanders throughout history, Washington heroically refused to take part in a corrupt military putsch. The movement collapsed.

However, Congress did grant officers a five-year pension, augmenting the federal debt and incentivizing militarists to push for an even stronger central government. In particular, Washington, Hamilton, Chief Artillery Officer Henry Knox, and Quartermaster General Timothy Pickering of Massachusetts now wanted a professional peacetime standing army. Morris heartily backed their endeavors. As a first step, high-ranking military officers formed the quasi-aristocratic and hereditary Society of the Cincinnati to lobby for such a government. Thomas Jefferson, Sam Adams, and Elbridge Gerry, fierce opponents of standing armies, trenchantly denounced the Society.

The nationalist James Madison spearheaded a second request for an impost in April 1783 so Congress could pay off its debts. But despite these efforts, the statist program was all but dead, and Morris

---

[33] Jackson Main, *The Anti-federalists* (Chapel Hill: The University of North Carolina, 2004), p. 81.

[34] Rothbard, *Conceived in Liberty*, 1–4, pp. 1501, 1512, 1515–17.

left office in disgust. By the end of 1783, the BONA only possessed its Pennsylvania charter; the federal government had paid off all loans and was no longer a partial owner.[35]

Thus, against Morris' drive for cronyism, pro-independence libertarians fought valiantly and stopped the entire counterrevolution dead in its tracks. Without their heroic efforts Morris would have successfully instituted the governing infrastructure—particularly the ability to tax—necessary to establish an Old Order American Empire.

The Libertarianism of the Revolution

The Treaty of Paris in 1783 ended the American Revolutionary War, recognizing the United States' secession. The costly conflict resulted in economic destruction through collapsing confidence in the currency, military confiscation of goods, British pillaging, and fleeing loyalists. But in the end, the highly radical conflict promoted liberty. It was truly a "People's War": when John Adams famously stated that only one-third of Americans actively supported the Revolution, he actually referred to the French Revolution. Groundswell libertarianism led to a highly successful war that achieved long-term reforms.

First, the Revolution dismantled feudalism as states split large aristocratic landholdings, distributing them to the homesteading farmers. Future sales greased the market economy's wheels and led to a more efficient allocation of resources. Second, the states dealt a devastating blow to the religious court intellectual by relaxing laws restricting religious worship. No longer could reactionaries enlist them to divinize statism. Third, the Revolution resulted in new state constitutions that increased suffrage and representation compared to the old colonial charters. With rotation in office and express prohibitions of interventions, higher suffrage weakened state officials' ability to enrich themselves at taxpayer expense. Fourth, the war encouraged similar European revolutions against absolutism, mercantilism, and feudalism. While they failed because of the Old Orders' entrenched power, the rebellions sent painful reminders to statists that their depredations faced limits.[36]

---

[35] Richard Kohn, *Eagle and Sword* (New York: The Free Press, 1975), pp. 10–11, 17–52; Rothbard, *Conceived in Liberty*, 1–4, pp. 1518–26.

[36] Jeffrey Rogers Hummel, "Benefits of the American Revolution," in *The Library of*

Finally, the Revolution contributed to the restriction of feudal slavery, a major step in the reduction of cronyism. The war encouraged the eradication of government protections for the slave trade and even slavery itself in several states. Crucially, and quite ominously, slavery prohibitions largely occurred in the North (particularly in New England, with the Mid-Atlantic trailing), though every southern state except South Carolina and Georgia restricted or banned slave importations. Virginia even relaxed laws regulating manumissions and allowed owners to free ten thousand slaves. In that state, the classical liberal slave owners such as Jefferson, Henry, and Mason optimistically hoped slavery would eventually—*somehow*—disappear. They believed slave-trade restrictions and diffusing slave populations across the West would end the practice, an unfortunate delusion because such restrictions also strengthened slavery by encouraging domestic breeding to maintain the ranks of the enslaved.

It is very important to understand sectional differences regarding slavery. Both northerners and southerners, disapproving of blacks, feared uncontrolled emancipation and integration. But the disparity in black population sizes (3 percent in the North versus 35 percent in the South) made northerners much less fearful of emancipation, though they expressed little desire to accept any blacks from the South's plantations.[37] Fatefully, because of the South's higher black population, slavery lingered on. Over time, the ignoble institution strengthened and corrupted classical liberal southerners.[38]

The ultimate catalyst for that corruption lay in the Treaty of Paris. Great Britain dubiously granted the Northwest and the right to navigate on the Mississippi River to the United States—empty actions because the British had only sparsely settled the Northwest and Spain essentially controlled the Mississippi River. But these acquisitions proved crucial to future foreign policy, because the imperial power of

---

Economics and Liberty (July 2018); William Marina, "The American Revolution and the Minority Myth," *Modern Age* (Summer 1976): 298–309; Rothbard, *Conceived in Liberty*, 1–4, pp. 1114, 1181–82, 1478, 1543–42, 1553–68; Rothbard, *Conceived in Liberty*, 5, pp. 49–50.

[37] Unless otherwise noted, all percentages are rounded.

[38] *Historical Statistics of the United States, Colonial Times to 1957* (Washington, DC, 1960), pp. 11–12; Hummel, "Benefits"; William Hyland, *George Mason* (Washington, DC: Regnery History, 2019), pp. 227–57; Kukla, *Patrick Henry*, pp. 123–26; Dumas Malone, *Jefferson the Virginian* (Boston: Little, Brown, 1948), pp. 264–68; Rothbard, *Conceived in Liberty*, 1–4, pp. 1548–52.

controlling the West tempted the nascent American confederation. For now, however, the republic shined bright.[39]

Only a significant political faction in favor of classical liberalism stopped the Grand Design and the reactionary counterrevolution. The libertarians destroyed the Grand Design by utilizing the extreme reform of secession, and they fought the counterrevolution—led by the very men who resisted secession—by weakening the Articles of Confederation and employing its unanimity requirement. Temporarily defeated, the statists plotted their next moves for an American Old Order.

---

[39] Rothbard, *Conceived in Liberty*, 1–4, pp. 1470–80.

CHAPTER 3

THE US CONSTITUTION: THE TRIUMPH OF POWER

The Postwar Depression

After the Revolutionary War, the country faced an economic crisis that interventionists used to launch another constitutional drive. Most historians attribute the 1780s economic disturbances to the weak Articles of Confederation, arguing that they led to poor economic growth and therefore the drive for stronger government was for the public interest.[1] In reality, the Articles limited special-interest legislation. Difficulties in the early 1780s came from the war's aftermath, and postwar interventions delayed recovery. Furthermore, the second—and this time successful—counterrevolution was really a crony putsch.

Strong evidence suggests that the American economy did not return to its pre-war levels until the beginning of the nineteenth century. First, industries had to recover from wartime destruction and rebuild damaged infrastructure. Second, manufacturers needed to experience a harsh but necessary correction: when peace arrived, Great Britain's better quality and lower-priced manufacturing exports returned to American shores. Consequently, Americans had to reallocate labor and other resources away from eastern manufacturing and back to agriculture and westward settlement. Third, Great Britain now restricted its purchases of American exports, forcing a redirection of exports to continental Europe and Asia. All three of these factors—recovering from wartime destruction, reallocating resources used in wartime production, and suffering from coercive foreign trade legislation—produced a postwar depression in 1784.[2]

---

[1] George Van Cleve, *We Have Not a Government* (Chicago: The University of Chicago Press, 2017).

[2] Jeremy Atack and Peter Passell, *A New Economic View of American History* (New York: W.W. Norton, 1994), pp. 112–15; Allan Kulikoff, "Such Things Ought Not to Be," in *The World of the Revolutionary American Republic*, ed. Andrew Shankman

Postwar tax and monetary policies aggravated this depression and hampered a quick recovery. The crucial problem for the federal and state governments was how to service their massive war debts. Unable to raise taxes, the Confederation Congress tried to prod states for requisitions. States attempted to fund their debts and make requisition payments by raising taxes and printing money, imposing distortions and misallocations onto an already depressed economy.[3]

States raised taxes by roughly three to six times their prewar levels and used an estimated 50 to 90 percent of tax revenue for debt repayment. Revenue from state tariffs was low, so most of this money came internally from excise and property taxes. Citizens complained loudly about the severe tax burdens they usually had to pay in specie. For example, the average citizen's taxes in Massachusetts increased from 2 to 10 percent of their income. Oligarchs designed the burden to regressively saddle poor interior farmers the most; they paid around 33 percent. The Massachusetts legislature needed the high taxes to pay the state debt at twice its prevailing market value to benefit speculators. The taxes eventually led to a severe tax revolt known as Shays' Rebellion from the fall of 1786 to early 1787. The sharp increase in Massachusetts' and other states' taxes reduced incentives to save and produce, thereby delaying recovery from the depression. On the other hand, Virginia paid off its debt at market values and state congressman Patrick Henry successfully pushed for lower taxes.[4]

Seven states—Pennsylvania, North and South Carolina, Georgia, New Jersey, New York, and Rhode Island—also printed money in 1785 and 1786 to pay off debts. While the printed money did reduce real debt burdens, some of these states also enacted legal tender laws. The result, Gresham's Law, aggravated the depression. In addition, higher prices caused by inflated credit by the three monopolistic state banks—the Bank of North America, the Bank of New York (BONY, est. 1784), and the Massachusetts Bank (est. 1784)—artificially increased

---

(New York: Routledge, 2014), pp. 134–64; Peter Lindert and Jeffrey Williamson, "American Incomes Before and After the Revolution," *Journal of Economic History* (September 2013): 725–65; Murray N. Rothbard, *Conceived in Liberty*, vol. 5, *The New Republic, 1784–1791* (Auburn, AL: Mises Institute, 2019), pp. 47–51.

[3] Rothbard, *Conceived in Liberty*, 5, pp. 66–81.

[4] Max Edling and Mark Kaplanoff, "Alexander's Fiscal Reform," *William and Mary Quarterly* (October 2004): 720; Jon Kukla, *Patrick Henry* (New York: Simon & Schuster, 2017), pp. 273–76; Kulikoff, "Such Things," 149; Rothbard, *Conceived in Liberty*, 5, pp. 68–69, 71–72, 111–26; Van Cleve, *Not a Government*, p. 76.

imports, causing a specie outflow that forced the banks to contract credit. It was the first real instance of the price–specie flow mechanism in the United States, an important self-correcting response of the free market articulated by Enlightenment economists and anti-bank Americans. When the banks contracted in 1784 and 1785 an additional readjustment process had to occur.[5]

Therefore, the depression inevitably resulted from a destructive war and government policies—foreign trade legislation, high taxes, debt monetization, and bank inflation. A stronger central government would not have been able to change any of these factors. However, despite this depression of the mid-1780s, many contemporaries still considered the period a time of growth. In fact, the 1780s experienced one of the greatest increases in population out of any decade in US history. Thus, by April 1786, Secretary of the Confederation Congress Charles Thomson could write to Thomas Jefferson, Minister to France, and declare that

> [t]here is not upon the face of the earth a body of people more happy or rising into consequence with more rapid stride. . . . Population is encreasing, new houses building, new lands clearing, new settlements forming, and new manufacture establishing with a rapidity beyond conception.[6]

Thomson's statement was a promising description of the young republic's capitalistic future.

The United States could have avoided raising taxes and printing money, and hence part of the depression, by repudiating its debts. The repudiation would not have hurt initial bond recipients because the vast majority had already sold their securities to speculators. Moreover, repudiation would have weakened the various governments' credit among domestic and foreign lenders, handicapping their borrowing capabilities and channeling savings to private industry. Some contemporaries argued for such a plan. In April 1786, "A Non-Impost Man" astutely wrote in the *American Herald*, "[T]he debt *need not be paid*;

---

[5] Pauline Maier, *Ratification* (New York: Simon & Schuster, 1020), pp. 224, 521; Curtis Nettels, *The Emergence of a National Economy* (New York: Holt, Rinehart and Winston, 1962), pp. 77–78; Rothbard, *Conceived in Liberty*, 5, pp. 52–56, 73–77.

[6] Gordon Wood, *Empire of Liberty* (New York: Oxford University Press, 2009), p. 14. See also Rothbard, *Conceived in Liberty*, 5, p. 125.

national credit is a proud fancy; funds are the means to *betray* our liberties; a revenue *impoverishes* the people; and the wisdom of Congress is the ambition of despots."[7] The Confederation Congress could have also divided up the federal debt among the states for retirement at realistic market values. Once again, some contemporaries argued for this, such as a special committee at the Confederation Congress in August 1786.

However, the United States eschewed both options and the federal and state debts, like the depression, provided the ultimate justification for a new central government. This time the reactionaries succeeded.[8]

The Reactionary Forces Regroup

In the 1780s, various groups favored a government stronger than the Articles of Confederation that could dispense special privileges, surpassing the previous followers of Robert Morris.

Revolutionary War holdovers constituted the most prominent group. The Confederation owed money to debt holders and ex-military officers connected with the Society of the Cincinnati. Virginia's James Madison, who wanted the federal and state debts funded at par, crucially pushed the 1783 impost through Congress. In contrast to Madison, radicals argued against a central taxing power and supported dividing the debt among the states. Despite their efforts, the states submitted to the amendment.

In Virginia, nationalists ardently backed the proposal. However, while Henry wavered, George Mason and Richard Henry Lee fiercely resisted. In the end, after Mason relented and George Washington exerted his influence, Virginia ratified in late 1783. Even Rhode Island relented in early 1786, over the protests of David Howell, and by August only New York remained. But the increasingly radicalized Governor George Clinton and his loyal political machine controlled the state. Clinton's critics argued that he wanted to protect the revenue accrued from the state's high tariffs. In reality, New York's tariffs ranged around 5 percent, similar to those of other states, and New York City enjoyed little competition with nearby ports.

---

[7] James Philbin, "The Political Economy of the Antifederalists," *Journal of Libertarian Studies* (Fall 1994): 99.

[8] Jeffrey Rogers Hummel, "The Consequences of a United States Default or Repudiation," in *Economic and Political Change after Crisis*, ed. Stephen Balch and Benjamin Powell (London: Routledge, 2016), pp. 108–13; Rothbard, *Conceived in Liberty*, 5, pp. 66–72, 78–81.

The Clintonian Abraham Yates led the state's opposition. Once the taxing power, "the only object of tyrants," was granted to the federal government, "it [would] eventually draw into its vortex all other powers" and destroy the people's liberties.[9] Alexander Hamilton and Philip Schuyler fought vigorously but failed to persuade Clintonians to abide by the impost's proposed terms. Once again the Article's unanimity requirement stymied any effort to centralize power through a national tax. Debt holders and military officials went back to the drawing board.[10]

The Articles also prevented the accrual of power in other ways, frustrating new special-interest groups. Recent events greatly distressed the banking interests. By 1783, the BONA had lost the Confederation's privileges and Pennsylvania radicals, led by William Findley and John Smilie, repealed its state charter in 1785 on constitutional grounds. Although reactionaries regained the legislature in 1786 and granted another charter, the corporation now possessed fewer privileges. Furthermore, Pennsylvania's paper money competed with the BONA's notes. Banking interests, led by Robert Morris, Gouverneur Morris, and James Wilson, desired to reestablish the crony partnership.[11]

Other business interests experienced setbacks. Inefficient northern manufacturers and shippers clamored for state tariffs and navigation laws to block other states' products and Great Britain's goods and ships. However, interstate competition minimized actual regulations: if one state imposed high restrictions, other states undercut them to acquire additional imports. In addition, the South's limited manufacturing and shipping motivated the region to pass milder regulations. On the national level, unanimity and supermajority requirements neutered mercantilist proposals: New York *had* defeated the 1783 impost and Congressman Lee successfully defeated a navigation act in 1785. Northern manufacturers and shippers wanted to outlaw state competition and set one large net to ensure uniform protection.[12]

---

[9] Jackson Main, *The Anti-federalists* (Chapel Hill: The University of North Carolina, 2004), p. 79.

[10] Irving Brant, *James Madison, Father of the Constitution* (New York: Bobbs-Merrill, 1950), pp. 306–07; Douglas A. Irwin, *Clashing over Commerce* (Chicago: The University of Chicago Press, 2017), p. 56; Maier, *Ratification*, pp. 324, 340, 536; Murray N. Rothbard, *Conceived in Liberty*, vols. 1–4 (Auburn, AL: Mises Institute, 2019), p. 1521; Rothbard, *Conceived in Liberty*, 5, pp. 60–65, 135; William Zornow, "New York Tariff Policies," *New York History* (January 1956): 44, 49, 61.

[11] Rothbard, *Conceived in Liberty*, 5, pp. 54–56, 73–74.

[12] Irwin, *Clashing over Commerce*, p. 56; Rothbard, *Conceived in Liberty*, 5, pp. 57–65.

Proponents of internal improvements failed to secure enough state subsidies. Washington, a particularly frustrated advocate, worked with transportation companies that wanted to improve westward navigation. He knew national assistance would foster centralization and increase his own wealth through higher stock prices and land values. Washington and others supported increased taxing power and authority to finance such improvements.[13]

Similarly, various groups yearned for a strong army and navy. Since the end of the Revolutionary War, the reactionary Hamilton and Washington supported a standing army, but the radical Congressmen Elbridge Gerry, Howell, and Lee blocked such proposals. Statists magnified their demands when Daniel Shays and others erupted in open rebellion against Massachusetts' onerous taxes. Although Massachusetts suppressed the rebellion, and men such as Jefferson remained unalarmed, the turmoil worried the reactionaries. Hamilton, Rufus King, and Henry Knox, the Confederation's Secretary at War and the Society of the Cincinnati's secretary, strongly castigated the rebels and urged for a stronger government that could suppress resistance.[14]

Furthermore, reactionary land speculators and merchants recognized that a reinvigorated military could coercively open up trade and territory, particularly in the Northwest, West Indies, Southwest, and Mediterranean Sea. After the war, land speculators lobbied the Confederation Congress to set a high minimum price and plot sizes for western lands to block out settlers. Consequently, the Ordinance of 1785 set the minimum price at $1 per acre and the tract size at 640 acres. The land speculators then lobbied Congress and secured large land grants, particularly in the Northwest, payable in cheap government debt. However, the British refused to leave their northwestern forts, because Americans had failed to pay prewar debts. Americans considered the obligations unjust, arguing that Great Britain's mercantilist regulations had forced them to borrow. Land speculators

---

[13] David Gordon, "George Washington," in *Reassessing the Presidency*, ed. John V. Denson (Auburn, AL: Mises Institute, 2001), pp. 36–37; John Larson, *Internal Improvement* (Chapel Hill: The University of North Carolina, 2001), pp, 10–20; Norman Risjord, *Chesapeake Politics* (New York: Columbia University Press, 1978), pp. 240–47; Rothbard, *Conceived in Liberty*, 5, p. 130.

[14] Richard Kohn, *Eagle and Sword* (New York: Alfred A. Knopf, 2003), pp. 45–72; Rothbard, *Conceived in Liberty*, 1–4, p. 1524; Rothbard, *Conceived in Liberty*, 5, pp. 111–26, 137.

wanted a powerful army that could force the British to leave the Northwest.[15]

Merchants also eyed Britain's West Indies' ports, which remained closed to American goods because of the debt controversy. They pushed for a navy that could incentivize the British to change their mind.[16]

Spain also refused to allow navigation on the Mississippi River, though it generously welcomed other trade arrangements, particularly the Jay-Gardoqui Treaty of 1786. But the proposed treaty did not secure the Mississippi, hurting land speculators and merchants. Furthermore, the stalemate caused Kentucky and Tennessee to toy with secession from Virginia and North Carolina, and prominent southern politicians to flirt with a southern confederation. One such politician was Governor Patrick Henry, who scorned the proposed treaty and believed it a northern plot to confine settlement in the East. When some New England reactionaries subtly threatened to form their own confederation to intimidate the South, Henry's hostility to centralized government increased. Interventionists wanted a nationalizing resolution on the Mississippi issue to stop secession and Henry's resistance. One option was a large army.[17]

In the Mediterranean, the Barbary States of North Africa (Morocco, Algiers, Tunis, and Tripoli) had always demanded tribute from American vessels. Previously, Great Britain paid them. But while the Confederation Congress conducted a favorable peace treaty with Morocco in 1787, the other Barbary States demanded higher taxes. Minister to France Jefferson, usually cognizant of the cost of war, urged armed confrontation. Far more cogent was Minister to Great Britain John Adams, who wisely noted that tribute was less expensive than war. Secretary for Foreign Affairs John Jay, reactionary to the core, hoped to exploit the opportunity and develop a strong navy.[18]

By 1786 and 1787, the Articles' discipline provided only two options: the states' rights Confederation must remain permanently weak or break up. Secession could possibly lead to separate New England, Mid-Atlantic, southern, and western confederacies. Such

---

[15] Michael Klarman, *The Framers' Coup* (New York: Oxford University Press, 2016), pp. pp. 349–50; Rothbard, *Conceived in Liberty,* 5, pp. 85–92.

[16] Rothbard, *Conceived in Liberty,* 5, pp. 48, 105–07, 127, 306.

[17] Kukla, *Patrick Henry,* pp. 285–306; Rothbard, *Conceived in Liberty,* 5, pp. 93–104.

[18] Rothbard, *Conceived in Liberty,* 5, pp. 60, 105–07.

libertarian decentralization would promote competition and weaken governments' ability to pass centralizing taxes, regulations, and subsidies to benefit favored interests. Recognizing that this would ruin their plans, reactionaries realized it was now or never.

The Constitutional Convention

The United States Constitution is often treated as a hallowed document for saving the country from the brink of total destruction. Even many modern-day proponents of limited government consider it a significant check on cronyism.[19] In reality, the Constitution was nothing more than the continuation of previous efforts to establish an American Old Order. It only acquired its laissez-faire meaning because of later strategic interpretations by libertarians.

In the mid-1780s the political spectrum coalesced into two groups. The reactionaries became bona fide *nationalists*, desiring to replace the confederation with a new government that could overpower the states and enact mercantilism. These nationalists swelled their ranks with the various disgruntled groups. On the other hand, the champions of liberty, who vigorously supported independence, became *federalists*. They secretly desired to either split up the confederation, maintain the weak Articles, or slightly strengthen them with amendments. Power would be spread out across the governments; hence the term *federalism*. Above all, these libertarians believed states' rights provided the best bulwark against special privileges. Nationalists hailed from the seaboard, federalists from the western regions of the states.

Three factors assured the nationalists' victory despite their minority status. First, the bulk of the country's prominent men supported nationalism, and these men closely communicated with each other. Second, some of the radical leadership had shifted into the nationalist camp, cornering federalist leaders into the defensive. Third, and most importantly, the nationalists deliberately lied to the public. Their most crucial obfuscation was to not call themselves nationalists, anathema to the public, but instead "Federalists" even though they secretly desired to crush states' rights. They called the true federalists "Anti-federalists" to sour their viewpoint in the public's mind. The linguistic sleight of hand was complete: Federalists championed a

---

[19] James Buchanan and Gordon Tullock, *The Calculus of Consent* (Ann Arbor: The University of Michigan Press, 1962).

stronger national government while Antifederalists stood for a weaker national government.[20]

In January 1786, the reactionary Madison proposed in the Virginia legislature a convention to strengthen Congress' regulatory powers. At the time, Patrick Henry was hesitatingly sympathetic, sending out a circular letter to the other governors. However, in September only a small group of Federalist delegates from five states met in Annapolis, Maryland. Despite this setback, Madison worked with Hamilton and planned for another convention, meeting next May in Philadelphia, to discuss *legal* amendments to the Articles.[21]

Federalists dominated the Philadelphia Convention because many Antifederalists disastrously declined to attend. Thus, many prominent Virginia and Massachusetts Antifederalists—Lee, Henry, Sam Adams, and John Hancock—were absent and only Mason and Gerry attended. Henry refused to participate because he "smelt a rat."[22] In addition, the radical theoretician Jefferson still served as Minister to France. Furthermore, Clinton absented and the staunchly Antifederal Rhode Island refused to send any delegates. Only a few hardcore libertarians attended: the obscure Clintonians Robert Yates and John Lansing, the nephew of Abraham Yates and the mayor of Albany, respectively, and Luther Martin, Maryland's attorney general. Despite their best efforts, the three would leave in disgust before the convention ended. These radicals, along with the more moderate Mason and Gerry, could not match the Federalists' heavy artillery: Robert Morris, Gouverneur Morris, and Wilson of Pennsylvania; Hamilton of New York; Madison and Washington of Virginia; and the wealthy planters Charles Pinckney and Charles Cotesworth Pinckney of South Carolina.[23]

The Federalist-dominated Constitutional Convention quickly scrapped the Articles and devised an entirely new government. Unsurprisingly, Robert Morris' ambit—Gouverneur Morris, Wilson, and Madison—played the largest role. Hamilton played a smaller part because Yates and Lansing continually outvoted him in the New York delegation and other Federalists balked at his monarchical tendencies. Robert

---

[20] Rothbard, *Conceived in Liberty*, 5, pp. 128–29.

[21] Kukla, *Patrick Henry*, p. 304; Rothbard, *Conceived in Liberty*, 5, pp. 129–32.

[22] Kukla, *Patrick Henry*, p. 320.

[23] John Kaminski, *George Clinton* (Madison, WI: Madison House Publishers, 1993), p. 119; Forrest McDonald, *We The People* (Chicago: The University of Chicago Press, 1958), pp. 80–81; Rothbard, *Conceived in Liberty*, 5, pp. 133–40, 212, 249.

Morris also sat on the sidelines because he knew his extensive involvement would generate too much controversy. Overall, the convention's Constitution laid the foundations for a corrupt American Empire.

To begin, the Federalists gave their new system the necessary political, legal, and military infrastructure. Instead of the Confederation's unicameral legislature, the new government contained three branches—a bicameral legislature, an executive, and a supreme judiciary—equipped with a host of formidable powers. Politicians possessed long terms with no limits, creating an oligarchical elite shielded from rotation in office. Hamilton and Gouverneur Morris even favored life tenure for some executive and legislative positions, though the convention only gave life tenure to the judicial branch.

A single president led the executive branch and could indefinitely win reelection by an Electoral College remote from state legislatures or congressional control. He had the power to veto legislation (susceptible to a two-thirds override), a colonial relic that made it harder to pass anti-crony reforms; create a formidable bureaucracy; and command the military. Hamilton, Gouverneur Morris, Madison, and Wilson advocated for a powerful executive against Mason's protests, who believed it would establish a monarchy. Hamilton and Wilson even wanted to give the executive an absolute veto, which would have erected an impenetrable bulwark against reform. Overall, the Federalists knew that a strong executive branch was indispensable for cronyism.[24]

A bicameral Congress possessed the unlimited power to tax, regulate, spend, and raise standing armies, all constitutionally justified by vague clauses. The Supremacy Clause made federal edicts "the supreme Law of the Land"; the general welfare clause sanctioned the collection of taxes, payment of debts, and provision "for the common Defence and general Welfare"; and the necessary and proper clause allowed for "all Laws which shall be necessary and proper."[25] Politicians and legal scholars later scrutinized these clauses, but at the convention relatively little debate occurred. The Federalists recognized the broad clauses easily facilitated special-interest legislation, shrewdly realizing that enumeration of such privilege granting would increase hostility toward the Constitution.

---

[24] Klarman, *Framers' Coup*, pp. 167–68; Rothbard, *Conceived in Liberty*, 5, pp. 145–52, 154–57, 162, 164, 167, 178, 185, 190–91.

[25] William Watkins, *Crossroads for Liberty* (Oakland, CA: Independent Institute, 2016), pp. 241–42, 248.

Martin introduced a weakened supremacy clause as a response to Madison's proposed congressional veto over any state's legislation. Although Martin intended the supremacy clause to limit power, the convention strengthened it so much that Martin ended up denouncing the final version as "worse than useless."[26] The convention approved the necessary and proper clause with little debate, though Gerry and Mason bitterly objected. Federalists strengthened the Articles' general welfare clauses. Men such as Gouverneur Morris and Wilson recognized that if those clauses allowed the Confederation Congress to charter the Bank of North America, a stronger clause could do far more. The ultra-reactionaries, from John Dickinson to the present, knew that vague clauses played an indispensable role in enhancing the central government's power.[27]

Finally, an elite Supreme Court, appointed by the president for life, lorded over the judicial branch and could review state and federal laws' constitutionality. In addition, Madison and Wilson enabled Congress to establish inferior courts to aid the Supreme Court. Through judicial review, the federal system would be the final arbiter of all constitutional questions, a fatal blow to states' rights. No real mechanism existed to check the unelected judges, nor could states and other federal branches challenge the judiciary's decisions. This monopolization of legal services indispensably furthered cronyism.[28]

One by one all the special interests received what they wanted. When it came to the debt speculators, Congress would assume the Confederation's debts. Furthermore, Madison and Hamilton successfully argued that the Constitution remain silent on state debts to provoke less opposition. Federalists then linked Congress' taxing power to payment of the public debt and general welfare. If Congress assumed federal as well as state debts at par, speculators would make a killing.[29]

---

[26] Bill Kauffman, *Forgotten Founder, Drunken Prophet* (Wilmington, DE: ISI Books, 2008), p. 52.

[27] Ibid., pp. 52–53; Klarman, *Framers' Coup*, pp. 152, 670; Rothbard, *Conceived in Liberty*, 5, pp. 187–88.

[28] Richard Ellis, *The Jeffersonian Crisis* (New York: Oxford University Press, 1971), pp. 7–12; Klarman, *Framers' Coup*, pp. 159–61; John Miller, *Hamilton and the Growth of the New Nation* (New York: Harper & Row, 1959), pp. 201–03; Rothbard, *Conceived in Liberty*, 5, pp. 156–57, 162, 206.

[29] Rothbard, *Conceived in Liberty*, 5, pp. 186–87; Klarman, *Framers' Coup*, pp. 383–84.

The Constitution also enshrined monetary mercantilism. The coinage clause authorized Congress to "coin money" and make legal tender laws in specie, thereby regulating the money supply.[30] In addition to a clause authorizing borrowing money, the Constitution initially allowed Congress to issue "bills on the credit of the United States" (i.e., paper money).[31] However, the Convention struck this paper money clause out. Gouverneur Morris argued that the lack of explicit enumeration just restricted issuance to a *"responsible* minister," while Nathaniel Gorham of Massachusetts and Madison recognized that the Constitution still implied "safe" emissions.[32] Crucially though, the Federalists made the prohibition of state paper money explicit, largely due to BONA stockholders Robert Morris and Gouverneur Morris. Pennsylvania's delegation wanted the Constitution to block out the competition of state paper money and instead funnel crony monetary privileges to their own banking interests.[33]

Quite crucially, the Federalists also secured the ability to charter a new central bank. Gouverneur Morris argued that the general welfare clause authorized Congress to grant "exclusive privileges to trading companies."[34] When Madison proposed explicit enumeration, Wilson remarked that such power was "already included in the power to regulate trade," to Mason's dismay.[35] The ultra-Federalists, the major players behind the constitutional drive, knew the vague clauses could always do the dirty work, just like with the BONA during the Revolutionary War.[36]

The Federalists did not leave out the manufacturers and shippers. The convention outlawed interstate tariffs, granting vague interstate

---

[30] S. Breckinridge, "Monetary Power and the Constitutional Convention," in Henry Holzer, *Government's Money Monopoly* (New York: Books in Focus, 1981), p. 37.

[31] Ibid., p. 37.

[32] Robert Natelson, "Paper Money and the Original Understanding of the Coinage Clause," *Harvard Journal of Law and Public Policy* (Summer 2008): 1054, 1056.

[33] Breckinridge, "Monetary Power," pp. 35–42; Farley Grubb, "Creating the U.S. Dollar Currency Union," *American Economic Review* (December 2003): 1788, 1790; Natelson, "Paper Money," pp. 1051–79.

[34] Max Farrand, *The Records of the Federal Convention of 1787* (New Haven, CT: Yale University Press, 1911), pp. 529–30.

[35] Ibid., p. 616.

[36] Steven Calabresi and Larissa Leibowitz, "Monopolies and the Constitution," *Harvard Journal of Law & Public Policy* (Summer 2013): 1009; Farrand, *Convention of 1787*, pp. 615–16; Calvin Johnson, "The Dubious Enumerated Power Doctrine," *Constitutional Commentary* (2005): 55–58.

regulatory oversight (the commerce clause) to only a simple majority in both chambers. This made it easier for Congress to cast a mercantilist net on all states to benefit select business groups. Some southern delegates bitterly protested the simple majority, such as the Federalist Charles Pinckney and the Antifederalists Martin and Mason. However, as Gorham bluntly explained: "If the Government is to be so fettered as to be unable to relieve the Eastern States what motive can they have to join in it."[37] The Constitution allowed the North to finally enact its preferred redistribution.[38]

Proponents of internal improvements secured successes as well. Armed with vast taxing capabilities, the delegates empowered Congress "to establish Post Offices and post Roads," an opening wedge for subsidized public works.[39] Although the delegates voted down a clause that explicitly enumerated the power to build "canals where deemed necessary," Gouverneur Morris and Wilson realized the broad clauses could perform the heavy lifting.[40]

Finally, land speculators and other proponents of a strong army and navy got their way. Congress could finance a military, and the president could command the army, enlist state militias, and govern any war departments Congress might establish. Gerry and Martin bitterly protested the pro-military provisions but to no avail: the Federalists adamantly demanded the expansionist commercial interests receive their military polity. Gouverneur Morris even wanted a simple majority for the Senate to ratify peace treaties instead of the agreed-upon two-thirds requirement to encourage Congress to declare war for the Mississippi River. Murray Rothbard remarks that Morris' desire "was a clear-cut indication of the neglected role that the power for aggressive war and any adventurous foreign policy played in the drive for the new Constitution."[41] After all, as John Rutledge of South Carolina remarked, "[w]e are laying the foundation for a great empire."[42]

[37] Rothbard, *Conceived in Liberty*, 5, pp. 196.

[38] Calvin Johnson, "The Panda's Thumb," *William and Mary Bill of Rights Journal* (October 2004): 1–56; Rothbard, *Conceived in Liberty*, 5, pp. 192–98.

[39] Watkins, *Crossroads for Liberty*, p. 241.

[40] Farrand, *Convention of 1787*, p. 615. See also Brant, *James Madison, Father*, pp. 149–50; Johnson, "Enumerated Power Doctrine," pp. 55–58.

[41] Rothbard, *Conceived in Liberty*, 5, p. 207.

[42] Ibid., p. 196.

As an extra sop to land speculators, Rufus King, Wilson, and Madison prevented the states from passing a "Law impairing the Obligation of Contracts."[43] Wilson, an attorney for Robert Morris, wanted to protect monopolistic corporate charters like that of the BONA. Federalists eagerly expected to use this contract clause to shield land grants.[44]

The major debates at the Constitutional Convention concerned who would control the Constitution's powers, particularly through representation in the bicameral Congress: greater political representation would increase a region's ability to control special-interest legislation. Large-state Federalists, such as Madison, Gouverneur Morris, and Wilson, squabbled bitterly with small-state Federalists, particularly Connecticut's Roger Sherman and Oliver Ellsworth, over states' proportional or equal representation. Concurrently, northern and southern states vehemently debated the *political* representation of slaves, which impacted the North's ability to pass tariffs and navigation acts.

After much debate, everyone shook hands. First, the Constitution sanctioned equal representation in the Senate (the upper oligarchical house) and proportional representation in the House (the lower democratic house) to give large and small states approximate parity. Second, and quite fatefully, the Constitution based House apportionment on the free population *and* three-fifths of slaves. Many envisioned that this clause, in conjunction with projected population trends, ensured southern dominance. Clearly, the North subsidized southern slavery in return for easier passage of tariffs and navigation acts in the short term. Hamilton later candidly admitted that the slave compromise resulted from the "spirit of accommodation which governed the convention; and without this indulgence no union could possibly have been formed."[45]

A related debate involved the country's first "corrupt bargain."[46] The convention strengthened southern slavery through a twenty-year protection of the slave trade. In return, the North could enact mercantilist tariffs and navigation acts through a simple majority vote. Furthermore, the Constitution contained a fugitive slave clause that required states to return escaped slaves, thereby socializing the enforcement

---

[43] Watkins, *Crossroads for Liberty*, p. 243.

[44] Merrill Jensen, *The Articles of Confederation* (Madison: The University of Wisconsin Press, 1940), p. 176; Rothbard, *Conceived in Liberty*, 5, pp. 185–86, 189–91, 206–07.

[45] Klarman, *Framers' Coup*, p. 303.

[46] Rothbard, *Conceived in Liberty*, 5, p. 192.

costs of slaveholding. Antifederal Luther Martin was especially critical of the Constitution's pro-slavery features, considering the document an *"insult to that God . . .* who views with equal eye the poor *African slave* and his *American master."*[47] The Constitution reduced anti-slavery sentiments and codified slavery across the country.[48]

The entire Constitution looked limited, democratic, and responsive to the people. In reality, it empowered a small elite, crippled states' rights, and created the groundwork for an Old Order American Empire. The Constitution was an especially suffocating document without any bill of rights that protected personal liberties and reserved power to the states.

Importantly, the Constitutional Convention was outside the Articles' amendment procedure. When the Annapolis Convention called for the Philadelphia meeting, they stated that its purpose was to revise the Articles and report any revisions "to the United States in Congress assembled, as when agreed to by them, and afterwards confirmed by the Legislatures of every State."[49] The Confederation Congress only agreed to the Philadelphia meeting "for the purpose of revising the Articles of Confederation . . . and reporting to the United States in Congress assembled and to the States respectively such alterations and amendments."[50] However, once the convention began, the delegates pledged a secrecy rule and quickly created an entirely new governmental structure. While one could charitably interpret the Constitution as an "amendment," Congress and the state legislatures still needed to ratify it. Instead, the Federalists decided to send the Constitution to state conventions. The reason, as admitted by Gouverneur Morris and Madison, was simple: it ensured a higher chance of ratification. Moreover, the Constitutional Convention scrapped unanimity, deciding that only nine out of the thirteen states (roughly three-fourths) needed to ratify.[51]

Many contemporaries recognized the bloodless coup d'état for special-interest spoils. In 1789, Abraham Yates, with only some rhetorical flair, accurately described the "legal revisions":

---

[47] Ibid., p. 198.

[48] Andrew P. Napolitano, *Dred Scott's Revenge* (Nashville, TN: Thomas Nelson, 2009), pp. 36–40; Rothbard, *Conceived in Liberty*, 5, pp. 159–76, 192–98.

[49] Rothbard, *Conceived in Liberty*, 5, p. 132.

[50] Ibid., p. 138.

[51] Ibid., pp. 146, 157, 199–203, 211–12.

The meeting at Philadelphia in 1787 for the sole and express purpose of revising the Articles of Confederation, got the name of a Convention (I believe before long that of a Conspiracy would have been more Significant), [and] paid no more regard to their orders and credentials than Caesar when he passed the Rubicon. Under an Injunction of Secrecy they carried on their works of Darkness until the Constitution passed their usurping hands.[52]

The Ratification Debates

Thanks to control of news outlets, malapportionment of delegates, and convention chicanery, Federalists rammed the Constitution through a resistant public. Massachusetts, Virginia, and New York put up fierce resistance, but not enough.

Once the convention finished in September 1787, only three remaining delegates refused to sign: Gerry, Mason, and Virginia Governor Edmund Randolph. They argued for a second constitutional convention and important structural amendments restricting taxation, regulations, standing armies, the ability to charter monopolies, and the vague clauses. Shrewdly, the Federalists realized that these proposals would cripple the new government's power, if not torpedo it altogether, and denied the need for additional work—the public-spirited Great Men in Philadelphia had accomplished everything.[53]

After the state legislatures received the Constitution in the fall, Federalists racked up their first major victory in Pennsylvania, where Wilson pushed for hasty ratification. Although infrequently discussed, the politics surrounding ratification were thoroughly crony. The states did not unanimously enter into the new government, ratification arose against the people's wishes, and the people could not amend the Constitution. In fact, while the population of some states clearly supported the Federalists, a majority of the population did not agree with the Constitution, a stark contrast with the mass-movement American Revolution.[54]

---

[52] Rothbard, *Conceived in Liberty*, 5, p. 273.

[53] Calabresi and Leibowitz, "Monopolies and the Constitution," p. 1009; Rothbard, *Conceived in Liberty*, 5, pp. 201–02, 212–13.

[54] Rothbard, *Conceived in Liberty*, 5, pp. 217–18, 221–30.

First, the Federalists maintained a massive advantage in the public relations department. They controlled the major newspapers and post offices, allowing them to delay, tamper with, or outright destroy Antifederalist mail. For example, between the critical New York and Virginia, Federalist communication took six to fourteen days to arrive while Antifederalist communication required six to ten *weeks*. The Federalist media organs also suppressed dissension at the ratification conventions. Nationalists spread the lie that the new "federal" government would be limited in *The Federalist Papers*, propaganda pieces written by Madison, Hamilton, and Jay. They waxed eloquently about the limited nature of the proposed government, including its taxing capabilities, vague clauses, and how states would retain their sovereignty. Many fell for the blatant lies, believing the Constitution strictly enumerated powers.

On the other hand, prescient Antifederalist writings criticized the Constitution. Pennsylvania's *Address of the Minority* warned of a standing army funded through a vast bureaucracy of tax collectors, and Massachusetts' "Agrippa" preached laissez-faire and criticized Congress' unlimited power over trade, taxes, and commerce. *Letters from the Federal Farmer* in Virginia and New York's *Cato* (potentially written by Lee and Clinton, respectively) stressed the benefits of small republics, warned of consolidation, and attacked the vague powers. Lastly, "Brutus" in New York criticized the necessary and proper clause. The author, channeling Adam Smith, castigated Congress' ability to incur a burdensome national debt. These writers, *not* Hamilton and Madison's divinized *Federalist Papers*, spoke the truth.[55]

Second, delegate malapportionment privileged the Federalists. Political representation of districts for state legislatures and the conventions heavily benefitted the eastern commercial districts. This favored the Federalists at the expense of the western and more numerous Antifederalistist districts. If accurate representation occurred, the Antifederal areas would have sent more delegates to the conventions and the Federal areas less. In some states the malapportionment remained egregious: in South Carolina, the percent of the population represented by convention delegates voting for the Constitution only

---

[55] Dumas Malone, *Jefferson and the Ordeal of Liberty* (Boston: Little, Brown, 1962), p. 397; Rothbard, *Conceived in Liberty*, 5, pp. 216–18, 228–29, 237–38, 255–56, 268–70; Thomas Slaughter, *The Whiskey Rebellion* (New York: Oxford University Press, 1986), p. 97; Robert Wright, *One Nation Under Debt* (New York: McGraw Hill, 2008), pp. 102–03, 118.

totaled 39 percent. In the crucial battleground states of Massachusetts, Virginia, and New York the numbers were the underwhelming 53, 50, and 34 percent. Importantly, even these numbers overstate support, because they assume the delegates voting for the Constitution actually represented their constituents' wishes, and many did not.[56]

Third, at the conventions the Federalists employed blatant lies, bribery, and dirty tricks to sway the radical moderates, the cautious Antifederalist-Federalist hybrid. In particular, they mendaciously promised structural amendments *after* ratification, particularly explicit enumeration and constraints on taxes, borrowing, and standing armies. This pledge became necessary after Pennsylvania radicals William Findley, John Smilie, and the Swiss immigrant Albert Gallatin protested ratification. Of course, promising something after ratification is much different than enacting it beforehand, and the Federalists quickly reneged on their agreement. Furthermore, Federalists corrupted key delegates with prospects of government power.[57]

The first battleground state, Massachusetts, was replete with such dirty tricks. In January 1788, the convention opened with Antifederalist strength at 60 percent. However, most Antifederalist delegates were poor westerners, and Federalists managed to prevent the election of Gerry. On the other hand, Federalist delegates had notable backgrounds. A prominent example was Fisher Ames, a member of the ultra statist Essex Junto, a group of reactionary and privilege-seeking merchants and lawyers around Boston. Crucially, the state only paid for the western delegates' trips *to* the convention, and wealthy Federalists offered to pay their return trips only if they ratified. Predictably, in many cases the Federalists never paid the delegates, or provided only a fraction of the reimbursement.

The Federalists also bribed and lied to prominent Antifederalist leaders. They promised John Hancock, the Antifederalist governor, either the presidency or vice presidency if he supported the Constitution and proposed various amendments—amendments that the Federalists gave him—for enactment *after* ratification. The corrupted Hancock fell for the trick, causing one Federalist to write: "Hancock is the ostensible puppet in proposing amendments; but they are the product

---

[56] Charles Roll, "We, Some of the People," *Journal of American History* (June 1969): 21–40; Rothbard, *Conceived in Liberty*, 5, p. 218.

[57] Rothbard, *Conceived in Liberty*, 5, pp. 226–30, 243–44; Gregory May, *Jefferson's Treasure* (Washington, DC: Regnery History, 2018), pp. 6, 18–21.

of the Feds in concert."[58] Hancock's support influenced crucial Antifederal delegates, and along with the betrayal of other important leaders such as Sam Adams, the Massachusetts convention ratified the Constitution in February. Federalist stratagems secured this victory.[59]

These three reasons—media control, malapportionment, and dirty tactics—assured a Federalist triumph. In June 1788, when New Hampshire became the ninth state to ratify, the new government illegally went into effect. New Hampshire's convention had actually met earlier in the year and planned to reject the Constitution until Federalists adjourned the meeting. Washington, upset at the adjournment, worried that the people might realize that the Constitution was not as popular "as they had been taught to believe."[60] Fortunately, his secretary reported that amendments did the trick in New Hampshire, which "were drawn up more with a view of softening & conciliating the . . . opposition than from an expectation that they would ever be engrafted in the Constitution."[61]

But, four states still failed to ratify: North Carolina, Rhode Island, Virginia, and New York. Federalists recognized that they needed Virginia and New York, the Antifederalist strongholds informally and ineffectively allied, for the new government's inauguration in 1789.

In Virginia, Henry, Mason, and Lee put up a good fight. Henry intuitively perceived that ratification impacted the great conflict between freedom and coercion, between an Empire of Liberty and an Empire of Power:

> If we admit this consolidated government, it will be because we like a great, splendid one. Some way or other we must be a great and mighty empire; we must have an army, and a navy . . . the American spirit, assisted by the ropes and chains of consolidation, is about to convert this country into a powerful and mighty empire.[62]

---

[58] Klarman, *Framers' Coup*, p. 439.

[59] Maier, *Ratification*, pp. 192, 212, 516; Rothbard, *Conceived in Liberty*, 5, pp. 236–46.

[60] Main, *Anti-federalists*, p. 211.

[61] Maier, *Ratification*, p. 317. See also Rothbard, *Conceived in Liberty*, 5, pp. 234–35, 253–54.

[62] Rothbard, *Conceived in Liberty*, 5, p. 263.

In Maryland, Martin emphasized a similar theme and declared that the Constitution would create "one great and extensive empire," but his efforts were for naught.[63]

Some historians have argued that Henry and other Virginian Antifederalists opposed the Constitution to covertly protect slavery.[64] This is not true. Like many southern libertarians, Henry abhorred slavery. He had worked to end Virginia's importation of slaves and ease manumission laws but did not know how to end the practice. At the convention, Henry admittedly argued that the Constitution could theoretically abolish slavery through its taxing power and general welfare clause. However, Henry's "slavery scare" remonstrance was a last-ditch effort to sway Federalists and radical moderates, and his proposed amendments made no mention of slavery. That Henry and others wanted restrictions on taxing power to prevent Congress from levying taxes on slaves is unsurprising: slaves were southerners' most valuable property. The fact that large slave-owning politicians in the Deep South states of South Carolina and Georgia, particularly Charles Cotesworth Pinckney, unhesitatingly supported ratification demonstrates that pro-slavery forces supported the Constitution. In reality, Henry was genuinely concerned about liberty.[65]

In the end, the Virginia Antifederalists could not surmount the betrayal of Governor Edmund Randolph, whom Federalists corrupted with the prospect of future employment; the threatened secession of the Federalists' Northern Neck region; and the lure of amendments after ratification. Over bitter opposition, in June enough wavering radical-moderates took the bait and ratified the Constitution by a margin of five votes. The feat was remarkable considering that 60 percent of the state's population was Antifederalist. Crucially, the radical moderate Jefferson, still away in France, supported the Constitution because of his friend Madison. However, Jefferson wanted structural amendments after ratification to constrain the government and achieve his Empire of Liberty.[66]

---

[63] Ibid., p. 263.

[64] Robin Einhorn, "Patrick Henry's Case Against the Constitution," *Journal of the Early Republic* (Winter 2002): 549–73.

[65] Klarman, *Framers' Coup*, pp. 297–304; Kukla, *Patrick Henry*, pp. 122–26, 238–40, 374, 506–07; Maier, *Ratification*, pp. 294–97.

[66] Klarman, *Framers' Coup*, p. 468; Rothbard, *Conceived in Liberty*, 5, pp. 255–66.

New York experienced a similar situation. While Governor Clinton and his loyal machine steadfastly opposed the Constitution, they recognized the uphill battle: by the summer of 1788 the choice was to either join the new union or remain outside of it. In May, Clinton tried to cooperate with Randolph to coordinate strategies and insist on amendments before ratification, but by this time the apostate Randolph mendaciously concealed Clinton's efforts at the Virginia convention. In New York, Antifederalists pushed hard for restrictive amendments, such as conditional ratification that allowed for possible secession, but Hamilton deep-sixed resistance. On this point, he read a letter to the Antifederalists written by Madison. "The Constitution requires an adoption in toto, and forever," wrote Madison, "[I]t has been so adopted by the other states. . . . In short, any condition whatever must vitiate the ratification."[67] Madison and Hamilton would not allow any secession whatsoever.

At the convention and in the press, Hamilton concealed his monarchical tendencies while waxing eloquently on the need for a formidable American Empire. In addition to Hamilton's strong-arming, district malapportionment and betrayal of Antifederalist delegates overwhelmed the opposition. Furthermore, like Virginia's Northern Neck, New York City, the capital of the existing Confederation Congress, threatened to secede. The motive was clear: if New York did not join, the capital would have to move and the city would lose the subsidies and privileges bestowed on the seat of power. In the end, staunchly Antifederalist New York barely ratified in July, by a razor-thin margin of two votes. But Antifederalists at least forced the Federalists to send a circular letter to other states requesting that Congress call a second constitutional convention. In addition, Governor Clinton planned to run for the vice presidency to secure restrictive amendments, anathema to Hamilton and the New York Federalists.[68]

In the summer of 1788 the old Confederation Congress, over the objections of Congressman Abraham Yates of New York, realized that the putsch had succeeded. The old Congress decided that the new Congress would assemble in March 1789. In addition, while they had not settled on a permanent capital, the temporary capital—to Hamilton's

---

[67] Klarman, *Framers' Coup*, p. 507.

[68] Kaminski, *George Clinton*, pp. 148–78; Rothbard, *Conceived in Liberty*, 5, pp. 255–57, 267–81.

delight and Madison's chagrin—remained in New York City. States would hold elections in the fall of 1788.

The congressional results were a bloodbath: the Antifederalists only won eleven of fifty-nine House seats and two of twenty-two Senate seats. The only two Antifederalist senators hailed from Virginia: Lee and the aging William Grayson. Henry deprived Madison of a Senate seat, but could not stop his nemesis from snatching a House spot at the expense of the Antifederalist James Monroe. The Federalists secured such crushing victories, because Federalists had won state elections and thus controlled the state legislatures. This allowed them to elect their own choices for senators and mandate at-large elections for members of the House instead of local district elections. At-large elections were insulated from the local constituencies and benefitted charismatic candidates, who tended to be Federalists. Virginia was an exception and Henry drew Madison's district so that it encompassed a large number of Antifederalist voters. Overall, the Federalists amassed enough representation in the elections to pass their special-interest legislation in the new Congress.[69]

Originally, the state legislatures decided how the Electoral College would be elected, such as by some form of popular vote or by state legislatures. The predominant choice was the latter. After electors were chosen, each cast two votes for president and the candidate with the majority would become president and the runner-up vice president. Washington, the legendary general of the Revolution, was guaranteed the exalted presidency. Since Washington hailed from southern Virginia, the electors felt obligated to choose a vice president from a major northern state. The Federalists realized that Pennsylvania was out of the question because of its proximity to Virginia and the only viable New Yorker was the staunchly Antifederalist George Clinton. This left Massachusetts, and the realistic choices were Governor Hancock and (now) Congressman John Adams. Although Hancock literally sold out for the vice presidency, he was still too Antifederalist and the Federalists easily double-crossed him. On the other hand, the reactionary Adams now exhibited monarchical and aristocratic tendencies. The choice was easy: the Federalists picked Adams.

Still, Hamilton, a major power broker in the Electoral College, suspiciously eyed the former radical. In January 1789 he wrote to Wilson:

---

[69] Klarman, *Framers' Coup*, pp. 559, 568, 623; Rothbard, *Conceived in Liberty*, 5, pp. 265–66, 282–83.

"[F]or God's sake . . . if risk is to be run on one side or on the other can we hesitate where it ought to be preferred?"[70] Hamilton was convinced that Adams could not be trusted, a fateful prediction that eventually proved correct. Therefore, to guarantee that Adams would not somehow miraculously win over Washington, Hamilton arranged for numerous delegates to "throw away" their votes instead. Washington won the presidency with sixty-nine electoral votes over Adams' thirty-four.

The Electoral College chose Washington and Adams in February, and in early March congressmen trickled into New York City. After Washington's inauguration, the new government effectively sprung into existence. The Federalists had successfully muscled through their mercantilist and empire-building Constitution against the will of the people. Power decisively triumphed over liberty.[71]

Prime Minister Madison

By spring 1789, the Federalist coup was complete. The new government created by the Constitution supplanted the Articles of Confederation and only insignificant North Carolina and Rhode Island remained outside the Union. Antifederalism was permanently weakened in Massachusetts and Pennsylvania, Martin returned to legal work, Henry brooded in Virginia, and Governor Clinton defended his control of New York against Hamilton. Their next step was a second constitutional convention that could devise the promised restrictive amendments. Unfortunately, the Federalists totally controlled the politically machinery and no laissez-faire coalition could stop them.

In the first year Madison exerted enormous influence over the politically inept Washington and Congress' legislation. In essence, he became the de facto prime minister, tallying a long list of goals. So far, only President Washington, Congress, and remnant posts from the confederation existed and the government lacked real executive and judicial branches. Most importantly, there was no money. Or, in the eloquent words of Congressman and Essex Junto man Ames, "[M]oney is power, a permanent revenue is permanent power."[72] Consequently, Madison and the Federalists moved to secure funding. Everyone agreed

---

[70] Manning Dauer, *The Adams Federalists* (Baltimore, MD: The John Hopkins Press, 1953), p. 81.

[71] Klarman, *Framers' Coup*, pp. 622–23; Rothbard, *Conceived in Liberty*, 5, pp. 284–87; Watkins, *Crossroads for Liberty*, p. 243.

[72] Fergus Bordewich, *The First Congress* (New York: Simon & Schuster, 2016), p. 74.

that revenue would primarily be raised by import duties and a navigation act, legislation the Constitution could secure more easily than the Articles.

In April, after Congress achieved a quorum, Madison introduced a revenue bill, provoking a sectional tension. Northern manufacturers wailed for protection while southern planters called for low rates. As the leading congressman, Madison tried to balance these concerns, but he surprisingly leaned to the North. The result, the Tariff Act of 1789, passed in July by an unrecorded vote. The law intended to raise revenue and protect industry, and rates as a percentage of total imports averaged 12.5 percent. In addition, Congress passed the Tonnage Act later in the month. This navigation act not only raised revenue but also shielded domestic shipping interests from foreign competition. While American ships had to pay six cents a ton on entry into a US port (and only once a year if employed in the fisheries or coastal trade), every foreign ship needed to pay fifty cents a ton. In the perceptive words of John Miller, Madison clearly "attempted to erect one all-embracing mercantilist system in place of the thirteen different systems that had hitherto existed in the United States."[73] But these policies siphoned the spoils to the North, much to southerners' dismay.[74]

Aside from raising revenue, Madison secured another stratagem to aggrandize central power: bill of rights amendments. This would deliver the *coup de grâce* to the reform opposition. It was not guaranteed that Henry and the other Antifederalists would stay on the outside. The New York convention circular letter that urged for a second constitutional convention and structural amendments gained ground in Virginia, North Carolina, and Rhode Island. To make matters worse, Henry and other Virginia Antifederalists devised a backup plan: they planned to buy southwestern lands claimed by Georgia and secede. Virginia's Antifederalist congressman, Theodrick Bland, hoped Henry's endeavors would create "an asylum from tyranny."[75]

Madison realized the realistic possibility of these threats and wanted to nip them in the bud with amendments. However, his goal

---

[73] Miller, *Alexander Hamilton*, p. 222.

[74] *Historical Statistics of the United States, Millennial Edition*, vol. 5, ed. Richard Sutch and Susan Carter. New York: Cambridge University Press, 2006, p. 510; John Miller, *The Federalist Era* (New York: Harper & Brothers, 1960), pp. 14–19; Irwin, *Clashing over Commerce*, pp. 73–77; Nettels, *Emergence of a National Economy*, pp. 109–11.

[75] Thomas Kidd, *Patrick Henry* (New York: Basic Book, 2011), p. 219. See also pp. 218–20; Rothbard, *Conceived in Liberty*, 5, pp. 297.

was not to pass structural amendments that crippled the Constitution but instead a bill of rights focusing on personal liberties such as freedom of speech and trials by jury. While these were certainly laudatory, Madison knew they would not weaken the Constitution. Moreover, these amendments would split the states' rights resistance by convincing many disgruntled Antifederalists that the new government was truly limited. In the words of Madison to Jefferson, his amendments would separate "the well meaning from the designing opponents . . . and give to the Government its due popularity and stability."[76] Madison also maintained a personal interest: a former foe of any amendments whatsoever, the electioneering Virginian had promised his constituents amendments.

Consequently, after Washington hinted that amendments could not be structural in his inaugural address (which Madison helped him write), the Virginia congressman introduced personal liberty amendments in May. Madison shrewdly made his announcement before Bland could introduce a resolution calling for a second constitutional convention. He skillfully navigated them through the House, deflecting criticism from arch-Federalists such as Ames who scorned the need for any amendments and disgruntled Antifederalists, particularly South Carolina's Thomas Tucker, who understood Madison's plan. The amendments met similar enemies in the Senate, particularly Federalist Senator Robert Morris and Antifederalists Lee and Grayson. The latter fumed to Henry that Madison intended "unquestionably to break the spirit of the Antifederalist party by divisions."[77] But in September Congress jointly approved the bill of rights amendments and sent them to the states for ratification. Three-fourths were required to consent.

Madison knew he had triumphed. In New York, the fiery Abraham Yates juxtaposed the "unimportant and trivial" personal liberty amendments with the promised structural amendments that were "intended either to explain or to restrict certain dangerous powers expressly or impliedly lodged in Congress."[78] Jefferson supported the amendments, though he still wanted structural amendments,

---

[76] Rothbard, *Conceived in Liberty*, 5, p. 298.

[77] Robert Rutland, *The Birth of the Bill of Rights* (London: Collier-Macmillan, 1962), p. 208.

[78] Alfred Young, *The Democratic Republicans of New York* (Chapel Hill: The University of North Carolina Press, 1967), p. 154.

particularly explicit prohibitions on monopoly grants and standing armies. The only structural amendment was what became the Tenth Amendment, which stated that "the powers not delegated to the United States by the Constitution, nor prohibited by it to the States, are reserved to the States respectively, or to the people."[79] This wording was similar to Article Two of the former Articles. But crucial differences existed. When Tucker, seconded by Gerry, tried to include the word "expressly," Madison sneered at such enumeration.[80] "It was impossible to confine a government to the exercise of express powers," the Virginian lectured, "there must necessarily be admitted powers by implication, unless the Constitution descended to recount every minutiae."[81] Once again, the new government would look federal when in reality it remained national, letting cronyism in through the back door.[82]

Madison's plan worked. Opposition to the new Constitution melted away once Antifederalists realized they had officially lost. After adjourning its convention in August 1788, heavily Antifederalist North Carolina met again in November 1789 and ratified the Constitution under intense Federalist propaganda emphasizing the bill of rights amendments. Henry was furious because North Carolina also ceded Tennessee to Congress, violating the rights of the actual settlers. He suffered another devastating setback in August 1790 after President Washington signed a treaty with Indians, invalidating the agreement between Georgia and the land company Henry participated in.

Even staunchly Antifederal Rhode Island ratified the Constitution. The little state refused to call a convention until early 1790 after the governor relented. But Antifederals adjourned the convention until late May. The US Senate responded by passing draconian trade legislation prohibiting all trade with Rhode Island. The appalled Senator William Maclay of Pennsylvania considered the threatened legislation the method of a tyrant, "meant to be Used the same Way That a Robber does a dagger or a Highwayman a pistol."[83] It strategically pended

---

[79] Watkins, *Crossroads for Liberty*, p. 251.

[80] Rothbard, *Conceived in Liberty*, 5, p. 300.

[81] Miller, *Federalist Era*, pp. 66–67.

[82] Bordewich, *First Congress*, p. 16; Calabresi and Leibowitz, "Monopolies and the Constitution," pp. 1009–12; David Moss, *Democracy* (Cambridge, MA: Belknap Press, 2017), p. 55; Rothbard, *Conceived in Liberty*, 5, pp. 297–301; Rutland, *Bill of Rights*, p. 202; Watkins, *Crossroads for Liberty*, pp. 227, 248.

[83] Bordewich, *First Congress*, p. 235.

in the House as Rhode Island "decided" its next steps. The little state barely relented with a 34-32 vote.[84]

In December 1791, after Rhode Island and the independent country of Vermont joined the Union, Virginia became the eleventh state to ratify the Bill of Rights and thereby put it into effect. Mason and Senator Lee admitted the need to compromise; in the latter's words, "if we cannot gain the whole loaf, we shall at least have some bread."[85] Defeated, the Virginia Antifederalist leadership suffered ignominious endings: Senator Grayson died in 1790, Henry returned to private law in 1791, Mason passed away in 1792, and Senator Lee followed in 1794. Madison achieved another victory for cronyism by crushing the reformers.[86]

Madison also used the Constitution to disburse privileges with the virtual creation of the executive and judicial branches. The executive branch would insulate bureaucrats and their regulations from the legislature and rotation in office. In May 1789, New Jersey's Federalist Congressman Elias Boudinot proposed the creation of executive departments, concentrating on a secretary of the treasury to manage the nation's finances. The battle in the House swirled around whether a group or a single person would run the department. Antifederalist Gerry argued for a board to defuse power, but Madison insisted that a single man would be more efficient. Madison won and only one secretary would manage the proposed Treasury Department.

Madison soon advocated the creation of war and foreign affairs departments to oversee the nation's military and international relations. The intense House debate focused on whether the president, who had the constitutional ability to appoint department heads with the Senate's consent, also had the ability to fire department heads without the Senate. Madison, ever fearful of the power of the Senate (i.e., *state legislatures*), interpreted the Constitution broadly and argued that the president alone had the removal power. Once again, Gerry defended the opposite view and maintained that the states had to consent to removal.

---

[84] Bordewich, *First Congress*, p. 48; Kidd, *Patrick Henry*, pp. 219–20; Klarman, *Framers' Coup*, pp. 517–30; Rothbard, *Conceived in Liberty*, 5, pp. 288–94.

[85] Henry Mayer, *A Son of Thunder* (New York: Grove Press, 1991), p. 460.

[86] Klarman, *Framers' Coup*, pp. 590–91; Kukla, *Patrick Henry*, p. 356; Mayer, *Son of Thunder*, pp. 460–61, 468; Rothbard, *Conceived in Liberty*, 5, pp. 107, 300–01.

Debate continued in the Senate until the upper house voted in July. The result could not have been more suspenseful: a dead tie. Predictably, the reactionary Vice President Adams voted for the ability to fire appointees at will, a power he hoped to exercise in the future. In response to this momentous decision, Senator Grayson thundered "consolidation is the object of the New Government, and the first attempt will be to destroy the Senate, as they are the Representatives of the State legislatures."[87] Grayson was right: the beginning of an independent executive bureaucracy had sprung into existence.[88]

Thus, Congress created the Treasury, War, and Foreign Affairs Departments (soon called the Department of State), along with the position of attorney general. When Washington appointed the heads, once again "Prime Minister" Madison assisted. Those knowledgeable correctly assumed that Knox would resume his position as Secretary of War. Washington initially wanted the arch-reactionary Jay to lead the State Department, but after Jay expressed his desire to serve on the new Supreme Court, the offer went to Jefferson, currently still abroad. Former governor of Virginia Edmund Randolph, Washington's close friend and a lawyer who betrayed his Antifederalist allies, received the attorney general position. Washington offered Robert Morris the powerful position of Secretary of Treasury. However, both Morris and Madison envisioned Hamilton for the job. To top the list off, the president appointed Gouverneur Morris as a "special agent" to Great Britain to secure favorable commercial arrangements.[89] Washington's appointments, save the radical moderate Jefferson, were ardent Federalists.[90]

Madison also supported the creation of the federal judiciary system. At first glance, the judiciary may seem separate from an analysis of cronyism. In reality, it was closely related: a strong oligarchical judiciary that could sanction the constitutionality of controversial legislation would be crucial to building a new American mercantilism. The Antifederalists had feared such a system, correctly believing that a federal court bureaucracy would transfer legal power from the states

[87] Bordewich, *First Congress*, p. 105.

[88] Bordewich, *First Congress*, pp. 56–64, 95–98, 104–05; Miller, *Federalist Era*, pp. 26–27.

[89] Miller, *Federalist Era*, p. 3.

[90] Bordewich, *First Congress*, pp. 59, 95, 160; Philip Burch, *Elites in American History*, vol. 1 (New York: Holmes & Meier, 1981), p. 49.

to the central government and monopolize law. It even worried those Federalists who feared that the creation of inferior courts would be going too far.

In April 1789, Connecticut's Federalist senator Ellsworth drafted a bill to create a Supreme Court with six justices and a system of lower courts. Madison played his part by adamantly denying that state courts could be trusted to enforce federal laws. Even Gerry supported the bill once he realized there was little hope of structurally amending the Constitution. In September, Congress passed the Judiciary Act of 1789, creating an entirely new legal structure *de novo*. It would take time for the court system to grow in power, but as Albert Jay Nock trenchantly pointed out, "of all the legislative measures enacted to implement the new constitution, the one best calculated to ensure a rapid and steady progress in the centralization of political power was the Judiciary Act of 1789."[91]

Washington shrewdly appointed three men from the South and three men from the North to the Supreme Court. For Chief Justice he chose the arch reactionary Jay, who believed that "those who own the country ought to govern it."[92] Robert Morris' ally Wilson also secured a justiceship and exerted considerable influence. Just like his executive appointments, Washington's Supreme Court choices were ultra-Federalist men.[93]

By fall 1789, Congress' first session had ended. Madison breathed life into the Constitution by enacting highly coveted sources of revenue the Articles previously denied, crushing Antifederalist opposition through the limp Bill of Rights, and establishing an independent executive bureaucracy and judicial system. He was at the peak of his power in the Federalist forces. However, much work remained, such as settling on the nation's permanent capital and figuring out debt assumption. Matters would rapidly change as Madison's old ally, Treasury Secretary Hamilton, brainstormed financial plans. It was now his turn to use the Constitution.

---

[91] Albert Jay Nock, *Our Enemy, The State* (Auburn, AL: Mises Institute, 2010), p. 169.

[92] Miller, *Federalist Era*, p. 32.

[93] Bordewich, *First Congress*, pp. 105–12, 141–43; Burch, *Elites in American History*, 1, pp. 60–61; Miller, *Federalist Era*, pp. 28–32; Nock, *Our Enemy*, pp. 169–70; Wood, *Empire of Liberty*, pp. 408–11.

PART II

THE HAMILTONIAN ERA, 1790–1801

CHAPTER 4

PRIME MINISTER HAMILTON: THE FISCAL PROGRAM

The Creation of a National Debt

The Hamiltonian Era was the nation's first decade of pure corruption. Secretary of the Treasury Alexander Hamilton embodied the court intellectual of the secularized altar, quickly supplanting James Madison as the nation's virtual prime minister. Unsurprisingly, Hamilton soon wrote of "my commercial system," a thoroughly mercantilist economy where the government privileged select business interests.[1] In particular, he desired a funded debt to benefit securities speculators, a monopolistic national bank to provide loans to favored businesses, subsidies and a moderately protective tariff to establish elite manufacturing firms, and internal improvements and land grants to aid speculators. Ever the economic and political genius, Hamilton realized that he could achieve his goals by using the Constitution. He first secured debt assumption with the Funding Act, made possible by a corrupt bargain that also determined the permanent location of the nation's capital. But in doing so he alienated Madison and caused the Antifederalists to devise new forms of resistance.

The United States grappled with three types of debt: $12 million in foreign debt, $42 million in domestic federal debt, and $25 million in domestic state debt. The Constitution empowered Congress to assume the Confederation's debts but said nothing about the particular value or assuming state debts. In his *Report Relative to a Provision for the Support of Public Credit*, delivered to Congress in January 1790, Hamilton argued that the federal government should assume all debts at face value. The Treasurer had no use for the anti-debt theories of Adam Smith, siding instead with James Steuart, who championed the blessings of public debt. Hamilton's rationale was straightforward:

---

[1] Thomas McCraw, *The Founders and Finance* (Cambridge, MA: Belknap Press, 2012), p. 90.

establish a near-permanent debt to increase government power and benefit Robert Morris–affiliated speculators who bought securities at a fraction of their face value. According to one historian, "Hamilton's precept was: Bind the rich to the government by self-interest."[2]

Indeed, the rich were eager for an alliance. After Congress passed revenue legislation in mid-1789, the Morris ambit bought up federal and state debts, accelerating their purchases later in the year once they secretly learned of Hamilton's plan. In New York, seventy-eight individuals acquired $2.7 million, or 31 percent, of various states' debts. Of this group, *eight* men alone gobbled up over half of that amount ($1.5 million). By 1790 the largest security holders owned an estimated two-thirds of federal debts. Furthermore, most of the federal debt (according to some estimates, four-fifths) was held by wealthy northerners, and the high-debt states hailed from the North, apart from South Carolina.

One notable purchaser was assistant Treasury Secretary William Duer, Hamilton's longtime friend, who speculated in land and other ventures. Duer was also close with Morris and William Constable, a prominent merchant who served as a director at Hamilton's Bank of New York. Constable and Duer forecasted to their associates a rise in security prices, which, in their words, was "based on something better than general optimism."[3] Other individuals close to Hamilton who speculated included Senators Morris, Philip Schuyler (Hamilton's father-in-law), Rufus King, and Oliver Ellsworth; and Congressmen Elias Boudinot and Jeremiah Wadsworth. Clearly, the old Morris clique hoped to make a killing.[4]

---

[2] Irving Brant, *James Madison, Father of the Constitution* (New York: Bobbs-Merrill, 1950), p. 291. See also McCraw, *Founders and Finance*, p. 97; Herbert Sloan, *Principle and Interest* (New York: Oxford University Press, 1995), pp. 95–96, 103–04, 113; Gordon Wood, *Empire of Liberty* (New York: Oxford University Press, 2009), pp. 95–97; Robert Wright, *One Nation Under Debt* (New York: McGraw Hill, 2008), pp. 36–39.

[3] Philip Burch, *Elites in American History*, vol. 1 (New York: Holmes & Meier Publishers, 1981), p. 76.

[4] *American Political Leaders* (Washington, DC: CQ Press, 2000), pp. 104, 314; Burch, *Elites in American History*, 1, pp. 54–56, 75–76; McCraw, *Founders and Finance*, p. 336; Murray N. Rothbard, *Conceived in Liberty*, vol. 5, *The New Republic: 1784–1791*, ed. Patrick Newman (Auburn, AL: Mises Institute, 2019), pp. 81, 87; Leonard White, *The Federalists* (New York: Macmillan, 1948), p. 360; Alfred Young, *The Democratic Republicans of New York* (Chapel Hill: The University of North Carolina Press, 1967), pp. 176–77.

However, in February 1790 Congressman Madison shockingly criticized the *Report*, stunning Hamilton and the ardent Federalists who expected to personally benefit. Madison's motivations had less to do with the debt measure itself than with the distribution of the benefits. He previously argued that the national debt should be paid off in full and the state debts assumed at face value. Moreover, Madison worked with Hamilton at the Constitutional Convention regarding debt assumption, lobbied for Hamilton's appointment to the Treasury, and in November 1789, when Hamilton asked for his old ally's views on financial matters, wrote nothing that alarmed the New Yorker. But now Madison argued that assuming all debts at par would benefit a few speculators and was unjust to states that had already paid off their debts. In place of Hamilton's scheme, Madison argued for a complex system of discrimination to make sure speculators did not unduly benefit.

Madison's reversal was political. Virginians barely elected Madison to the House for a two-year term, and after a year they loathed him. Madison had sided with the North on tariffs and navigation acts, and infuriated many Antifederalists with his limp Bill of Rights, which the state had received in the fall of 1789 and was vigorously debating. Crucially, Hamilton's plan would have furthered northern power at the expense of Virginia. Combined with the controversial discussion over the location of the permanent capital—which appeared to be headed somewhere outside of the South—the government was rapidly taking a pro-North position. For Virginia this was unacceptable, which meant it was unacceptable for Madison too, if he wanted to save his political hide and continue to serve in Congress.

Madison was not reversing his position on cronyism so much as reaffirming his belief in Virginia's supremacy. When Madison earlier proposed that the Confederation pay off its debts in full and assume state debts, this was before northern speculators purchased securities and Virginia paid off its debt. In fact, in response to Hamilton, Madison proposed that Congress assume state debts where they stood at the end of the war to make sure Virginia gained, which would increase the debt more than what Hamilton desired. Madison wanted Virginia to get her slice of the pie. But to Hamilton and the Federalists, his position was "a perfidious desertion of the principles which he was solemnly pledged to defend," and they accused him of fearing "Patrick Henry's shade."[5]

---

[5] Fergus Bordewich, *The First Congress* (New York: Simon & Schuster, 2016), p. 208 and John Miller, *The Federalist Era* (New York: Harper & Brothers, 1960), p. 41.

Gridlock descended over Congress as Madison's discrimination pro-posals suffered humiliating defeats and Hamilton's legislation stalled.[6]

To make matters worse, the government's paralysis over the per-manent location of the nation's capital grew worse. In the waning days of the Confederation Congress, Hamilton managed to keep New York City as the temporary capital. Now, "Hamiltonople" fought Pennsyl-vanians and southerners over the capital's permanent location, with southerners especially adamant given the recent northern successes.[7] Of course, many relevant players focused on the handsome profits they would make from their real estate speculations. Unsurprisingly, Senator Morris wanted the capital in a Philadelphia suburb, such as the aptly named Morrisville, proposing to invest $100,000 of Penn-sylvania taxpayer funds in the cause. Even President Washington speculated in land around northern Virginia, where the capital could lie.[8]

By the summer of 1790 the two contentious issues—debts and capital city—lay prostrate and unresolved, with both northerners and southerners rumbling threats of secession. Matters quickly changed when Secretary of State Thomas Jefferson invited Madison and Ham-ilton to dinner. Jefferson, who returned to the United States in Novem-ber 1789, was still playing his role as the preeminent radical moder-ate, the Antifederalist-Federalist hybrid. The Virginian still desired the Empire of Liberty: he was strenuously anti-debt, opposed assum-ing state debts, and was previously willing to default on some foreign debts. However, at this crucial juncture he moderated and agreed with the Federalists. But like Madison he was not about to acquiesce to northern domination.

At dinner, the three men struck the nation's second corrupt bar-gain. First, the federal government would assume state debts and pay all debts at face value. Second, President Washington received the privilege of choosing the capital's permanent location on the Poto-mac (its temporary residence moved to Philadelphia), and there was a

---

[6] Richard Beeman, *The Old Dominion and the New Nation* (Lexington: The University Press of Kentucky, 1972), pp. 58–64; Brant, *James Madison, Father*, pp. 306–07; Bordewich, *First Congress*, pp. 190–93, 207–12; Miller, *Federalist Era*, pp. 36, 46–47; John Miller, *Alexander Hamilton and the Growth of the New Nation* (New York: Harper & Row, 1959), pp. 239–40.

[7] Miller, *Alexander Hamilton*, p. 248.

[8] Bordewich, *First Congress*, pp. 149–50, 154, 230; Rothbard, *Conceived in Liberty*, 5, p. 283.

strong chance he would place it near his landholdings. Shortly there-after, Congress passed the Residence Act and the Funding Act. The libertarian Jefferson decided not to seize the opportunity but instead moderated to strengthen the new government. Power, as always, cor-rupts.[9]

But there was still one libertarian unsatisfied: Patrick Henry. The radical was apoplectic over the Funding Act, especially the assump-tion of state debts. In November 1790 he introduced a resolution into the Virginia legislature, declaring assumption "repugnant to the Con-stitution, as it goes to the exercise of power not expressly granted to the General Government."[10] Against Federalist resistance, the resolu-tion passed. The Virginia legislature then adopted an address blast-ing the Funding Act for encouraging British mercantilism, benefitting privileged speculators, injuring Virginia, and exceeding constitutional authority. The House version of the *Address of 1790* even declared that "the consent of the State legislatures ought to be obtained before the said act can assume a constitutional form."[11] This provision bordered on nullification and threatened to severely weaken the new govern-ment. Unfortunately, the Senate struck it out at the last minute.

Clearly, Henry and the Virginia Antifederalists strategically inter-preted the Constitution as a document of enumerated powers. This, of course, was the lie the Federalists used during the ratification debates. "Expressly" was nowhere in the Constitution or the pending Bill of Rights (still in the Virginia legislature), but that did not stop Henry. The *Address of 1790* was the opening shot in the Antifederalist strug-gle to cease outright resistance and revolutionize the Constitution to weaken the central government. In Henry's words to James Monroe in January 1791, "it is natural to care for the crazy machine, at least so long as we are out of sight of a port to refit."[12] The Virginia Antifed-eralists, set on their new strategy, agreed to ratify the Bill of Rights in 1791. Yet Henry would abandon the movement he was destined to lead, retiring in disgust from the Virginia House. He tried to form an alliance with Madison and Jefferson in late 1791, but Jefferson hated Henry and was decidedly lukewarm to the *Address of 1790*. Madison

---

[9] Bordewich, *First Congress*, pp. 174, 242–53, 269–70; Miller, *Federalist Era*, p. 47; Sloan, *Principle and Interest*, pp. 46–47, 153, 181.

[10] Beeman, *Old Dominion*, p. 78.

[11] Ibid., p. 80.

[12] Thomas Kidd, *Patrick Henry* (New York: Basic Book, 2011), p. 223.

turned the offer down, leaving the old radical fuming. Instead of working with Henry, Jefferson championed the constitutional position by himself.[13]

It is important to emphasize the compromise's debt largesse, one reason Henry fumed at the deal. The Funding Act caused the fortunes of elites to explode by almost $60 million. Prominent beneficiaries included the aforementioned speculators Morris, Duer, Boudinot, King, and Schuyler as well as Ames, Philip Livingston, Pinckney, Washington, and Willing. The public debt surged to $80 million in 1792 and increased to $83 million by 1795, and interest payments helped augment spending by 48 percent (14 percent per year). When one recognizes that by 1795 the available records suggest 5 percent of security holders of $10,000 or more claimed ownership of *65 percent* of the federal debt, and a quarter of a percent (0.25 percent) of security holders ($100,000 or more) held *30 percent*, it becomes clear that Hamilton's funding program was a massive redistribution racket that siphoned taxpayer money to the rich. Or, more specifically, the gains flowed to the old rich, the plan of the nationalists since the early 1780s.[14]

Indeed, in the absence of any libertarian resistance, Henry's protests notwithstanding, Hamilton was just starting to exploit the Constitution. The Federalists had achieved their first special-interest policy, a goal they wanted since the days of the Revolutionary War. Next on the plate was another leftover—a monopoly bank.

The Bank of the United States

After Congress adjourned in mid-1790, the government moved from New York City to Philadelphia. The transition was fitting, since Hamilton now wanted to charter a central bank in the city, drawing

---

[13] Beeman, *Old Dominion*, pp. 64–66, 77–82, 113–14; Jon Kukla, *Patrick Henry* (New York: Simon & Schuster, 2017), pp. 257–60, 356, 365–68; Dumas Malone, *Jefferson and the Rights of Man* (Boston: Little, Brown, 1951), p. 337; Norman Risjord, *Chesapeake Politics* (New York: Columbia University Press, 1978), pp. 408–09; Rothbard, *Conceived in Liberty*, 5, p. 301; Sloan, *Principle and Interest*, pp. 169–70.

[14] E. James Ferguson, *The Power of the Purse* (Chapel Hill: The University of North Carolina, 1961), p. 284; *Historical Statistics of the United States, Colonial Times to 1957* (Washington, DC, 1960), pp. 80, 91; Allan Kulikoff, "Such Things Ought Not to Be," in *The World of the Revolutionary American Republic*, ed. Andrew Shankman (New York: Routledge, 2014), pp. 153, 164; Miller, *Federalist Era*, p. 50; Curtis Nettels, *The Emergence of a National Economy* (New York: Holt, Rinehart and Winston, 1962), p. 122; Wright, *One Nation Under Debt*, p. 308.

inspiration from the Bank of North America and the Bank of England. The central bank plan bore many similarities to his debt assumption program: both provoked heated political discussion related to the debate over the nation's capital and benefited the northern financial elite. Significantly, the famous controversy over the Bank of the United States' (BUS) constitutionality led to two distinct interpretations of the Constitution—strict versus broad construction—that fueled the forces of liberty and power by inhibiting or facilitating cronyism. Furthermore, the Bank's consequences—increasing corrupt bank charters on the state level and fostering a nationwide business cycle—influenced future special-interest legislation and reform efforts.

Hamilton introduced his *Report on a National Bank* to Congress in December 1790. The Senate referred the banking report to an extremely receptive committee: Morris, Schuyler, Ellsworth, South Carolina's Pierce Butler, and Massachusetts' Caleb Strong. All staunch Federalists, four presided with Hamilton at the Constitutional Convention and three owned stock in other banks. They unsurprisingly drafted a bill along Hamilton's recommendations.

Essentially, the projected BUS would be a privileged corporation partially owned by the government, evoking bad memories of colonial British corporations. First, the institution received a twenty-year federal monopoly with the exclusive ability to open branches outside Pennsylvania. Second, Congress capitalized it at $10 million, a massive sum considering that the combined capital of existing banks totaled only $2 million. Third, the federal government planned to own one-fifth ($2 million), and another fifth ($2 million) of the Bank's capital consisted of specie, and while the rest could be purchased with government bonds. This favoritism increased the price of government securities and tied rich speculators to the central government. Lastly, the federal government would deposit most of its money in the Bank, a munificent subsidy. In return for such cronyism, the Bank would make loans to the government and favored business interests. In short, similar to Hamilton's debt plan, the proposed BUS subsidized northern commercial interests. More than that: it strikingly reestablished the alliance between banking interests and the federal government.[15]

---

[15] Hammond, *Banks and Politics*, p. 115; McCraw, *Founders and Finance*, pp. 110–13; Miller, *Federalist Era*, p. 56; Nettels, *Emergence of a National Economy*, pp. 128–29; Murray N. Rothbard, "The History of Money and Banking Before the Twentieth Century," in *A History of Money and Banking in the United States*, ed. Joseph Salerno (Auburn, AL: Mises Institute, 2002), p. 68.

Hamilton's Bank received a far more controversial reception than his concurrent *Report on the Establishment of a Mint*, which resulted in the 1792 Coinage Act that defined the American dollar in terms of specie and set the country on a dollar accounting system. While the Senate passed the bank bill without much difficulty in January 1791, it faced strong House opposition. Most criticism came from Madison, who understood Hamilton's intentions. Madison clearly recognized that the bank bill was another attempt by northern elites to dominate the federal government and control its patronage. Southerners already worried that Pennsylvanians would attempt to keep the capital, and establishing a massive corporation in Philadelphia aided their cause. As a Virginia nationalist, Madison wanted nothing of it.

On the House floor, Madison argued that not only would the Bank benefit northern speculators, but it was also *unconstitutional*. In particular, the Constitution nowhere explicitly stated that the government could incorporate a bank, and it did not fit the criterion of the necessary and proper clause. Not only that: the bill violated the Bill of Rights' Tenth Amendment (which Virginia had still not ratified), as powers of incorporation belonged exclusively to the states.

Although Madison displayed some consistency in the 1780s and 1790s regarding federally chartered banks, his position on the enumeration of powers conveniently shifted. In 1789 Madison argued that the president alone, not the Senate, possessed the constitutional power to remove appointed officials. He also disapproved including the word "expressly" in the Tenth Amendment for fears that it would shackle the Constitution. Now, Madison opportunistically read the Constitution very narrowly to thwart Hamilton. This tactic—arguing whatever was needed for a particular audience—was familiar to both constitutional theoreticians, who artfully employed it during the ratification debates, especially in *The Federalist Papers*.

However, despite the Virginian's efforts, the House passed Hamilton's bank plan in February by a significant margin, 39-20. This embarrassed Madison, since it showed that Prime Minster Hamilton controlled both the government and the North; thirty-three of the thirty-nine ayes came from the North while fifteen of the twenty nays hailed from the South. The fracturing of the Federalist forces started to draw new political battle lines.[16]

---

[16] Bordewich, *First Congress*, pp. 59–63, 290–94; Miller, *Federalist Era*, pp. 57–58, 66–67; Rothbard, "History of Money," pp. 65–68.

While the Bank bill had passed both chambers, Washington still needed to sign it. The president was close to Hamilton, but still worried over Madison's constitutional arguments. Moreover, he understood that the Bank might delay, if not prevent, the establishment of the nation's capital in the South. The president could not refer the matter to the Supreme Court, because it was still setting up shop and would only make decisions by hearing legal cases. Although Washington had never vetoed legislation, he could exercise that option now, thereby transforming the power into an anti-crony tool. In light of this, Washington turned to three Virginians: Congressman Madison, Attorney General Edmund Randolph, and Secretary Jefferson. All three sided against the Bank, but Jefferson made the most radical and sophisticated argument.

Jefferson, who never presided at the Constitutional Convention or any ratification debate, articulated a strict interpretation of the Constitution. Of course, he would never acknowledge Henry's previous efforts. Jefferson, the great theoretician, argued that nothing in the Constitution allowed for a bank charter, nor was there anything "necessary" about such an institution. For something to be "necessary and proper," it had to actually be necessary, not just "convenient and proper." Nor did it meet the "general welfare" clause, for that provision only concerned taxes. Jefferson also grounded his case on the proposed Tenth Amendment and argued the Constitution was an agreement by the states. Unfortunately, Jefferson moderated at the end. Although he thought the Bank should be vetoed, if Washington remained on the fence, Jefferson advised submitting to Congress—the executive must defer to the legislature.[17]

After receiving the opinions of Madison, Randolph, and Jefferson, Washington turned to Hamilton. The Treasurer skillfully responded in a long document intended to overwhelm the president. Essentially, Hamilton maintained the ultra-Federalist position articulated by Gouverneur Morris and James Wilson: "necessary" meant whatever legislators want it to mean (i.e., convenient), implied powers existed alongside any enumerated powers, and the Constitution allowed anything that promoted the (subjectively decided) "general welfare." In addition, Hamilton shrewdly used Madison's own words in *The Federalist Papers* to show the change in the Virginian's position.

---

[17] Bordewich, *First Congress*, pp. 293–95; Malone, *Jefferson and the Rights of Man*, pp. 337–44.

Overall, in contrast to Jefferson's strict constructionism, Hamilton's remarks formed the basis for what came to be known as the "broad" interpretation of the Constitution so instrumental in facilitating cronyism. The Treasurer even influenced the Supreme Court's later rulings.

It cannot be emphasized enough that Hamilton's broad constructionism was undoubtedly the logical motivation behind the Constitution. Hamilton was *not* perverting the document; he used it in the way the ultra-Federalists of Robert Morris, the main group that spearheaded statism, had intended. They had always wanted to provide vague and omnipresent power to the federal government, first in the Articles and now in the Constitution, for their own selfish ends. Jefferson, away in France and relying on Madison's information, naïvely believed otherwise. In fact, on top of his and Hamilton's earlier lies in *The Federalist Papers*, Madison now engaged in an outright fabrication: according to legal historian Mary Bilder, he "subtly created an alternative interpretation of the [Constitutional] Convention" by rewriting his notes to convince Jefferson that he supported limited government.[18]

Despite Hamilton's best efforts, Washington remained unconvinced, leaning toward a veto. But Hamilton and the northern Federalists kept one crucial ace up their sleeve: they could block Washington's desire to amend the Residence Act. In late January 1791 Washington announced his decision for the site of the capital: he wanted the federal district to move slightly outside of the agreed-upon location and include 200 acres of his land, along with some buildings he owned in Alexandria. He had already dispatched three of his close chums, none of whom had any experience in city building, to survey the area. But the northern Federalists would not sign on without a price. If Washington wanted greater convenience and higher prices for his land, he must give northern Federalists their Bank. In the end, personal cronyism tipped him over into signing the bank bill in late February, and the president relegated the executive veto to minor matters. Congress amended the Residence Act, which reportedly increased the value of Washington's property by an astounding 1000 percent. Once again, power corrupted.[19]

---

[18] Mary Bilder, *Madison's Hand* (Cambridge, MA: Harvard University Press, 2015), p. 239.

[19] Bilder, *Madison's Hand*, pp. 202–22; Bordewich, *First Congress*, pp. 293–300; Malone, *Jefferson and the Rights of Man*, pp. 344–50.

Morris and other commercial elites quickly dominated the BUS. Stock subscriptions became available in July, but only in block shares of $400, effectively limiting purchases to the wealthy. Duer, who had resigned as assistant secretary in April 1790, led the speculative mania during the summer. In fact, speculation mounted so much that Hamilton had to use his BONY to prevent a crash. Thirty members of Congress bought shares, or roughly one-third of the legislature's total membership and half of the congressmen who had voted for the Bank. Ownership concentrated in the large commercial cities—Boston, New York City, Philadelphia, and Charleston. In October, the shareholders elected directors: twenty of the twenty-five men hailed from Pennsylvania, New York, and Massachusetts. By 1795, two-thirds of directors resided in Philadelphia, associates of Morris' BONA. Willing, Morris' business associate, beneficiary of the Funding Act, and former head of the BONA, became president. A reestablishment of the partnership indeed!

Directors wanted to use the BUS' exclusive interstate banking privilege to expand operations and increase profits. Some Federalists actually hoped that it would drive the existing banks—the Bank of North America, Bank of New York, Massachusetts Bank, Bank of Maryland, and Providence Bank—out of business. Aside from then securing a monopoly, this control would reduce states' rights. However, Hamilton disapproved of branching because he believed it would overextend the Bank. Hamilton also knew that if the BUS opened a branch in New York it would bankrupt his BONY. The Treasury Department already maintained cozy relations with Hamilton's BONY, and Hamilton wanted the two to monopolize together by holding each other's stock. But in this case, Hamilton's creature overruled him. The directors of the BUS quickly opened up branches in Boston, New York, Baltimore, and Charleston. Secretary Hamilton ended up saving his BONY largely by funneling local Treasury transactions and deposits to the institution.[20]

Pro-central bank historians have long asserted that the judicious BUS restrained risky state banks.[21] In reality, during the 1790s the BUS wildly inflated and encouraged state banks' credit expansion.

---

[20] Bray Hammond, *Banks and Politics in America* (Princeton, NJ: Princeton University Press, 1957), pp. 122–27, 144; Burch, *Elites in American History*, 1, pp. 57, 77; Miller, *Alexander Hamilton*, pp. 246, 270–71, 273–77; Andrew Shankman, *Crucible of American Democracy* (Lawrence: University Press of Kansas, 2004), pp. 31–32.

[21] Roger Lowenstein, *America's Bank* (New York: Penguin Press, 2015), pp. 2–3.

Normally, bank competition restrains credit expansion because of a feedback loop similar to the price–specie flow mechanism, called the adverse clearing mechanism: if one fractional reserve bank engages in credit expansion beyond its specie reserves, competing banks will redeem the notes and deposits, forcing the bank to contract credit. Unless specie reserves significantly increase, only government intervention, such as privileges to bank notes and deposits, restrictions on entry, sanctioning the suspension of note convertibility, and increases in non-specie reserves, will enable banks to expand credit for significant periods of time.

In the case of the BUS, government forces encouraged inflation. First, the Bank accumulated artificially large reserves because of its federal charter and monopoly on government deposits. Second, monopoly privileges allowed it to exclusively branch across state lines: the BUS could enter other banks' local monopolies, but not the other way around. As time progressed, the Bank's inflation led to credit expansion by state banks. This occurred because the BUS' federal deposits often consisted of state bank notes. Instead of redeeming notes and restricting state banks' credit expansion, the BUS accumulated them, thereby granting de facto loans to these institutions which they used to expand credit. The friendly environment for state banks' credit expansion is seen in the fact that from 1791 to 1796 bank charters increased from six to twenty-two.[22]

Partisanship and bribery existed in the chartering of local monopolies. Unsurprisingly, Federalists spearheaded this process and controlled many of the new state banks. In some states, opponents chartered their own banks to combat the burgeoning Federalist monopolies. In 1793, the former Antifederalist Albert Gallatin pushed for the Bank of Pennsylvania's charter to create competition for the Federalist-controlled BUS. Gallatin argued that the state should invest its current surplus into one-third bank ownership to limit future taxes. Pennsylvanians agreed and the institution soon had five branches spread across the state. Opposition groups across the country looked forward to the day when they would control state legislatures and break Federalist bank monopolies.[23]

---

[22] Hammond, *Banks and Politics*, pp. 144, 197–202; Rothbard, "History of Money," pp. 69–70.

[23] Howard Bodenhorn, *State Banking in Early America* (New York: Oxford University Press, 2003), pp. 12–14; Hammond, *Banks and Politics*, pp. 164–65; Gregory May,

Unsurprisingly, Hamilton and other Federalists supported the new soft money position: central banking, bank charters, and inflationary credit expansion. In stark contrast, Jefferson and likeminded critics of corruption formed the hard money and laissez-faire bulwark. Unfortunately, Enlightenment thinkers were generally unhelpful because they split over what constituted laissez-faire in monetary affairs and did not articulate a theory of free banking. Some theorists supported 100 percent reserves (notable examples include Joseph Harris, David Hume, and Jacob Vanderlint), while others, particularly Adam Smith, favored fractional reserve banking and even some aspects of the BOE (Hamilton actually alluded to Smith's BOE apologetics in his *Report*). Accordingly, Jeffersonians favored some rudimentary form of no government involvement; championed the hard money position of hostility to fractional reserve banking; or simply supported their own charters to weaken the Federalists.[24]

The BUS recklessly expanded credit when it first opened in December 1791. Throughout its existence the Bank channeled loans to favored interests: the government and large Federalist businesses, speculators, landowners, and merchants. This favoritism earned it the ire of southern planters and smaller interests. By the first two weeks of operation, the Bank had loaned $1 million to the private sector and $2 million to the government, and its surging inflation led to a hesitant public redeeming bank notes and deposits for specie. The Bank quickly contracted credit, collapsing security prices in March. This Panic of 1792 ruined Duer and other speculators who borrowed from the Bank. While Hamilton had bailed Duer out in the summer of 1791, he would not help his old friend again. The BUS learned its lesson and expanded credit at a much steadier, though still thoroughly expansionist, pace after 1792.[25]

Jefferson's Treasure (Washington, DC: Regnery History, 2018), pp. 33–34; Young, *Democratic Republicans*, pp. 211–30.

[24] Joseph Dorfman, *The Economic Mind in American Civilization*, vol. 1 (New York: Viking Press, 1946), pp. 301–04; Miller, *Federalist Era*, p. 62; Fritiz Redlich, *The Molding of American Banking* (New York: Johnson Reprint, 1968), p. 29; Murray N. Rothbard, *An Austrian Perspective on the History of Economic Thought*, vol. 1, *Economic Thought Before Adam Smith* (Auburn, AL: Mises Institute 2006), pp. 332–35, 428, 462–69; Richard L. Timberlake, *Monetary Policy in the United States* (Chicago: The University of Chicago Press, 1993), pp. 5, 8; Lawrence White and George Selgin, "Laissez-Faire Monetary Thought in Jacksonian America," in *Perspectives on the History of Economic Thought*, ed. Donald Moggridge (Aldershot, UK: Edward Elgar, 1990), pp. 20–21.

[25] Burch, *Elites in American History*, 1, pp. 57–58, 77–78; Nicholas Curott and Tyler

The federal- and state-induced credit expansion led to a massive inflation and an economic bubble. Estimates vary, but from 1791 to 1796 the money supply increased by 48 percent (8 percent per year). Predictably, the inflation led to higher prices. After gently declining from 1785 to 1791 by 8 percent, wholesale prices surged 72 percent from 1791 to 1796 (11 percent per year). Industrial production and real gross domestic product (GDP) figures, which are only available after 1790, increased by 49 percent (8 percent per year) and 44 percent (7.5 percent per year). The credit expansion artificially pushed down interest rates, ostensibly increasing the profitability of long-term investments, and a speculative mania in transportation, manufacturing, and real estate projects blossomed.[26]

In addition, Great Britain and France, resuming war in 1793, stimulated exports and the shipping industry. From 1790 to 1793, total exports (including re-exports, or goods imported from one country and subsequently exported to another) increased by 29 percent (9 percent per year). But from 1793 to 1799 they increased by 201 percent (20 percent per year). Federalists gleefully took credit for the prosperity, though their Constitution and economic program had little to do with it. To the extent that Federalist policies increased economic growth, it came at the price of a future economic downturn.[27]

Such a government-induced downturn was inevitable. The higher prices increased imports and set in motion the price–specie flow mechanism. When specie reserves flowed out of the country, banks contracted credit and ended the speculative investment boom. A bust resulted, and by 1797 business failures mounted. From 1796 to 1798 industrial production declined by 7 percent (3.5 percent per

Watts, "A Monetary Explanation for the Recession of 1797," *Eastern Economic Journal* (June 2018): 384–86; Richard Sylla, Robert Wright, and David Cowen, "Alexander Hamilton, Central Banker," *Business History Review* (Spring 2009): 73–86.

[26] Curott and Watts, "Monetary Explanation," pp. 384–87, 390–91; Joseph Davis, "An Annual Index of U.S. Industrial Production," *Quarterly Journal of Economics* (November 2004): 1189; *Historical Statistics of the United States*, vol. 3, ed. Richard Sutch and Susan Carter (New York: Cambridge University Press, 2006), pp. 180–81; Louis Johnston and Samuel Williamson, "What Was the U.S. GDP Then?" *Measuringworth.com*; Peter Rousseau and Richard Sylla, "Emerging Financial Markets and Early US Growth," *Explorations in Economic History* (January 2005): 24.

[27] Jeremy Atack and Peter Passell, *A New Economic View of American History* (New York: W.W. Norton, 1994), p. 77; Nettels, *Emergence of a National* Economy, pp. 324, 396.

year), real GDP increased by only 6 percent (3 percent per year), and prices sharply dropped by 16 percent (8.5 percent per year).[28]

In the midst of the Panic of 1797, Jefferson, well versed in hard money economics, articulated a rudimentary analysis of the credit-induced business cycle:

> The banks may be considered as the primary source of this catastrophe. In order to increase their circulating paper and of course their profits, they issued it to every pretender in commerce, gave them thereby the appearance of capitals which these people did not possess, and . . . overspeculating themselves . . . in lands, in canal schemes, town lot schemes, manufacturing schemes and whatever could hit the madness of the day . . . in the height of their delirium, the balloon bursts, lets them drop from the clouds, and ends as such phrensies ought always to end.[29]

In other words, the BUS' loans to favored businesses engineered the nation's first boom-and-bust business cycle, misleading businesses about the supply of savings and the profitability of investment projects. Jefferson knew that to stop future downturns, he needed to eliminate the BUS.

Morris elites dominated Hamilton's Bank. The chartering of the BUS contributed to opposing constitutional doctrines, benefited the northern financial elite, and bound them to the federal government. Their next goal in the Hamiltonian Era promised to continue this trend.

The Report on Manufactures

By 1791, with the assumption of federal and state debts at face value and the establishment of a monopolistic national bank, the Hamiltonian fiscal program was well under way. The Treasurer soon devised additional special-interest legislation: subsidizing manufacturing businesses controlled by the Morris elite.

In his first annual message to Congress in January 1790, Washington promoted manufactures necessary for national defense. The

---

[28] Curott and Watts, "Monetary Explanation," pp. 391–94; Davis, "Annual Index," p. 1189; *Historical Statistics*, 3, p. 181; Johnston and Williamson, "GDP."

[29] Curott and Watts, "Monetary Explanation," pp. 395–96.

House responded by requesting Hamilton to report on American manufacturing and provide policy recommendations. The Treasurer happily agreed, spending nearly two years developing his *Report on Manufactures*. Assistant Treasurer Tench Coxe of Philadelphia, ardent protectionist, brother-in-law of BUS President Willing, and a former Tory during the Revolutionary War, provided crucial assistance. In addition, Hamilton relied on his formidable Treasury bureaucracy that he had scattered across the country.

Contrasting with Jefferson, who praised Adam Smith, the Treasurer dismissed the Invisible Hand as unrealistic in an age of Colbertian mercantilism. He argued that two wrongs—combatting mercantilist restrictions with even more mercantilist restrictions—do make a right. Hamilton opined that the relatively agrarian United States economy needed government assistance to develop its infant manufacturing sector because unlike Great Britain, already engaging in large-scale production, the US' relative advantage remained in agriculture. To the extent that Americans produced manufactures, it was accomplished by small "firms" composed of self-employed artisans and craftsmen.

Hamilton argued that the Visible Hand could propel American manufacturing to greatness with subsidies and tariffs—monopolistic privileges the Constitution sanctioned. Unlike some contemporaries, Hamilton did not want high protective tariffs, because they would assist smaller firms, hamper relations with Great Britain, and threaten government revenue by inducing smuggling. Instead, Hamilton wanted moderate tariffs that only protected elite manufacturing interests and raised enough revenue for debt assumption and lucrative subsidies to large firms. This was not the only competitive disadvantage Hamilton's system hoisted upon smaller firms; he wanted an elaborate system of government inspection to ensure products adhered to an arbitrary standard of quality.[30]

In 1791, around the same time he drafted his *Report on Manufactures*, Hamilton established a large manufacturing firm for wealthy northern interests. With the help of New Jersey Governor William Paterson, an ardent Federalist delegate to the Constitutional Convention, Hamilton steered a corporate charter through the New Jersey

---

[30] Burch, *Elites in American History*, 1, p. 73; Thomas J. DiLorenzo, *Hamilton's Curse* (New York: Three Rivers Press, 2008), pp. 101–06; Douglas A. Irwin, *Clashing over Commerce* (Chicago: The University of Chicago Press, 2017), pp. 68–73, 80–83; Miller, *Alexander Hamilton*, pp. 282–93; Miller, *Federalist Era*, pp. 63–65.

legislature in November and created the Society for Establishing Useful Manufactures (SEUM). The same New York City and Philadelphia elite who benefited from Hamilton's earlier plans financed the SEUM: governor of the society Duer, Congressman Boudinot, Secretary of War Henry Knox, Federalist delegate at the New York ratifying convention Nicholas Low, and New York oligarchs Livingston and former Senator Schuyler. Many members of the New Jersey legislature also bought shares, and throughout its existence Hamilton took time away from his official duties to advise the company. The SEUM founded the town of Paterson (named after the governor) right outside of New York City. The legislature capitalized the corporation at $1 million, a sum far larger than any existing manufacturing firm.[31]

New Jersey graciously granted the company a host of privileges. First, the charter bestowed on the SEUM a monopoly over using the corporate form to produce various manufactured goods, including cotton products, which it decided to concentrate on. Second, the SEUM's stock, sold in expensive blocks of $100, could be bought with federal debt, increasing the prices of said debt and indirectly subsidizing the company through the government's interest payments. Third, the legislature granted the SEUM exclusive rights to use the water power near Paterson, along with the power to use eminent domain. Fourth, New Jersey bought $10,000 of stock, a small amount relative to its size but a sign that the company might get larger subsidies from the state and Congress in the future.[32]

Unsurprisingly, just two weeks after New Jersey chartered the company, Hamilton submitted his *Report on Manufactures* to Congress in December 1791. The *Report* provided an extensive account of manufacturing (he selectively highlighted the successful ventures), his philosophy of mercantilist intervention, and concrete policy recommendations. For the latter, Hamilton requested tariff increases on twenty-one manufactured goods (from roughly 5 to 10 percent) and tariff decreases on five inputs manufacturers used. In addition, Hamilton wanted to subsidize five goods: coal, raw wool, sailcloth, glass, and

[31] *American Political Leaders* (Washington, DC: CQ Press, 2000), pp. 104, 280; Burch, *Elites in American History*, 1, pp. 78, 255; Miller, *Alexander Hamilton*, pp. 160, 209, 300–01, 309; Nettels, *Emergence of a National Economy*, p. 124.

[32] Dorfman, *Economic Mind*, 1, p. 292; Miller, *Alexander Hamilton*, p. 300; Nettels, *Emergence* of a *National Economy*, p. 124; Shankman, *Crucible*, pp. 35–40; Andrew Shankman, "A New Thing on Earth," *Journal of the Early Republic* (Autumn 2003): 331–35.

cotton products. Clearly, Hamilton envisioned funneling the subsidies for cotton production to the SEUM. In fact, many of the corporation's promoters bought shares because they anticipated federal subsidies and knew the mammoth project could only succeed with such crony assistance. Hamilton even alluded to the corporation in his report when he wrote that "measures are already in train" for the "making and printing of cotton goods."[33] In other words, Hamilton wrote his *Report on Manufactures* to help subsidize the large New Jersey monopoly that planned to invest in cotton products. Smaller artisans and other commercial interests that had supported the Constitution quickly became disillusioned with Hamilton.[34]

Unfortunately for Hamilton, his subsidy program encountered stiff resistance from Secretary of State Jefferson and Congressman Madison, who by this time had completely split with Hamilton. Jefferson and Madison now led the Antifederalist proponents of small government, regrouping under the emerging Republican Party, while Hamilton marshalled the reactionary Federalists. Hamilton justified subsidies' constitutionality by broadly construing the general welfare clause. Jefferson and Madison strictly interpreted the clause, arguing that it only referred to the taxing power. In this battle, Congress sided with Madison and Jefferson, balking at the subsidies. It was Hamilton's first real defeat, and thus a small victory for liberty.

However, Congress did follow up on Hamilton's tariff recommendations. In March 1792 the legislature asked Hamilton for advice on raising revenue to aggress on frontier Indians. Hamilton complied, using it as an opportunity to advance tariff increases he thought would stimulate manufacturing. Southern congressmen, such as ex-Antifederalist John Mercer of Maryland, realized that Hamilton was using an alleged military emergency to execute his *Report* "by extensive duties operating as indirect [subsidies], under the pressure of providing for an Indian war."[35] But the military justification amplified the fears of enough congressmen that Hamilton won out. As in the bank bill, the vote on the Tariff of 1792 followed sectional lines: the House voted

---

[33] Drew McCoy, *The Elusive Republic* (Chapel Hill: The University of North Carolina Press, 1980), p. 159.

[34] Irwin, *Clashing over Commerce*, pp. 82–83; Miller, *Alexander Hamilton*, pp. 282–90, 308–09; Nettels, *Emergence of a National Economy*, p. 124; Shankman, *Crucible*, pp. 36, 39–40.

[35] Irwin, *Clashing over Commerce*, p. 85.

37-20, with the North mostly for the tariff increases and the South against them. Congress passed eighteen of the twenty-one increases and three of the five decreases Hamilton recommended. Throughout the decade, Federalists continued to raise tariffs, and as a percentage of total imports they climbed from an average of 12.5 percent in 1790 to 24 percent in 1797 and 30 percent by 1800.[36]

Trouble with Indians led to additional cronyism. At the behest of Washington, under the sway of mercantilist thought, the federal government constructed a factory system of trading posts where US agents could buy furs from Indians to compete with the British in the region. In 1795, Congress appropriated $50,000 for this purpose and soon increased appropriations to $300,000. The government inefficiently managed the factory system and experienced difficulty competing with British companies and private American firms.[37]

Yet, Congress still granted no subsidies to the SEUM, dooming it to failure. The company already suffered a rocky start when Duer and others crashed to bankruptcy during the Panic of 1792. To make matters worse, New Jersey wisely followed Congress' footsteps and refused to contribute further largesse. Hamilton indirectly subsidized the company out by getting the BONY to provide it loans, financed by government deposits to the bank. But it was not enough. Shorn of taxpayers' money, the company spent too much on expensive machinery for its inexperienced labor force and did not save enough for operating costs. Poor management plagued the SEUM, because its founding members did not know how to profitably run a manufacturing company. The SEUM only completed its plant in 1794 and by 1796 had failed, a warning sign of the Panic of 1797. Patterson turned into a ghost town.[38]

While Hamilton's system of direct federal subsidies to privileged businesses failed, at least tariffs increased. The increase in tariffs was yet another way the federal government augmented its power and distributed crony benefits to northern business interests. Once again, the source lay in Hamilton's fiscal program, which depended upon the Constitution.

---

[36] *Historical Statistics*, 5, p. 510; Irwin, *Clashing over Commerce*, pp. 83–87; Jackson Main, *The Anti-federalists* (Chapel Hill: The University of North Carolina, 2004), p. 213.

[37] Burton Folsom, *Empire Builders* (Traverse City, MI: Rhodes & Easton, 1998), pp. 9–11.

[38] Miller, *Federalist Era*, p. 67; Miller, *Alexander Hamilton*, pp. 302, 308–10; Nettels, *Emergence of a National Economy*, p. 125.

Internal Improvements and Land Speculation

During the 1790s, Federalists wanted to use the Constitution to construct internal improvements and protect speculators' land claims. The policies were intricately linked: speculators bought public lands and then pushed for government transportation projects, whether on the federal or state level, to raise the value of their holdings. Prominent Federalists engaged in this practice, including Morris, who stuck his hand into nearly every special-interest racket; Schuyler; and Washington. In his *Report on Manufactures*, Hamilton supported internal improvements and later used his broad constructionism to sanction crony land speculations.

Government aid on the state and local level to transportation projects had existed for many decades. Prior to 1790, towns built roads with a local labor tax that compelled citizens to devote a certain number of days to a project. Unsurprisingly, without any profit incentive and a transient labor force, the governments poorly built the roads and frequently delayed repairs. This infeasible system led to private turnpike charters creating corporations that built roads and collected profits by charging fees. Private enterprise provided most of the investment funds; state and local assistance played a secondary role. In addition to turnpikes, states granted charters to other transportation businesses, such as bridges and canals. With each passing year the number of charters increased, and by 1800 the states had chartered seventy-three turnpikes, seventy-one bridges, and sixty-five canals.[39]

Investors, particularly the middling farmers and artisans in the Mid-Atlantic and New England, preferred turnpikes to canals. Southern commercial interests eschewed both, relying on the region's navigable river systems. Typically, turnpikes suffered losses. First, state and local governments often attached restrictive regulations to charters that hampered productivity: maintenance laws, minimum mileage between tolls, price ceilings on toll rates, limits on charging for other services, restrictions on appealing to state legislatures for punishing toll evaders, and coerced free passes for select citizens. Second,

---

[39] Albert Fishlow, "Internal Transportation in the Nineteenth and Early Twentieth Centuries," in *The Cambridge Economic History of the United States*, vol. 2, ed. Stanley Engerman and Robert Gallman (New York: Cambridge University Press, 2000), pp. 548–50; Daniel Klein and John Majewski, "Economy, Community, and Law," *Law & Society Review* (Fall 1992): 472–75; Robert Wright, "Rise of the Corporation Nation," in *Founding Choices*, eds. Douglas Irwin and Richard Sylla (Chicago: The University of Chicago Press, 2011), pp. 220–21.

investors from nearby commercial centers recognized that the turn-pikes could be unprofitable because of the innate difficulty in monitoring users. They treated stock purchases as equivalent to paying for the roads, a cost covered by the additional revenue they estimated their businesses would accrue. On the other hand, private toll bridges generally earned profits because owners experienced little restraints on pricing and could easily monitor users.[40]

Some transportation companies clearly abused their charter privileges. For example, in April 1792, New York chartered the Northern and Western Inland Lock Navigation Companies as part of a broad vision for a canal system linking the Hudson River with Lake Erie or Lake Ontario, bordering Canada. Each maintained eminent domain rights and $12,500 in state subsidies. The prominent Federalist Schuyler dominated the companies. Fifteen of the original thirty-six directors were land speculators, and their only goal was to maintain the appearance of credible businesses long enough to profitably speculate in land. One notable example, attorney Robert Troup, spent $3,000 acquiring interests in nearly two hundred thousand acres the canals planned to travel through. When construction began, the value of his holdings exploded to $130,000. Troup and other land speculators then sold their landholdings. Predictably, the inefficient and poorly managed companies, which continually clamored for more state money, received state bailouts in the late 1790s. Such shenanigans soured the public on partnerships between states and private firms; they recognized that these problems would only magnify with federal assistance.[41]

Hamilton and other Federalist proponents of internal improvements argued that the Constitution's general welfare clauses provided justification for subsidies and government construction of internal improvements, and the post roads were necessary and proper. Once again, broad constructionism performed the dirty work. However, though Congress subsidized coastal navigation and other small projects

---

[40] Daniel Klein, "The Voluntary Provision of Public Goods?" *Economic Inquiry* (October 1990): 788–812; Klein and Majewski, "Economy, Community, and Law," pp. 469–512; Daniel Klein and John Majewski, "Turnpikes and Toll Roads in Nineteenth-Century America," *EH.Net Encyclopedia*, ed. Robert Whaples (February 2008); Wood, *Empire of Liberty*, p. 471.

[41] John Larson, *Internal Improvement* (Chapel Hill: The University of North Carolina Press, 2001), pp. 26–28; Brian Murphy, *Building the Empire State* (Philadelphia: University of Pennsylvania Press, 2015), pp. 56–59, 68–72.

in the 1790s, controversy over the *Report on Manufactures*, the constitutionality of assistance, concerns over excessive government expenditure, and problems relating to regional favoritism proved insurmountable obstacles. The Republican Jefferson, well steeped in the free market economics that generally, though not always, shunned government subsidies, led the resistance. He understood that government investment corrupted politicians through favoritism and bribery, led to profligate spending, and required future taxes. Furthermore, Republicans' strict constructionism reasoned that internal improvements were unconstitutional and required an amendment. But Jefferson had to fight some of his closest allies on the matter.

In 1796 the ex-Federalist Madison introduced a measure in the House to appropriate some of the Post Office's surplus for a national survey of postal routes, "the commencement of an extensive work."[42] But Jefferson bitterly criticized the proposal and it died in the Senate. For the remainder of the decade Jefferson and the Republican Party remained hostile to federal internal improvements, considering them the embodiment of government cronyism. They stood in stark contrast with Hamilton, who in 1799 proposed federally funded transportation projects, which he coincidentally pushed for alongside other plans to reduce states' rights.[43]

Morris and his coterie also supported federal and state land policies that benefited speculators, and Hamilton predictably justified their constitutionality. With the advent of the Constitution, the Federalists did not change the Confederation's land policies, because Hamilton thought selling land in large tracts to speculators would quickly bring in revenue. However, Jefferson's Republicans wanted the land sold to actual homesteading settlers in small plots. Congress eventually passed a law in 1796 that raised the minimum price to $2 and maintained the large plot size of 640 acres. Crucially, it also allowed settlers to borrow on credit, which increased dependency on the government. While the high price kept land out of speculators' hands, the price, along with the large plot size, still discouraged settlers and stymied western migration. Under the new policy sales remained small, at less than fifty thousand acres. This stunting of western migration boosted real estate values

---

[42] Joseph Harrison, "'Sic Et Non,'" *Journal of the Early Republic* (Winter 1987): 339.

[43] Manning Dauer, *The Adams Federalists* (Baltimore, MD: The John Hopkins Press, 1953), pp. 202–04; DiLorenzo, *Hamilton's Curse*, p. 113; Harrison, "'Sic Et Non,'" pp. 338–40; Larson, *Internal Improvement*, pp. 45–52.

along the coast, property usually owned by the Federalists.[44]

However, Federalists actively dispensed state land grants and used the federal government to legalize their plunder. The most prominent case concerned the infamous Yazoo land scandal. In the 1780s Georgia claimed ownership of a large swath of Indian land west of the state, the so-called Yazoo lands (the upper portion of modern Alabama and Mississippi). By 1789, the state legislature wanted to sell ownership to various land speculator companies, particularly the South Carolina Yazoo Company, the Tennessee Yazoo Company, and the Virginia Yazoo Company.

The three corporations wanted to buy the mostly unappropriated land, or Indian land, to make money, but the Virginia Yazoo Company also maintained an additional goal. Recall that some Antifederalist Virginians, notably Henry, contemplated relocating to the southwest to set up a new independent government. In December 1789 the Georgia legislature sold a massive twenty-five million acres to the companies for a bargain $200,000 (less than one cent an acre), payable in debt certificates. But in 1790 the deal with the three companies collapsed after Georgia demanded payment in specie and Washington, cognizant of Henry's motives, made a treaty with the Creek Indians living in the region that invalidated the sale.

Although Henry and the original companies failed, speculators without any desire for independence reopened negotiations in a couple of years. In 1795, four new corporations—the Upper Mississippi Company, Tennessee Company, Georgia Mississippi Company, and Georgia Company—bribed the Georgia legislature to purchase a gargantuan *thirty-five million acres* of land for $500,000 (roughly 1.5 cents an acre). Many prominent Federalists invested in the companies, including the ineffable Senator Morris and his lackey, the Supreme Court Justice Wilson. These companies quickly sold their land claims to prospective buyers, particularly northern speculators, at handsome profits. For example, the Georgia Mississippi Company dispensed part of its grant for $1,138,000, over an original cost of $155,000, to the New England Mississippi Land Company.

---

[44] Daniel Feller, *The Public Lands in Jacksonian Politics* (Madison: The University of Wisconsin Press, 1984), pp. 7–8; May, *Jefferson's Treasure*, pp. 35, 126–28; Nettels, *Emergence of a National Economy*, pp. 146–49.

The new Federalist speculators hoped to reap astounding profits when they resold their ill-gotten gains to actual settlers. But the people of Georgia, discovering that their bribed legislature sold millions of acres on bargain terms, nearly revolted. They voted existing representatives out of office and the new legislature of 1796 promptly repealed the act. Since the Federalists controlled the state machinery, the Yazoo scandal virtually destroyed the Federalist Party in Georgia and ruined the political career of Governor George Mathews.

Speculators ranted against the Georgia legislature. They did not care that their claims resulted from an illicit deal; the Federalists thought a private contract of any kind was irrevocable. They hoped to defend their claims by invoking the ever-reliable Constitution, particularly the contract clause. Of course, protecting government privileges was the clause's original motivation at the Constitutional Convention, especially by Wilson—who later became a Supreme Court justice and acquired an interest in the Yazoo lands! In 1797, some speculators turned to the pre-eminent hermeneutician, Hamilton, and requested his opinion. The father ordained that the legislature had no right to rescind prior land grants and conjectured the Supreme Court would uphold his view. Thus, in Wilsonian fashion, Hamilton used the Constitution to protect the privileged claims of land speculators sold by a corrupt state legislature. In 1798 Congress organized the region below the Yazoo lands and above Spanish Florida as the Mississippi Territory, but problems relating to the Yazoo lands, which Georgia still claimed, remained unresolved. Eventually, the Hamiltonian Supreme Court sided with the speculators.[45]

Overall, the early years of the Hamiltonian Era were a victory for Morris. With the libertarian Antifederalists out of the government, power hungry Federalists had nothing standing in their way. Treasury Secretary Hamilton used his broad constructionism to enact northern cronyism. Against Hamilton's broad constructionism, Jefferson interpreted the Constitution strictly to limit favor granting. But Jefferson's political support was still too weak, and Hamilton continued to pursue his program unchecked. He now turned to military cronyism.

---

[45] James Broussard, *The Southern Federalists* (Baton Rouge: Louisiana State University Press, 1978), p. 248; G. Herndon, "George Mathews," *The Virginia Magazine of History and Biography* (July 1969): 324; Kidd, *Patrick Henry*, pp. 218–20; Miller, *Alexander Hamilton*, pp. 547–48; Nettels, *Emergence of a National Economy*, pp. 149, 154; Aaron Sakolski, *The Great American Land Bubble* (New York: Harper & Brothers, 1932). pp. 125–41.

CHAPTER 5

PRIME MINISTER HAMILTON: THE IMPERIAL PROGRAM

The Whiskey Rebellion

By President George Washington's second term, "Prime Minister" Alexander Hamilton enacted the crony Federalist economic program, solidifying the allegiance of Robert Morris. But the Hamiltonian Era was nowhere near finished. While the power of Morris waned during the Adams administration, the New Yorker's rose, and Hamilton surpassed his old mentor. During the Quasi-War with France he strove to establish the United States as a world superpower along the lines of Great Britain. In other words, he wanted an Old Order Empire that could grant even larger privileges. Perhaps most crucial of all, he wanted to lead it. The resurgent classical liberal forces resisted Hamilton's drive for an Empire of Power and first tried to reform the government illegally through nullification and resistance—the so-called Whiskey Rebellion of 1794.

Treasurer Hamilton's debt assumption, designed to benefit Morris and other speculators, called for revenues larger than what Madison secured in 1789. Hamilton reasoned that internal taxes, such as excise taxes, must play a crucial role in making up the difference. In *The Federalist Papers* Hamilton previously argued that unpopular internal taxes would be "confined within a narrow compass."[1] This fit in well with the dictum his idol, the mercantilist Jean-Baptiste Colbert, preached: "the art of taxation consists in so plucking the goose as to obtain the largest amount of feathers with the least amount of hissing."[2] Of course, after ratification Hamilton could conveniently drop

---

[1] Thomas Slaughter, The *Whiskey Rebellion* (New York: Oxford University Press, 1986), p. 97.

[2] Murray N. Rothbard, *An Austrian Perspective on the History of Economic Thought*, vol. 1, *Economic Thought Before Adam Smith* (Auburn, AL: Mises Institute 2006), pp. 246.

his promise, because the hissing no longer mattered. In May 1790, Congress debated a bill calling for excise taxes on domestically distilled spirits to pay for the planned assumption of debts. The bill failed, but Hamilton, Assistant Secretary Tench Coxe, and fellow ally Congressman Fisher Ames of the Essex Junto remained optimistic about its future prospects.

Lo and behold, after the Funding Act passed, Congress debated a similar bill in early 1791. Opponents reasoned that an invasive whiskey tax would remind too many people of similar depredations Great Britain previously inflicted. One congressman argued that the tax would impose a "swarm of harpies" disguised as "revenue officers," who will pry "into every man's house and affairs" like a "Macedonian phalanx."[3] Ames could only sneer at such hissing, considering the protests of the Pennsylvania State Assembly as "anarchy" because state legislatures had no business in federal matters—the Constitution established apodictic federal supremacy![4] Congress passed the whiskey tax bill in March 1791, with opposition located in every state outside of New England and especially among western delegates from Antifederalist regions.[5]

Westerners considered the whiskey tax devastating. First, whiskey formed the lifeblood of the isolated frontier economy, transported more easily than grain, and could be exchanged for eastern goods. In addition, the law empowered the authorities to search property for illegal distilling operations and contraband. Second, the tax forced distillers to cough up nine cents per gallon of whiskey. However, they could instead pay a fixed rate on their distillery's capacity, which for larger enterprises translated to six cents per gallon. Thus, the tax favored large eastern distilleries over small western distilleries. Clearly, Hamilton's oppressive and regressive tax extracted money away from poor westerners and redistributed it to rich easterners who held government debt—a clear instance of cronyism.[6]

To the formerly Antifederalist West, the tax embodied eastern dominance. Since the Confederation days, the West frequently complained of unfair taxes, inadequate help with Indians, speculative land grants, and lack of eastern concern for securing navigation on

---

[3] Slaughter, *Whiskey Rebellion*, p. 99.

[4] Ibid., p. 101.

[5] Ibid., pp. 95–105.

[6] Ibid., pp. 71–73, 131–49.

the Mississippi River. The tax aggravated their secessionism, since they saw no reason to continue the present arrangement. In the words of the Mingo Creek Society of western Pennsylvania in 1794: "To be subject to all the burdens and enjoy none of the benefits arising from government is what we will never submit to."[7]

In the summer of 1791, resistors in western Pennsylvania organized a Pittsburgh meeting. At the conference, the libertarian reformers criticized the assumption of state debts, the national bank, and the high salaries of government officials. They urged popular nullification of the whiskey tax by urging citizens to not become tax collectors. Former Pennsylvania Antifederals John Smilie, Albert Gallatin, and William Findley attended a second Pittsburgh meeting in 1792 and urged further protests. Similar discontent occurred in other states, and by the summer the tax remained unpaid. Irate at such recalcitrance, the reactionary Hamilton banged the war drums and urged military force to suppress some tax resistors, choosing North Carolina. Hamilton had previous experience using military threats, such as the Newburgh Conspiracy of 1783. Fortunately, Washington demurred.

But resistance continued through the summer of 1794, with sporadic instances of disobedience and violence turning more organized. Hamilton believed that Gallatin, a frequent Republican critic of his fiscal policies, masterminded everything. The Pennsylvanian had good reason to be upset: he briefly served as a US senator earlier in the year, before the Federalists expelled him on citizenship grounds. A ragtag band of seven thousand rebels started harassing Pittsburgh, and similar discontent appeared in central Pennsylvania and the western regions of many southern states. Resistance mounted, secession threatened, and Hamilton and Washington realized that open rebellion in the entire West stared them in the face. Power needed to make an example of liberty.[8]

Since 1789, the Federalists itched for a European standing army. After all, the Constitution empowered the federal government with the unambiguous ability to create a strong military and nationalize state militias. Secretary of War Henry Knox's grand plan for military greatness was to create a Roman army composed of three "corps"

[7] Ibid., p. 164. See also pp. 36–74, 163–64.

[8] Gregory May, *Jefferson's Treasure* (Washington, DC: Regnery History, 2018), pp. 35–37, 44–52; Slaughter, *Whiskey Rebellion*, pp. 117–20, 186–89.

(Advanced, Main, and Reserved), all subdivided into legions.[9] Congress would force men in the youngest corps (the Advanced) out of their occupations for one month a year for training in Spartan-style camps. After their inculcation, they would graduate to the Main corps, the first line of defense.

Against such flagrant militarism, a furious public shot down Knox's ridiculous proposal, a program projected to require enormous appropriations—the annual cost for the Advanced corps alone was $400,000. The public understood the Antifederal argument that standing armies lead to greater government tyranny and suppression of resistance. DeWitt Clinton, nephew of the New York governor, considered Knox's plan "so palpably absurd and impolitic."[10] Defeated, the Federalists still managed to pass the Uniform Militia Act of 1792, requiring middle-aged men to enroll in their state's militia or pay a large fine if they failed to report for national service. If the president wanted to call forth the militias, a justice of the Supreme Court had to approve. Congress had created its first peacetime army.[11]

With the emerging "Whiskey Rebellion," Hamiltonian Federalists urged for an army to suppress the hissing goose, and the state militias the president could call forth looked suitable. In August 1794, ultra-reactionary Supreme Court justice James Wilson rose to the task. Consequently, Washington dragooned a massive thirteen thousand–man army to suppress the delinquent taxpayers. In the words of Harlow Giles Unger, this "was Patrick Henry's worst nightmare."[12] Like Henry, other Antifederalists had previously raised concerns about the Constitution's potential to create a militaristic Old Order Empire. The Pennsylvanian Antifederalists made particularly prescient remarks in 1787, when they warned of a "standing army," supported by "tax-gatherers" and "revenue officers," that could "swarm over the land . . . impoverishing and desolating all before them."[13]

---

[9] Fergus Bordewich, *The First Congress* (New York: Simon & Schuster, 2016), p. 195.

[10] Richard Kohn, *Eagle and Sword* (New York: The Free Press, 1975), p. 130.

[11] Bordewich, *First Congress*, p. 195; Jeffrey Rogers Hummel, "The American Militia and the Origin of Conscription," *Journal of Libertarian Studies* (Fall 2001): 45–46; Kohn, *Eagle and Sword*, pp. 128–38; Murray N. Rothbard, *Conceived in Liberty*, vol. 5, *The New Republic: 1784–1791*, ed. Patrick Newman (Auburn, AL: Mises Institute, 2019), p. 269; Slaughter, *Rebellion Whiskey*, pp. 192–93.

[12] Harlow Giles Unger, *Lion of Liberty: Patrick Henry and the Call to a New Nation* (Cambridge, MA: Da Capo Press, 2010), p. 263.

[13] Rothbard, *Conceived in Liberty*, 5, p. 229.

Washington and Hamilton traveled with the army as it trudged westward. The Federalist swarm encountered no resistance and realized the tax protestors had scattered. Washington left for Philadelphia and placed General Henry Lee of Virginia in charge. In reality, Hamilton called the shots, itching to make an example of the delinquent taxpayers. In his words, "the insurrection will do us a great deal of good and add to the solidity of every thing in this country."[14] The Treasurer, who admitted that he had "long since . . . learnt to hold popular opinion of no value," pushed the army through the Appalachian Mountains, reminding some disgruntled soldiers of Hannibal of Carthage traveling through the Alps.[15] The lavish living quarters and food supplies of the Treasurer further upset them. But the Federalists bribed soldiers with whiskey to drunkenly stumble along, harassing and intimidating all in their wake while they sniffed out rebels. In the most prominent roundup, troops kidnapped one hundred and fifty half-dressed men in the middle of the night and dragged them into a forced march, starving, humiliating, and assaulting them along the way.

The Hamiltonian dragnet interrogated the roundups to find prominent rebels, try them for treason, and execute them. The Treasurer ranked Gallatin and Findley high on his list, wanting to make examples for everyone to see. Unfortunately for Hamilton, after the investigations ended there remained only about twenty obscure men to imprison. Most of the army left while the remaining contingent continued to harass and steal from the local populace. Hamilton preferred to station a standing army until westerners' loyalty increased, but Washington wisely realized the political ramifications and eventually disbanded the troops.[16]

However, with Hamilton's prodding, Washington blamed the uprising on the new democratic societies, the voluntary organizations that had recently formed and associated with the Republican Party. Pro-British Federalists accused the organizations of allying with the French revolutionaries sparking European discontent, but in

---

[14] Gordon Wood, *Empire of Liberty* (New York: Oxford University Press, 2009), p. 138.

[15] Kohn, *Eagle and Sword*, p. 172.

[16] May, *Jefferson's Treasure*, p. 55; Brion McClanahan, *How Alexander Hamilton Screwed Up America* (Washington, DC: Regnery History, 2017), pp. 57–72; John Miller, *Alexander Hamilton and the Growth of the New Nation* (New York: Harper & Row, 1959), pp. 408–11; Slaughter, *Whiskey Rebellion*, pp. 190–220.

reality "their objective was simply to conduct a constitutional opposition to Hamiltonianism in the name of liberty and democracy."[17] Furthermore, Washington conveniently neglected his participation in the Society of the Cincinnati, an elitist organization he and his Treasurer rewarded with patronage in the bloated Federalist bureaucracy: of their roughly five hundred federal appointees old enough to have fought in the Revolutionary War, 28 percent served as officers, and 15 percent affiliated with the aristocratic Society. Put another way, Hamilton and Washington thought that only societies supporting statism and militarism, not liberty and low taxes, promoted the public interest. Of course, Hamilton also pinned blame on Jefferson and Madison even though the two remained neutral to the democratic societies and unsympathetic to the rebellion (though against how Federalists suppressed it).[18]

Significantly, Gallatin emerged unscathed. He publicly denounced the rebellion, but this only earned him the suspicion of Treasury Comptroller Oliver Wolcott, who believed that Gallatin had done so to avoid punishment. Pennsylvanians rewarded the Republican with a House seat in the fall 1794 elections, and the free market Gallatin soon turned into Hamilton's worst nightmare.[19]

The Whiskey Rebellion highlights Hamilton's penchant for power. Unlike the more hesitant Washington or Knox, Hamilton fixated on the military and its ability to coerce the public into doing his bidding. Richard Kohn perceptively remarks:

> To [Hamilton] force was a positive tool. The display of military power in the Whiskey Rebellion made the government a grander machine, more impressive and more permanent. Force . . . spoke a language of its own, imparting confidence to friends and threatening punishment to enemies, endowing its wielders with prestige and with respect. The threat of force could be used,

---

[17] Miller, *Alexander Hamilton*, p. 412.

[18] Richard Ellis, *The Jeffersonian Crisis* (New York: Oxford University Press, 1971), p. 273; Miller, *Alexander Hamilton*, pp. 411–14; Murray N. Rothbard, "Bureaucracy and the Civil Service in the United States," *Journal of Libertarian Studies* (Summer 1995): 24–28; Slaughter, *Whiskey Rebellion*, p. 221; Sean Wilentz, *The Rise of American Democracy*, (New York: W.W. Norton & Co., 2005), pp. 40–71; Wood, *Empire of Liberty*, p. 108.

[19] Kohn, *Eagle and Sword*, pp. 201–02; May, *Jefferson's Treasure*, pp. 55–59.

as he had used it [at Newburgh] in 1783, to frighten men
into agreeing to specific policies.[20]

Historians sympathetic to Hamilton argue that his tax program actually decreased burdens because Congress now collected most revenue from tariffs, allowing states to drastically reduce internal taxes after their spending declined from debt assumption.[21] However, Congress still needed regressive internal taxes to fund largesse to speculators, and these taxes provoked intense hostility. The Whiskey Rebellion was *not* an isolated occurrence, if Washington and Hamilton had not sent a massive army to western Pennsylvania, the entire West would have revolted. Furthermore, the subsequent lack of taxpayer resistance compared to what occurred in the Confederation Era—aside from the important Fries Rebellion in 1799—does not mean that taxpayers rested easy. In reality, the federal government's ability to raise a large army intimidated them. This hardly demonstrates the public's agreement with the tax structure.

Unfortunately for the taxpaying public, the Whiskey Rebellion only inaugurated Hamilton's military cronyism. He now set his sights on foreign policy.

Taking the Frontier

Throughout the 1790s Hamilton clandestinely conducted relations with British officials and expanded the western domain to benefit commercial interests. The pro-British Jay's Treaty, or what one historian called "Hamilton's Treaty," especially raised a firestorm of criticism that induced Washington to retire from office, allowing Hamilton to increase his power after John Adams assumed the presidency.[22]

Since Hamilton modeled his economic program along the lines of Great Britain, in matters of foreign policy he predictably supported the British. He deeply admired their monarchical government and wanted a partnership to increase government revenue from tariffs for his debt assumption largesse. The pro-British High Federalists, the extreme reactionaries connected with Hamilton and the Massachusetts-based

---

[20] Kohn, *Eagle and Sword*, p. 171.

[21] Max Edling and Mark Kaplanoff, "Alexander Hamilton's Fiscal Reform," *William and Mary Quarterly* (October 2004): 713–44.

[22] Samuel Bemis, *Jay's Treaty* (New York: Macmillan, 1923), p. 271.

Essex Junto, vigorously supported him. After all, these men, during the American Revolution, only begrudgingly supported independence. In stark contrast, the anti-British Republicans supported the worldwide adoption of free market policies, championed isolationism and non-interventionism, and desired Jefferson's Empire of Liberty. However, the free trade Republicans, under the sway of Adam Smith's deviations into mercantilism, occasionally supported commercial sanctions to break down trade barriers and weaken Old World institutions. Their retaliation derived from the colonial era boycotts, only now backed by the coercive force of a central government.[23]

Hamiltonian doctrine dominated the government from the outset. In 1789, before Jefferson became secretary of state, Hamilton clandestinely conducted diplomatic relations with Major Gordon Beckwith, an unofficial British ambassador. Beckwith soon realized that Hamilton desired to preserve the revenue stream at all costs, which naturally strengthened Great Britain's hand in future negotiations. Diplomatic relations worsened when France, in the midst of a deteriorating revolution, declared preemptive war on Britain in February 1793, causing both nations to seize American ships destined for enemy ports. Hamilton and Jefferson wisely advocated neutrality, and President Washington issued his Proclamation of Neutrality in April. However, under the sway of Hamiltonianism, the president did so without Congress' consent. Jefferson and Madison considered this executive aggrandizement, and Hamilton defended Washington through his broad constructionism. By the end of the year Jefferson had resigned.[24]

Without Jefferson, Hamilton's grip strengthened. In early 1794, when the US heard of the new British policy to seize American ships trading with the French West Indies, the infuriated Hamilton advocated an armed force of fifteen to twenty thousand troops, harbor

[23] Philip Burch, *Elites in American History*, vol. 1 (New York: Holmes & Meier Publishers, 1981), p. 49; Manning Dauer, *The Adams Federalists* (Baltimore, MD: The John Hopkins Press, 1953), p. 62; Joseph Dorfman, *The Economic Mind in American Civilization*, vol. 1 (New York: Viking Press, 1946), pp. 286–87, 304–06; John Nelson, *Liberty and Property* (Baltimore, MD: The Johns Hopkins University Press, 1987), pp. 119–21; Wood, *Empire of Liberty*, pp. 92–93.

[24] Julian Boyd, *Number 7* (Princeton, NJ: Princeton University Press, 1964), pp. 21–33; Burch, *Elites in America*, I, pp. 49, 252; McClanahan, *Hamilton Screwed Up America*, pp. 73–87; Curtis Nettels, *The Emergence of a National Economy* (New York: Holt, Rinehart and Winston, 1962), pp. 324–25; Wood, *Empire of Liberty*, pp. 181–83, 204, 239.

defenses, and a naval force. Republicans opposed these measures because they threatened freedom and instead advocated the use of militias and privateers. Fortunately, the British changed their policy and an opening for diplomatic negotiations emerged. For advice, the president spoke with the omnipresent Senator Morris. Washington proposed Vice President John Adams, Hamilton, Jefferson, or Chief Justice John Jay. Morris quickly dismissed Adams and Jefferson to recommend Hamilton, but Washington realized the potential backlash and settled on Jay. As a close friend of Hamilton, Jay did not differ too much from Morris' first choice—Hamilton even drew up his instructions.

The result was Jay's Treaty, which benefited American expansionists and Great Britain. Northwestern land speculators and other affiliated interests received what they long desired: the evacuation of the British forts in the Northwest. But to get this land, Jay completely acquiesced to Britain's version of "neutrality," leading to greater French seizures of American ships. After Republican senator Stevens T. Mason of Virginia, a former Antifederalist and nephew of George Mason, leaked the treaty, the public nearly revolted and critics threatened secession. Despite the intense controversy, Washington signed the treaty in August 1795 and in the following March refused to let the House see documents relevant for appropriating funds.[25]

The pro-British treaty caused Spain to fear an outright alliance between the two countries, and the Federalists moved in for the kill. They handed the intimidation job to the wealthy planter Thomas Pinckney, the brother of Charles Cotesworth Pinckney and a former South Carolina governor. Pinckney's Treaty of 1795 allowed the US to transport goods on the Mississippi with the right of deposit (the ability to transfer goods from one ship to another without paying port fees) for three years, renewable after unless a party rejected. This pleased Morris, the inveterate land speculator, who recognized the treaty "doubles or trebles the value of the lands bordering upon the Western Waters of the Ohio." [26]

---

[25] Burch, *Elites in American History*, 1, pp. 59–60, 78; Norman Risjord, *Chesapeake Politics* (New York: Columbia University Press, 1978), pp. 449, 454; Miller, *Alexander Hamilton*, pp. 390, 415–22; Wood, *Empire of Liberty*, pp. 192–99, 239.

[26] Wood, *Empire of Liberty*, p. 201. See also Burch, *Elites in American History*, 1, p. 52; Alexander DeConde, *This Affair of Louisiana* (New York: Charles Scribner's Sons, 1976), pp. 61–62.

Significantly, Jay's Treaty provided an opening for Hamilton to tighten his power. The intense backlash induced Washington to retire and Hamilton set upon a new front man for his empire building, choosing the ever-pliable Thomas Pinckney over the stubborn Vice President Adams. However, his plan failed and in 1796 Adams barely defeated the Republican Jefferson, who became vice president. Although Adams despised Hamilton and the Treasurer no longer served in the federal government, Hamilton controlled the administration. This was due to two reasons. First, Adams decided to retain Washington's cabinet: Treasurer Wolcott, Hamilton's former subordinate; Secretary of War James McHenry, the best man at Hamilton's wedding; Secretary of State Timothy Pickering, a Hamiltonian businessman of the Essex Junto; and British Ambassador Rufus King, a Hamiltonian lawyer and former director at the Bank of New York and the Bank of the United States. Second, Adams frequently left Philadelphia for Massachusetts. While Washington was away during his eight years for 181 days, the single-term Adams worked from home for 385 days. This clearly opened a power vacuum, with Hamilton now "the recognized leader of the Federalist party . . . there were no secrets from him."[27]

Even better for Hamilton, the Panic of 1797 financially devastated Morris, sending him to prison. Justice Wilson also followed. Previously, Hamilton worked for Morris and helped him earn money in return for sharing power. Now, with Morris out of the picture, Hamilton could control all the power himself. He enlisted new subordinate allies, the High Federalist Essex Junto merchants, and embarked on building an international empire.[28]

Hamiltonian Militarism

When Adams became president, Hamilton utilized a foreign crisis to advocate a military buildup. By the end of the decade he favored a vast expansion into Louisiana and South America, an invasion that would augment the commercial fortunes of internationalist New England merchants. Hamilton even secured command of the new

---

[27] Dauer, *The Adams Federalists*, p. 122.

[28] Burch, *Elites in American History*, 1, pp. 49–52, 65–66, 74; John Miller, *The Federalist Era* (New York: Harper & Brothers, 1960), p. 256; Miller, *Alexander Hamilton*, pp. 447–48, 516; Leonard White, *The Federalists* (New York: Macmillan, 1948), pp. 42–43, 237–41; Wood, *Empire of Liberty*, p. 206.

empire's military. Republicans resisted the measures but lacked the strength to stop Hamilton's machinations.

After the presidential election of 1796, France announced the seizure of all American ships carrying British cargo. While Jefferson and the Republicans stressed peace, Adams urged a military expansion, particularly in the navy, and Congress authorized the president to call forth eight thousand militiamen if necessary. In mid-1798 the public learned that the peace commission had spectacularly failed: Foreign Minister Charles Talleyrand tried to extort a bribe and a loan prior to negotiations—the infamous XYZ Affair. The Federalists exploited the Republicans' embarrassment and commenced the unofficial naval "Quasi-War" with France.[29]

If the goal is to create an Old Order Empire, the first step is to enlarge the army. Hamilton called for regular and provisional armies of fifty thousand, the construction of a formal navy, and imprisoning recalcitrant militiamen or subjecting them to forced labor on public works. To his chagrin, Congress only raised a smaller regular army of twelve thousand (the "New Army") and a provisional army of ten thousand.[30] But Congress also created the Navy Department for the ensuing conflict on the high seas. Republicans, including Senator Andrew Jackson of Tennessee (which that entered the Union in 1796) and Congressmen John Williams of New York, Gallatin, and Nathaniel Macon of North Carolina, bitterly resisted. They rightfully argued that the navy subsidized Federalist merchants and standing armies crippled the economy. However, Republicans lacked the political numbers to block the legislation, and the budget exploded. From 1795 to 1800, spending in the Departments of War and Navy increased by 108 percent (16 percent per year), pushing up federal spending by 43 percent (7.5 percent per year). Military spending as a percent of spending grew from 38 percent to a bloated 56 percent.[31]

The second step is to pay for the bloated army expenditures. Federalists levied taxes on houses, land, slaves, and even stamps, eerily reminding the country of former British taxes. Even worse, Federalists

---

[29] Wood, *Empire of Liberty*, p. 245. See also pp. 239–45.

[30] Ibid., p. 263.

[31] *Historical Statistics of the United States*, vol. 5, ed. Richard Sutch and Susan Carter. New York: Cambridge University Press, 2006), pp. 80, 91; Miller, *Alexander Hamilton*, pp. 467–68; Norman Risjord, *The Old Republicans* (New York: Columbia University Press, 1965), pp. 13–14; Wood, *Empire of Liberty*, pp. 245–46, 262–64, 701.

created a swollen bureaucracy to assess property values and collect revenue. For example, in Pennsylvania they employed a suffocating nine commissioners, forty-one principal assessors, four hundred and twenty assistant assessors, four inspectors of revenue, thirty-nine supervisors of the collection, fourteen surveyors of revenue, and twenty-five collectors. Americans resented the depredations. The funding measures even caused the Fries Rebellion in early 1799, led by John Fries and German immigrants in southeastern Pennsylvania. From 1795 to 1800, government revenue surged by a crippling 77 percent, but the national debt remained at $83 million.[32]

The third, and most important step, is to appoint someone to lead the army. As Richard Kohn explains, Hamilton wanted to rule the intimidating military from a position that "did not have to be elected" while continuing "to pull the strings of power, influencing key Federalists, plotting strategy with the congressional leadership, manipulating the cabinet—without the slightest personal worry about public opinion."[33] Hamilton wrote to the retired Washington, exhorting the Virginian to accept nominal command while recommending second-in-command for himself. After some additional exhortations by Hamilton's de facto cabinet, Washington agreed that Hamilton should receive second-in-command. President Adams resisted, but Washington and the cabinet refused to have it any other way. In the words of Secretary Pickering to Washington, Adams did not realize that Hamilton had to be "the *Second* to you—and the *Chief in your absence*."[34] By October 1798 Adams had capitulated and Inspector General Hamilton was "second"-in-command. To any objective observer, Hamilton's self-serving overtures came dangerously close to bringing about his preferred monarchical government and smacked of personal cronyism.[35]

Now that Hamilton and the Essex Junto had implemented their military machinery, funding, and hierarchy, they dreamed grandiose ideas of empire, or at least apologetically of "defensive" empire. A war

---

[32] *Historical Statistics*, 5, p. 82; Andrew Shankman, *Crucible of American Democracy*, (Lawrence: University Press of Kansas, 2004), p. 64; Daniel Sisson, *The American Revolution of 1800* (New York, Alfred A. Knopf, 1974), pp. 283–86; Wood, *Empire of Liberty*, p. 265.

[33] Kohn, *Eagle and Sword*, p. 254.

[34] Ibid., p. 232.

[35] Ibid., pp. 230–38; White, *Federalists*, pp. 243–47; Wood, *Empire of Liberty*, pp. 264–67.

with France would allow the Federalists to work with Britain, possibly in a formal alliance, and seize Spanish Florida (West Florida and East Florida), Louisiana, and South America—to prevent the French from laying their lands on them. The conquest of Louisiana would also crush secessionist plans and reduce western support for the Jeffersonian Republicans.

Of course, for the Essex Junto, naval aggression would prod open foreign markets, subsidizing trading interests and bringing new natural resources under US control. As early as July 1797, a Federalist gazetteer wrote that both France and Spain had to be "driven into the Gulf of Mexico" and the wealth gained from this plundering "would be the cream of the War."[36] George Cabot of Massachusetts, member of the Essex Junto, agreed, "fully persuaded" that Great Britain and the United States should "enjoy exclusively the commerce of all Americas & Africa & the best part of Asia & Europe."[37] Perhaps the frankest statement came from the High Federalist *Gazette of the United States*, which frequently advocated suppression of Republican opposition, war with France, and an alliance with Great Britain. The periodical "demand[ed]" war "against France" and Spain, belligerently proclaiming:

> It is in vain to disguise the truth that America is essentially and naturally a commercial nation; and that from her location on the map of the world she must ever remain so. It ought therefore to be the undeviating care of the Government . . . to procure admission to our flag, in ports whence it is now excluded; to obtain it by right where it now rests on the ground of sufferance; and to establish it on a regular and permanent footing.[38]

Translation: Congress must subsidize commerce by strengthening the navy, prying open the ports of resistant countries, and securing discriminatory trade deals.

Hamilton eagerly looked forward to participating in the new imperial conquests. When it came to South America and the "riches of *Mexico* and *Peru*," he frankly declared, "[T]he command in this

---

[36] DeConde, *Affair of Louisiana*, p. 69.

[37] Dauer, *Adams Federalists*, p. 191.

[38] Ibid., p. 194.

case would very naturally fall upon me."[39] By January 1799 Hamilton itched for war with France. He wrote to Massachusetts Congressman Harrison Gray Otis and demanded Congress guarantee war by the end of July if France did not get negotiations moving. At the same time, Hamilton made sure the empire crushed civilian uprisings at home. During Pennsylvania's anti-tax Fries Rebellion, he advised McHenry to use excessive troops and "appear like Hercules" without any "consideration of expense."[40] Hamilton wanted Fries and other leaders to be convicted of treason and executed, but to his dismay Adams ended up pardoning them.[41]

Some historians have argued that Hamilton did not actually want to lead the country's military in an elitist fashion and differed from the High Federalists.[42] In reality, Hamilton, in both writing and action, excelled at personal appearances. He shrewdly tried to avoid military escalations over trifling issues, official alliances with Great Britain, or blatantly offensive military measures. The Inspector General recognized that such actions reduced public support for war and strengthened Republican opposition. In other words, he was covert. Ames of the Essex Junto, while favoring an outright alliance with Great Britain, exhorted a similar strategy: "Wage war and call it self defense . . . tell the citizens of danger & bring them to war gradually."[43]

The Antifederalists' fears about the Constitution rapidly materialized. After first establishing a mercantilist system, Hamilton stifled taxpayer resistance and pushed the country closer to a belligerent Old Order Empire. The forces of power achieved success after success, because the Republican Party lacked political strength and the Federalists easily capitalized on a purported military crisis. There seemed to be nothing that could stop the Hamiltonian juggernaut.

---

[39] Ibid., pp. 188, 196.

[40] Miller, *Alexander Hamilton*, p. 505.

[41] Dauer, *Adams Federalists*, pp. 172–97; Miller, *Alexander Hamilton*, pp. 495–98, 505–07.

[42] Aaron Coleman, "'A Second Bounaparty?'" *Journal of the Early Republic* (Summer 2008): 183–214.

[43] Dauer, *Adams Federalists*, p. 195. See also Miller, *Alexander Hamilton*, p. 470; Rothbard, *Conceived in Liberty*, 5, p. 241.

CHAPTER 6

THE JEFFERSONIAN REVOLUTION AND THE DEFEAT OF HAMILTON

The Republican Opposition Emerges

During the Adams administration, the battle between liberty and power entered its next phase. The Republican Party, composed of Antifederalists, Thomas Jefferson's radical moderates, and James Madison's disgruntled Federalists, developed the political infrastructure necessary to combat Alexander Hamilton. Jefferson refined the Antifederalist theoretical rationale—the compact theory—needed to justify nullification and secession. While the Republicans eschewed these anti-crony reforms, they successfully mobilized their political constituents in 1800 to seize control of the government *legally*. This highly significant victory—the so-called Revolution of 1800—ousted Hamilton and the High Federalists from power and changed the course of history.

Hamilton's emerging economic and military program extremely worried the Antifederalists. But the suppression of the Whiskey Rebellion made it clear that the Federalists would not tolerate resistance. Consequently, the classical liberals licked their wounds and went back to the drawing board. In the spirit of Patrick Henry and the *Address of 1790*, they interpreted the Constitution and Bill of Rights in a strictly enumerated fashion. These former Antifederals, such as William Findley, George Clinton, and Abraham Yates, now argued that the Constitution—*properly interpreted*—actually preserved the balance of power between the states and the central government. In other words, they championed the lie that Federalists such as Hamilton and Madison repeated during ratification. Such newfound admiration for the Constitution infuriated the Federalists. In 1792 Fisher Ames complained: "We hear, incessantly, from the old foes of the Constitution, 'this is unconstitutional, and that is,' . . . If the Constitution is what they affect to think it, their former opposition to such a nonentity was improper."[1] Ames was completely right.[2]

Examples of Antifederalists now supporting the Constitution abound: the staunch advocate of the free market John Taylor of Caroline, senator for Virginia from 1792 to 1794 (he succeeded Richard Henry Lee), particularly stood out. Taylor, well-steeped in Enlightenment thought and Adam Smith's economics, articulated strict constructionism to defend liberty against power, particularly in his *A Definition of Parties* and *An Enquiry into the Principles and Tendency of Certain Public Measures* (both published in 1794). He favored structural amendments to weaken the Hamiltonian program, especially to prohibit federal debt holders and Bank of the United States stockowners from holding office, limit government borrowing, and remove the vague clauses. The Virginia theorist fiercely opposed the BUS and went so far as to argue that all paper money was a fraudulent special privilege.[3]

Another prominent Antifederalist, Congressman Albert Gallatin, turned into a strict constructionist and fierce critic of Hamilton. In 1796 he published the libertarian *A Sketch of the Finances of the United States*, striking at the heart of the Hamiltonian system: the national debt. Unlike Hamilton, Gallatin realized that deficit spending was dangerous since governments inevitably borrow and spend *ad nauseam*. He lashed out at Hamilton's debt assumption because it funded state debts at face, and not market, value, an enormous privilege to the financial elite. In a similar vein, *A Sketch* reasoned that Hamilton's BUS favored eastern stockholders and lent excessively to the federal government. Gallatin, a harsh critic of military expenditures, made the Smithian argument that wartime expenditures reduce the nation's capital stock and burden the economy by diverting funds away from

---

[1] Richard Kohn, *Eagle and Sword* (New York: The Free Press, 1975), p. 197.

[2] Saul Cornell, *The Other Founders* (Chapel Hill: The University of North Carolina Press, 1999), pp. 169–70, 200–12; Alfred Young, *The Democratic Republicans of New York* (Chapel Hill: The University of North Carolina Press, 1967), pp. 331–32.

[3] *American Political Leaders* (Washington, DC: CQ Press, 2000), pp. 216, 241, 302; Paul Conkin, *Prophets of Prosperity* (Bloomington: Indiana University Press, 1980), pp. 52, 56; Joseph Dorfman, *The Economic Mind in American Civilization*, vol. 1 (New York: Viking Press, 1946), pp. 301–04; Kevin Gutzman, *Virginia's American Revolution* (Lanham, MD: Lexington Books, 2007), pp. 118–19, 141–42; Herbert Sloan, *Principle and Interest* (New York: Oxford University Press, 1995), pp. 109, 191, 193, 308; Joseph Stromberg, "Country Ideology, Republicanism, and Libertarianism," *Journal of Libertarian Studies* (Winter 1982): 35–48.

private enterprise. He concluded with several economic reforms: reduce military spending, sell western lands, revise the tax system, and pay off the public debt.[4]

Antifederalists, especially Gallatin and Taylor, loyally followed Jefferson, the preeminent radical moderate. He strictly interpreted the necessary and proper and general welfare clauses, along with the (weakened) Tenth Amendment. Furthermore, he wanted structural amendments to enumerate the Constitution's powers even more. In 1792, the secretary of state drafted the private *Note of Agenda to Reduce the Government to True Principles*, laying out a hard-core libertarian program to reduce cronyism and implement the Empire of Liberty: abolish the BUS, repeal excise taxes, lower tariffs, condemn the *Report on Manufactures*, downsize the debt, divide the Treasury Department and require greater congressional oversight, and make the government deal only in specie and not bank money. In November 1798 he even wrote to Taylor and advocated an amendment to prevent Congress from borrowing to reduce the military's power and the chance of war. It is easy to see why former Antifederalists followed Jefferson, with the glaring exception of the bitter Henry. However, they rightfully remained less enchanted with Madison, the inveterate opportunist, and the Federalists he brought with him.[5]

The disparate groups—former Antifederalists, radical moderates, and disgruntled Federalists—joined forces to create the Republican Party. The Republican alliance centered in New York and Virginia, the two former Antifederalist states that squandered their chance to officially collaborate during ratification. While the Federalists maintained a powerful grip on New England, the Republicans mustered formidable strength in the South (though as late as 1798 40 percent of southern congressmen were Federalists), and the middle states remained toss-ups. In the 1790s, the minority Republicans controlled the House only once (1793–95) and the Senate not at all. However, time was on their side: Republicans had developed better organizational skills than their Antifederalist ancestors and embraced democracy, unlike the elitist Federalists. By the end of the decade the Republicans formed

[4] Gregory May, *Jefferson's Treasure* (Washington, DC: Regnery History, 2018), pp. xxv, 74–76; Thomas McCraw, *The Founders and Finance* (Cambridge, MA: Belknap Press, 2012), pp. 205–14; John Nelson, *Liberty and Property* (Baltimore, MD: The Johns Hopkins University Press, 1987), pp. 119–21.

[5] Sloan, *Principle and Interest*, pp. 184, 196, 347, 352.

the requisite machinery to fight the Federalists, developing a full-scale libertarian opposition.[6]

Hamiltonian Federalists stood for an Empire of Power ruled by the elites, or more specifically, broad constructionism, centralization, bureaucratic entrenchment, central banking, protectionism, internal improvements, land grants, and international aggression. On the other hand, the Jeffersonian Republicans favored the Empire of Liberty: strict constructionism, states' rights, rotation in office, hard money, free trade, opposition to federally funded internal improvements, settlers' rights, and peace. Gordon Wood brilliantly describes how the radical Whig theories in John Trenchard and Thomas Gordon's *Cato's Letters* and the threat of Hamiltonianism bound the new Republican coalition together:

> This Republican ideology, involving a deep hatred of overgrown central power and a fear of the political and financial mechanisms that sustained such power—inflated executive authority, high taxes, standing armies, and perpetual debts—had been inherited from the English radical Whig "country-opposition" tradition that had been sharpened and Americanized during the Revolution. . . .
>
> To those steeped in this radical Whig ideology, Hamilton's system threatened to re-create the kind of government and society that many Americans thought they had destroyed in 1776.[7]

It is extremely important to note that slavery was *not* a party division. Although antislavery advocates filled both parties' ranks, Federalists and Republicans defended the Constitution's slavery protections. Throughout the 1790s, High Federalists worked to strengthen slavery because they wanted to establish an Empire of Power and secure favorable commercial regulations. In 1789 they

---

[6] James Broussard, *The Southern Federalists* (Baton Rouge: Louisiana State University, 1978), p. 16; Noble Cunningham, *The Jeffersonian Republicans* (Chapel Hill: The University of North Carolina Press, 1957), pp. 46–49, 256; *Historical Statistics of the United States*, vol. 5, ed. Richard Sutch and Susan Carter (New York: Cambridge University Press, 2006), p. 200; John Miller, *The Federalist Era* (New York: Harper & Brothers, 1960), pp. 99, 125.

[7] Gordon Wood, *Empire of Liberty* (New York: Oxford University Press, 2009), p. 172.

scuttled the Pennsylvania Abolition Society's petition to Congress so the legislature could concentrate on the nation's finances. In 1793 they eagerly voted for a crony fugitive slave law that made it easier for slave owners to capture runaway slaves. Five years later, Essex Junto man Secretary Timothy Pickering and Congressman Harrison Gray Otis crushed a House proposal to ban slavery in the Mississippi Territory. During his time in power Hamilton made no serious effort against slavery, continually courting the ardently pro-slavery South Carolina Federalists, particularly the Pinckneys. The Federalists only complained about the slavery clauses (not slavery per se) after they lost political power in the early 1800s.[8]

Overall, the new laissez-faire Republican Party was genuinely concerned about stopping the Federalists' accretion of power and distribution of cronyism, a goal they hoped to accomplish through strict constructionism. The Republicans faced their toughest test during the foreign policy controversies of the late 1790s.

The Kentucky and Virginia Resolutions

During the Quasi-War's frenzied atmosphere, Federalists insinuated that Republicans were French agents subversively destroying the federal government. In mid-1798, they enacted a series of highly controversial laws known as the Alien and Sedition Acts. Jefferson responded by developing the radical anti-crony reform tools necessary to thwart the legislation.

The Alien Acts increased immigration barriers and empowered the president to expel "hostile" aliens. The Sedition Act allowed the government to fine and imprison those critical of either the president or Congress. Crucially, the position of vice president—currently held by the Republican Jefferson—was exempt. The Federalists justified the acts with the necessary and proper and general welfare clauses, and with utter disdain for the First Amendment that supposedly protected free speech and the press. Inspector General Hamilton and President Adams approved the measures, but ever prescient, Hamilton worried

---

[8] James Banner, *To the Hartford Convention* (New York: Alfred A. Knopf, 1970), pp. 105–07; Thomas J. DiLorenzo, "Yankee Confederates," in *Secession, State and Liberty*, ed. David Gordon (New Brunswick, NJ: Transaction Publishers, 1998), pp. 145–46; Miller, *Federalist Era*, pp. 125, 200–01, 259–61; Sean Wilentz, *The Rise of American Democracy* (New York: W.W. Norton, 2005), pp. 219–20; Sean Wilentz, *No Property in Man* (Cambridge, MA: Harvard University Press, 2018), pp. 154–72, 316–17.

of the vigor with which his High Federalists pursued their objectives because it could rouse intense Republican opposition.

Federalists did not use the Alien Acts to deport a single person, because Adams strictly interpreted the laws. However, Federalists did employ the Sedition Act to crack down on Republican newspapers that opposed the Federalist dispensation. Secretary Pickering assiduously sniffed out dissent, arrested twenty-five people for criticizing the government, and brought seventeen indictments of seditious libel against Republican journalists and editors. Federalists levied fourteen of the indictments under the new legislation (even before the Sedition Act they arrested people for seditious libel), convicting and punishing a total of ten men. The most prominent examples include the English lawyer and scientist Thomas Cooper, who sympathized with the Republican cause, and the editor of the radical Philadelphia *Aurora,* William Duane.[9]

In the spring of 1798 Taylor despairingly wrote to Jefferson that the Federalists would suffocate the country with high taxes and standing armies, advocating secession. Corresponding again in June, Taylor warned Jefferson of the impending danger and in the spirit of Patrick Henry and the *Address of 1790,* articulated the compact theory. This theory argues that the people, working through their respective states, ratified the Constitution in a contract. The people agreed to give up some of their autonomy in return for possessing the ability to judge when the federal government overstepped its boundaries and therefore violated said contract. Consequently, states could nullify federal laws, or, if this was not enough, they could withdraw from the compact and secede. The theory was a novel Antifederalist twist on the mendacious Federalist argument during the ratification debates that the states would be able to check unconstitutional federal legislation. It formed a significant defense against cronyism by elevating the state governments to a legal authority that could break the federal judiciary monopoly: no longer would a centralized oligarchy determine the legality of laws. The worried Jefferson accepted and refined Taylor's ideas, because they fit in with his own radical moderate views, though of course he gave no credit to Henry.

Jefferson considered the Alien and Sedition Acts tyrannical, believing they portended more drastic measures: Congress would

---

[9] John Miller, *Alexander Hamilton and the Growth of the New Nation* (New York: Harper & Row, 1959), pp. 484–85; William Watkins, *Crossroads for Liberty* (Oakland, CA: The Independent Institute, 2016), p. 194; Wood, *Empire of Liberty,* pp. 247–62.

make the president and Senate elected for life, and with it, finally extinguish the American Revolution. Jefferson was pushed to the radical brink; desperate times called for desperate measures. Consequently, in late 1798, Jefferson and Madison anonymously drafted the respective Kentucky and Virginia Resolutions, two radical documents that protested federal tyranny (Kentucky had entered the Union in 1792).[10]

Unsurprisingly, Jefferson's original Kentucky Resolutions were far more radical and pro–states' rights than the lukewarm Madison's. In his Resolutions, Jefferson trenchantly criticized the Alien and Sedition Acts as unconstitutional and outside the federal government's enumerated powers. The similarity in Jefferson's thought over the years on competing legal jurisdictions was evident. In his earlier Declaration of Independence Jefferson argued that

> governments are instituted among men, deriving their just powers from the consent of the governed . . . whenever any form of government becomes destructive of these ends, it is the right of the people to alter or to abolish it, and to institute new government.[11]

Put another way, in the Empire of Liberty the people had a right to compete with their government and decide what should be legal. By 1798, Jefferson echoed the same principle when he wrote

> that whensoever the General government assumes undelegated powers, its acts are unauthoritative, void, and of no force . . . the government created by this compact was not made the exclusive or final judge of the extent of the powers delegated to itself . . . each party has an equal right to judge for itself, as well of infractions as of the mode and measures of redress.[12]

Jefferson continued to echo his revolutionary roots: whenever the federal government assumes powers not enumerated, thereby

---

[10] Cornell, *Other Founders*, p. 239; Norman Risjord, *Chesapeake Politics* (New York: Columbia University Press, 1978), p. 240; Wood, *Empire of Liberty*, pp. 267–69.

[11] Murray N. Rothbard, *Conceived in Liberty*, vols. 1–4 (Auburn, AL: Mises Institute 2019), p. 1292.

[12] William Watkins, *Reclaiming the American Revolution* (Oakland, CA: The Independent Institute, 2004), p. 67.

breaking the compact, "a nullification of the act is the rightful remedy."[13] Jefferson radicalized as the months progressed. By August 1799, he privately toyed with secession—the logical continuation of the compact theory—if the federal government did not change its ways . Unfortunately, the reactionary Madison swayed the theoretician from this preeminently radical option.

Jefferson dropped the Antifederalist bombshell—the states' rights and strictly construed Tenth Amendment compact theory. It was the "Spirit of 1798," a perfect complement to his *Note of Agenda* and Empire of Liberty. He continued the Antifederal tradition by arguing that the states could best stop power's depredations. When the Kentucky legislature received Jefferson's Resolutions in November 1798, it struck out nullification to facilitate passage. But in November 1799, the legislature repeated its opposition to the Alien and Sedition Acts and stated "a Nullification of those acts by the States to be the rightful remedy."[14]

On the other hand, Madison's Virginia Resolutions, while certainly evidence of his outward radicalization, were more moderate than Jefferson's Kentucky Resolutions. While he did argue for a watered-down compact theory, he objected to Jefferson's argument that the state legislatures could nullify federal laws. Ultimately, Madison wrote a protest, rather than an actual call for radical resistance. After all, unlike Jefferson, Madison participated in the Constitutional Convention and the Virginia ratification debate. However, Jefferson made some last-minute changes to Madison's draft before Taylor introduced it into the Virginia legislature, declaring the Alien and Sedition Acts *"utterly void, and of no force or effect."*[15] Taylor happily agreed with this defiance of federal law, which he hoped would lead to a second constitutional convention. Unfortunately, a coalition of Virginia Federalists and hesitant Republicans struck it out.[16]

The respective legislatures adopted the Kentucky and Virginia Resolutions in late 1798. While the resolutions fell flat in the other

---

[13] Ibid., p. 68.

[14] Wood, *Empire of Liberty*, p. 271. See also Watkins, *Reclaiming the American Revolution*, pp. 67–71; Wood, *Empire of Liberty*, pp. 269–70; Thomas E. Woods Jr., *Nullification* (Washington, DC: Regnery, 2010), pp. 44–50.

[15] Richard Beeman, *The Old Dominion and the New Nation* (Lexington: The University Press of Kentucky, 1972), pp. 190–91.

[16] Ibid., pp. 191–94; Cornell, *Other Founders*, pp. 241–45; Wood, *Empire of Liberty*, pp. 269–70.

state legislatures, which the Federalists mostly controlled, local support emerged: Virginia's Dinwiddie County issued similar resolutions that protested the Alien and Sedition Acts as well as the standing army, naval buildup, formal alliances, and government borrowing. Other Virginia counties followed, and counties from New York, Kentucky, and Tennessee proclaimed similar sentiments. Republican newspapers in Philadelphia and Vermont joined the cause by printing related protests.[17]

Notably, the young John Randolph of Roanoke, a former Antifederalist and Jefferson's distant cousin, radically urged the stockpiling of weapons. While running for Congress in 1799, he defended the Republican creed against a Federalist candidate for the Virginia legislature: Patrick Henry. Cognizant of his hatred of Jefferson and Madison, Federalists had previously offered Henry multiple position of power, such as original negotiator for Pinckney's Treaty, chief justice, and even the presidency, but the old radical turned them down. But when Washington asked Henry to run for the lowly position of state congressman, Henry agreed to forsake his principles so he could spite his enemies. Against Randolph, Henry correctly stated that the Alien and Sedition Acts logically resulted from the Constitution but unfortunately attacked the Kentucky and Virginia Resolutions. Still the radical, he argued that the proper response to oppression was to "overturn the government," but only after provocation.[18] Virginians elected both, though Henry died before he assumed office, an odd ending for the diehard Antifederalist. Unfortunately, Henry, blinded by his acrimonious relationship with Jefferson and Madison, could not see that the Kentucky and Virginia Resolutions logically resulted from the *Address of 1790*. But Randolph would preserve Henry's legacy by forcefully defending states' rights and the principles of 1798 in Congress.[19]

---

[17] Daniel Sisson, *The American Revolution of 1800* (New York, Alfred A. Knopf, 1974), pp. 299–302, 324–25; Wood, *Empire*, pp. 269–70.

[18] David Johnson, *John Randolph of Roanoke* (Baton Rouge: Louisiana State University Press, 2012), p. 41.

[19] Ibid., pp. 39–41, 55; Thomas Kidd, *Patrick Henry* (New York: Basic Books, 2011), pp. 237–43; Jon Kukla, *Patrick Henry* (New York: Simon & Schuster, 2017), pp. 367–68; Harlow Giles Unger, *Lion of Liberty: Patrick Henry and the Call to a New Nation* (Cambridge, MA: Da Capo Press, 2010), pp. 264–72; Nicholas Wood, "John Randolph of Roanoke and the Politics of Slavery in the Early Republic," *Virginia Magazine of History and Biography* (Summer 2012): 110–11.

Naturally, Hamilton viewed the anonymous Kentucky and Virginia Resolutions as "signs of a gangrene begun" because they dared "to unite the State Legislatures in a direct resistance to certain laws of the Union."[20] The Inspector General insisted that the states did not create the federal government and had no ability to resist or judge the constitutionality of federal laws. Hamilton completely contradicted *The Federalist Papers*, particularly when he described the "State legislatures" as "jealous guardians of the rights of the citizens against encroachments from the federal government."[21] Hamilton even urged new interventions to Speaker of the House Jonathan Dayton, declaring that Congress should strengthen the federal judiciary, subsidize internal improvements, increase taxes, make the current armies permanent, pass an amendment breaking up Virginia and other large states, strengthen the sedition laws, and employ the alien laws to deport foreign Republicans. Hamilton also wrote to another Federalist and urged confrontation with Virginia. Clearly, the corrupt Hamilton wanted to tighten the Federalist noose and further establish his Old Order Empire.

However, neither the Federalist Congress nor Virginia and Kentucky took any action. The Republicans instead channeled their rebellion into peaceful political revolution. The "Spirit of 1798" served as an important radical impetus for the presidential election of 1800 and the coming decades.[22]

The Revolution of 1800

By 1799, the corrupt Federalists had created a mighty imperial edifice; in March 1801, it all came crashing down. A personal feud between Adams and Hamilton split the Federalist Party. Consequently, the organization failed to stop the Jeffersonian Republicans from engineering a peaceful and popular political revolution. The Hamiltonian Federalists contemplated blocking the political winds by interfering with elections, incapacitating President Adams, and obstructing an overtime presidential election. They only succeeded in enacting a new law that maintained their grip on the federal judiciary.

---

[20] Sisson, *American Revolution of 1800*, p. 312.

[21] Dumas Malone, *Jefferson and the Ordeal of Liberty* (Boston: Little, Brown and Co., 1962), p. 397.

[22] Manning Dauer, *The Adams Federalists* (Baltimore, MD: The John Hopkins Press, 1953), pp. 202–04; Malone, *Ordeal of Liberty*, p. 397; Miller, *Alexander Hamilton*, pp. 489–91; Sisson, *American Revolution of 1800*, pp. 302–15.

With the Revolution of 1800, the Republicans secured a deafening victory against cronyism.

Jefferson had developed his *Note of Agenda* and "Spirit of 1798," but knew the Republicans still needed a campaign platform that promoted the Empire of Liberty. In early 1799, he wrote to Republican Elbridge Gerry and championed "a government rigorously frugal and simple . . . relying . . . on our militia solely, till actual invasion, and for such a naval force only as may protect our coasts and harbors . . . for free commerce with all nations; political connection with none."[23] The radical Philadelphia *Aurora* repeated similar free market sentiments in 1800. Against the Federalist "increase of public debt, additional taxes, further loans, new excises, higher public salaries, and wasteful expenditure of public money," the Republicans supported "decrease of public debt, reduced taxes, no loans, no excises, reduced public salaries, and a system of economy and care of the public money."[24] In the same year, Gallatin published his *Views of the Public Debt* attacking Federalist fiscal policies, and for campaign distribution Jefferson ordered Cooper's free trade *Political Arithmetic*, which blasted the Federalists' naval protection of the mercantile community. Clearly, the Republicans had their laissez-faire platform.[25]

In the fall 1799 elections, a political crack surfaced after Republican Thomas McKean defeated Federalist US Senator James Ross for the Pennsylvania governorship, capitalizing on the recent Fries Rebellion and utilizing the Jeffersonian anti-tax, anti-standing army, and anti-elitism platform. Pennsylvania Federalists tried to plug the fissure by blocking attempts to choose the method for selecting electors for the upcoming presidential election (state legislature, state-wide elections, or district elections), a move that could prevent the state from choosing any electors at all. Senator Ross even tried to create a congressional committee overseeing electoral returns to guarantee Federalist electors.[26]

---

[23] Cunningham, *The Jeffersonian Republicans*, p. 211.

[24] Ibid., p. 214.

[25] Joyce Appleby, *Capitalism and a New Social Order* (New York: New York University Press, 1984), pp. 88–89; Cunningham, *Jeffersonian Republicans*, p. 163; May, *Jefferson's Treasure*, 91.

[26] Malone, *Ordeal of Liberty*, pp. 462–64; John Miller, *The Federalist Era* (New York: Harper & Brothers, 1960), pp. 255–57.

An even bigger crack emerged from the grisly fight between President Adams and Inspector General Hamilton. Adams had had enough of the "second"-in-command and his imperial visions. In February 1799 the former Revolutionary radical unexpectedly and courageously decided to send a new peace commission to France without discussing the matter with his cabinet. Hamilton, Pickering, and James McHenry understood that ending the Quasi-War would cripple their efforts to further enlarge the military, invade other countries, and suppress the Republicans. While Adams was away from Philadelphia in the summer of 1799, Hamilton flirted with a "voluntary" coup d'état. The cabinet (i.e., Hamilton's men) would take effective control of the government per the president's cooperation. When Adams refused, Hamilton personally stressed the need to delay peace. Adams later famously recalled that "never in my life did I hear a man talk more like a fool."[27] With some minor concessions, by November Adams had secured his commission. The High Federalists realized that Adams simply had to go. Hamilton unsuccessfully tried to drag Washington out of retirement before he died in December. Instead, the Inspector General set his sights on Charles Cotesworth Pinckney.

In May 1800, the breakages grew more numerous. The Republicans secured the New York legislature in the spring elections, thanks to the political renegade and former Antifederalist Aaron Burr, whom Hamilton detested. Burr won the state by catering his new Bank of the Manhattan Company to disgruntled Republican merchants and entrepreneurs who groaned under the established Federalist monopolies. Since the state legislature chose the New York electors, the Republicans now controlled the state's electors. The mortified Hamilton wrote to Governor John Jay, asking him to call into session the lame-duck Federalist legislature and demand it change the state's electoral rules to ensure a Federalist victory. This blatant cronyism and flirting with illegality was too much even for the reactionary Jay, who refused to respond to Hamilton's order.[28]

Soon enough, all hell broke loose. For the first time, the Republicans and Federalists formally nominated their presidential candidates

[27] Miller, *Hamilton*, p. 502.

[28] Cunningham, *Jeffersonian Republicans*, pp. 182–85; Bray Hammond, *Banks and Politics in America* (Princeton, NJ: Princeton University Press, 1957), pp. 149–58; Miller, *Federalist Era*, pp. 258–60; Miller, *Hamilton*, 500–03; Sisson, *American Revolution*, pp. 369–74; Wood, *Empire of Liberty*, pp. 271–74.

in congressional caucuses. Jefferson initially asked George Clinton to be his vice president, but when the New Yorker declined, the Virginian choose the maverick Burr. For the Federalists, Hamilton engineered the ticket to be between President Adams and Pinckney *equally*, secretly planning for Pinckney to win. Adams, insulted by the equality, surmised that Hamilton schemed to deprive him of the presidency. Adams quickly summoned Pickering and McHenry and demanded their resignations. McHenry obliged, but when the Essex Junto man refused, Adams fired him and filled the vacancy with Virginia's John Marshall. To make matters worse for the High Federalists, Congress winnowed the army down, thereby crippling the military establishment. In October, with the High Federalists at total war with the moderate Adams Federalists, Hamilton arrogantly circulated a hysterical diatribe against the president to secure electoral support for Pinckney. This further split the Federalists and alienated many leaders from Hamilton. "Prime Minister" Hamilton was no more.[29]

During this time, states held elections for presidential electors and congressional delegations. In Congress, the results were a total smash for the Republicans, up and down the coast. For the first time, the Republicans controlled Congress, and the Federalists never again secured either chamber, proving that the Election of 1800 was truly a people's revolution. Clearly, the Federalist system—excessive government spending, high taxes, standing armies, and the Alien and Sedition Acts—along with the Spirit of 1798 led to this spectacular victory. With the war crisis over, the public saw little need to maintain the Federalist measures and the Republicans brilliantly capitalized on their concerns. The proponents of liberty finally secured a reform tool—the party system and electoral change—to topple Federalist cronyism.

However, the Revolution of 1800 also concerned the presidency. Due to the various methods states could use to choose electors, the results for president were much closer, a clear demonstration of how the Federalists' Electoral College weakened the public's will. New England strongly voted for the Federalists, New York for the Republicans, Pennsylvania compromised and cast slightly more votes for Jefferson, and the South and West voted staunchly Republican. In the

---

[29] Cunningham, *Jeffersonian Republicans*, pp. 162–66; Kohn, *Eagle and Sword*, pp. 266–67; Malone, *Jefferson, Ordeal*, pp. 473–75; Miller, *Federalist Era*, pp. 259–63; Miller, *Hamilton*, pp. 514–24; Sisson, *American Revolution of 1800*, pp. 384–85; Wood, *Empire of Liberty*, pp. 271–75.

end, Jefferson and Burr tied with seventy-three votes while Adams and Pinckney trailed with sixty-five and sixty-four votes, respectively. The Republicans seized the presidency.[30]

There was only one problem: against the plan, all the Republican electors voted equally. Per the Constitution, the Federalist lame, duck House would decide whether Jefferson or Burr would be president. Each state delegation had to cast one vote, with the majority (nine states of sixteen) picking the winner. Republicans controlled eight state delegations, Federalists six, and two states were divided.[31]

At the very best, the situation was gloomy for the Federalists. They definitively lost control of the legislative branch and now had to choose between two Republicans for the executive. Despondent, they quickly passed the Judiciary Act of 1801, an old Hamiltonian plan, in the waning days of Adams' presidency. This crucial piece of legislation increased the number and jurisdiction of inferior courts, allowing Federalists to protect their special privileges. Soon after, Adams made a number of "midnight appointments" to fill the new positions. Crucially, one of these late-term appointments was the elevation of Secretary of State John Marshall to the Supreme Court. A prominent lawyer and land speculator, Marshall worked for Robert Morris and helped consolidate his financial empire (Marshall's younger brother even married Morris' daughter). He would soon act as Hamilton's reincarnation in the Supreme Court and protect the Federalists' special-interest legislation.[32]

But this only softened the blow: the Federalists still had to choose the next Republican president. The Federalists thought that if they elected Burr he would forever be indebted to them. But the people wanted Jefferson, and if the Federalists managed to elect Burr or elect no one at all, there was a serious chance the country would plunge into a severe constitutional crisis, if not outright civil war. On the other hand, Hamilton abhorred his New York rival. Swallowing his pride, Hamilton urged congressmen to vote for Jefferson, though he only thought it proper to "throw out a line for [Burr] . . . and then *lay the*

---

[30] Dauer, *Adams Federalists*, pp. 256–59; *Historical Statistics*, 5, p. 200; Miller, *Federalist Era*, pp. 267–68.

[31] Miller, *Federalist Era*, pp. 268–71; Watkins, *Crossroads for Liberty*, pp. 243–44.

[32] Philip Burch, *Elites in American History*, 1 (New York: Holmes & Meier Publishers, 1981), p. 107; Richard Ellis, *The Jeffersonian Crisis* (New York: Oxford University Press, 1971), p. 15; Miller, *Alexander Hamilton*, pp. 535–36; Wood, *Empire of Liberty*, p. 419.

foundation of dissension between the two chiefs."[33] Thus, while Hamilton still committed to Jefferson, he wanted to provoke a fissure in the Republican ranks and potentially cause a serious constitutional crisis. Moreover, the reactionary urged his party to accept Jefferson only on the condition that he preserve Federalist cronyism: the fiscal system, foreign relations, army, and bureaucratic personnel. But Hamilton could not convince his congressional allies to elect Jefferson, a stark example of his fall from grace.

When the voting began in February, the first thirty-five ballots produced no victor. The gridlock had to be resolved before March to avoid a political crisis—the country could not be permitted to go without a chief executive for a couple of days! The lone congressman from Delaware, the moderate Federalist James A. Bayard, finally surmounted the impasse. Bayard, cognizant of the violent threats mounting against Federalists, realized that they could not elect Burr. In addition, Bayard received confidential assurances from Congressman Samuel Smith of Maryland, an ex-Federalist turned Republican, that most of the Federalist program would be maintained; a dark stain that symbolized the upcoming clash between the radical and moderate Republicans. The thirty-sixth ballot averted the crisis—the Federalists elected Jefferson.[34]

The peaceful Revolution of 1800 ended the Hamiltonian era. In eleven short years the Constitution created a polity that led to many Antifederalists' fears: mercantilism on a grand scale, high taxes, standing armies, and repression of personal freedom. This "monarchical program," writes Wood, was "counter to the libertarian impulse of America's republican ideology."[35] Consequently, Jefferson rallied the people and stopped the Federalist tyranny dead in its tracks. The recent move of the nation's capital from the bustling metropolis of Philadelphia to the new backwater Federal City on the Potomac River (soon called Washington, DC) symbolically marked the Republican triumph. With the Federalists finally out of the way, the Republicans could now reform the government, roll back cronyism, and establish their Empire of Liberty.

---

[33] Sisson, *American Revolution of 1800*, pp. 412–13.

[34] Burch, *Elites in American History*, 1, p. 90; Miller, *Federalist Era*, 270–76; Sisson, *American Revolution of 1800*, pp. 411–14; Wood, *Empire of Liberty*, pp. 282–86.

[35] Wood, *Empire of Liberty*, p. 276. See also pp. 287–89.

PART III

THE FAILED JEFFERSONIAN REVOLUTION, 1801–1817

CHAPTER 7

PRESIDENT JEFFERSON: THE SUPREMACY OF MODERATION

Reforming the Judiciary

Unfortunately, the Republican Party quickly split into two factions, the Old Republicans who wanted to institute Antifederalist reforms and amend the Constitution, and moderates who desired only a slight trimming and reconciliation with the Federalists. President Thomas Jefferson, coveting an ever-expanding coalition, dropped his libertarian *Note of Agenda* and Spirit of 1798, eschewing Old Republicans John Randolph and John Taylor for James Madison and his ex-Federalist moderates. He appointed moderates to his cabinet and only partially dismantled the Federalist bureaucracy. Congress repealed internal taxes and decreased spending, but maintained land polices, tariffs, and naval expenditures. The Republicans let the Bank of the United States and state-level banking partnerships remain. Although Jefferson, an Old Republican at heart, tried to establish his Empire of Liberty, the corrupting nature of power ensured the survival of Federalist cronyism. Jefferson's first corruption concerned appointing moderates, acquiescing to existing bureaucrats, and allowing Chief Justice John Marshall's use of judicial review to protect the special privileges granted by prior administrations.

In March 1801, Jefferson filled upper-level executive positions with moderates. Secretary of state unsurprisingly went to the president's Virginia ally, Madison, the preeminent moderate and opportunist. Secretary of the Navy wound up in the lap of Robert Smith of Maryland, the younger brother of the Congressman Samuel Smith, who previously gave assurances that Jefferson would not dismantle the Hamiltonian system. The Smiths, ex-Federalist merchants, planned to dominate maritime policy. Rufus King remained as minister to Great Britain while Jefferson awarded Robert Livingston and Charles Pinckney, ex-Federalists from New York and South Carolina instrumental in the election, ambassador posts to France and Spain. For the party press, the president passed over the radical William Duane and his Philadelphia *Aurora* for the moderate Samuel Harrison Smith (no relation) and his *National Intelligencer*. Secretary of the Treasury Albert Gallatin, a former Antifederal, stood out as the major exception. However, like Jefferson, Gallatin would support both Old Republican and moderate positions while in office.[1]

Jefferson faced a more important task regarding rank-and-file appointments, particularly the Federalist judicial branch. For years, Hamilton employed staunch partisans to ensure loyal henchmen ran the government. Federalists passed the Judiciary Act of 1801 and engaged in midnight appointments to solidify their control, particularly by appointing judges, which the Constitution entrenched with lifetime tenure. Now playing the defense, the Hamiltonian Marshall planned to deploy judicial review (i.e., determining laws' constitutionality) so he could protect Federalist cronyism, establish the Supreme Court as the sole constitutional authority, and declare Republican policies unconstitutional. In the face of this judicial cronyism, Old Republicans urged rotating out officials, repealing the Judiciary Acts of 1789 and 1801, and amending the Constitution so Congress could remove judges. But moderates only wanted Jefferson to limit the number of removals.[2]

In this controversy Jefferson straddled the middle. He removed many midnight officials, bureaucrats who visibly abused their positions, and all attorneys and marshals. He also refused to acknowledge any of Adams' undelivered commissions to various midnight appointments, a fateful decision. However, these removals, though admirable, were virtually all that Jefferson carried out, totaling roughly one-fourth of presidential class officials. The moderates in Jefferson's cabinet reacted negatively when he attempted to make more removals. Jefferson's moderation infuriated Old Republicans and even failed to

---

[1] *American Political Leaders* (Washington, DC: CQ Press, 2000), p. 290; Philip Burch, *Elites in American History*, vol. 1 (New York: Holmes & Meier Publishers, 1981), pp. 86–92; Noble Cunningham, *The Jeffersonian Republications in Power* (Chapel Hill: The University of North Carolina, 1963), p. 15; Richard Ellis, *The Jeffersonian Crisis* (New York: Oxford University Press, 1971), pp. 19–24, 31–32, 51, 57; Sean Wilentz, *The Rise of American Democracy* (New York: W.W. Norton, 2005), pp. 105–08.

[2] Ellis, *Jeffersonian Crisis*, pp. 19–24, 235, 276; Murray N. Rothbard, "Bureaucracy and the Civil Service in the United States," *Journal of Libertarian Studies* (Summer 1995): 28–31.

please the Federalists he tried to court, who wailed at how the president dared to remove anyone at all. The president also vacillated over repealing the Judiciary Acts and grew silent on amendments.

Fortunately, Federalist hubris in December 1801 radicalized Jefferson. Four of the midnight justices whom Jefferson never appointed, including one William Marbury, initiated a lawsuit before the Supreme Court to ask for writs of mandamus requiring Secretary Madison to deliver their commissions. The Federalists arrogantly wanted to show the Republicans their firm grip on the judiciary. But their gall backfired horrendously, incensing Old Republicans and the president. Despite moderates' waffling, in early 1802 the Republicans repealed the Judiciary Act of 1801. The repeal did count as a great reform, because Congress repealed the act and revoked new judges' lifetime tenure by eliminating their offices, but Old Republicans remained upset Congress went no further. The judicial edifice of the Constitution and the 1789 Judiciary Act stood unperturbed, and Congress exercised no greater authority over removing entrenched federal judges than before.

Lo and behold, Marshall exploited this moderation. In *Marbury v. Madison* of February 1803, the Chief Justice declared that the four judges had a right to commissions but the court's jurisdiction did not allow it to issue writs of mandamus. In it, Marshall utilized judicial review: the Supreme Court maintained the right to declare various acts of the federal government unconstitutional. *Marbury v. Madison* marked the beginning of the enormous growth in the Supreme Court's power and influence—authority Marshall would use to solidify special-interest privileges.[3]

Subsequent efforts to reform the judiciary and amend the Constitution proved to be equally unsatisfactory. Jefferson supported legally impeaching federal judges to provide openings for Republicans. Congressional Old Republicans removed Federal District Judge John Pickering in 1804, but after they failed to remove Supreme Court justice Samuel Chase future impeachment efforts evaporated. Even worse, after Chase's acquittal Randolph called for an amendment that allowed Congress and the president to remove judges, but Jefferson gave it short shrift. The Republicans only passed the Twelfth Amendment in 1804, allowing electors to designate the president and vice president on their ballots to prevent another near-fiasco from happening again.

---

[3] Ellis, *Jeffersonian Crisis*, pp. 32–39, 43–51, 57–66, 235; Rothbard, "Bureaucracy," pp. 28–29.

The Twelfth Amendment did nothing to strike at Federalist judicial cronyism, let alone any cronyism: Hamilton favored it and actually went further, advocating that the people, and not the state legislatures, directly choose presidential electors. Most importantly, Jefferson only appointed moderates to fill Supreme Court vacancies, respectively in 1804, 1806, and 1807. He eschewed appointing strict construction-ists and compact theorists, such as Old Republicans Judge Spencer Roane of the Virginia Court of Appeals or the law professor St. George Tucker of Virginia. He instead recommended moderates who quickly became acolytes of Marshall.

In the end, Jefferson's desire to placate the opposition proved critical for the Empire of Liberty. The Federalist bureaucracy and Marshall's dominance of the Supreme Court (and hence Hamiltonian constructionism) remained largely untouched. The Old Republicans grew disgruntled and began to drift away from the administration—an ominous sign for President Jefferson.[4]

The Gallatinian Economic Program

Against the moderates, the Old Republicans strove to implement laissez-faire by decreasing revenue, cutting spending, defaulting on the debt, and passing a constitutional amendment to limit borrowing. Unfortunately, Jefferson forgot his 1792 *Note of Agenda* and earlier calls for a debt amendment. While Secretary Gallatin and Congress repealed the internal tax system, they limited action on tariffs and land policy and introduced no borrowing amendment. In addition, they only grad-ually cut spending, because a foreign war preoccupied Jefferson. These decisions resulted from Jefferson's desire to appeal to Federalists—a classic illustration of power corrupting politicians into moderation.

At his inaugural, President Jefferson disavowed default but prom-ised the people a "wise and frugal" government, and with Gallatin at the helm he did not disappoint.[5] The former Antifederalist prepared his fiscal policy before Congress opened in December 1801, devising a tax-and-spend program that paid off the public debt. While this in itself

---

[4] Burch, *Elites in American History*, 1, pp. 108–09; John Miller, *Alexander Hamilton and the Growth of the New Nation* (New York: Harper & Row, 1959), p. 567; Norman Ris-jord, *The Old Republicans* (New York: Columbia University Press, 1965), pp. 24–28; H. Arthur Scott Trask, "Thomas Jefferson," in *Reassessing the Presidency*, ed. John V. Denson (Auburn, AL: Mises Institute, 2001), pp. 72–77.

[5] Dumas Malone, *Jefferson the President, First Term* (Boston, MA: Little, Brown, 1970), p. 22.

was laudatory, Jefferson's decision not to take the Old Republican route and build momentum for a borrowing amendment limited reform. Jefferson's moderate decision can ultimately be traced back to his role in the 1790 debt assumption compromise and his desire to appeal to Federalist creditors, who worried about default and a debt ceiling.[6]

Gallatin outlined his Antifederalist fiscal-military program in a November 1801 letter to Jefferson: "pretended tax-preparations, treasure-preparations, and army-preparations against contingent wars tend only to encourage wars."[7] The Treasurer understood that "defense" spending creates a vested interest group that benefits from outright war and promotes its continuance. Gallatin's embrace of Adam Smith's Invisible Hand starkly contrasted with Hamilton, who continued to support the Visible Hand's higher taxes, subsidization of industry, expensive internal improvements, and militarism. Unfortunately for Hamilton and his imperial dreams, Gallatin flexed his Old Republican muscle in Congress: Speaker of the House Nathaniel Macon and Chairman of the House Ways and Means Committee John Randolph.[8]

The first item on the Republican agenda was revenue, particularly the hated internal taxes, such as the whiskey tax. Removing them *in toto* was not only popular; wholesale removal would cripple the Federalists' civil service by eliminating the justification for employing so many government bureaucrats. Although a stern opponent of internal taxes, the moderate Gallatin was so fixated on paying off the national debt that he urged postponement. But Jefferson and the Old Republicans were adamant, and rightfully so, since as the years progressed wholesale removal would lose momentum and become more difficult to enact. Against this reform, Federalists argued that repealing internal taxes would increase dependency on tariffs, currently hovering around 30 percent. They tried to push for tariff cuts instead, using the argument that they disproportionately burdened the poor (Federalists conveniently forgot that they previously erected these burdens).

[6] Ellis, *Jeffersonian Crisis*, p. 276; Gregory May, *Jefferson's Treasure* (Washington, DC: Regnery History, 2018), p. 400; Rothbard, "Bureaucracy," pp. 30–31; Herbert Sloan, *Principle and Interest* (New York: Oxford University Press, 1995), p. 196.

[7] Thomas McCraw, *The Founders and Finance* (Cambridge, MA: Belknap Press, 2012), p. 235.

[8] Cunningham, *Jeffersonian Republicans in Power*, pp. 73–74; Joseph Dorfman, *The Economic Mind in American Civilization*, vol. 1 (New York: Viking Press, 1946), p. 416; May, *Jefferson's Treasure*, pp. 74–76, 107–10.

However, what the Federalists really desired was to maintain some *structure* of internal taxes: it would be much harder to raise unpopular internal taxes in the future if Republicans repealed the entire system and whittled down the bureaucratic miasma.

Despite the protests, Randolph shepherded the repeal law through Congress in 1802. The result was dramatic: in 1800 internal taxes brought in 7 percent of revenue but by 1804 less than 1 percent. This confirmed the Federalist fears: the whittling down of the Treasury bloat was so severe that the total Treasury staff in 1801 (1,285 men) was actually greater than in 1826 (1,075 men). Thus, the Republican tax policy served as a quasi-structural reform.[9]

But moderation still occurred. Even though Gallatin agreed with the Old Republicans' free trade sentiments, he had no intention of lowering tariffs from 30 percent, because he wanted to pay off the national debt. The other major component of revenue—land sales—hardly provided the government a serious source of income. Admirably, Gallatin wanted to reform the land system by decreasing the minimum price and acreage as well as eliminate land sales on credit. Although he convinced Congress to reduce minimum acreage to 160 acres, he failed to eliminate sales on credit or lower the minimum price from $2 an acre. The desire to pay off the debt stymied the Republicans: they wanted to repeal the credit system and lower the $2 price, but the decrease in tax revenue would postpone debt payment. In the end, they moderated and maintained land prices while encouraging settlers to rack up debts. The compromise did not even raise much money: from 1801 to 1812, the US government sold a modest four million acres.[10]

Second on the agenda was reducing spending and paying off the debt. Gallatin told Jefferson that given lower taxes, debt extinguishment required stringent military cuts. Secretary Smith naturally resisted, covetous of his budget. Gallatin frequently clashed with Smith, which meant he clashed with Smith's older brother, Congressman Samuel

---

[9] *Historical Statistics of the United States*, vol. 5, ed. Richard Sutch and Susan Carter. New York: Cambridge University Press, 2006), p. 82; David Johnson, *John Randolph of Roanoke* (Baton Rouge: Louisiana State University Press, 2012), pp. 55–58; May, *Jefferson's Treasure*, p. 106; Trask, "Thomas Jefferson," pp. 49–50; Leonard White, *The Jeffersonians* (New York: Macmillan, 1951), p. 139.

[10] Jeremy Atack and Peter Passell, *A New Economic View of American History* (New York: W.W. Norton, 1994), pp. 258–59; Daniel Feller, *The Public Lands in Jacksonian Politics* (Madison: The University of Wisconsin Press, 1984), pp. 10–12; *Historical Statistics*, 5, pp. 82, 510; McCraw, *Founders and Finance*, p. 250.

Smith, chairman of the pro-merchant Committee on Commerce and Manufactures. The elder Smith actually supported increased military spending during the Quasi-War, because the US Navy's subsidization of the shipping trade lowered his insurance rates. This was the very cronyism Republicans wanted to avoid. But Gallatin successfully slashed the military budget: from 1800 to 1802, government spending decreased 27 percent and the share of military spending declined from 56 to 27 percent. Unfortunately, moderation set in after the president fixated on a foreign war.[11]

When Tripoli of the Barbary States demanded more tribute, the new president refused and the US entered another naval war. Jefferson failed to secure a congressional declaration of war, setting an atrocious precedent for executive overreach. In vain, Gallatin and Randolph protested to Jefferson that Congress should pay Tripoli because the cost of war would be greater than tribute and interfere with their retrenchment goals. But the adamant Jefferson pushed military spending back up. After collapsing 73 percent from 1800 to 1802, naval expenditures had increased 75 percent by 1805. Gallatin believed part of the splurge was due to Secretary Smith's shipping background and he later accused the Smiths of embezzling war appropriations to their mercantile firm Smith & Buchanan. In addition, the Tripoli War forced Gallatin to request a slight increase in tariffs. Proponents argued for the tariff increases on the grounds that they would only be temporary, but Congress ended up making them permanent.

In 1803, Randolph perceptively noted that Federalists and moderate Republicans "who pant for military command and the emoluments of office" caused the war.[12] Indeed, Randolph was on the mark, for Jefferson wanted to boost America's standing in the world and win over pro-navy Federalists, especially northern merchants. Old Republicans could detect Jefferson's courting from the beginning. In 1801, he appointed one of the Smith brothers to his cabinet and in 1802 appointed as Commodore of the Mediterranean Fleet the unqualified Richard Valentine Morris, nephew of ultra-Federalist Gouverneur Morris and brother of Lewis Robert Morris, a former Federalist congressman who helped Jefferson win in the 1801 House election. Once

[11] Frank Cassell, *Merchant Congressman in the Young Republic* (Madison: The University of Wisconsin Press, 1971), pp. 90, 110, 113, 117–18; *Historical Statistics*, 5, pp. 80, 91; May, *Jefferson's Treasure*, p. 82; McCraw, *Founders and Finance*, p. 250.

[12] Risjord, *The Old Republicans*, p. 36.

again, power corrupted a reformer: preserving Federalist military cronyism and using it abroad to win over a special-interest group. By June 1805, Tripoli sued for peace and ended tribute, but the US continued to make payments to the other Barbary States until 1816.

In addition to the Tripoli War, the Louisiana Purchase of 1803 stymied fiscal retrenchment. However, despite both moderations, the Jeffersonian Republicans still shrunk the federal government. From 1800 to 1808, tax revenue increased by 57 percent (from growing international commerce and not tax hikes), spending decreased by 8 percent, and the public debt fell by 31 percent. Thus, while the decrease in the national debt, from $83 million to $57 million (31 percent), resulted primarily from increases in tariff revenue rather than drastic spending cuts, the frugal-minded Republicans admirably did not use the revenue as a justification to increase spending and instead devoted it to paying off government loans.[13]

However, the corrupting nature of power once again limited the extent of reform. Republicans failed to dismantle the Hamiltonian fiscal system they previously criticized by defaulting, utilizing severe budgetary reforms, and enacting structural amendments. It should come as no surprise, then, that the Old Republicans lamented the lack of significant change. Notably, the laissez-faire Taylor wanted to know why the Republicans previously complained of the Hamiltonian debt "paper systems" when they now "neglect[ed] to provide against them."[14]

The Bank Charter Struggle

Attacking the privileged BUS had always been Jefferson's hobbyhorse: in *Notes of Agenda* the hard money advocate wanted to repeal the charter and prohibit the government from dealing in bank money to end the crony partnership with banking interests. The anti-paper money Old Republicans optimistically believed the president would push for repeal and an amendment that would forbid future central banks. In addition, they eagerly looked forward to breaking the Federalist state-level bank monopoly by creating new state banks, taking over existing institutions, or destroying them. But moderation reigned

---

[13] Cassell, *Merchant Congressman*, p. 122; *Historical Statistics*, 5, pp. 80, 91; May, *Jefferson's Treasure*, pp. 145–47, 183–84; McCraw, *Founders and Finance*, pp. 237–38; Risjord, *The Old Republicans*, p. 22; Glenn Tucker, *Dawn Like Thunder* (New York: Bobbs-Merrill, 1963), pp. 152–53; Trask, "Thomas Jefferson," pp. 52–56, 79.

[14] Risjord, *The Old Republicans*, pp. 37–38.

supreme. Secretary Gallatin believed the BUS could be properly harnessed and state-level Republicans succumbed to the Federalists' chartering practices, realizing that banks could provide financial support in elections. Republicans only failed to renew the BUS during the first term of Madison, Jefferson's anointed successor, due to a rift among state banking interests. As usual, power corrupted liberty and the reform movement broke down.

When he entered office, Jefferson remained hostile to the Bank, the centralizing agent of Federalist corruption and corporate privilege. He supported weakening the "powerful enemy" and placing it on an "equal footing only with other banks, as to the favors of the government."[15] Jefferson still believed in his 1792 plan, envisioning a system where the government would eventually hold its own funds and separate from the banking business altogether. In the meantime, the federal government should transfer its deposits in the BUS and other Federalist institutions to new Republican state banks, which would counteract the Federalists' influence. The president vividly demonstrated his sentiments in Rhode Island. In 1791, Federalists chartered the Providence Bank and the new institution operated as the only bank in the city for a decade. In July 1803, Gallatin received a letter from Providence Republicans currently establishing a Republican bank, requesting that the Jefferson administration transfer federal deposits from the Providence Bank to the new Roger Williams Bank. Jefferson enthusiastically agreed and transferred the funds.[16]

However, Gallatin did not share Jefferson's antipathy to central banking, much to the enmity of Old Republican Randolph and his monetary mentor Taylor. Gallatin argued that the bank's branches allowed the government to easily transfer money across the country. In addition, though previously critical of the BUS' lending practices, he now argued the institution could make loans to Congress when it was in trouble. Overall, he convinced Jefferson not to divorce the federal government from banking. This was an important failure, because by sanctioning the BUS, Jefferson implicitly sanctioned the Hamiltonian constructionism that birthed it in the first place. The BUS lived out the rest of its twenty-year charter undisturbed by the Jefferson

---

[15] Cunningham, *Jeffersonian Republicans in Power*, p. 64.

[16] Howard Bodenhorn, *State Banking in Early America* (New York: Oxford University Press, 2003), pp. 13–14; Cunningham, *Jeffersonian Republicans in Power*, pp. 64–65.

administration. The lure of being able to use the bank for their own needs corrupted the Republicans into continuing its existence.

While President Jefferson unsuccessfully destroyed the central bank outright, at least the government's involvement decreased and the institution partially privatized. By 1802 the federal government had sold all of its BUS stock. Moreover, from 1804 to 1812 the national debt declined 50 percent; correspondingly, the Bank's holdings of federal debt fell 64 percent. The Federalist bank maintained a relatively high reserve ratio of 40 percent and operated cautiously to avoid political backlash from the Republicans in control.[17]

Overall, the BUS' conservative practices and the adverse clearing mechanism led to limited inflation: from 1800 to 1810 the money supply grew by only 15 percent (1.5 percent per year). Prices likewise increased by less than 2 percent overall. However, the Bank still remained a crucial depository for coveted federal funds. This sizable subsidy from the federal government caused jealousy among the new state banking interests.[18]

State banking blossomed during the Jefferson years as hard money Republicans realized that chartering new banks weakened existing Federalist banks and alleviated the problems they perceived were inherent to fractional reserve banking. In other words, while they did not support the laissez-faire solution of free banking, they admirably wanted to break bank monopolies by chartering additional competition, a quasi-reform. As Republicans battled Federalists in local political arenas, the number of state banks exploded from twenty-eight in 1800 to sixty-four in 1804, and then to 102 by 1810. However, when the Republicans tried to reform the monetary system they got their hands dirty. The crony corporate charter continued to exist, because banks provided valuable political support. The desire to increase their political base corrupted Republicans into granting the same type of

---

[17] John Devanny, "A Loathing of Public Debt, Taxes, and Excises," *Virginia Magazine of History and Biography* (Winter 2001): 406–07, 409–10; Bray Hammond, *Banks and Politics in America* (Princeton, NJ: Princeton University Press, 1957), p. 207; May, *Jefferson's Treasure*, pp. 112–14; McCraw, *Founders and Finance*, p. 211; Richard Timberlake, *Monetary Policy in the United States* (Chicago: The University of Chicago Press, 1993), pp. 9–10.

[18] *Historical Statistics of the United States*, vol. 3, ed. Richard Sutch and Susan Carter. New York: Cambridge University Press, 2006), p. 181; Peter Rousseau and Richard Sylla, "Emerging Financial Markets and Early US Growth," *Explorations in Economic History* (January 2005): 24.

monopoly charters the Federalists previously doled out. This can be seen in various states, particularly New York, Pennsylvania, and Virginia.[19]

Since the Constitution, New York politics had devolved into a brutal struggle between the Clintonian Republicans and Federalists. Banking was not separate from this process, and to maintain control Republicans gave out bank patronage. In 1803, Republicans controlled the legislature. On behalf of Aaron Burr's Bank of the Manhattan Company, they refused to charter Hamilton's Merchants Bank in New York City. However, the Republican legislature granted a charter to the New York State Bank in Albany on the grounds that the existing Bank of Albany was too Federalist. The Republicans realized that the New York State Bank would be a loyal political supporter while the Merchants Bank would not. But politicians still wanted something from the New York State Bank, particularly bank stock they could later sell. Republicans eagerly accepted the rewards of playing favorites.

To make matters worse, Republicans kept new Federalist cronyism. When the Federalists regained control of the legislature in 1804, on behalf of the chartered banks they passed the monopolistic Restraining Act, which forbade unincorporated banks from issuing notes, a fatal hamstring to unchartered competition. The Federalist Merchants Bank did secure a charter in 1805, but only after they out-bribed the other state banks, and a physical altercation between two judges in the state senate occurred. When Republicans regained control of the legislature, they kept the restraining law to solidify banking support.[20]

Pennsylvania experienced similar sordid politics. By 1803, the formerly Antifederalist Bank of Pennsylvania succumbed to Federalist control. Republican businesses and merchants complained that the existing three banks—the Bank of North America, the Bank of Pennsylvania, and the BUS—catered only to Federalist entrepreneurs. In response, Republicans created the Philadelphia Bank as an unincorporated association in September 1803. The Philadelphia *Aurora* heartily supported the institution's plans for a charter, because the new bank would decrease the influence of other banks and grant loans

[19] Murray N. Rothbard, "The History of Money and Banking Before the Twentieth Century," in Rothbard, *A History of Money and Banking in the United States*, ed. Joseph Salerno (Auburn, AL: Mises Institute, 2002), p. 70; Timberlake, *Monetary Policy*, p. 16.

[20] Bodenhorn, *State Banking*, pp. 14, 186; Hammond, *Banks and Politics*, pp. 158–61.

to small businesses. But the Federalist Bank of Pennsylvania was prepared to fight.

In December 1803 the Philadelphia Bank applied for a state charter and offered various pecuniary incentives to the state: $15,000 for a ten-year charter or $20,000 for a fourteen-year charter. When a House committee reported favorably on the application, the Bank of Pennsylvania struck back, wailing about the reduction in profits. The House then submitted the charter application and the Bank of Pennsylvania's protests to another committee, which ruled in January 1804 to not incorporate the newcomer. The committee endorsed an egregious Bank of Pennsylvania proposal: in exchange for a $200,000 down payment, the legislature would extend the bank's charter to 1827, forbid any additional charters (except rechartering the BONA), and place restrictions on unincorporated banks.

But the Philadelphia Bank countered and insisted that its earlier proposal was "misunderstood"—the state misinterpreted the amount of money the business was offering! That sealed the deal, and in early 1804 the legislature debated a ten-year charter for the Philadelphia Bank in return for the more appropriately understood *$135,000*—not the misunderstood $15,000. The Bank of Pennsylvania protested by offering a $100,000 interest-free loan if the legislature blocked the charter. To the bank's dismay, the state turned down the offer and Philadelphia Bank now operated with a charter.

To its credit, the Pennsylvania legislature soon recognized the basics of free banking, cogently declaring that the "evils" of the banking system "will probably find their most effectual remedy in . . . rivalship . . . [and] the fear of being called upon for specie."[21] Unfortunately, power, particularly the temptation of monetary bribes, corrupted the legislature. When the Bank of Pittsburgh and the Bank of Northern Liberties (in Philadelphia) opened in 1810 without charters, the legislature forbade unincorporated associations from various banking activities and later denied charters to the two institutions, forcing them to operate illegally.[22]

---

[21] Anna Schwartz, "The Beginning of Competitive Banking in Philadelphia," in Schwartz, *Money in Historical Perspective* (Chicago: The University of Chicago Press, 1987), p. 15.

[22] Bodenhorn, *State Banking*, pp. 3, 141–42; Schwartz, "Competitive Banking in Philadelphia," pp. 10–15; Andrew Shankman, *Crucible of American Democracy* (Lawrence: University Press of Kansas, 2004), pp. 119–20.

Banking in Virginia was also deeply intertwined with political favoritism. At the beginning of Jefferson's presidency, Virginia Federalists controlled the BUS' Norfolk branch and the Bank of Alexandria. Hard money Republicans deprived the latter of its recharter in 1800 against strenuous Federalist protests. In 1805, the Republican legislature even forbade notes issued by the Bank of the Potowmac, a company in Washington, DC, technically outside the state.

The bigger battle concerned the Bank of Virginia's charter. Initially, Federalists supported the institution more than the Republicans, who split over providing cheap credit to the business community and adhering to John Taylor's anti-bank principles. In February 1803, while Republicans evenly split in the Assembly, Federalists overwhelmingly supported the bank bill and gave it the crucial margin of victory. However, Republicans killed the measure in the Senate. Despite this, in the following year pro-bank forces passed the bill, which might have been related to the bank's promise to lend $300,000 to the state in exchange for one-fifth ownership. The corrupted Republicans proved to be no better than Federalist legislators, injecting partisanship in the Bank of Virginia: the Republican state treasurer overwhelmingly voted for Republican directors, recognizing that Republican directors wedded the party to the bank, a helpful ally in future elections. Clearly, Republicans stooped to granting charter privileges in Virginia.[23]

Congress only eliminated the BUS in early 1811, during Madison's first term, when the twenty-year charter had to be reissued. By this time, the ex-Federalist conveniently changed his mind on the Bank's constitutionality. Interestingly, the battle lines split through the forces of liberty and power. Libertarians were torn, but not because of corruption. Old Republicans recognized that some moderates fought the recharter simply to embarrass Treasurer Gallatin, who was far too frugal for their liking. Old Republicans had to choose which poison—end the BUS or protect Gallatin—they thought would do the least harm. On the side of cronyism, state banking interests split over what privileges they preferred. Some, particularly in Philadelphia and New York, benefited from the BUS' credit expansion. On the other hand, other state banks faced competition from the Bank's interstate branches and desired the subsidy of government deposits. It is no coincidence that Senators Samuel Smith and Henry Clay fought recharter, because

---

[23] Bodenhorn, *State Banking*, pp. 15, 219, 222; James Broussard, *The Southern Federalists* (Baton Rouge: Louisiana State University Press, 1978), pp. 334–40.

they heavily invested in Maryland and Kentucky banks. Prominent financial backers of the moderate Republicans also split, such as merchants John Jacob Astor and Stephen Girard. Astor opposed renewal because the BUS failed to provide adequate loans while Girard favored continuation because he had recently become the Bank's largest stockholder in anticipation of recharter.[24]

In this unusual stalemate, liberty won out, thanks to an aging Antifederalist. After the Senate voted 17-17, Vice President George Clinton decided in the negative on constitutional grounds. The government withdrew its deposits and divided them among twenty-one state banks—the goal of many anti-bank proponents. Despite much clamor, no financial crisis occurred, and the number of state banks increased from 102 in 1810 to 117 in 1811. The BUS finally died. However, by not repealing the charter and only failing to renew it, Republicans left open the door for the creation of another central bank that could more appropriately serve their interests. This happened in 1816.[25]

During the early years of the Jefferson administration, the Republicans' urge to expand their political coalition blunted bureaucratic, judicial, fiscal, military, and banking reforms. But they moved in the correct direction, and the long-run trend of intervention pointed downward. The Republicans had laissez-faire in their grasp; the Empire of Liberty was on the horizon. Unfortunately, matters quickly changed in 1803.

---

[24] Irving Brant, *James Madison, Father of the Constitution* (New York: Bobbs-Merrill, 1950), pp. 137, 269–70; Burch, *Elites in American History*, 1, pp. 97, 120–21; Hammond, *Banks and Politics*, pp. 212–13; May, *Jefferson's Treasure*, pp. 185–88; Risjord, *The Old Republicans*, pp. 110–17.

[25] John Kaminski, *George Clinton* (Madison, WI: Madison House Publishers, 1993), p. 290; Timberlake, *Monetary Policy*, p. 16; John Holdsworth, *The First Bank of the United States* (Washington, DC: Government Printing Office, 1910), p. 105.

CHAPTER 8

PRESIDENT JEFFERSON: THE CORRUPTION OF LAND

The Louisiana Purchase

Hamilton's death in 1804 hammered the nail into the Federalist coffin. But while the reactionary forces decayed, their special-interest policies lived on, for slowly but surely the libertarian Republicans embraced statism. The primary reason was the Louisiana Purchase of 1803, a five hundred million acre acquisition that corrupted Jefferson into embracing broad constructionism for his Empire of Liberty. To keep his enlarged empire from fracturing, Jefferson and moderate Republicans utilized numerous special-interest policies. Appealing to New England Federalists flirting with secession after the Louisiana Purchase, Republicans favored a payout to speculators in the Yazoo scandal, later sanctioned by the Hamiltonian Supreme Court. Jefferson acquired bribe money for West Florida to protect the enlarged southern frontier. Republicans covetously eyed the federal surplus for internal improvements to nationalize the West. They also supported trade restrictions to privilege manufacturing and mercantile constituents. The Louisiana Purchase truly wrecked the Republican Party.

In the 1790s, the Federalists aggressively pushed for expansion to strengthen their corrupt empire. Fortunately, their exile from political power in 1801 dashed any hopes of such conquest. But a new Federalist war threat quickly emerged. In 1800, King Carlos IV of Spain agreed to transfer Louisiana to France if Napoleon gifted Queen Maria Luisa's brother, the current Duke of Parma in northern Italy, Tuscany and other Italian territories, making him the king of Etruria. Consequently, France and Spain signed the secret Treaty of San Ildefonso transferring Louisiana to France. Two additional facts about the treaty bear emphasis: Spain refused to yield Florida (which France never included in Louisiana) and demanded France never transfer Louisiana to either the US or Great Britain.

Rumors of the treaty's existence reached the US in 1801, though by the fall of 1802 the actual Louisiana transfer had still not occurred. When he learned of the negotiation, Jefferson expressed his desire for West Florida and New Orleans, some land on the lower Mississippi River for an American port, or a French guarantee of free navigation on the Mississippi. The anxiety heightened when Spain failed to renew Pinckney's Treaty and ended the right of deposit in New Orleans on the grounds that Americans continually smuggled goods through the city and showed little respect for Spanish sailors in American ports. Although Spain did nothing illegal and Americans could still smuggle or ship goods legally through New Orleans, it caused a fury.[1]

It was at this moment, under the potential wartime crisis, that the battle between liberty and power reemerged in full force. Hamilton and the Federalists wanted to first enter into a war and *then* negotiate, hoping to use the crisis as an opportunity to exploit fears, weaken the Republicans, and springboard back into prominence. On the other hand, Jefferson and the Republicans aimed to first try peaceful negotiation *before* entering into hostilities, though they were not above backing diplomatic maneuvers with the velvet glove of potential force and even an alliance with Great Britain. Despite this, the Republican policy was undeniably more peaceful and libertarian than the Federalist approach.

In his December 1802 congressional message, Jefferson did not mention the crisis over the deposit, though he implied that recent changes in foreign relations could make a war necessary. Hamilton criticized Jefferson's timidity and dreamed of an expansionist war for "the *unity of our Empire.*"[2] Federalists then castigated Jefferson's appointment of James Monroe to help Ambassador Livingston and Republican attempts to voluntarily purchase the Mississippi River. In February 1803, Hamilton continued the assault and urged that the country should "seize" Florida and New Orleans before negotiating.[3]

Randolph and western Republican senators, particularly those from Kentucky and Tennessee, defended the president's diplomacy,

---

[1] Alexander DeConde, *This Affair of Louisiana* (New York: Charles Scribner's Sons, 1976), pp. 95–96, 119–21; Walter Nugent, *Habits of Empire* (New York: Vintage Books, 2009), pp. 54–61; H. Arthur Scott Trask, "Thomas Jefferson," in *Reassessing the Presidency*, ed. John V. Denson (Auburn, AL: Mises Institute, 2001), p. 57; Gordon Wood, *Empire of Liberty* (New York: Oxford University Press, 2009), p. 369.

[2] DeConde, *Affair of Louisiana*, p. 128.

[3] Ibid., p. 139.

holding back Federalist warmongers. Westerners recognized that a war would increase the federal government's debt and taxes, reduce opportunities to trade with the French and Spanish, and lead to heavy requests for western troops. Republican Senator DeWitt Clinton of New York also criticized the Federalist machinations and Virginia's Republican senator, Stevens T. Mason, accurately summed up their imperial fantasies:

> Presently we shall be told we must have Louisiana; then the gold mines of Mexico—these would be good things, if come by honestly—then Potosi—then St. Domingo, with their sugar, coffee, and all the rest. . . . But what have we to do with the territories of other people? Have we not enough of our own?[4]

Fortunately, Spain restored the right of deposit. The Republicans resisted the corruption of westward empire.[5]

But in the meantime, Napoleon's plans for Louisiana changed. By January 1803, his efforts to reassert control in the West Indies had failed, and war with Great Britain loomed on the horizon. Importantly, to facilitate the war effort Napoleon needed his troops in Europe, a neutral US, and money. He made a momentous decision: France would sell *all* of Louisiana for a bargain $15 million. Monroe and Livingston, mesmerized by the windfall that landed on their lap, hastily agreed in April.

It is imperative to understand that the Louisiana Purchase, from top to bottom, was crony. First, neither France nor Spain really owned most of the land since they failed to adequately homestead it. The only people who could be considered partial owners were the scattered Europeans and the Indian hunters. True ownership required the gradual process of settlement, a core plank of Jefferson's Empire of Liberty. But, similar to the gift King James I endowed to the speculating Plymouth and Virginia companies, France planned to transfer its dubious

---

[4] Ibid., p. 140.

[5] Ibid., pp. 127–28, 134–35, 138–40; Joseph Dorfman, *The Economic Mind in American Civilization*, vol. 1 (New York: Viking Press, 1946), pp. 316–17; Dumas Malone, *Jefferson the President, First Term* (Boston, MA: Little, Brown, 1970), pp. 277–81; Nugent, *Habits of Empire*, pp. 60–62; Steven Siry, *DeWitt Clinton and the American Political Economy* (New York: Peter Lang, 1990), pp. 93–95; Frederick Tolles, *George Logan of Philadelphia* (New York: Oxford University Press, 1953), pp. 234–36.

ownership to a government that also had no legitimate claim over the area. Second, to actually acquire Louisiana, France was legally obligated to elevate the Duke of Parma to the King of Etruria and forgo selling the land to another foreign power. Napoleon never made him the independent King of Etruria and clearly reneged on the other stipulation. He never even obtained the consent of the French legislature. Walter Nugent correctly described the Louisiana Purchase as a "dirty deal"—a sordid benefit to the US and France at the expense of Louisiana's inhabitants and the Spanish.[6]

Jefferson received the treaty in July. Before submitting it to the Senate for ratification, the strict constructionist faced an enormous dilemma. Nowhere did the Constitution explicitly enumerate the power to purchase territory from another government and bring the land and its residents into the Union. Jefferson despaired the precedent he would set by broadly reading the Constitution to justify territorial acquisition. He had previously spent the past decade fighting such a Hamiltonian exegesis and the special-interest legislation it led to.

According to the Federalists who actually drafted the Constitution, they intended the new polity to wield implied powers that could enact privilege granting-policies. Senator Gouverneur Morris, one of the major Federalists at the Convention still alive, certainly considered territorial acquisition constitutional: "I knew as well then as I do now, that all North America must at length be annexed to us—happy, indeed, if the lust for dominion stop there."[7] The Louisiana Purchase *was* constitutional, because the vague clauses sanctioned vast government power. However, Jefferson and his Republicans interpreted the Constitution in the way the Federalists actually promised, requiring its powers to be confined to those explicitly enumerated, expandable only with amendments. So, according to the Republicans, the Louisiana Purchase should have been unconstitutional.

But it was a lot of land. In fact, it was just *too* much land. Throughout 1803, the president ruminated on the constitutionality with his close advisors. Jefferson wanted an amendment that would have explicitly given the federal government the power to acquire and annex territory. But his cabinet disagreed, and even Secretary

---

[6] Nugent, *Habits of Empire*, p. 63. See also Malone, *Jefferson, First Term*, pp. 293–96; Nugent, *Habits of Empire*, pp. 62–66.

[7] DeConde, *Affair of Louisiana*, p. 191.

Gallatin sounded Hamiltonian when he argued that treaty-making power implied the ability. Torn, Jefferson called for an early session of Congress to meet in October, because Napoleon stipulated that the treaty would have to be ratified within six months of the original signing in France.[8]

Jefferson's anxiety escalated when he received a secret letter from Livingston in August reporting that Napoleon was having second thoughts. The president, alarmed at the letter, now urged minimizing the constitutionality issue. In reality, Livingston misread Napoleon. War had broken out in Europe, and Napoleon needed money. He understood that his country was in no position to defend the territory: some way or another, the superior British Navy or the inexorable tide of American settlers would take Louisiana. It was better to get some money than nothing at all. Even Madison and Gallatin estimated that the French would not renege on their agreement, though they saw no reason for delay. Realistically, the Jefferson administration could have pressed for an amendment and secured one by the end of the year. Napoleon would have waited.

But Jefferson did not make Napoleon wait and rushed to ratify the treaty. Even with his haste, Jefferson still toyed with an amendment, perhaps after the Senate ratified the treaty. In September, Jefferson admirably wrote:

> I had rather ask an enlargement of power from the nation where it is found necessary, than to assume it by a construction which would make our powers boundless. Our peculiar security is in possession of a written Constitution. Let us not make it a blank paper by construction. I say the same as to the opinion of those who consider the grant of the treaty making power as boundless. If it is, then we have no constitution.[9]

Unfortunately, after delivering this brilliant statement of constitutional reform, Jefferson once again acquiesced to broad constructionism.[10]

---

[8] David Carson, "Blank Paper of the Constitution," *Historian* (March 1992): 478–80; DeConde, *Affair of Louisiana*, pp. 177–84; Malone, *Jefferson, First Term*, pp. 272, 311–15.

[9] Malone, *Jefferson, First Term*, p. 318.

[10] Irving Brant, *James Madison, Secretary of State* (New York: Bobbs-Merrill, 1953),

In October, Jefferson did not mention the constitutional controversy to Congress. Instead, two groups raised the issue: envious Federalists and principled Republicans. The Federalists split into two groups. Some Federalists desired the land and simply attacked the Jefferson administration. Other Federalists, particularly the High Federalists in New England, realized the potential loss of influence their region would suffer if Congress could admit new states from the West. In Madisonian fashion, the High Federalists strictly interpreted the Constitution. They did not generally criticize the right to acquire territory by purchase or conquest. Instead, they questioned whether the executive could compel Congress to accept the territory's inhabitants into the Union and admit new states from territory acquired after the Constitution's ratification without the consent of the existing states. The High Federalists wanted any new land the US acquired to remain as subjugated territories in their empire. For his part, Hamilton remained a broad constructionist: the nationalist supported both the constitutionality and implicit consequences of the Louisiana treaty.[11]

Although Federalist senators protested, the Senate hastily ratified the treaty. The allure of land corrupted the even most doctrinaire of Republicans: Old Republican Senator John Taylor of Virginia, the supposed strict constructionist (back in the Senate from June to December 1803, after Senator Mason died) defended the legitimacy of the purchase against High Federalists Timothy Pickering and others. Even the strict constructionist and laissez-faire advocate Senator George Logan of Pennsylvania remained silent. It was hypocrisy of the highest level, though the Republicans at least highlighted the opportunism of the previously bellicose Federalists who earlier advocated outright conquest.

However, much like Jay's Treaty nearly a decade earlier, the treaty would not be official until the House approved appropriations. Congressman Randolph, loyally serving the president, defended the constitutionality, though he wrote to his superior that "the constitutionality

---

pp. 141–43; Carson, "Blank Paper," pp. 480–82; DeConde, *Affair of Louisiana*, pp. 184–86; Malone, *Jefferson, First Term*, pp. 315–24.

[11] DeConde, *Affair of Louisiana*, pp. 186–89; Richard Ellis, *The Union at Risk* (New York: Oxford University Press, 1987), pp. 5–6; Reginald Horsman, "The Dimensions of an 'Empire for Liberty'," *Journal of the Early Republic* (Spring 1989): 7; Jon Kukla, *A Wilderness so Immense* (New York: Alfred A. Knopf, 2003), pp. 290–93, 308; John Miller, *Alexander Hamilton and the Growth of the New Nation* (New York: Harper & Row, 1959), pp. 562–63.

[issue] is the theme of the opposition."[12] But House Federalists pressed for proof of French ownership. If the House had passed resolutions toward this end, it would have delayed appropriations and thrown the entire transaction into doubt. Almost enough Republicans joined with the Federalists to stop the entire illicit purchase dead in its tracks: a vote to demand proof of ownership failed by just *one* vote, 57-59.

In the end, the die was cast: Jefferson and the Republicans muscled a bargain through Congress that violated their own constitutional principles, augmented the national debt, and blatantly contradicted Republicans' plans to amend the Constitution. Nugent accurately writes that for the Republicans, "the temptation, the opportunity, was too great. . . . Imperialism trumped honesty."[13] With this decision, strict constructionism died and Jefferson increasingly supported broad constructionism to solidify his empire. The entire episode highlights the corrupting nature of power and the difficulty of reform. To make the central government behave in the limited manner envisioned, Jefferson and the Republicans had to tie their own hands behind their backs. But once the opportunity to broadly interpret the Constitution presented itself—in the form of a massive land acquisition—nothing constrained them from untying the knot.[14]

The consequences of the Louisiana Purchase were seismic, bursting the Empire of Liberty at the seams. High Federalists fretted that it provided the potential to create western states populated by settlers sympathetic to the Republicans. They also feared that southern slave owners would now dominate the central government forever, pinning the blame on the three-fifths clause. Their criticism had nothing to do with the plight of slaves: over the next two decades High Federalists in Massachusetts spearheaded the tightening of poor laws, blocking black migration into the state, and segregating schools and churches. Instead, their criticism concerned how the clause boosted Republican political representation. Pickering, now one of the staunchest critics of the three-fifths clause, even flirted with secession and a northern confederacy, but the preeminent nationalist Hamilton torpedoed the

---

[12] David Johnson, *John Randolph of Roanoke* (Baton Rouge: Louisiana State University Press, 2012), p. 65.

[13] Nugent, *Habits of Empire*, p. 68.

[14] *American Political Leaders* (Washington, DC: CQ Press, 2000), pp. 228, 248, 302; Carson, "Blank Paper," pp. 484–88; DeConde, *Affair of Louisiana*, pp. 189–90; Nugent, *Habits of Empire*, pp. 65–66; Tolles, *George Logan*, pp. 240–42; Wood, *Empire of Liberty*, pp. 371–72.

idea before he suddenly died. The Republicans now needed to mollify New England.[15]

As for Louisiana, Republicans embraced the means used by the British Old Order they previously despised. In 1804, Congress divided it into the Territory of Orleans (modern-day Louisiana) and the District of Louisiana (everything else). It also passed a bill that turned the Territory of Orleans into a vassal state. Unlike the Northwest Territory and Mississippi Territory, whose people had the right to an elected legislature against a presidentially appointed governor, the Territory of Orleans' interim government included only a presidentially appointed governor and legislative council, a clear return to the antiquated colonial approach. To make matters worse, Jefferson chose for the governor of the region William C.C. Claiborne of Tennessee. During the heated presidential gridlock of 1801, Claiborne, the state's sole representative, voted for Jefferson. The new president had rewarded him with the governorship of the Mississippi Territory. Now, in 1804, Jefferson again rewarded Claiborne with the far more important position of governor of the Territory of Orleans, giving him near-dictatorial power over the region's inhabitants. Although Congress eventually granted the Territory of Orleans the right to a representative assembly and admitted the region as the state of Louisiana in 1812, the entire experience did not bode well for future Republican territorial ambitions.[16]

However, Congress did enact one saving grace, forbidding the importation of foreign slaves into the Territory of Orleans. A similar anti-crony victory occurred in 1807, when Congress abolished the international slave trade for the whole country. Although antislavery advocates championed the decision, it caused little fanfare because every state save South Carolina had already banned the practice. Jefferson and many antislavery southern Republicans continued to sanguinely believe that ending the slave trade and diffusing slaves into

---

[15] James Banner, *To the Hartford Convention* (New York: Alfred A. Knopf, 1970), pp. 105–07; Thomas J. DiLorenzo, "Yankee Confederates," in *Secession, State and Liberty*, ed. David Gordon (New Brunswick, NJ: Transaction Publishers, 1998), pp. 138–41, 145–46; Richard Ellis, *The Jeffersonian Crisis* (New York: Oxford University Press, 1971), p. 89; Miller, *Alexander Hamilton*, pp. 563–66, 575; Sean Wilentz, *No Property in Man* (Cambridge, MA: Harvard University Press, 2018), p. 174.

[16] James Broussard, *The Southern Federalists* (Baton Rouge: Louisiana State University, 1978), pp. 60–61; Kukla, *Wilderness So Immense*, pp. 311–13; Malone, *Jefferson, First Term*, p. 361; Wood, *Empire of Liberty*, pp. 372–73, 529.

the West would weaken the institution and reduce antipathy toward blacks. They failed to properly appreciate that slave breeding could maintain populations and perpetuate the practice. Slavery continued to grow.[17]

The Old Republican Randolph quickly regretted his decision. He realized it set a bad constitutional precedent, enhanced executive power, and led to western clamor for federally funded internal improvements. By 1805 he considered the acquisition "the greatest curse that ever befell us."[18] It was a crucial victory for power, and the reform movement had utterly collapsed by the end of Jefferson's first administration. The Empire of Liberty took a turn for the worse.[19]

Satisfying Land Speculators

After the Louisiana Purchase, Randolph and other Old Republicans increasingly criticized Jefferson and the moderates. Their first serious dispute regarded the Yazoo land scandal and corrupt Federalist speculators from secessionist-leaning New England. Against Randolph, moderate Republicans sanctioned a federal bailout that the Marshallian Supreme Court later protected.

Georgia formally ceded the Yazoo lands in 1802, which Congress soon organized into the Mississippi Territory. To settle the speculators' disputed land titles, the president appointed a commission led by Madison and Gallatin. In a classic case of moderation, the commission's report of February 1803 recommended Congress set aside five million acres to divide among the speculators. Moderates wanted compromise because most of the claimants hailed from New England, an area the Republicans desired to court.

When the House reviewed the commission's report in early 1804, Randolph fumed. He regarded the 1795 sale as crony, considered the corrupt land speculators no better than the security owners who benefited from Hamilton's debt-funding scheme, and maintained that the decision to allot land to claimants violated the Georgia legislature's

---

[17] Broussard, *Southern Federalists*, pp. 314–15; Wilentz, *Property in Man*, pp. 174–75; Wood, *Empire of Liberty*, pp. 523–24; Nicholas Wood, "John Randolph of Roanoke and the Politics of Slavery in the Early Republic," *Virginia Magazine of History and Biography* (Summer 2012): 115–17.

[18] John Devanny, "A Loathing of Public Debt, Taxes, and Excises," *Virginia Magazine of History and Biography* (Winter 2001): 400.

[19] Ibid., pp. 400–01; Russell Kirk, *John Randolph of Roanoke* (Indianapolis, IN: Liberty Fund, 1997), pp. 204–05.

right to rescind their own special-interest contract. It did not help Randolph's temper that moderate Republicans had invested in the New England Mississippi Land Company, and Postmaster General Gideon Granger of Connecticut served as their agent. By denouncing the commission's report, Randolph broke with the Jefferson administration. He managed to postpone the issue until the next congressional session in early 1805.

The problem for Randolph, however, was that in the aftermath of the Louisiana Purchase moderate Republicans grew even more eager to compromise on Yazoo because of rumors that New England Federalists contemplated secession. Moderates did not want to risk splitting up their new empire and looked forward to working with the speculators. They allied with Federalists, narrowly defeating Randolph's motion to repudiate the compromise by 63-58. But the vote total revealed that more Republicans actually sided with Randolph than with their president, including the majority of Virginia's delegation. It was a sign that many Republicans remained uneasy with the Jefferson administration's moderation. However, Congress postponed the legislation embodying the compromise, and Randolph blocked payments in subsequent sessions. For the time being, moderation failed and Old Republicans put the Yazoo question on the backburner.[20]

But Yazoo speculators did not give up: they followed Hamilton's original advice and tried legal avenues. By 1810, during Madison's presidency, their case landed in the Supreme Court. The Federalists still controlled a majority of the bench, ably commanded by the Hamiltonian Marshall. As Hamilton predicted, Marshall based the ruling in *Fletcher v. Peck* (1810) on the contract clause. For the first time, the Supreme Court used judicial review to overturn a state law and declared that Congress had to reward the Yazoo claimants. By overturning a state law, the Supreme Court dramatically increased its own power, an extremely disturbing development. In 1814, when enough Federalists resided in Congress and Randolph no longer served as a representative, moderate Republicans granted a payout of $4.75 million to the claimants. Unsurprisingly, it mostly benefited new speculators who had bought

---

[20] Ellis, *Jeffersonian Crisis*, pp. 87–89, 93–94, 213; Paul Goodman, *The Democratic-Republicans of Massachusetts* (Cambridge, MA: Harvard University Press, 1964), pp. 183–84; David Johnson, *John Randolph of Roanoke* (Baton Rouge: Louisiana State University Press, 2012), pp. 83–86; Curtis Nettels, *The Emergence of a National Economy* (New York: Holt, Rinehart and Winston, 1962), p. 149; Norman Risjord, *The Old Republicans* (New York: Columbia University Press, 1965), pp. 38–42.

depreciated ownership claims in anticipation of a government bailout. Randolph lost and the moderate Republicans and Federalists won. It was official: the Republicans embraced land speculation.[21]

It bears emphasizing that Marshall adhered to the tradition of former Supreme Court Justice James Wilson and was motivated to protect his own pockets. In the 1790s Marshall and his brother worked with speculator Robert Morris in acquiring a land grant, the Fairfax Estate, which the Virginia legislature subsequently rescinded. In 1809, after legal delays, Spencer Roane at the Court of Appeals declared the Marshalls' titles invalid. Marshall appealed Roane's decision and sent it to the Supreme Court. The high court declared in *Fairfax's Devisee v. Hunter's Lessee* (1813) that the Marshalls justly owned the titles. To be fair, Marshall recused himself from the ruling due to conflict of interest, but the same could not be said for President Madison's recent appointee, Justice Joseph Story, who delivered the ruling. He previously worked as an attorney for New England's Yazoo claimants and the Crowninshield merchant interests. Clearly, Story wanted to help Marshall and strengthen the speculator interests he served. Thus, Marshall's declaration in *Fletcher v. Peck* (1810) provided legal precedent that allowed Story to legitimize the Chief Justice's prior land speculations. This was the exact type of judicial and land speculator cronyism Randolph previously warned about, which Republicans now embraced.[22]

Clandestine Operations for Florida

The Yazoo land scandal was not the only territorial issue that alienated Randolph. Jefferson, corrupted by Louisiana, pressed for expanding the American frontier, envisioning all of North America and eventually South America free from any European presence whatsoever. But the eternal contradiction remained: to remove the Old Order

[21] *American Political Leaders*, p. 425; Philip Burch, *Elites in American History,* 1 (New York: Holmes & Meier Publishers, 1981), p. 111; Johnson, *John Randolph*, p. 86; Brion McClanahan, *How Alexander Hamilton Screwed Up America* (Washington, DC: Regnery History, 2017), pp. 104–10; Nettels, *Emergence of a National Economy*, p. 154; Aaron Sakolski, *The Great American Land Bubble* (New York: Harper & Brothers Publishers, 1932), pp. 139–41.

[22] Burch, *Elites in American History*, 1, pp. 110–12, 125–26; Goodman, *Democratic-Republicans of Massachusetts*, pp. 183–84; Daniel Howe, *What Hath God Wrought* (New York: Oxford University Press, 2007), pp. 122–23; John Larson, *Internal Improvement* (Chapel Hill: The University of North Carolina Press, 2001), pp. 123–24.

Jefferson increasingly resorted to its means. In this vein, Jefferson and Madison used bribes and supported insurrections to obtain parts of Florida.

Moderate Republicans wanted Florida to increase the government's newfound control over the Gulf of Mexico and Caribbean trade, prevent fugitive slaves from escaping Georgia, and weaken frontier Indians. Jefferson first targeted West Florida, the highly coveted panhandle east of New Orleans. The administration dubiously argued that the Louisiana Purchase included it, a claim France and Spain rightfully denied. In November 1803, Randolph, still supportive of the land acquisition, introduced the administration's Mobile Act, which proposed to annex West Florida into the Mississippi Territory. Although Jefferson signed it in 1804, Spain and France bitterly protested and the law remained a dead letter. Later in the year, a group of thirty Americans tried to capture a Spanish fort. US officials detained the men but did not turn them over to Spain.[23]

From a broader vantage point, Jefferson only needed to convince Napoleonic France, which currently controlled the Spain. In late 1805, in a move reminiscent of the XYZ Affair, Foreign Minister Talleyrand admitted France would oversee the transfer of West Florida as well as East Florida (the peninsula) provided that the Jefferson administration provide a bribe as compensation for intimidating Spain.

In November, Jefferson's cabinet decided to purchase all of Florida from Spain with the "help" of France. However, in his December message to Congress, the president adopted a very bellicose tone, desiring a troop buildup because negotiations to purchase Florida had supposedly failed. At the same time, Jefferson sent a confidential message: Congress should pass vague resolutions that could be made public while clandestinely authorizing money for diplomacy, hinting that it needed to approve $2 million to pay off France into coercing Spain. In essence, the corrupt Jefferson wanted Congress to do his dirty work and supply a slush fund without even asking for it.

Speaker Macon, a dedicated Old Republican, referred the confidential message to a select committee chaired by Randolph. The Old Republican wanted no part in Jefferson's sordid bribery. While Randolph supported acquiring Florida through open and honorable measures (including defensive force in this category), he considered

---

bribery the crony Yazoo scandal all over again. He believed the extortion money would push the neutral US into Napoleon's warmongering hands if Great Britain ever discovered the clandestine payoff. Private exhortations by the president, Madison, and his close friend Gallatin did not change Randolph's mind.

The committee's report rejected the $2 million appropriation, considering the purchase as unnecessarily adding to the debt and violating neutrality. Randolph favored open settlement, and instead of the payoff recommended additional troops on the southern border to mimic what Jefferson actually advocated to the public. Despite this, Barnabas Bidwell of Massachusetts, a moderate Republican who dissented on the committee, countered with a resolution to appropriate $2 million for "extraordinary expenses."[24] In the congressional debates, the apoplectic Randolph thundered that this slush fund would "grease the fists of Napoleon with American gold."[25] But the House accepted Bidwell's resolution, 77-54. Federalists, fighting anything the Republican Party did, and twenty-seven Republicans, concerned over the direction of their party, formed the opposition. The Senate passed the Two Million Dollar Act in February 1806, and only four Republicans voted in opposition. However, greater Republican dissatisfaction existed because Randolph's ally Senator George Logan and three others absented rather than publicly rebuke the president. Instead, Logan wrote a critical letter to Jefferson.[26]

Randolph pinned the blame for his stinging defeat on the Federalist-in-disguise, whispering in Jefferson's ear: Madison. The Old Republican seethed: "I consider this matter as fairly at issue, whether this nation is to be governed by a secret Machiavellian, invisible, irresponsible Cabinet, or the principles of the Constitution."[27] Though defeated, Randolph did not give up. Congress planned to appropriate bribe money from the unpopular salt tariff. In April, Randolph moved to repeal the tax to eliminate the funds, a cunning tactic because the public hated it. Although Congress repealed the tax, moderate Republicans countered by appropriating money from budgets for the Tripoli

---

[24] Risjord, *The Old Republicans*, p. 48.

[25] Dumas Malone, *Jefferson the President, Second Term* (Boston MA: Little, Brown, 1974), p. 75.

[26] Johnson, *John Randolph*, pp. 100–04; Malone, *Jefferson, Second Term*, pp. 69–78; Risjord, *The Old Republicans*, pp. 43–50.

[27] Adam Tate, *Conservatism and Southern Intellectuals* (Columbia: University of Missouri Press, 2005), p. 24.

War. In the end, delays by Randolph, publicity over the act, and war in Europe postponed negotiations. Congress suspended efforts to buy Florida in 1807, when Jefferson thought the money might be needed for an upcoming clash with Great Britain.[28]

The corrupting desire to acquire more land by whatever means necessary troubled many Republicans. During the Two Million Dollar Act debates, Senator Stephen Bradley of Vermont proposed an amendment that allowed the president to obtain Florida, Canada, and Nova Scotia by purchase or force. Clintonian Samuel Mitchill of New York dissented, diagnosing the nascent republic with "a land mania": "What next, why all the Globe—why this rage—Have we an inhabitant for every acre?"[29] The empire developed an insatiable urge to expand. By 1809, Jefferson greedily insisted to Madison that the empire must include Canada, Cuba, and Mexico's provinces.[30]

But the Empire of Liberty first had to conquer the siren song of Florida. During the Madison administration, Republicans warned that Great Britain, a recent ally of the crumbling Spanish Empire, would occupy the region. In reality, the British were not interested, but that did not matter to the expansionists: President Madison moved beyond Jefferson's bribery method and simply invaded Florida by clandestinely inspiring "local" revolts.

First, in April 1810, Claiborne, governor of the Territory of Orleans, visited Madison and insisted that the US could easily capture West Florida. Madison agreed, and Secretary of State Robert Smith stood ready to call out the Mississippi Territory's militia. In September, eighty insurgents seized the environs near New Orleans, creating the independent Republic of West Florida. Governor of the Mississippi Territory David Holmes quickly sent troops to the border in anticipation of an annexation request. Once received, he cheerfully noted to the president that "the views of our government have been in great measure realized."[31] Holmes fortunately made this remark privately because Secretary Smith swore "on [his] honor as a gentleman" to the French Minister that the US was ignorant to the entire affair.[32]

---

[28] Johnson, *John Randolph*, pp. 112–13; Malone, *Jefferson, Second Term*, p. 93.

[29] Horsman, "Dimensions of an 'Empire for Liberty'," p. 11.

[30] John Kaminski, *George Clinton* (Madison, WI: Madison House Publishers, 1993), pp. 280–81, 332; Wood, *Empire of Liberty*, pp. 375–76.

[31] Nugent, *Habits of Empire*, p. 107.

[32] Ibid., p. 108.

Madison, ever concerned about fabricating his reputation as a strict constructionist, fretted that Congress might consider it unconstitutional. Conveniently, the president defended annexation with the necessary and proper clause. When the US annexed the little republic into the Territory of Orleans, upset insurgents protested that they wanted to form their own independent state, ignorant that the Madison administration had used them. Their resistance dissipated after Claiborne's soldiers arrived in December 1810. Ecstatic, Senator Henry Clay of Kentucky, an auspicious moderate Republican, supported the West Florida takeover and triumphantly proclaimed: "Ere long, the *new* United States . . . embracing . . . the entire country east of the Mississippi, including East Florida and some of the territories to the north of us also."[33]

Madison had only acquired the portion of West Florida close to New Orleans, even though the federal government declared that it owned all of West Florida, authorizing a formal takeover if local insurgents approved it. However, the Spanish still maintained control of the rest of West Florida. The administration then shifted its attention to East Florida, particularly near Georgia's border.[34]

Although the US never had the audacity to claim East Florida as part of the Louisiana Purchase, in January 1811 Madison secretly met with General George Mathews, the former corrupt governor of Georgia discredited by the Yazoo land scandal. The president gave Mathews vague instructions to explore potential "discontent" in East Florida, promising military and financial support. Madison did not bother to even inform his Secretaries of War or Navy. Mathews agreed and wrote to Secretary of State James Monroe, the former Antifederalist now comfortably ensconced in the halls of power, declaring that the region teemed with rebels (he lied). Unsurprisingly, he requested military supplies.

In March 1812, despite not hearing back, Mathews used his seventy-man strike force of "rebels"—which included only nine actual residents from East Florida—to move in near St. Augustine, a clear act of aggression. When the public found out, the administration saved its hide by disavowing Mathews. Despite this convenient disassociation,

---

[33] Horsman, "Dimensions of an 'Empire for Liberty'," pp. 12–13.

[34] Robert Higgs, "Not Merely Perfidious but Ungrateful," *The Independent Review* (Fall 2005): 303–10; Horsman, "Dimensions of an 'Empire for Liberty'," p. 12; Nugent, *Habits of Empire*, pp. 104–10.

Madison appointed Governor David Mitchell of Georgia to occupy the area with troops. While the president gave Mitchell orders to withdraw, he was to do it as slowly as possible to continue American occupation.

Thus, the Madison administration continued Jefferson's machinations to illicitly acquire Florida. By early 1812, the United States snatched the extremities of West and East Florida. Slowly but surely, the Republican Party moved away from moderation and into the outright embrace of power.[35]

Public Works Largesse

After the Louisiana Purchase, Republicans embraced a vast network of internal improvements to solidify the empire. In doing so, Jefferson abandoned his laissez-faire instincts and constitutional scruples. The entire episode provides another example of power's corrupting influence.

By the second Jefferson administration, government provision of public works became paramount. First, many thought that after Congress extinguished the debt it could use surpluses for positive investment. Second, politicians reasoned that internal improvements would stimulate economic development in the Northwest, Southwest, and Louisiana, reducing secessionist impulses. In other words, if the West was going to remain in the Union, it needed a sweetener.

Thus far, states had done their part by granting corporate charters to transportation companies at an increasing rate. For example, by 1811 New York had chartered 137 turnpikes, and by 1820 eight Pennsylvania turnpikes and three bridge companies handled the route between Philadelphia and Pittsburgh. Southern states continued to rely on navigable river streams. However, many thought federal subsidies and construction, especially in the West, should supersede state involvement.[36]

Gallatin was one such vocal proponent, building off Adam Smith and other Enlightenment economists, who unfortunately had admitted that governments could embark upon these projects when the market "underprovided" infrastructure. Evidently, Gallatin did not

---

[35] Nugent, *Habits of Empire*, pp. 111–14; Silverstone, *Divided Union*, pp. 105–11.

[36] Albert Fishlow, "Internal Transportation in the Nineteenth and Early Twentieth Centuries," in *The Cambridge Economic History of the United States*, vol. 2, ed. Stanley Engerman and Robert Gallman (New York: Cambridge University Press, 2000), p. 550; Gregory May, *Jefferson's Treasure* (Washington, D.C.: Regnery History, 2018), pp. 133–34; Wood, *Empire of Liberty*, p. 484.

understand that to the extent supposed "under provision" occurred in the United States, it resulted from the Napoleonic Wars. The conflict artificially increased the profitability of the transatlantic trade and misallocated scarce resources in the shipping industry. The prominent Republican engineer B. H. Latrobe explained this fact when he wrote in June 1806 that the "suspension of the internal improvements of the country, is the absorption of all our active capital by . . . the foreign trade, which revived with the new War."[37] Latrobe, whose excellent analysis also applies to the earlier Anglo-French wars and the unofficial Quasi-War in the late 1790s, unfortunately favored government investment to make up the shortfall in private capital. These followers of Adam Smith and other Enlightenment theorists did not yet realize that like wartime spending, government "investment" in infrastructure also misallocates scarce resources because it is not based on profit and loss, thereby breeding economic inefficiency.[38]

Jefferson initially resisted his Treasurer. In 1802, the president worried about the federal erection of piers, because they were unconstitutional, promoted cronyism, and led to wasteful spending. But earlier in the year, to displace the Federalist establishment in Ohio and prevent the seizure of land on federal credit, he moderated. The president approved the Enabling Act, a statehood bill which included a Gallatin provision that set aside 10 percent (later reduced to 5 percent) of revenue from land sales for internal improvements. Jefferson's earlier remarks regarding corruption and inefficiency proved to be prescient: soon enough, local politicians siphoned the Enabling Act's funds to parochial boondoggles for local constituents.[39]

By his second inauguration in 1805, Jefferson expanded his interventionism when he declared that surpluses could "by a just repartition among the states, and a corresponding amendment of the constitution, be applied *in time of peace*, to rivers, canals, roads, arts, manufactures, education, and other great objects within each

---

[37] Talbot Hamlin, *Benjamin Henry Latrobe* (New York: Oxford University Press, 1955), 211–12.

[38] Joseph Harrison, "'Sic Et Non'," *Journal of the Early Republic* (Winter 1987): 342; Larson, *Internal Improvement*, pp. 59–63; John Nelson, *Liberty and Property* (Baltimore, MD: The Johns Hopkins University Press, 1987), pp. 119–21; Wood, *Empire of Liberty*, p. 332.

[39] Harrison, "'Sic Et Non,'" pp. 338–41; Larson, *Internal Improvement*, p. 54; George Taylor, *The Transportation Revolution* (New York: Holt, Rinehart and Winston, 1951), p. 19.

state."[40] Toeing the nationalist line, in 1806 he stressed the burgeoning empire: "the lines of separation [between the states] will disappear, their interests will be identified, and their union cemented by new and indissoluble ties."[41] Jefferson at least maintained some semblance of his reform principles by requesting an amendment, the distribution of federal revenue to the states, and the limiting of spending to periods of peace and surplus.

But Jefferson's call for an amendment was meaningless. In early 1806, Congress, building off the Enabling Act, passed a law to construct a national road from Maryland to the Ohio River. The fact that Jefferson hoped the states would ratify an amendment before construction commenced was an empty restraint. Even strict constructionism provided no help: congressmen argued that the road would be useful for national defense and postal routes, goals the Constitution sanctioned. The National Road proceeded undisturbed, and Jefferson's amendment died in Congress.

Preliminary work on the National Road began in 1806 and 1807. The act authorized Jefferson to appoint commissioners to design the road, establish routes, and request permission from the relevant states. The problems with government internal improvements that Jefferson once tried to emphasize rose to the surface. Thus, in December 1806 the commissioners reported that inhabitants living in Maryland, Pennsylvania, and Virginia districts argued they were "entitled to a preference."[42] Translation: Congress must stimulate their local commerce, land values, and election returns at the expense of other taxed regions. Pennsylvania stipulated consent conditional on requiring that the road run through Uniontown and Washington. Jefferson fretted over this local special-interest pleading, but Gallatin persuaded him to accept the constraint because the road was "a national object of great importance (particularly as a bond of union)."[43] As for Uniontown and Washington specifically, Gallatin lived in the former and insisted that the Republicans needed the latter for the upcoming 1808 elections. Once again, Jefferson acquiesced.

---

[40] Harrison, "'Sic Et Non,'" p. 341.

[41] Wood, *Empire of Liberty*, p. 484.

[42] Carter Goodrich, *Government Promotion of American Canals and Railroads* (New York: Columbia University Press, 1960), p. 25.

[43] May, *Jefferson's Treasure*, pp. 134–35.

Unsurprisingly, cronyism caused construction delays, excessive costs, districting constraints, and poor management by political appointees. Workers struck ground only in 1811, used expensive stone, and developed a meandering route that finally reached Wheeling on the Ohio River in 1818. In the end, the lack of a profit incentive killed the project, and a network of state-assisted private roads and canals filled the gap. As the decades progressed, the National Road fell into desuetude.[44]

As it commenced construction, Congress eyed even greater largesse. Since 1805, assistance to the Chesapeake and Delaware Canal and a proposed canal in Louisville, Kentucky, had floated around the legislature. In 1807, it dawned upon Senator Clay that he could increase support for the Kentucky canal if he supported funding for the Delaware canal. In other words: "Support my project and I'll support yours." This parochial logrolling appalled Federalist Senator John Quincy Adams of Massachusetts, son of the former president and who was rapidly transforming into the preeminent moderate Republican. Instead, Adams proposed much more broad and visionary logrolling, envisioning a vast network of internal improvements that gave each region of the empire a slice of the pie. When support for the two canals fizzled, the Senate adopted such a plan and instructed Gallatin to prepare a report.

In April 1808, Gallatin delivered his *Report on Roads and Canals*, recommending a massive system of canals and turnpikes. The Treasurer estimated the cost at an enormous $20 million, financed over ten years by annual appropriations of $2 million from surplus tax revenue and land sales. But even this would be inadequate, for construction on similar projects demonstrated that Gallatin vastly underestimated expenses. Much like Hamilton's *Report on Manufactures* twenty years earlier, Gallatin's boondoggles, which special interests covetously eyed, went nowhere. Collapsing revenue from recent trade restrictions, threats of war, and ideological resistance from Old Republicans killed the plan. Despite this setback, moderate Republicans continued to dream of internal improvements financed by the federal trough.[45]

---

[44] Burton Folsom and Anna Folsom, *Uncle Sam Can't Count* (New York: HarperCollins Publishers, 2014), pp. 4–7; Goodrich, *Government Promotion*, pp. 25–26; Harrison, "'Sic Et Non,'" pp. 341–43; May, *Jefferson's Treasure*, pp. 134–35; Wood, *Empire of Liberty*, p. 482.

[45] Goodrich, *Government Promotion*, pp. 26–37; Harrison, "'Sic Et Non,'" pp. 342–43;

Most notably, in 1811 the Federalist Gouverneur Morris and Republican DeWitt Clinton lobbied Congress for funds to build a New York canal to the Great Lakes, a longtime goal of New Yorkers and a project Gallatin previously proposed. Fellow New Yorker and ex-Federalist turned moderate Republican Congressman Peter B. Porter assisted their endeavors. He had his own interests in mind, though, hoping that the canal would benefit his mercantile Porter, Barton & Company. The men from New York failed for the same reasons as Gallatin's *Report*.[46]

The Republicans' embrace of federally funded public works, justified by broad constructionism, heavily shifted the party into the big government camp. They no longer even tried to adhere to the party's former libertarian principles.

Protecting Merchants and Manufacturers

Foreign diplomacy and international trade constituted the most disastrous policies of Jefferson's second term. The anti-war Jefferson slowly but inexorably supported a military buildup and aggressive trade legislation against Great Britain—the age-old enemy—and dismissed the peaceful 1806 Monroe-Pinkney Treaty. The primary rationale once again concerned land: conquering Canada and Florida for the empire. In addition, Jefferson and his moderate Republicans wanted to privilege anti-British shippers and manufacturers. While Jefferson's Embargo Act was too excessive of a restriction for merchants, the law, along with Madison's protective tariffs, pleased manufacturers. Old Republicans harshly criticized the moderates but could not stop the trends.

In May 1803, Great Britain and France resumed hostilities, benefiting America's shipping trade: in a pattern reminiscent of the 1790s, total exports shot up 94 percent from 1803 to 1807. However, as in that decade, Great Britain and France focused on crippling each other (and benefitting their own merchants) by stepping up seizures of American ships and personnel trading with the enemy. In this regard,

---

Larson, *Internal Improvement*, pp. 58–59; Thomas McCraw, *The Founders and Finance* (Cambridge, MA: Belknap Press, 2012), p. 419.

[46] Goodrich, *Government Promotion*, p. 36; Brian Murphy, *Building the Empire State* (Philadelphia: University of Pennsylvania Press, 2015), p. 177; J. Stagg, "Between Black Rock and a Hard Place," *Journal of the Early Republic* (Autumn 1999): 386, 394–96, 403–05.

Britain was the bigger aggressor: while France seized 558 ships from 1803 to 1812, the former mother country seized 917 ships. Concerning their impressments, which increased from 2,400 in 1792 to 6,000 in 1802. The British stood on somewhat solid ground since over a third of American sailors were actually British. Britain even recognized the impressment controversy, making efforts to placate the US as much as feasible. Thus, in July 1804, Ambassador to England James Monroe confidentially reported "the truth is that our commerce never enjoyed in any war, as much freedom, and indeed favor from this govt. as it now does."[47]

Although the situation remained unfortunate, America had few realistic options. The Republicans cogently recognized that war would be too costly, but unfortunately did not realize that commercial retaliation, which they yearned to try, would not soothe tensions. In late 1807, Jefferson succinctly described the available policies as "War, Embargo or Nothing."[48] Unfortunately, as in all cases of government intervention, the insatiable desire for politicians to do something was a cure worse than the supposed disease of doing nothing.

In 1805, when Great Britain authorized a greater seizure of American ships engaged in the re-export trade, the situation escalated. Although Britain released many seized vessels to "tranquilize" the country, in Monroe's wording, costly delays caused American merchants to suffer heavy losses and a quadrupling of insurance rates.[49] In 1806, an embarrassed Britain restored the American re-export trade to its old status (still liable to seizure, but with less restrictions). Despite this, American merchants demanded one of their old crony desires, a larger navy to mitigate market risk.[50]

Jefferson and the moderate Republicans always remained open to enlarging their political base. They had increasingly taken advice on commercial matters from Massachusetts merchants, particularly Congressman Jacob Crowninshield. The president even offered Crowninshield the secretary of the Navy position in 1805. Although

---

[47] Donald Hickey, *The War of 1812* (Chicago: University of Illinois Press, 2012), p. 10. See also p. 10; Douglas A. Irwin, *Clashing over Commerce* (Chicago: The University of Chicago Press, 2017), pp. 99–100; McGraw, *Founders and Finance*, pp. 272–73; Nettels, *Emergence of a National Economy*, p. 396; Wood, *Empire of Liberty*, pp. 642, 646.

[48] Malone, *Jefferson, Second Term*, p. 469.

[49] Hickey, *War of 1812*, p. 10.

[50] Ibid., pp. 10–11.

he declined, Madison awarded his brother Benjamin the position in 1815. To please these commercial interests, the president's bellicose message to Congress in December 1805 advocated increasing seaport town fortifications and gunboats, constructing formal navy ships, and creating a naval militia reserve. Jefferson also wanted to assist northern manufacturers. In his 1805 inaugural speech, when discussing the budget surplus, Jefferson dismissed lower tariffs, insisting manufacturers needed protection, a stark contrast from the Jefferson of the 1790s, who supported free trade and condemned Hamilton's *Report on Manufactures*.[51]

In early 1806 the House bypassed Randolph so it could do something about the British question. Pennsylvania Republican Andrew Gregg introduced a sweeping resolution banning all British imports. Another proposal, written by Senator Samuel Smith, only banned British goods Americans could domestically produce. The mercantilist Smith also wanted a new navigation act restricting British merchants but found little support for his measure. Maryland's Joseph Nicholson introduced Smith's nonimportation bill in the House. Both the Gregg and Nicholson proposals created an umbrella that protected northern manufacturers and merchants.

Randolph blasted Gregg's Resolution and reminded Republicans of their traditional principles, especially their attacks on merchant protections in the Quasi-War. Randolph, devoted to Adam Smith's free trade principles, declared that the Resolution supported the manufacturing North at the expense of the importing South, sacrificing cheap imports to protect merchants engaged in the re-export trade. Furthermore, the measure violated American neutrality and "plung[ed] [the country] at last into war," increased the president's power, and violated the Constitution.[52] Lastly, he mentioned moderate Republicans' hidden desire to conquer Canada. Speaker Macon supported Randolph on the floor, criticizing the warmongering patriotism and protectionism infecting the Republican Party. Although Randolph and Macon defeated Gregg's Resolution, the House passed Nicholson's Resolution against Federalists and a crumbling minority of Old Republicans. Senator Logan failed to stop the bill's passage in the Senate. However, the Non-Importation

---

[51] *American Political Leaders*, p. 136; Burch, *Elites in American History*, 1, pp. 98, 273; Hickey, *War of 1812*, 10–11; Larson, *Internal Improvement*, p. 57; Wood, *Empire of Liberty*, p. 644.

[52] Johnson, *John Randolph*, p. 108.

Act only started at the end of 1806; Congress subsequently pushed back the date to December 1807.[53]

With his resistance, Randolph forever severed links with Jefferson. Even the free trader Thomas Cooper sided with the moderate Republicans, supporting retaliatory measures and protection for manufacturers. Significantly, Cooper later justified his stance by appealing to the ideas of Adam Smith, a demonstration that the classical liberal economists did not always offer the Invisible Hand solution. Dreams of war, conquest, and national might shifted more and more members of the Republican Party away from their cherished libertarian principles.[54]

There is no clearer demonstration of Jefferson's transformation than his decision to torpedo peaceful negotiations with Great Britain. When the president sent a commissioner to assist Monroe, he dismissed recommendations to appoint Randolph and sent Maryland Federalist William Pinkney, another courting of the opposition. Despite this, the Monroe-Pinkney Treaty of 1806 was a sensible compromise, decidedly improving over the one-sided Jay's Treaty that lapsed in 1803. Britain refused to yield on impressment but instead offered to observe greater caution and a quicker rectification of mistakes. Furthermore, Britain promised not to interfere with the re-export trade if Americans paid a minor transit duty when they stopped in the US, a fee smaller than what they normally paid; narrowed classification of contraband; offered to give notice of blockades; agreed to refrain from seizures or impressments five miles from the American coast; reduced taxes on American ships in British ports; continued American access to the British Indies; and even granted a quasi-insurance clause that required indemnification of improperly violated American merchants. The US only had to relinquish the ability to employ discriminatory commercial sanctions (i.e., those that applied unequally to Great Britain, such as the Non-Importation Act of 1806).

However, Jefferson and Madison wanted to end impressment and keep the right to employ commercial sanctions. Although unstated, Jefferson might have also realized that a treaty with Britain made it harder for the US to take over Canada. "To tell you the truth,"

---

[53] *American Political Leaders*, p. 224; Cassell, *Merchant Congressman*, pp. 127–29; Devanny, "Loathing of Public Debt," pp. 391, 411; Johnson, *John Randolph*, pp. 107–10; Kirk, *John Randolph*, p. 326; Risjord, *The Old Republicans*, pp. 53–64; Wood, *Empire of Liberty*, pp. 644, 649.

[54] Joseph Dorfman, *The Economic Mind in American Civilization*, vol. 2 (New York: Viking Press, 1946), pp. 529, 531–32, 535–36.

Jefferson reportedly admitted to a close friend, "I do not wish any treaty with Great Britain."[55] Madison and Jefferson refused to even submit the Monroe-Pinkney Treaty to the Senate for potential ratification, deeply disturbing Senator Logan. Donald Hickey rightfully considers the rejection "a great turning point in the Age of Jefferson."[56] The Republican Party decided to forgo a peaceful resolution in favor of aggressive actions.

Relations with Great Britain sharply deteriorated in 1807, after the infamous attack on an American ship, the *Chesapeake*, by the British *Leopard*. The incident caused a furious uproar in America, though Macon and Gallatin wisely supported peace. Great Britain realized the gravity of the situation: they disavowed the attack, recalled the commander of the *Leopard* and gave him another assignment, offered to pay reparations, and returned three of the four impressed men. Unfortunately, Jefferson wanted more, such as an end to all impressments, and this demand delayed settlement for years. Of course, what Jefferson really desired was Canada.[57]

By the time Congress convened in October 1807, the Old Republicans' strength had crumbled, particulary after moderate Republicans ousted Macon and Randolph from the Speaker of the House and the Ways and Means Committee. In addition, Logan retired, and the newly elected William Crawford of Georgia succeeded him as the pre-eminent Old Republican in the upper house. The forces of liberty could do little to stop Jefferson's plans.

By December, Jefferson decided that a draconian embargo was somehow the best option. He planned to block trade with Great Britain and France, particularly withholding American exports, to make them realize their dependence on the young empire. The mercantilist Madison predictably favored the idea while Gallatin strenuously opposed it, recognizing that an embargo would do little to change Europe while devastating the US economy. Ever influenced by Smithian laissez-faire, the Treasurer reasoned that "Government prohibitions do

---

[55] Hickey, *War of 1812*, p. 15.

[56] Ibid., p. 15.

[57] Hickey, *War of 1812*, pp. 13–16; Irwin, *Clashing over Commerce*, p. 101; Malone, *Jefferson, Second Term*, pp. 400–10; May, *Jefferson's Treasure*, pp. 159–63; Murray N. Rothbard, "Report on George B. DeHuszar and Thomas Hulbert Stevenson, *A History of the American Republic*, 2 vols," in Rothbard, *Strictly Confidential*, ed. David Gordon (Auburn, AL: Mises Institute, 2010), pp. 108–09; Tolles, *George Logan*, pp. 279–80; Wood, *Empire of Liberty*, pp. 647–48.

always more mischief than had been calculated; and it is not without much hesitation that a statesman should hazard to regulate the concerns of individuals, as if he could do it better than themselves."[58]

However, Jefferson was convinced of his righteousness. In December, with the Non-Importation Act finally in effect, the president fatefully recommended additional commercial retaliation, a regulatory net too restrictive even for the merchants. In the name of impressed sailors and seized goods, the Embargo Act ended all foreign trade on American ships "except vessels under the immediate discretion of the President."[59] Moderate Republicans loyally supported the policy while Federalists, defensive of Great Britain and connected with the northern commercial trade, balked. The Senate secretly passed the bill within hours of Jefferson's message, with only Crawford and Federalists opposed. Despite greater resistance by Old Republicans and Federalists in the lower chamber, the House followed three days later.[60]

Republicans poorly conceived the Embargo Act, and many resisted it. Ironically, Federalist shippers criticized it as too harsh a retaliatory policy, though some prominent Republican merchants managed to secure benefits. John Jacob Astor lobbied for a ship's exemption on account that its trade with China would improve foreign relations. He earned $200,000 from the voyage. Stephen Girard transferred his foreign wealth to the US by purchasing government bonds and stock in the Bank of the United States. The mercantile Crowninshield family and William Gray, reportedly the wealthiest merchant in America, publicly supported the embargo. Critics attributed Crowninshield and Gray's support to cronyism: they planned to gobble up smaller merchants' businesses at artificially low prices and obtain a monopoly. But, these exceptions aside, the mercantile class heavily opposed the law and their resistance only grew as 1808 progressed.[61]

---

[58] Trask, "Thomas Jefferson," p. 91.

[59] William Watkins, *Reclaiming the American Revolution* (Oakland, CA: The Independent Institute, 2004), p. 87.

[60] *American Political Leaders*, p. 224; Irwin, *Clashing over Commerce*, pp. 102–03; May, *Jefferson's Treasure*, pp. 63–66; Risjord, *The Old Republicans*, pp. 80–83; Watkins, *Finance and Enterprise in Early America* (Philadelphia: University of Pennsylvania Press, 1978) pp. 86–87; Wood, *Empire of Liberty*, pp. 649–50.

[61] Donald Adams, *Finance and Enterprise in Early America* (Philadelphia: University of Pennsylvania Press, 1978), pp. 7–11; Dorfman, *Economic Mind*, 1, p. 320; Goodman, *Democratic-Republicans of Massachusetts*, pp. 192–95; John Haeger, *John Jacob Astor* (Detroit, MI: Wayne State University Press, 1991), pp. 104–05; Nettels, *Emergence of a National Economy*, p. 340.

Over the year, Congress passed a patchwork of additional regulations and the Treasury issued a flood of directives to stop smuggling.
But smuggling only grew, particularly in New York and Vermont. Jefferson even declared the regional militia needed to suppress an "insurrection."[62] The president had come a long way from his free trade and
anti-war principles. By early 1809, a disparate coalition had formed to
drastically reduce the restrictions. Matters got so bad in New England
that the rank and file supported nullification and secession, something the Federalist leaders quickly quashed. But the Federalist congressmen still joined Clintonians and Old Republicans to create what
Jefferson dismissively described as an "unaccountable revolution of
opinion."[63] Congress ended the Embargo, substituting it with a Nonin-
tercourse Act that reopened trade with all nations except Great Britain
and France (if either country suspended restrictions, Congress could
restore trade). Jefferson bitterly signed the Embargo Act's repeal in
March. For now, the nation avoided continued economic calamity.[64]

The Embargo was an unmitigated disaster. America's commercial retaliation caused no political changes in either Great Britain or
France, only an unambiguous decline in the economy. Over 1808,
exports collapsed by 80 percent and imports 60 percent. Unemployed
sailors and ships languished on the coast. From 1808 to 1809, the
federal government's revenue decreased 55 percent. Industrial production decreased 17 percent in 1808 alone, while real GDP did not
change at all.[65]

However, a silver lining emerged, at least for moderate Republicans. When he left office, Jefferson praised the Embargo Act because
it encouraged domestic manufacturing. In particular, the number of
cotton mills increased from fifteen to eighty-seven from 1807 to 1809.
Notably, Baltimore industrialists formed the Union Manufactory, a

---

[62] Trask, "Thomas Jefferson," p. 87.

[63] Ibid., p. 97.

[64] Banner, *Hartford Convention*, pp. 294–306; Irwin, *Clashing over Commerce*, pp. 104–
10; May, *Jefferson's Treasure*, p. 168; Trask, "Thomas Jefferson," pp. 89–90, 96–99;
Watkins, *Reclaiming the American Revolution*, pp. 87–88; Thomas E. Woods Jr., *Nullification* (Washington, D.C.: Regnery, 2010), pp. 60–65.

[65] Joseph Davis, "An Annual Index of US Industrial Production," *Quarterly Journal
of Economics* (November 2004): 1189; *Historical Statistics*, 5, p. 80; Johnson, *John
Randolph*, p. 134; Louis Johnston and Samuel Williamson, "What Was the US GDP
Then?" *Measuringworth.com*; May, *Jefferson's Treasure*, p. 171; Wood, *Empire of Liberty*, p. 655.

million-dollar chartered corporation that became the largest cotton factory in the country. In 1809 and 1811, Massachusetts and New York enacted general incorporation statutes that allowed some manufacturers to create companies without a formal legislative charter. While these limited general incorporation statutes were anti-crony, most of the new companies depended on the embargo privilege and soon advocated increased restrictions on foreign goods.

The corrupt Republicans were ready to listen to this constituency, in particular Madison, who supported *"permanent* duties for encouraging manufactures."[66] In April 1810, at the behest of congressional Republicans, Gallatin presented his *Report on Manufactures*. Unlike Hamilton, the Smithian Gallatin shied away from moderately protective tariffs and outright subsidies. However, he argued that Congress should create a gargantuan fund of $5–20 million for loans to manufacturers. If enacted, the federal government could pick winners and losers based on political favoritism, and the largesse would morph into an engine of Republican cronyism far greater than what Gallatin (and Jefferson) once trenchantly criticized. Fortunately, this expensive boondoggle died in Congress. But the undeterred Madison pushed ahead with protective tariffs. By 1812, Congress had increased the average rate on total imports from 30 percent to 37 percent. Northern manufacturing, particularly large mills and factories, quickly blossomed. Thus, ironically, the Republicans, not the Federalists, enacted the mercantilism necessary to protect manufacturing interest groups.

Jefferson assumed office carrying the torch of the libertarian Revolution of 1800. But he abandoned his constitutional scruples for the immense Louisiana land grab, a corrupting acquisition for his Empire of Liberty. To benefit new constituencies and prevent the enlarged empire from breaking apart, he and other moderate Republicans embraced bailouts to speculators, aggression in Florida, public works subsidies, and various layers of privileges for merchants and manufacturers. They transitioned from fighting Federalist privileges, to sanctioning them, to actually pursuing their own. This trend only continued to worsen.[67]

---

[66] Irwin, *Clashing over Commerce*, p. 111.

[67] *Historical Statistics*, 5, p. 510; Irwin, *Clashing over Commerce*, pp. 121–24; May, *Jefferson's Treasure*, pp. 194–98; Lawrence Peskin, *Manufacturing Revolution* (Baltimore, MD: The John Hopkins University Press, 2003), pp. 134, 166–67, 170–73, 185; Wood, *Empire of Liberty*, p. 702.

CHAPTER 9

PRESIDENT MADISON: THE EMPIRE OF POWER

Conquering Canada

James Madison, the preeminent moderate Republican, fulfilled the power-aggrandizing trends Thomas Jefferson accomplished after the Louisiana Purchase. During the attempted conquest of Canada and Florida—the War of 1812—the Republicans wholeheartedly sponsored Federalist cronyism for the Old Order Empire: a protective system for manufacturers, favorable terms for debt speculators, and banking privileges. After the war, the new National Republicans—the direct descendants of the moderate Republicans—continued to enact Federalist policies: another central bank, peacetime protective tariffs, and plans for a federal transportation network. Madison came full circle: he began his career laying the groundwork for a Federalist government and ended it by adding the finishing touches.

Once he acquired Louisiana, Jefferson increasingly fixated on Canada. Most prominently, the conquest would monopolize the lucrative Great Lakes and St. Lawrence River trade. Aside from bringing additional revenue into the Treasury's coffers, this would allow American commercial interests to ship goods through an American-controlled St. Lawrence River or a canal that connected one of the Great Lakes with the Hudson River. In addition, controlling Canada would benefit the New England fishing industry, which the Republicans wanted to court; eliminate British fur trade competition around the upper Mississippi River; and ensure continental dominance. Lastly, annexation weakened western Indians, whom Republicans accused of aggressing on frontier settlements. In reality, though, the hunters only farmed on a fraction of the land, Americans undeniably encroached, particularly William Henry Harrison, inveterate land speculator and governor of the Indiana Territory.[1]

After the *Chesapeake* incident, Jefferson banned British warships from American ports and recalled American ships from abroad. He recommended a military buildup, particularly an increase in harbor defenses and gunboats, one hundred thousand militia, and a Canadian offensive. The president insisted to the public that the embargo was necessary to prevent war. At the same time, he ratcheted up military expenditures for a secret invasion. From 1805 to 1808, Congress augmented the Departments of War and Navy's combined budgets by 107 percent. In late 1808, Secretary of War Henry Dearborn recommended an army appropriation of $2.1 million. Careening toward an offensive strike in early 1809, the House passed a bill that called for a special session to meet in May, tasking it with ending the embargo and declaring war. But everything came to a crashing halt: the makeshift coalition of Clintonians, Old Republicans, and Federalists that repealed the embargo also rejected Dearborn's request.[2]

Defeated, expansionists postponed imperial war until the 1810 midterm elections, when moderate Republicans increased their strength and two new bellicose factions emerged. John Randolph appropriately labelled the first group, the proponents of a land war, the War Hawks. Prominent War Hawks included Congressmen Henry Clay, Tennessee's Felix Grundy, Peter B. Porter, and John C. Calhoun of South Carolina. War Hawks contrasted with the bellicose war faction Nathaniel Macon labelled the Invisibles, who preferred a naval war to subsidize shipping interests. Prominent Invisibles included Senators Samuel Smith and William Branch Giles of Virginia. However, War Hawks amassed the greater political strength, so the war drive focused on their goals. The War Hawks wanted war to seize British Canada in the North and Spanish Florida in the South.

---

[1] Roger Brown, *The Republic in Peril* (New York: Columbia University Press, 1964), pp. 120–21; Bruce De Mesquita and Alastair Smith, *The Spoils of War* (New York: Public Affairs, 2016), pp. 68–72; Reginald Horsman, "On To Canada," *Michigan Historical Review* (Fall 1987): 17; Stanley Lebergott, *The Americans* (New York: W.W. Norton, 1984), pp. 13–16; Walter Nugent, *Habits of Empire* (New York: Vintage Books, 2009), pp. 75–78.

[2] *Historical Statistics of the United States, Colonial Times to 1957* (Washington, DC, 1960), p. 91; H. Arthur Scott Trask, "Thomas Jefferson," in *Reassessing the Presidency*, ed. John V. Denson (Auburn, AL: Mises Institute, 2001), pp. 93–100; Gordon Wood, *Empire of Liberty* (New York: Oxford University Press, 2009), pp. 647–48.

The Madison administration already worked toward the latter goal by encouraging "revolts." In December 1811, Grundy privately summed up the War Hawks' plans: "the Canadas & Floridas will be the Theatres of our offensive operations."[3]

When arguments to seize Canada leaked into the public discourse, War Hawks anxiously defended their bellicosity. They described the Canadian conquest as an "occupation" designed to force the British to repeal their maritime restrictions, insisting that after the war the US would seamlessly return Canada. Thus, Clay famously wrote in December 1813 that "Canada was not the end but the means, the object of the War being the redress of injuries, and Canada being the instrument by which that redress was to be obtained."[4] Many historians take the War Hawks' words at face value and argue that conquering Canada was not a major motivation for war against Britain.[5]

In reality, the War Hawks had no intention of returning Canada: British maritime issues provided a convenient front to sell war to a hesitant public. In the same letter Clay wrote that "it has ever been my opinion that if Canada is conquered it ought never to be surrendered if it can possibly be retained."[6] In December 1811, War Hawk Congressman Richard Johnson of Kentucky proclaimed that he would die unhappy unless Canada was "incorporated [into] the United States."[7] Secretary of State James Monroe spoke for the administration in 1812 when he tried to get the British to end the war quickly because it would be "difficult to relinquish Territory which had been conquered."[8] Of course, even if the British quickly surrendered, the Republicans would have still kept land they seized.[9]

---

[3] Julius Pratt, *Expansionists of 1812* (New York: Macmillan, 1925), p. 122. See also *American Political Leaders* (Washington, DC: CQ Press, 2000), p. 290; David Johnson, *John Randolph of Roanoke* (Baton Rouge: Louisiana State University Press, 2012), pp. 140–41; John Pancake, *Samuel Smith and the Politics of Business* (Tuscaloosa: University of Alabama Press, 1972), p. 79; Pratt, *Expansionists of 1812*, pp. 49–50, 120; Wood, *Empire of Liberty*, pp. 660–62.

[4] De Mesquita and Smith, *Spoils of War*, p. 81.

[5] Richard Maass, "'Difficult to Relinquish Territory Which Had Been Conquered'," *Diplomatic History* (January 2015): 70–97.

[6] De Mesquita and Smith, *Spoils of War*, p. 81.

[7] Horsman, "On To Canada," p. 12.

[8] Ibid., p. 14.

[9] Ibid., pp. 11–17.

In mid-1811, Madison eagerly called for an early session of Congress. Treasurer Gallatin, anxious to avoid war, toned down Madison's aggressive message. But the War Hawks still got the picture and elected Clay to the important Speaker of the House position. Speaker Clay reorganized House committees to his faction's liking. War Hawks Porter, Calhoun, and Grundy dominated the important Foreign Relations Committee and allocated their time to invasion plans. In November, Chairman Porter, with his own ill-gotten interests in mind, delivered the committee's report. It called for filling up army and navy vacancies, increasing the army to ten thousand men, augmenting the supply of volunteers by fifty thousand, readying the militia, and preparing the navy. The resolutions were to "make preparations" for war.[10]

The former Federalist Porter was a businessman in New York near Lake Ontario. Porter had a vested interest in the crop, livestock, and shipping potential in the adjacent Canadian land (Upper Canada), which he considered "immensely valuable."[11] Porter created Porter, Barton & Company to acquire land and control trade in the region, actively supporting Federalist Gouverneur Morris and Republican DeWitt Clinton's previous efforts to link the Hudson River to the Great Lakes with a canal. Unfortunately for Porter, the New York State Canal Commission recognized that ships trafficking in Lake Ontario would still be incentivized to ship down the Canadian-controlled St. Lawrence River (Lower Canada). It made more sense for New York to build a canal to Lake Erie, where such competition did not exist. If only the United States owned Canada, Porter strategized, it could divert traffic away from the St. Lawrence River and make a Lake Ontario canal feasible—thereby boosting the profits of Porter, Barton & Company! Porter envisioned making Lower Canada a vassal territory while incorporating Upper Canada, geographically closer to his business interests, into the United States. He did not play games with his report: "Do not let us raise armies unless we intend to employ them."[12]

---

[10] Norman Risjord, *Chesapeake Politics* (New York: Columbia University Press, 1978), p. 129.

[11] J. Stagg, "Between Black Rock and a Hard Place," *Journal of the Early Republic* (Autumn 1999): 392.

[12] Donald Hickey, *The War of 1812* (Chicago: University of Illinois Press, 2012), p. 31. See also pp. 28–29; Nugent, *Habits of Empire*, pp. 75–82; Risjord, *The Old Republicans*, pp. 128–29; Stagg, "Black Rock," pp. 386, 394–96, 402–03, 405, 412–14; Sean Wilentz, *The Rise of American Democracy* (New York: W.W. Norton, 2005), p. 154; Wood, *Empire of Liberty*, pp. 666–67.

Congressman Randolph fought the report in a valiant stand on behalf of liberty. He blasted the entire proposal as preparing for a "war of conquest, a war for the acquisition of territory and subjects" driven by "agrarian cupidity [and] not maritime right."[13] He accused Porter of wanting to attack Canada because his businesses "on the Hudson and the Lakes would be enriched by supplies for the troops, which they alone can provide."[14] He reasoned that a Canadian war would not improve the nation's maritime rights and relations with the Indians, who were angry because of "our own thirst for territory [and] our own want of moderation."[15] Furthermore, the territorial expansion would shift the nation's capital to the West. Above all, Randolph hurled a devastating thunderbolt against his Republican-In-Name-Only opponents when he stated that the party had once

> vaunted of paying off the national debt, of retrenching useless establishments; and yet had now become as infatuated with standing armies, loans, taxes, navies, and war, as ever were the Essex Junto. What Republicanism is this?[16]

In essence, with this damning statement Randolph brilliantly encapsulated the corrupting nature of power that infected the Republican Party.

Strategically, and quite ominously, Randolph raised the specter of slave insurrections. However, his protest was not a thinly veiled protection of slavery. Like other southern classical liberals, slavery tormented Randolph. Consequently, the same man who wrote committee reports supporting bans on slavery in the Indiana Territory and the foreign slave trade into the Louisiana Purchase, futilely brought the up the issue to dampen southern War Hawks' ardor. Although the "slavery scare" was a grisly tactic, desperate times called for desperate measures, and in his speech against the war Randolph used every tool in his arsenal, much like Patrick Henry during the Virginia ratification debates. Nationalistic southerners disagreed with the Old Republican's sectional maneuvers: the ardent War Hawk Calhoun, who longed for

---

[13] Johnson, *John Randolph*, p. 144 and Nugent, *Habits of Empire*, p. 81.

[14] Stagg, "Black Rock," p. 386.

[15] Johnson, *John Randolph*, p. 144.

[16] Adam Tate, *Conservatism and Southern Intellectuals* (Columbia: University of Missouri Press, 2005), p. 69.

the "day when the British will have no Halifax on this continent," stated the upcoming war would not threaten slavery.[17] The war of conquest was still on.[18]

In the end, the House approved the committee's resolutions by overwhelming margins. Even many Federalists voted for them, which one described as "measures of the old federal school."[19] In early 1812, Congress increased the army to thirty-five thousand. Randolph tried to fight this, stating it would lead to Republicans adopting "Federal doctrine to its full extent."[20] The corrupting nature of power—the drive for more land to expand the empire—had really transformed the Republican Party of the 1810s into the Federalist Party of the 1790s.[21]

But at this moment, the Republican war machine drew the line, for it quickly became clear that the War Hawks and Invisibles were *not* a unified front willing to adopt the Federalist system—a strong army and navy, military bureaucracy, and high taxes. The War Hawks naïvely believed that land forces could quickly conquer Canada and Florida, balking at extensive war preparations. At the same time, they fought against any attempts to strengthen the navy. They reasoned that the navy would largely benefit Federalists (of course, their downplaying of the navy justly exposed them to the criticism that they neglected maritime issues). On the other hand, the Invisibles wanted greater war preparedness and favored a naval war to help shipping interests.

However, one thing Republicans happily agreed on was the cost: they strenuously fought against tax increases—the public must not recognize the cost of war! When Secretary Gallatin, who opposed the war but resigned himself to it, proposed tariff increases and a revival of the internal tax system, War Hawks and Invisibles castigated him for trying "to chill the war spirit."[22] After all, 1812 was an election year, and higher taxes could lead to bad outcomes at the polls. Congress eventually agreed on future tariff increases and navigation duties but

---

[17] Nugent, *Habits of Empire*, p. 81.

[18] Johnson, *John Randolph*, pp. 143–46; Nugent, *Habits of Empire*, pp. 80–81; Tate, *Conservatism and Southern Intellectuals*, pp. 67–69; Nicholas Wood, "John Randolph of Roanoke and the Politics of Slavery in the Early Republic," *Virginia Magazine of History and Biography* (Summer 2012): 113–16.

[19] Hickey, *War of 1812*, p. 31.

[20] Risjord, *The Old Republicans*, p. 134.

[21] Hickey, *War of 1812*, pp. 31–32; Wood, *Empire of Liberty*, p. 672.

[22] Hickey, *War of 1812*, p. 33.

postponed internal taxes. Republicans settled on financing their militarism by borrowing.

In addition, the Republican Party still agreed on the basics: a war of some kind against Britain. That country also agreed on the basics: it did *not* want a war against the United States. In the spring, the British ordered increased care toward American ships, removed their boats from the American coast, and offered to give the former colonies an equal share of their licensed trade with Napoleonic Europe. But the US did not consider this adequate appeasement. In early June, Madison delivered his war message to Congress, strategically emphasizing maritime issues without mentioning Canada or Florida. He hoped for a war to rally the War Hawks behind his reelection bid against the challenger DeWitt Clinton, who tried to ally with pro-liberty Republicans and Federalist opponents of the upcoming war.[23]

In a closed session, Congressman Calhoun introduced a bill to declare war, which the House quickly and secretly passed by a relatively underwhelming vote. Republicans were for and Federalists against, and the South and West were strongly for while the North—the area most affected by the British seizures of goods and impressment—was against. Only a handful of Old Republicans in the South and Clintonian Republicans in the North voted against their party. The bill stalled in the Senate until the upper chamber passed it by a thin margin of 19-13, less than the two-thirds required for a treaty. While Federalists and Clintonians opposed the motion, the pro-naval war Invisibles provided the margin of victory.

The declaration of war flummoxed the British, who had announced earlier in the month that they would repeal their restrictions if the US dropped its ban on British imports. Furthermore, the British soon scrapped their restrictive system. To be fair, communication took longer than a month and the British had stumbled into these concessions with no plans to announce them to the US in advance. But once the Republicans learned of the British repeals, they could have abandoned the war effort. However, this was not to be, for Madison wanted the British government to completely renounce the right to impose restrictions.

---

[23] Brown, *Republic in Peril*, pp. 131–57; De Mesquita and Smith, *Spoils of War*, pp. 81–84; Hickey, *War of 1812*, pp. 33, 39, 46–47, 100–04; Nugent, *Habits of Empire*, p. 82; Risjord, *The Old Republicans*, pp. 136–37.

Walter Nugent perceptively describes the real reason for the war: "'True patriotism' required that it continue, without a reason—except to invade and annex Canada? So it did, for almost two and a half years."[24] Indeed, ten days into the war, Jefferson wrote that "the *cession* of Canada . . . must be a sine qua non at a treaty of peace."[25] He followed this up with an even more aggressive remark in August: "The acquisition of Canada . . . will give us experience for the attack of Halifax the next, and the final expulsion of England from the American continent."[26] The Empire of Liberty was now an Empire of Power.[27]

The War of 1812

Although splits between Invisibles and War Hawks dashed Republican dreams for imperial aggrandizement, the War of 1812 still led to various special privileges, including protective restrictions for manufacturers, generous terms for debt speculators, and subsidies to banking interests. It was the high tide of cronyism.

The War of 1812 differed from the American Revolutionary War, because the United States clearly aggressed in the new conflict. Although Britain did not completely eliminate maritime grievances, it made notable concessions that should have prevented or at least delayed hostilities. Of course, this had nothing to do with the real motive: conquering British Canada and Spanish Florida. If the Revolutionary War was a "just war," to quote Murray Rothbard, it is clear that the War of 1812 was an "unjust war."[28]

During these dark days, Randolph stood virtually alone in opposition among the Republicans—even Macon reluctantly supported the administration's efforts. In January 1813, he delivered a speech in Congress and blasted the pro-power Republicans for betraying their true libertarian principles:

> Love of peace, hatred of offensive war, jealousy of the
> State governments towards the General Government

---

[24] Nugent, *Habits of Empire*, pp. 82–83.

[25] Ibid., p. 85.

[26] Ibid., p. 73.

[27] Hickey, *War of 1812*, pp. 39–43; Nugent, *Habits of Empire*, pp. 82–83; Risjord, *The Old Republicans*, pp. 144–45; J. Stagg, *Mr. Madison's War* (Princeton, NJ: Princeton University Press, 1983), pp. 118–19.

[28] Murray N. Rothbard, "America's Two Just Wars," in *The Costs of War*, ed. John V. Denson (New Brunswick, NJ: Transaction Publishers, 1999), p. 119.

and of the influence of the Executive over the coordinate branches of the Government; a dread of standing armies; a loathing of public debt, taxes, and excises; tenderness for the liberty of the citizen; jealousy, Argus-eyed jealousy of the patronage of the President.[29]

Unfortunately, for this brilliant restatement of the Republican Party's founding doctrine, Randolph's Virginia constituents rewarded the Old Republican by voting him out of office in April 1813. It looked as if nothing would stop the War Hawks from total domination.[30]

But all was not well in the expansionist war. War Hawks hoped the military could quickly snatch Canada and Florida for the empire, but the Republicans disagreed over what to do with their newfound acquisition. Ironically, the major problem was that southern and western War Hawks coveted the conquest far more than their northern allies. While War Hawks wanted a land war, Invisibles stressed the naval campaign.

Recall that the Senate only barely agreed to declare war, thanks to the Invisibles. Shortly thereafter, the House passed a resolution pledging that the federal government would protect Canadians' "lives, liberty, property, and religion" in the same manner as US citizens, a clear step toward annexation.[31] However, it failed in the Senate. Although southerners supported the measure, Federalists and anti-war Clintonians, aided by the swing pro-naval war Invisibles, defeated the bill. Then, with Randolph opposing, the House passed legislation authorizing the occupation of Florida. Senator William Crawford, former Old Republican turned War Hawk, attached to the Florida bill an amendment authorizing the president to establish a temporary government in Canada to enlist the north for the Florida war. Even though southern senators supported the final bill, it failed by the razor-thin margin of 14-16 after most of the North opposed the measure. In the end, pro-power Invisibles provided a slim majority to declare war, but not a war of land conquest.

Undeterred by the rebuff, Madison fixated on the Florida question. In early 1813 Secretary Monroe continued the government's clandestine operations, conquering the last segment of West Florida. In a

---

[29] Risjord, *The Old Republicans*, p. 19.

[30] Johnson, *John Randolph*, pp. 152–54.

[31] *History of Congress* (June–July 1812), p. 322.

virtual side affair to the War of 1812, General Andrew Jackson of Tennessee fought the Creek Indians, allies of the Spanish, in the Mississippi Territory and Florida. While the United States never conquered Canada, slowly but surely the empire bit away at Florida.[32]

Despite the territorial setbacks, Republicans still used the war to distribute new special privileges. First came the manufacturers. In July 1812 Congress followed up on its earlier pledge to raise revenue by increasing tariffs until a year after hostilities ended and a new navigation act that taxed goods on foreign ships. The legislature also continued nonimportation of British products and restricted exports to Canada. When combined with the British blockade of the coast, the trade legislation resulted in economic autarky. From 1811 to 1814, exports collapsed by 89 percent, imports 75 percent, and customs revenue 55 percent. The trade and shipping barriers subsidized domestic manufactures and inefficient methods of land transportation. In particular, Francis Cabot Lowell of the Boston Associates, wealthy businessmen descendent from the old Essex Junto, founded the Boston Manufacturing Company in 1813, quickly earning a profit of 25 percent. The Federalist Boston Associates eagerly looked forward to continued federal assistance after the war.[33]

The debt speculators stood next in line. Federal expenditures exploded 330 percent to pay for increases in the army, navy, and war bureaucracy. Several states, especially New York and Pennsylvania, lived on the government fat and experienced wartime booms in their manufacturing and real estate sectors. Pennsylvania returned the favor by reelecting Madison in 1812. If Congress could not raise revenue from taxes to finance such spending, it had to resort to other means, allowing the Treasury to issue long-term debt securities. Banks and wealthy citizens in the Mid-Atlantic cities of New York, Philadelphia,

---

[32] Brown, *Republic in Peril*, pp. 126–29; *History of Congress*, pp. 298, 322–26, 1683, 1691–94; Nugent, *Habits of Empire*, pp. 115–20; Wood, *Empire of Liberty*, pp. 686–87.

[33] Adam Bellow, *In Praise of Nepotism* (New York: Doubleday, 2003), pp. 320–21; Stuart Brandes, *Warhogs* (Lexington: The University Press of Kentucky, 1997), p. 55; *Historical Statistics, Colonial Times to 1957*, p. 538; *Historical Statistics of the United States*, vol. 5, ed. Richard Sutch and Susan Carter (New York: Cambridge University Press, 2006), p. 82; Douglas A. Irwin, *Clashing over Commerce* (Chicago: The University of Chicago Press, 2017), pp. 120–21; Curtis Nettels, *The Emergence of a National Economy* (New York: Holt, Rinehart and Winston, 1962), pp. 275–76, 338–40; Lawrence Peskin, *Manufacturing Revolution* (Baltimore, MD: The Johns Hopkins University Press, 2003), pp. 134, 209; George Taylor, *The Transportation Revolution* (New York: Holt, Rinehart and Winston, 1951), p. 234.

Baltimore, and Washington, DC, gobbled the investments up. The public debt, after declining from $57 million in 1808 to $45 million in 1811 (21 percent), increased to $127 million in 1815 (182 percent).

Most prominently, in 1813, a private syndicate led by Stephen Girard and John Jacob Astor subscribed to two-thirds of a $16 million loan. On top of earning a 0.25 percent commission, they purchased the bonds below face value (at eighty-eight cents on the dollar) and with depreciated state bank notes (an estimated specie value of forty-two cents on the dollar). If they could use the government to eliminate their investment's risk, they would reap a massive profit. Similar to Robert Morris' debt speculators, they pushed for the chartering of a new central bank whose stock could be purchased with government securities to increase the value of their bond holdings. The influential financiers embarked on their goal by first lobbying for their Philadelphia lawyer, Alexander J. Dallas, to be appointed Treasurer in October 1814.[34]

Finally, Republicans pleased the state banking interests. The exigencies of wartime finance led the Treasury to print money in the form of interest-bearing notes redeemable in specie in one year. The people could use them to pay taxes, though they were not legal tender for private transactions. However, the public did not use the high-denomination Treasury notes. Instead, banks primarily purchased the notes and held them as reserves. From June 1812 to February 1815, Treasury notes in circulation increased to $15.5 million. This subsidy to the banks—increasing their reserves—led to significant inflation. While the money supply had remained constant from 1810 to 1812, from 1812 to 1814 it increased 29 percent (14 percent per year). Similarly, though the cost of goods stayed constant in the two years prior to the war, the increase in the money supply and collapse in imports increased prices by 39 percent from 1812 to 1814 (18 percent per year).

Historians often argue that the demise of the Bank of the United States in 1811 caused the prevailing free-banking system to recklessly expand credit during the war years.[35] In reality, though the estimated number of total banks increased from 117 to 247 between 1811 and

[34] Brandes, *Warhogs*, p. 61; Philip Burch, *Elites in American History*, vol. 1 (New York: Holmes & Meier Publishers, 1981), pp. 97–99, 269; Hickey, *War of 1812*, pp. 104, 118–19, 235–38; *Historical Statistics*, 5, p. 80; Nettels, *Emergence of a National Economy*, pp. 331–32, 335; Gregory May, *Jefferson's Treasure* (Washington, DC: Regnery History, 2018), pp. 215–17.

[35] Roger Lowenstein, *America's Bank* (New York: Penguin Press, 2015), p. 3.

1815, no system of free banking existed and state governments still intervened. The government's augmentation of bank reserves, not deregulation, caused the monetary expansion and increase in prices. With or without the BUS, the same inflation would have occurred.

The central government's policy to increase bank reserves in the form of Treasury notes would have resulted in a sustained credit expansion were it not for the antiwar New England Federalist banks, who refused to purchase any debt. After banks in the Mid-Atlantic, South, and West purchased the Treasury notes with banknotes and deposits, the federal government spent this money on New England goods to facilitate the war. New England financial institutions then presented the notes and deposits for specie redemption at their subsidized rivals' branches in the rest of the country. The adverse clearing mechanism caused specie to flow to the Northeast. If this continued indefinitely, then to avoid illiquidity the expanding banks outside of New England would have to contract credit, jeopardizing the wartime funding measures. But the federal and state governments allowed banks to breach contract and suspend specie payments in August 1814.

Thus, the Republicans subsidized banks by first increasing their reserves and then bailing them out when they should have failed. Shorn of specie redemption, the banks continued to engage in credit expansion and made lucrative profits of 12 to 20 percent in 1815. Suspension lasted until February 1817, and those who sued banks for failing to honor their obligations rarely succeeded in court. The banks looked forward to future assistance from a more permanent relationship with the federal government.[36]

During the war, New England remained upset. States' rights doctrine flourished and the rank and file contemplated radical nullification and secession reforms. But the result of their leaders' efforts, the Hartford Convention of December 1814, called for only "moderation and firmness" and amendments to incentivize New England to remain

---

[36] *Historical Statistics*, 3, p. 181; Nettels, *Emergence of a National Economy*, pp. 332–35; Murray N. Rothbard, "The History of Money and Banking Before the Twentieth Century," in Rothbard, *A History of Money and Banking in the United States*, ed. Joseph Salerno (Auburn, AL: Mises Institute, 2002), pp. 73–84; Peter Rousseau and Richard Sylla, "Emerging Financial Markets and Early US Growth," *Explorations in Economic History* (January 2005): 24; Richard Timberlake, *Gold, Greenbacks, and the Constitution* (Berryville, VA: The George Durell Foundation, 1991), p. 16; Richard Timberlake, *Monetary Policy in the United States* (Chicago: The University of Chicago Press, 1993), pp. 13–18.

in the Union.[37] Prominent Federalist leaders, such as the venerable John Jay, Congressman Daniel Webster of New Hampshire, and Timothy Pickering, praised the convention's report. On the other hand, the mass populace complained bitterly because they hoped for more radical measures.[38]

Thanks to diplomatic skill and British war fatigue, the Republicans emerged relatively unscathed. The Treaty of Ghent, ratified by the Senate in February 1815, restored the status quo, mentioning none of the maritime issues that supposedly drove America to declare war against Great Britain (the end of the Napoleonic Wars made these issues dead letters). The United States believed it emerged the unambiguous winner after General Jackson smashed the British in his defense of New Orleans in the month prior.

Overall, the policies Republicans pursued during the War of 1812 impacted the nation's history more than the war itself. The corrupted Republican Party totally embraced statism to expand their empire. With the conflict over, Madison and his new National Republicans could turn to adopting what Norman Risjord describes as "the old Hamiltonian system" and "the final abandonment of 'the principles of 1798'": a national bank, a protective tariff, and a national system of internal improvements.[39] Indeed, the Republicans had long discarded the compact theory and laissez-faire economics, embracing Hamiltonian policies with little restraint.[40]

Postwar Economic Nationalism

The rest of Madison's second term witnessed the National Republicans fortifying their Old Order Empire: a second central bank, peacetime restrictive tariffs, and transportation subsidies. They only suffered defeat on the internal improvement issue because Madison envisioned an even grander system. Overall, the corrupted party hammered the final nails in the reform coffin brought by the Jeffersonian Revolution of 1800.

---

[37] Hickey, *War of 1812*, p. 281.

[38] *American Political Leaders*, p. 318; James Banner, *To the Hartford Convention* (New York: Alfred A. Knopf, 1970), pp. 308–18, 327–46; Hickey, *War of 1812*, pp. 222, 274–83, 291–300, 306; William Watkins, *Reclaiming the American Revolution* (Oakland, CA: The Independent Institute, 2004), pp. 90–93.

[39] Risjord, *The Old Republicans*, p. 161.

[40] Hickey, *War of 1812*, pp. 284–301, 316; Nugent, *Habits of Empire*, pp. 85–90.

Madison's December 1815 message to Congress discarded the fashionable laissez-faire theories the Republican Party paid lip service to: "However wise the theory may be which leaves to the sagacity of individuals the application of their industry and resources, there are . . . exceptions to the general rule."[41] But the free market Randolph, now back in Congress, mustered "a desperate, tho feeble stand against the new system which *out-Hamiltons* Alexander Hamilton."[42]

First, National Republicans desired a second national bank. During the war, Astor and Girard initiated the drive to increase the value of government debt by making securities exchangeable for bank stock. Astor even nixed concurrent proposals that allowed investors to capitalize a new bank with real estate mortgages. In the fall of 1814, their new pawn, Treasurer Dallas, outlined plans for a central bank along their recommendations. However, Congress resisted because of the blatant profits Astor and Girard would amass, greatly emasculating Dallas' proposal into a privately owned commercial bank. However, Madison vetoed the bill because the projected bank was not close enough to the government. Congress responded with a new bill in February 1815 that met the president's objections, but news of peace postponed efforts to create another central bank.[43]

Madison revived the plan in December. By this time, the country's monetary affairs had sunk calamitously, because the state banks had not yet resumed specie payments. Since the war's beginning, banknotes and deposits had increased far beyond the available supply of gold and silver, posing a major problem for returning to the specie standard. Contemporaries did not even consider the option of dollar devaluation and this left Congress with the options of either deliberately contracting the money supply by retiring Treasury notes, waiting for increased production of goods and services to lower prices and bring specie into the country, or engaging in a sleight of hand with a new central bank that could lend to state banks and continue inflating. Given the lack of hard money sentiment among National

---

[41] George Dangerfield, *The Awakening of American Nationalism* (New York: Harper & Row, 1965), p. 6.

[42] Daniel Peart, *Lobbyists and the Making of US Tariff Policy* (Baltimore, MD: The Johns Hopkins University Press, 2018), p. 25.

[43] John Haeger, *John Jacob Astor* (Detroit, MI: Wayne State University Press, 1991), pp. 143–44; Bray Hammond, *Banks and Politics in America* (Princeton, NJ: Princeton University Press, 1957), pp. 231–32; Hickey, *War of 1812*, pp. 256–58.

Republicans, they unsurprisingly chose the last path.[44]

After Madison's message, Speaker Clay, who publicly recanted his past heresies by recognizing the benefits and constitutionality of central banking (as did Congressman Samuel Smith), started the process to charter a new institution. He instructed the inveterate nationalist Calhoun, chairman of the House Committee on a National Currency, to work with Secretary Dallas. Calhoun, whom Joseph Dorfman accurately characterizes as proclaiming "the policies of high Federalism," introduced the bill in January 1816.[45] It was in most respects a replica of Hamilton's old BUS, only larger. The proposed bank in Philadelphia possessed a twenty year monopoly charter with one-fifth government ownership and a capitalization of $35 million (instead of $10 million). The bill also required the bank to give the government a payment of $1.5 million. Of the $28 million in private capital, $21 million could be purchased with government securities and $7 million with specie—thereby boosting the prices of government debt. Similar to Hamilton's Bank, Dallas' Bank received most government deposits, a vast subsidy.

Quite importantly, Calhoun, among other National Republicans, defended its constitutionality using the moribund coinage clause. In spirit with the ultra-Federalists who led the Constitutional Convention, Calhoun argued that the coinage clause empowered the federal government to regulate the nation's currency. Moreover, he declared that since the Constitution forbade states from issuing paper money, it also forbade states from chartering banks that could issue paper money. Therefore, a national bank was the proper method by which the federal government could constitutionally regulate the nation's money supply.[46]

Randolph answered Calhoun, blasting the bank as unnecessary and contributing to the formation of "one great consolidated nation, under one form of law."[47] To the Old Republican, it "would be an engine

---

[44] Hammond, *Banks and Politics*, pp. 232–33; Murray N. Rothbard, *The Mystery of Banking* (Auburn, AL: Mises Institute, 2008), p. 198; Timberlake, *Monetary Policy*, pp. 18–22.

[45] Joseph Dorfman, *The Economic Mind in American Civilization*, vol. 1 (New York: Viking Press, 1946), p. 362.

[46] Hammond, *Banks and Politics*, pp. 233–39, 243–44, 253–54; Susan Hoffman, *Politics and Banking* (Baltimore, MD: The John Hopkins University Press, 2001), pp. 46–48.

[47] Risjord, *The Old Republicans*, p. 163.

of irresistible power in the hands of any administration" aggravating, not inhibiting, state banks' credit expansion.[48] Still under the sway of the hard money John Taylor, Randolph favored a purely private bank that would sever what he called the "monstrous alliance," conceiving an institution somewhat similar to that of Jefferson's earlier *Note of Agenda* to make the government deal only in specie and not bank money.[49] Similarly, Senator Nathaniel Macon "still [could not] find the authority for a bank in the constitution of the US"[50]

Unlike earlier attempts, Astor and Girard did not express any public support for fear of increasing opposition, privately communicating with Dallas and Madison during the legislative process. Consequently, Congress was more sympathetic, but the House still narrowly passed the bill. Fifteen Federalists provided the crucial margin of victory, disgusting Randolph for demonstrating their lack of "courage, . . . talent, [and] integrity to conduct an opposition."[51] The Senate followed up in April and Madison soon signed the bill. The government-bank partnership was back in full force: National Republicans birthed the Second Bank of the United States into existence. The Bank's inflationary capabilities pleased Astor and Girard, businesses eager for cheap credit, and state banks hungry for additional reserves.[52]

After chartering a new central bank, Congress turned to protective tariffs. Jefferson and Madison's mercantilist trade policies protected inefficient manufacturers at the expense of more economical British firms and the public. In particular, the number of textile mills increased from eighty-seven in 1809 to 243 in 1814. Despite the continuation of wartime tariffs, many manufacturing companies suffered losses after commerce revived with Great Britain: though wholesale prices declined 9 percent from 1814 to 1815, prices of domestically produced goods actually remained constant while prices of imported products plummeted 17 percent. Americans accused British manufacturers of "dumping," or selling below their cost of production. Some

---

[48] Rothbard, *Mystery of Banking*, p. 200.

[49] Risjord, *The Old Republicans*, p. 166.

[50] Ibid., p. 167.

[51] Ibid., p. 167.

[52] John Devanny, "A Loathing of Public Debt, Taxes, and Excises," *Virginia Magazine of History and Biography* (Winter 2001): 406–11; Haeger, *John Jacob Astor*, p. 199; Hammond, *Banks and Politics*, pp. 239–44; Risjord, *The Old Republicans*, pp. 162–63, 167–68; Rothbard, *Mystery of Banking*, pp. 200–01; Arthur A. Schlesinger Jr., *The Age of Jackson* (Boston, MA: Little, Brown and Company, 1945), pp. 228–29.

statements by British politicians gave credibility to such a claim. In reality, more efficient British manufacturers only tried to sell their wares at market prices after international trade reopened. But US companies continued to complain, and the National Republican Party wanted to assist this constituency.[53]

In February 1815, the House directed Dallas to write a new peace-time tariff schedule that could replace wartime rates. The Treasurer's report, which paid homage to Hamilton's *Report on Manufactures*, proposed new tariffs that would raise revenue and protect industries. Dallas explicitly wanted to protect existing manufacturing interests, particularly cotton and woolen textiles, but not new industries, such as luxury goods. His rates were lower than the wartime schedule's but still very generous in a time of peace: most importantly, 33.33 percent and 28 percent on cotton and woolen textiles, respectively. Significantly, Dallas stressed a twenty-five-cent minimum valuation on cotton textiles, which meant any imported cotton product priced lower, say at nine cents, would be assessed as if its price were twenty-five cents. In other words, instead of a three-cent duty on a nine-cent cotton cloth (the 33.33 percent rate), there would be a duty of eight and one-third cents on the nine cent cloth—a whopping rate of 93 percent. This blatantly regressive tax, lobbied for by Boston Associate Francis Cabot Lowell of the Boston Manufacturing Company, drastically raised actual tariff rates on cheap imported cloth relative to expensive cloth.

However, other interests, particularly New England shippers and southern planters, wanted low tariffs. At this time, only the Mid-Atlantic staunchly favored high tariffs on industrial products. When the Chairman of the Ways and Means Committee, South Carolina's William Lowndes, received Dallas' report, the moderate protectionist revised some rates downward. In particular, Lowndes reduced the rates on cotton and woolen textiles to 25 percent. Happily for Dallas (and Lowell), the minimum valuation remained in place.

The House debated the new tariff schedule in March 1816. Interestingly, southern National Republicans, though their economic interests should have pushed them to lower tariffs, supported moderate protectionism. They did so for national defense reasons and from the expectation that the South might embark on manufacturing in the

---

[53] *Historical Statistics*, 3, p. 193; Irwin, *Clashing over Commerce*, pp. 126, 132–33; Wood, *Empire of Liberty*, pp. 702–03.

future. The free trade Randolph bitterly fought the minimum valuation, which the Boston Associates' lackey, Congressman Daniel Webster of New Hampshire, strenuously defended. Randolph tried to strike the privilege out because it taxed merchants and slaveholders to benefit cotton manufacturers—a clear attempt to rally New England shippers and southern National Republicans against the bill. But Calhoun rebuffed Randolph, declaring that cotton manufacturers warranted protection, including the minimum valuation. The House passed the tariff and the Senate followed shortly thereafter.

Thus, the National Republicans adopted another Federalist policy; enough politicians could see the resemblance between old and new. In June 1816, Federalist Senator Rufus King wrote: "As respect Taxes, Army, Navy, and some other points, the practice of the Republicans now seems to be the same as that of the Federalists formerly, but I am not inclined to oppose measures proposed or done by Republicans, which the Federalists proposed and did in former times."[54]

The new peacetime Tariff of 1816 boasted an average duty of 27 as a percentage of total imports and benefitted manufacturers more than prewar rates in many respects, particularly the minimum valuation. But for the industrialists, moderate mercantilism did not go far enough. New societies soon sprouted and clamored for more assistance, such as the New York-based American Society for the Encouragement of Domestic Manufactures, which included among its members Presidents Adams, Jefferson, and Madison. Protectionist periodicals, such as the *Niles Weekly Register*, also increased their circulation.[55]

After enacting tariff legislation, Congress prepared for the upcoming presidential election. Everyone understood that the Republican candidate would crush his Federalist opponent, and the Republican nomination in the congressional caucus proved to be more important than the election itself. Two Virginians led the race: Secretary of War William Crawford, who had long resided in Georgia, and the National Republican Secretary of State James Monroe. Although Crawford supported the SBUS, moderately protective tariffs, and federally funded transportation projects, the former Old Republican championed frugality and advocated stringent budget cuts. His followers, particularly

---

[54] Peart, *Making of US Tariff Policy*, p. 27.

[55] *Historical Statistics*, 5, p. 510; Irwin, *Clashing*, pp. 126–35; Dangerfield, *Awakening*, p. 15; Peart, *Making of US Tariff Policy*, pp. 13–30; Murray N. Rothbard, *The Panic of 1819* (Auburn, AL: Mises Institute, 2007), p. 210.

Martin Van Buren's Albany Regency, were known as "Radicals." However, Crawford sabotaged his chances when he withdrew his name two months before the caucus, with the apparent understanding that he succeed Monroe in eight years. But when Crawford reentered his name at the last minute, the contest was still on. One hundred and nineteen Republicans voted; sixty-five for Monroe, fifty-four for Crawford. Unsurprisingly, Monroe destroyed Rufus King in the fall.[56]

But not all was well for the National Republicans. Before the election, they passed the Compensation Act. This law raised the salary of congressmen, which had not increased since 1789, from $6 to $12 per day. But they got greedy: the pay raise was effective immediately, meaning the current Congress voted to double its own pay and present the taxpayers with the bill. The people, struggling in the war's aftermath, would not stand for what they considered blatant cronyism. In the fall elections, the furious voters kicked out two-thirds of congressmen. Many of the new representatives, while not doctrinaire Old Republicans, championed reform more than their predecessors. The stunned lame-duck Congress returned in December for one final session before Monroe's inauguration in March 1817. It repealed the Compensation Act and the legislature later settled on $8 per day.[57]

Momentously, Congress decided to push forward with the final piece of the Hamiltonian program: federally funded internal improvements. In his 1816 congressional message, Madison recommended such a system but stressed that an amendment accompany the legislation. The president maintained multiple reasons for this stipulation. First, the opportunist had already contradicted himself on central banking, and if he wanted to cement his legacy as the nation's preeminent strict constructionist he had to require an amendment. Even on this point Madison was inconsistent, because earlier in the year he signed a bill appropriating $100,000 to continue constructing the National Road without raising any constitutional objections. Second, Madison wanted the amendment to clear up any ambiguities and pave the way for a clear expansion of interventionism. Unlike the

[56] Andrew Browning, *The Panic of 1819* (Columbia: University of Missouri Press, 2019), pp. 208, 294; Burch, *Elites in American History*, 1, pp. 268, 272; Dangerfield, *Awakening of American Nationalism*, pp. 22–23, 30; Risjord, *The Old Republicans*, pp. 228–31.

[57] Daniel Howe, *What Hath God Wrought* (New York: Oxford University Press, 2007), pp. 86–87; Risjord, *The Old Republicans*, pp. 180–82; Wood, *Empire of Liberty*, pp. 718–21.

original Jeffersonian approach, which demanded amendments as a roadblock to restrict government power, Madison wanted to use them as enabling devices.[58]

However, Madison failed to convince National Republicans, who thought the Constitution already contained the power. One such nationalist was Calhoun, an enthusiastic proponent of federal handouts to transportation companies. The South Carolinian responded to Madison's plea with a bill that would use the government's SBUS bonus ($1.5 million) and future dividends from stock ownership to subsidize roads and canals. In this way, Congress would divert revenue from paying down the bloated federal debt to land speculators, transportation companies, and mercantile businesses. Calhoun defended its constitutionality with the general welfare clause and precedent—the Louisiana Purchase. His argument for broad constructionism practically mimicked Hamilton's: the Constitution "was not intended as a thesis for the logician to exercise his ingenuity on. It ought to be construed with plain good sense."[59] In addition, the Hamiltonian buttressed his case with the argument that federally funded internal improvements would "bind the republic together" and prevent "the greatest of calamities—*disunion*."[60]

But here, as always, the topic of internal improvements ran into difficulties. While Clay firmly supported the bill, Randolph fought it as expected. In addition, the young Philip Barbour of Virginia, rapidly shaking off his previous wartime nationalism and transforming into one of the state's preeminent Old Republicans, bitterly attacked the proposed legislation on constitutional grounds. In the end, the House moved that the funds had to be distributed to the states according to population and the states had to concede to distribution. After a bitter struggle, Congress barely passed the bill before Monroe's inauguration. Voting divided along sectional lines—National Republicans desired federal improvements to bind the empire, but did not want rival states to benefit more than their home turf. New England voted nay because the region had already constructed roads and wanted to prevent western migration; the Mid-Atlantic, particularly canal-hungry New York, enthusiastically voted yea; the Upper South opposed;

---

[58] Howe, *What Hath God Wrought*, p. 86; Risjord, *The Old Republicans*, p. 168.

[59] John Larson, *Internal Improvement* (Chapel Hill: The University of North Carolina Press, 2001), p. 65.

[60] Dangerfield, *Awakening of American Nationalism*, p. 18.

and the Lower South split. Vocal opposition came from the new Old Republican senator from South Carolina, William Smith, a vehement opponent of the statist Calhoun and Lowndes.

But Madison shockingly responded with a veto. According to the president, the bill was too decentralized and Congress failed to pass an amendment. He arrogantly sent the bill back to Congress, confident the legislature could produce an even more nationalist bill and an amendment. Madison, as usual, wanted to have it both ways: a National Republican who harkened back to old-school Federalism, and a nominal adherent to Jeffersonian principles. In the end, believing his legacy secured, the president retired "without denying either his nationalist instincts or his deep suspicion of laissez faire."[61]

The Republican Revolution of 1800 ended in a resounding failure. Jefferson and Madison threw the Federalist Party out of power on the basis of strict constructionism, limited government, and states' rights. But power corrupted the Republican Party into moderation and then outright privilege granting. As the libertarian Republicans morphed into moderate Republicans, then War Hawks and Invisibles, and finally National Republicans, cronyism reversed its gradual decline and lurched upwards. National Republicans eagerly looked forward to continuing the trend.

---

[61] Dangerfield, *Awakening of American Nationalism*, p. 20. See also William Belko, *Philip Pendleton Barbour in Jacksonian America* (Tuscaloosa: University of Alabama Press, 2016), pp. 55–56, 66–67; Dangerfield, *Awakening of American Nationalism*, pp. 18–20; Howe, *What Hath God Wrought*, p. 88; Larson, *Internal Improvement*, pp. 63–69, 274; Risjord, *The Old Republicans*, pp. 168–74, 186.

PART IV

THE ERA OF CORRUPTION, 1817–1829

CHAPTER 10

ERECTING THE AMERICAN SYSTEM: THE MONETARY INFRASTRUCTURE

The Panic of 1819

In what Robert Remini describes as the "Era of Corruption," Speaker Henry Clay's "American System" resurrected the Federalists' empire-building policies: central banking to coordinate inflation, protective tariffs to subsidize manufacturers, federally funded internal improvements to bind the country together, greater authority of Washington, DC, over settlers' rights, and imperialist diplomacy to enlarge the domain.[1] In the process, National Republicans and friendly Federalists systematically looted the public purse for private enrichment. However, the Panic of 1819 complicated their plans. The central blame can be laid on the Second Bank of the United States, which continued the wartime inflation and fostered a business cycle. In the aftermath, National Republicans protected the Bank and increased its control over the economy, rekindling controversy over monetary and banking policy.

Stephen Girard, who previously lobbied for the central bank to increase the value of his bond holdings, estimated that the profits from the new Bank "will be immense."[2] Girard turned into the largest shareholder, and John Jacob Astor ascended to the New York branch's presidency. Both men also became two of the five government directors, along with William Jones, a former Philadelphia merchant and prior secretary of the Navy; James Buchanan, investment partner of Congressman Samuel Smith in the Baltimore mercantile firm Smith

---

[1] Robert Remini, *Andrew Jackson,* vol. II (New York: History Book Club, 1998), p. 15 and Robert Remini, *Henry Clay* (New York: W.W. Norton & Company, 1991), pp. 174, 225.

[2] Donald Adams, *Finance and Enterprise in Early America* (Philadelphia: University of Pennsylvania Press, 1978), p. 57.

& Buchanan and soon to be president of the SBUS' Baltimore branch; and Pierce Butler, a former delegate to the Constitutional Convention.

Unfortunately for Girard and Astor, they suffered a setback with the election of the main office's president. No shareholder could control more than thirty votes, but Baltimore financiers circumvented this restriction with proxies. Lawyer George Williams, the most notorious example, owned 1,172 shares under different clients, allowing him to amass thirty-nine times the voting power allowed. In fact, just *fifteen* individuals controlled 75 percent of the Baltimore branch's shares legally held by sixteen thousand individuals, allowing the group to elect the inexperienced Jones to the presidency. Astor and Girard bitterly resented the election, realizing it weakened their influence over the Bank.[3]

Under Jones' aegis, the SBUS opened in January 1817 and inflated, increasing its notes and deposits from $13.1 million in 1817 to $20.6 million by 1818 (57 percent). In particular, it lent $6 million to the large state banks in New York, Philadelphia, Baltimore, and Virginia to help them resume specie payments, which became federal policy in February. The SBUS' loans provided an enormous windfall to the fractional reserve institutions, because they used the loans not to return to gold and silver convertibility but instead as reserves for further expansion. No wonder, then, that the number of state banks grew from 212 in 1815 to 338 in 1818. In total, from 1815 to 1817 the money supply increased from $75 million to $94 million, or by 25 percent (12 percent per year). The SBUS' southern and western branches led the credit expansion, but in Baltimore, the swashbucklers who previously captured the SBUS engaged in outright fraud.[4]

---

[3] *American Political Leaders* (Washington, DC: CQ Press, 2000), pp. 127, 290; Andrew Browning, *The Panic of 1819* (Columbia: University of Missouri Press, 2019), pp. 147–48, 314; John Haeger, *John Jacob Astor* (Detroit, MI: Wayne State University Press, 1991), p. 201; Bray Hammond, *Banks and Politics in America* (Princeton, NJ: Princeton University Press, 1957), pp. 231–32, 251–52.

[4] Browning, *Panic of 1819*, pp. 152–54; *Historical Statistics of the United States*, vol. 3, ed. Richard Sutch and Susan Carter (New York: Cambridge University Press, 2006), p. 632; Murray N. Rothbard, "The History of Money and Banking Before the Twentieth Century," in Rothbard, *A History of Money and Banking in the United States*, ed. Joseph Salerno (Auburn, AL: Mises Institute, 2002), pp. 82–84; Peter Rousseau and Richard Sylla, "Emerging Financial Markets and Early US Growth," *Explorations in Economic History* (January 2005): 24; Richard Timberlake, *Monetary Policy in the United States* (Chicago: The University of Chicago Press, 1993), p. 30.

Branch President Buchanan and bank cashier James McCulloch initially loaned themselves $673,000 to speculate in the Bank's stock. Not satisfied with this investment on the Bank's behalf, they continued to dig into the public trough. Buchanan and Williams, the deceptively large shareholder, loaned $2.5 million to themselves and McCulloch $574,000. To do so, they falsely claimed to secure their loans with collateral and insisted that the directors approved their actions. In reality, they did not, but Buchanan and Williams paid off President Jones with $18,000 of hush money, who later made a cool $250,000 off his own stock speculation. The two also bribed the Baltimore branch's bank teller with $50,000. Buchanan, McCulloch, and Williams severely violated the Bank's charter for their own personal aggrandizement.[5]

The federal government added to the SBUS' largesse with its own reckless land policies. Congress pushed back due dates for land debts and issued $4 million of "Mississippi stock" as payment for the old Yazoo land claims, receivable as cash for land purchases in the soon-to-be states of Alabama and Mississippi.[6] When combined with SBUS' monetary expansion, Congress' policies exploded land indebtedness. The US only sold 4.5 million acres by 1813, with total indebtedness to the government at $2.1 million. In 1815, it sold 1.1 million acres and the total unpaid balance stood at $3.7 million. But speculators soon borrowed from banks to make initial down payments to the government, anticipating endlessly rising prices. Land purchases totaled 5.6 million acres in 1819 alone and total indebtedness ballooned to $24 million, a 548 percent increase from 1815. Land prices increased from $2.20 to $3.37 per acre (53 percent).[7]

The credit expansion led to abnormally low interest rates, which caused an economic boom in farm improvement projects, land speculation, buildings, slaves, turnpikes, ships, and steamboats. Stock transactions increased so much that traders formed the New York Stock Exchange in March 1817. Even though overall prices fell 3 percent from 1816 to 1818 (1.5 percent per year), prices in the aforementioned sectors actually rose. Overall, real GDP and industrial production increased by 6 percent and 10 percent, respectively (3 percent and 5 percent per year).

---

[5] Browning, *Panic of 1819*, pp. 314–15; Hammond, *Banks*, p. 261.

[6] Daniel Feller, *The Public Lands in Jacksonian Politics* (Madison: The University of Wisconsin Press, 1984), p. 18.

[7] Ibid., pp. 11–12, 18, 20, 22; Sarah Quinn, *American Bonds* (Princeton, NJ: Princeton University Press, 2019), pp. 25–29.

However, the economic boom was unsustainable, because the Treasury concurrently attempted to resume specie convertibility. Secretary of the Treasury William Crawford, leader of the small-government Radicals, recognized that the monetary contraction necessary for such a goal required retiring the Treasury notes currently serving as bank reserves. After 1815, resuming trade and winding down the wartime apparatus caused Congress to run surpluses from 1816 to 1819, the first time since 1811. Consequently, as the public debt decreased, the supply of the wartime Treasury notes declined from $15.5 million to zero.

This decline would have led to credit contraction if it had not been for the SBUS pumping new reserves into the system. The federal government attempted to have it both ways: a resumption of specie payments and an easy adjustment process for the state banks. But this could not continue forever, thanks to the adverse clearing mechanism. The state banks still refused to resume specie payments while the SBUS' notes and deposits remained redeemable. Consequently, by mid-1818, specie reserves at the Bank began to decline. If conditions stayed the same, the breaking point would come sooner rather than later. The SBUS had to contract credit, and contract it did.[8]

From mid-1818 to mid-1819, a revolution occurred at the SBUS. First, the financial institution sharply contracted credit, calling in loans, refusing to make new loans, and pressing upon state banks for specie. Its notes and deposits declined from $20.6 million in 1818 to $12.3 million in 1819, a contraction of 41 percent. The contraction caused the money supply to deflate from $94 million in 1817 to $84 million in 1818 (11 percent). Second, Congress investigated the Bank's illicit practices, culminating in the corrupt Jones' resignation in January 1819. By March, the public discovered the Baltimore branch's fraudulent dealings and its $1.5 million loss. These revelations were enormously bad timing for Congress, because a month earlier it had rejected proposals to repeal the Bank's charter.

---

[8] Joseph Davis, "An Annual Index of US Industrial Production," *Quarterly Journal of Economics* (November 2004): 1189; *Historical Statistics*, 3, p. 181; *Historical Statistics of the United States*, vol. 5, ed. Richard Sutch and Susan Carter (New York: Cambridge University Press, 2006), p. 80; Louis Johnston and Samuel Williamson, "What Was the US GDP Then?" *Measuringworth.com*; Remini, *Andrew Jackson*, 2, p. 42; Rothbard, "History of Money," pp. 86–89; Murray N. Rothbard, *The Panic of 1819* (Auburn, AL: Mises Institute, 2007), pp. 7–14; Timberlake, *Monetary Policy*, pp. 15, 18–26.

Although analysts subsequently described it as the Panic of 1819, no stock market crash or dramatic bank runs occurred. Despite this, everyone could see that a crash had happened, and Thomas Jefferson wrote to his old friend John Adams: "the paper bubble is then burst."[9] Wholesale prices collapsed 15 percent from 1818 to 1819 and bottomed out in 1821, for a total decline of 31 percent. Prices for exports also plummeted, crushing the indebted South. After rising 57 percent from 1815 to 1818, abundant crop harvests in Europe and a concurrent British contraction caused export staple prices in Charleston to plummet 40 percent from 1818 to 1819, for a total decline of 54 percent by 1821.[10]

The severe monetary and price pressure led to massive bankruptcies as interest rates increased and borrowers defaulted. Public land sales, slave trading, agricultural improvements, steamships, turnpikes, and other projects floundered. The distress was the most acute in the cities, where widespread unemployment afflicted factory workers, artisans, mechanics, and craftsmen. From 1818 to 1819, daily agricultural wage rates shrunk 65 percent, and wages for unskilled turnpike workers dropped 84 percent. Many westerners returned to barter conditions and used grain and whiskey as money. Although the number of state banks increased from 338 in 1818 to 341 in 1819, the total had dropped to 267 by 1822, a decline of 22 percent. In *A Short History of Paper Money and Banking* (1833), William Gouge aptly summed up the crisis: "The Bank was saved, and the people were ruined."[11]

Some state banks were also saved, thanks to a suspension of specie payments. The states, Janus-faced about the privileges they continually granted to their financial institutions, aided them in their latest breach of contract. For instance, while Maryland and Pennsylvania passed laws compelling state banks to resume specie payments or forfeit their charters, they allowed them to suspend redemption to money brokers, the traveling arbitrageurs most likely to press banks for convertibility. In addition, Maryland required a crippling $500

---

[9] George Dangerfield, *The Awakening of American Nationalism* (New York: Harper & Row, 1965), p. 86.

[10] Browning, *Panic of 1819*, p. 183; *Historical Statistics*, 3, p. 181; *Historical Statistics of the United States, Colonial Times to 1957* (Washington D.C., 1960), p. 120; Rothbard, "History of Money," pp. 88–89; Rothbard, *Panic of 1819*, p. 20; Rousseau and Sylla, "Emerging Financial Markets," p. 24; Timberlake, *Monetary Policy*, p. 30.

[11] William Gouge, *A Short History of Paper Money and Banking* (Auburn, AL: Mises Institute, 2007), p. 10.

license for money brokers and a \$20,000 bond to operate a money broker business. Commenting on the banking situation, in April 1821 the Philadelphia merchant and State Senator Condy Raguet wrote to the British economist David Ricardo, a free trade and hard money follower of Adam Smith, admitting "the whole of our population are either stockholders of banks or in debt to them. It is not the *interest* of the first to press the banks and the rest are *afraid*."[12] Banks only resumed specie payments in the early 1820s.[13]

Thanks to the liquidation process, the downturn did not appreciably affect real economic activity. Real GDP and industrial production only declined by 1.9 percent and 4.1 percent in 1819 before increasing from 1819 to 1822 by 4.4 percent and 6.3 percent per year. Even the high unemployment in the cities insignificantly affected the overall country, because most people still worked in agriculture, and a modern study estimates the nationwide unemployment rate at only 4 percent in 1819. However, many members of the public truly believed they experienced a severe depression, because they either lived in the cities or focused on nominal prices. They failed to understand that the decline in nominal values was an illusion and did not accurately correspond with changes in real values.[14]

In fact, nominal values have even fooled modern economic historians. In a recent analysis of the panic, one historian argued that GDP per capita declined by 48 percent (6.3 percent per year) from 1814 to 1824.[15] However, this was only *nominal* GDP per capita. In reality, the behavior of real GDP performed differently. In the panic year of 1819, nominal GDP per capita did decrease by 4.4 percent, but real GDP per capita fell by only 1.1 percent. Crucially, from 1819 to 1824 nominal GDP per capita declined 10 percent while real GDP per capita actually *rose* 8 percent (1.5 percent per year). As Joseph Davis explains, falling prices and decreased spending do not necessarily imply reduced economic activity:

---

[12] Rothbard, *Panic of 1819*, p. 16.

[13] Hammond, *Banks and Politics*, pp. 258–62; *Historical Statistics*, 3, p. 632; Murray N. Rothbard, *An Austrian Perspective of Economic Thought*, vol. 2, *Classical Economics* (Auburn, AL: Mises Institute, 2006), pp. 81–82, 97, 193; Rothbard, "History of Money," pp. 79–82, 89–90; Rothbard, *Panic of 1819*, pp. 22–25.

[14] Stanley Lebergott, "Changes in Unemployment," in *The Reinterpretation of American Economic History*, ed. Robert Fogel and Stanley Engerman (New York: Harper & Row, 1971), pp. 77–78.

[15] Browning, *Panic of 1819*, pp. 185–86.

One plausible explanation for the disparity [in nine-teenth-century depressions] may be that the media confused commercial crises with financial ones, because the latter were better characterized by falling commodity and security prices, rather than declines in real industrial activity.[16]

Regardless of its actual economic impact, the Panic of 1819 stirred up intense debate over government power. In particular, the SBUS' monetary authority caused nationwide resentment.

The Rebirth of Monetary Reform

The crisis generated two diametrically opposed perspectives: the hard money view in favor of abolishing cronyism, particularly the SBUS, and the soft money side that espoused the American System's easy credit. Anti-bank forces filled the ranks of the Crawfordite Radicals while the credit expansion faction coalesced into the National Republicans. Ultimately, the soft money group reigned supreme because of the SBUS' corrupting influence and the landmark case *McCulloch v. Maryland*.

The hard money theories of new Smithian economists, particularly Jean-Baptiste Say and Destutt de Tracy, provided an antidote to the country's woes. Significantly, the Frenchmen influenced politicians, businessmen, and intellectuals to embrace radical laissez-faire thought over the next several decades. Tracy considered irredeemable paper money "the most fatal of all fraudulent bankruptcies" and attacked the "radically vicious" banks the government "privileged."[17] Say echoed similar sentiments, desiring 100 percent reserves or freely competitive fractional reserve banks. The two writers provided important ideological ammunition for the assault on the corrupt partnership between banking and government.[18]

---

[16] Joseph Davis, "An Improved Annual Chronology of US Business Cycles since the 1790s," *Journal of Economic History* (March 2006): 115. See also Johnston and Williamson, "US GDP Then?"

[17] Timothy Terrell, "The Economics of Destutt de Tracy," in *Destutt de Tracy, A Treatise on Political Economy*, ed. Thomas Jefferson (Auburn, AL: Mises Institute, 2009), pp. vi–vii.

[18] Rothbard, *Austrian Perspective of Economic Thought*, 2, pp. 6–8, 11, 37–40; Rothbard, *Panic of 1819*, pp. 248–49.

Classical liberals quickly translated Tracy and Say's anti-bank theories for public consumption. Jefferson, back in the saddle for laissez faire, edited Tracy's *A Treatise on Political Economy* (1817), persuading the College of William and Mary to adopt it as a textbook. He praised its "sound principles of Political Economy" and hoped Tracy would be placed "in the hands of every reader."[19] The free trade Clement C. Biddle of Philadelphia annotated Say's identically titled *A Treatise on Political Economy* (1821). Jefferson also lauded Say's book because it communicated Smith's *Wealth of Nations* in a "shorter compass and more lucid manner."[20] In fact, Say's work served as an extremely popular economics textbook. Consequently, in the 1820s, some American economists, such as John McVickar of New York and the 100 percent reserve advocate Condy Raguet, devised rudimentary free banking proposals. In 1826, the redoubtable Thomas Cooper, now at South Carolina College and a key Crawfordite Radical, attacked bank charters for conferring "exclusive privileges upon [one] class, upon motives and pretenses often fraudulent, seldom excusable, never justifiable."[21] However, it would take time for such revolutionary theories to affect politics.[22]

In the meantime, the hard money contingent restricted fractional reserve state banks. According to Murray Rothbard, "controls over banks were not considered interference in the market but rather an exercise of the government's sovereign rights over the money supply and a prevention of bank interference with the market. The most

---

[19] Terrell, "The Economics of Destutt de Tracy," p. xii.

[20] Joseph Dorfman, *The Economic Mind in American Civilization*, vol. 2 (New York: Viking Press, 1946), p. 514.

[21] Howard Bodenhorn, *State Banking in Early America* (New York: Oxford University Press, 2003), p. 188.

[22] William Belko, *The Triumph of the Antebellum Free Trade Movement* (Gainesville: University Press of Florida, 2012), p. 52; Michael Bordo and William Phillips, "Faithful Index to the Ambitions and Fortunes of the State," in *Economists and Higher Learning in the Nineteenth Century*, ed. William Barber (New Brunswick, NJ: Transaction Publishers, 1993), p. 49; Norman Risjord, *The Old Republicans* (New York: Columbia University Press, 1965), p. 252; Rothbard, *Austrian Perspective of Economic Thought*, 2, pp. 8, 11; Rothbard, *Panic of 1819*, pp. 193–95; Joseph T. Salerno, "The Neglect of the French Liberal School in Anglo-American Economics," *Review of Austrian Economics* (December 1988): 132–33, 141–43; Lawrence White and George Selgin, "Laissez-Faire Monetary Thought in Jacksonian America," in *Perspectives on the History of Economic Thought*, ed. Donald Moggridge (Aldershot, UK: Edward Elgar, 1990), pp. 22–26.

cogent upholders of this view were the leading Virginians."[23] Jeffer-son anonymously wrote a *Plan for Reducing the Circulating Medium* to achieve "the eternal suppression of bank paper."[24] He envisioned grad-ually reducing banknotes and eliminating banking entirely, in essence adopting a 100 percent specie standard. Virginia Governor Thomas Randolph, a son-in-law of Jefferson, pushed for a state-established 100 percent reserve program and the collection of taxes only in specie. Old Republican Spencer Roane lashed out at the SBUS and supported a prohibition on new state bank charters. Some writers even argued for eliminating all limited liability banks, an idea they erroneously attributed to Adam Smith. Virginia's hostility to banking remained so strong after the panic that it did not charter any new banks for the next fifteen years.

New Yorkers advocated similar policies. Angered at the SBUS' harsh contraction and blatant corruption, two New York congressmen remarked that they regretted their votes for the "incorporation of that *now-swindling monster.*"[25] The crisis jolted both Republican factions, the Clintonians of Governor DeWitt Clinton and the Regency of State Senator Martin Van Buren (a key Radical), into the hard money posi-tion. Believing the increase in state banks caused the depression, they attacked the chartering system. The 1820 New York Constitution even required a two-thirds majority for any new bank charter.

Unfortunately, both Virginia and New York's reformers failed to realize that their policies entrenched credit expansion and crony-ism by increasing banking interventions. Free entry reduces credit expansion because of the adverse clearing mechanism. On the other hand, restricting bank entry creates regional monopolies that can eas-ily expand credit and corrupt politicians. The free banking solution of unchartered and laissez-faire competition still eluded reformers.[26]

On the other hand, various western states enacted soft money policies, including state-owned banks and government agencies that issued inconvertible paper. In Tennessee, wealthy merchant Felix Grundy pushed for a government loan office that could issue paper

---

[23] Rothbard, *Panic of 1819*, p. 247.

[24] Ibid., p. 184.

[25] Browning, *Panic of 1819*, p. 325.

[26] Browning, *Panic of 1819*, pp. 127, 179, 325; Donald Cole, *Martin Van Buren and the American Political System* (Princeton, NJ: Princeton University Press, 1984), p. 88; Risjord, *The Old Republicans*, pp. 229–30; Rothbard, *Panic of 1819*, pp. 31, 181–85, 190–93, 207, 243.

money. But the hard money Andrew Jackson sent a memorial to the state legislature citing "judicious political economists" who had demonstrated that the "large emissions of paper from the banks by which the country was inundated, have been the most prominent causes of those distresses of which we at present complain."[27] Although the legislature nixed the loan office bill, it created the Bank of the State of Tennessee, which that floundered throughout the 1820s.

Crucially, the business downturn turned Jackson into an ardent opponent of government-subsidized banking and fractional reserve banking in general. A similar conversion experience affected the young Tennessee politician and planter, James K. Polk. Jackson grounded his arguments upon strict constructionism, arguing that the moribund coinage clause allowed only a specie currency and prohibited Congress and the states from chartering note-issuing banks. In contrast to John Calhoun's broad constructionism—the coinage clause sanctioned a national bank to regulate the money supply—Jackson's strict constructionism required a specie currency. The new interpretation neatly tied in with the growing free market economic thought, heavily influencing opponents of cronyism. Jackson already showed his anti-bank proclivities in 1827, when he supported a Tennessee law that levied a tax on banks chartered outside the state, fuming at the SBUS' newly established branch. He thundered that the people of Nashville would now be "cursed" with the SBUS' "attendant evils and corruption."[28]

Missouri, another state with intense monetary debate, suffered from severe deflation. Responding to the state's new loan office (later declared unconstitutional because the Constitution explicitly forbids states from issuing money), Senator Thomas Hart Benton argued for a purely specie currency. He viciously attacked the SBUS, charging that citizens were now "mortgaged to the money power" and "in the jaws of the Monster."[29] Another western politico who shifted to hard money was Amos Kendall, editor of the Kentucky *Argus* and an economic theorist. Kendall now called banks "disgusting" and supported a constitutional amendment prohibiting them, along with a fallback

---

[27] Rothbard, *Panic of 1819*, p. 128.

[28] Remini, *Andrew Jackson*, 2, p. 47. See also Hammond, *Banks and Politics*, pp. 235–38, 349; Paul Kahan, *The Bank War* (Yardley, PA: Westholme Publishing, 2016), pp. 31–32; Remini, *Andrew Jackson*, 2, pp. 43–48; Rothbard, *Panic of 1819*, pp. 68, 127–31, 202; Sean Wilentz, *The Rise of American Democracy* (New York: W.W. Norton, 2005), p. 244.

[29] Browning, *Panic of 1819*, p. 217.

plan for a 100 percent reserve system.[30] The Panic of 1819 turned the younger Radicals—particularly Van Buren, Jackson, Polk, Benton, and Kendall—into hard money advocates and fierce opponents of the corrupting hydra, the SBUS.[31]

Indeed, the SBUS corrupted many. First, it recruited intellectuals, the Hamiltonian economists and newspapermen who sprouted up to justify central banking and attack free market economics. Their ranks included Hezekiah Niles of the *Niles Weekly Register*, Mathew Carey, the protectionist Friedrich List, and the Federalist Daniel Raymond. In addition, the National Republicans' establishment periodical, the *National Intelligencer*, supported the Bank for loans. The paper embodied the modern secularization of the alliance of throne and altar: the *National Intelligencer* received lucrative contracts to print congressional documents in return for sponsoring congressmen's interventionist policies. A cozy partnership indeed! It did not help that the paper's editors spent lavishly and poorly managed the enterprise.[32]

Second, the highly skilled Nicholas Biddle worked for the institution. A former Federalist who married into a wealthy Philadelphia family, Biddle was appointed by his friend Monroe as a government director in January 1819. Smart and arrogant, just like his ideological mentor Hamilton, Biddle firmly believed in the American System. He thought that the war proved the indispensability of a central bank to regulate state banks and supported cheap credit to alleviate the panic, particularly to manufacturers and transportation companies. Unsurprisingly, the interventionist rejected Adam Smith. In early 1823, Biddle started his new job as president of the SBUS.[33]

Third, the Bank bribed high-profile politicians, particularly Henry Clay and Daniel Webster, to serve as corporate lobbyists. Clay, the son-in-law of a wealthy Kentucky businessman, fixated on funneling cheap credit to his state. At the Bank's inception, the Speaker befriended President Jones and persuaded the main office to establish

---

[30] Rothbard, *Panic of 1819*, p. 202.

[31] Rothbard, *Austrian Perspective of Economic Thought*, 2, pp. 130–32, 210–16; Rothbard, *Panic of 1819*, pp. 115–17, 121, 202–03, 247–49.

[32] Stephen Campbell, *The Bank War and the Partisan Press* (Lawrence: University Press of Kansas, 2019), pp. 23–25, 60; Dorfman, *Economic Mind*, 2, pp. 566–97; Leonard White, *The Jacksonians* (New York: Macmillan, 1954), pp. 290, 293–94.

[33] Thomas Govan, *Nicholas Biddle* (The University of Chicago Press, 1959), pp. 45, 50–52, 59, 65, 70, 77–78; Robert Remini, *Andrew Jackson and the Bank War* (New York: W.W. Norton & Company, 1967), pp. 33–34.

branches in Lexington and Louisville, exerting enormous influence in choosing their directors. After the panic, Clay temporarily retired from his Speakership to work for the SBUS and pay off his $40,000 debt. Astor assisted him with a $20,000 loan that an anonymous benefactor only paid off in 1845. The central bank paid Clay an annual retainer of $6,000, more than the secretary of state's salary, to collect outstanding debts (Clay could also acquire foreclosed property). Critics continually accused Clay of favoritism. For example, while filing four hundred suits in Ohio and Kentucky's federal courts to collect $2 million in debts, he tried to exempt Senator Richard Johnson's $200,000 obligation. He also earned $2,000 for his legal services defending the SBUS in the federal courts.

Webster adhered to one principle his entire life: follow the money. The Boston Associates and Biddle ranked among his biggest contributors. Thanks to Webster's influence, the Boston Associates dominated the Boston branch's board (Webster's brother-in-law also served as a director). Unsurprisingly, they secured "kissing privileges," or easy credit terms, for their businesses.[34] Webster owned stock, performed legal work, and, thanks to his good friend Biddle, served as a director. Furthermore, the congressman received a retainer that he frequently wanted "renewed or *refreshed* as usual."[35] This retainer was in addition to the $32,000 in no-fee loans he had accumulated over the years.[36]

Fourth, and perhaps most importantly, Chief Justice John Marshall protected the Bank from legal assaults. Marshall, a stockholder in the institution, recognized that the Bank protected federal power over the states. This became especially apparent when Maryland and Ohio tried to weaken its influence. The states reasoned that since they taxed their own state banks, they could also tax the SBUS, viewing it as an expression of their sovereign rights against federal encroachment. Most notably, Maryland enacted a $15,000 annual tax on all non-state-chartered banks, including the SBUS. The embezzling

---

[34] Carl Prince and Seth Taylor, "Daniel Webster, the Boston Associates, and the US Government's Role in the Industrializing Process," *Journal of the Early Republic* (Autumn 1982): 293.

[35] Robert Remini, *Daniel Webster* (New York: W.W. Norton & Company, 1997), p. 262.

[36] Maurice Baxter, *Henry Clay and the American System* (Lexington: The University Press of Kentucky, 1995), pp. 228, 303–05; Philip Burch, *Elites in American History*, 1 (New York: Holmes & Meier Publishers, 1981), pp. 104, 148, 169; Prince and Taylor, "Daniel Webster," pp. 292–93; Remini, *Daniel Webster*, pp. 261–62.

McCulloch unsurprisingly refused to pay, sending the case *McCulloch v. Maryland* to the Supreme Court and onto the arch-Federalist's lap.

Old Republicans had long grown wary of the Supreme Court. Over the years Marshall and his protégé, Joseph Story increasingly empowered the federal government through judicial review, particularly in *Marbury v. Madison* (1803), *Fletcher v. Peck* (1810), and *Fairfax's Devisee v. Hunter's Lessee* (1813). Recall that in the last case, Story declared that the Marshalls indeed owned titles to the Fairfax Estate, thereby overruling Virginia. However, Spencer Roane used the Spirit of 1798 to nullify the decision. He declared part of the 1789 Judiciary Act unconstitutional, insisting that Virginia could decide the constitutionality of its legislation better than the Supreme Court. Of course, Marshall did not accept this Antifederalism for an answer, filing an appeal to his Supreme Court. After Marshall once again recused himself, Justice Story declared in *Martin v. Hunter's Lessee* (1816) that only the high court, not the states, could interpret the Constitution. The decision shocked many Virginians and reawakened their devotion to states' rights. For example, Thomas Ritchie of the Richmond *Enquirer* shook off the nationalism he espoused during the War of 1812 and joined Roane in vigorous resistance.[37]

McCulloch v. Maryland, argued from February to March 1819, shocked the Virginians even more. Webster served as a key member of the SBUS' legal team and argued its constitutionality on the grounds of the necessary and proper clause. In striking contrast to the venal Webster, Luther Martin, the former Antifederalist who heroically opposed the Constitutional Convention's nationalism, led the states' rights legal team. The venerable Marylander brought out all the old Antifederalist arguments about the Constitution's power, combining them with the Spirit of 1798. Martin even quoted Marshall at the Virginia Ratifying Convention when he mendaciously insisted on the limited nature of the proposed government.

Marshall, who sold his shares right before the court case, protected the citadel with his broad constructionism and judicial review. Skirting recent interpretations of the coinage clause (as well as Martin's damning quote), the Hamiltonian used the reliable necessary and

---

[37] Hammond, *Banks and Politics*, pp. 263–64, 266; John Larson, *Internal Improvement* (Chapel Hill: The University of North Carolina Press, 2001), pp. 123–26; Brion McClanahan, *How Alexander Hamilton Screwed Up America* (Washington, DC: Regnery History, 2017), pp. 132–36.

proper clause. Marshall did not merely rule that Maryland could not tax the Bank; he ordained that Congress could enact virtually any desired legislation. The Chief Justice even argued that the federal government was not a confederation of states but a national government responsible only to the people. Thirty years after the Constitution, Marshall's decision embodied every Antifederalist's fear—the Constitution had created a powerful and omnipresent empire.

McCulloch v. Maryland struck like a thunderclap. It did not help the central bank's reputation that right after the decision, investigations revealed the cashier McCulloch as a massive embezzler. To add insult to injury, McCulloch, Buchanan, and Williams never suffered any serious legal penalties. Federalists lauded the court's decision, but to the rest of the public, Marshall's ruling and Baltimore's malfeasance highlighted the SBUS' egregious privileges. Most notably, John Taylor of Caroline, in *Construction Construed and Constitutions Vindicated* (1820), declared states' rights the only recourse to defending liberty from power. One of Taylor's next works, *New Views of the Constitution* (1823), took a decidedly neo-Antifederalist turn after the publication of Robert Yates' *Secret Proceedings* (1821), which presented a negative perspective on James Madison, the Constitutional Convention, and *The Federalist Papers*.[38]

Westerners especially heaped scorn on Marshall's decision. Ohio, where the SBUS previously engaged in massive credit expansion, watched the central bank rapidly foreclose on real estate. The state auditor dismissed the ruling and insisted that the Bank had to pay Ohio's tax. In 1820, the state legislature even praised "the doctrines asserted by the Legislatures of Virginia and Kentucky, in their resolutions" and the Republican Revolution of 1800.[39] When the SBUS refused to pay, Clay and Webster defended the Bank. In *Osborn v. the Bank of the United States* (1824), Marshall once again ruled in the Bank's favor.[40]

---

[38] Browning, *Panic of 1819*, pp. 317–18, 328–31; Saul Cornell, *The Other Founders* (Chapel Hill: The University of North Carolina Press, 1999), pp. 278–94; Thomas J. DiLorenzo, *Hamilton's Curse* (New York: Three Rivers Press, 2008), pp. 87–88; Hammond, *Banks and Politics*, pp. 264–72; McClanahan, *Alexander Hamilton*, pp. 115–27; Remini, *Daniel Webster*, p. 165; David Schwartz, "Coin, Currency, and Constitution," *Michigan Law Review* (2020): 1019–22.

[39] Thomas E. Woods Jr., *Nullification* (Washington, DC: Regnery, 2010), pp. 71–72.

[40] Baxter, *Henry Clay*, pp. 42–43; Browning, *Panic of 1819*, p. 303; DiLorenzo, *Hamilton's Curse*, pp. 64–65; Remini, *Jackson and the Bank War*, pp. 31–32.

Biddle, protected by Marshall, set about making the larger commercial cities "the principal scene of our operations."[41] In 1823, Biddle arranged for the election of four Philadelphians to the main board of directors, along with four others from New York and Boston. The central banker decided to nationalize the empire's monetary system and coordinate bank credit expansion through the SBUS' non-redemption of state banks' notes and deposits. In 1822, the country's money supply stood at $81 million, but by 1829 it had increased to $105 million, a 30 percent increase (4 percent per year). The number of state banks similarly increased from 267 to 369. The SBUS spearheaded the inflation, accounting for 64 percent, in addition to granting loans to state banks.[42]

But supporters of liberty did not give up. In December 1827, Virginia's Congressman Barbour, a Crawfordite Radical, introduced a resolution requesting the government to contemplate selling its SBUS stock. Barbour wanted to pay down the national debt and believed Congress should privatize the institution. Unfortunately, pro-SBUS forces crushed the resolution. Joseph Gales, editor of the *National Intelligencer*, reassured Biddle, triumphantly proclaiming "this vote as definitely settling . . . in advance" the recharter question in 1836.[43] The next year, Treasurer Richard Rush praised the central bank and its ability to coordinate banknote expansion across the country. Unsurprisingly, Rush hailed from a wealthy Federalist family close to the Girard interests and other Philadelphia elites. His boss, President John Quincy Adams, was Biddle's friend and a SBUS shareholder.

With the president, Congress, and the Supreme Court on board, it looked as if the National Republicans had permanently fastened the SBUS onto the American economy. They soon turned to other key planks of the American System, enriching new special-interest groups in the process.[44]

---

[41] Remini, *Jackson and the Bank War*, p. 37.

[42] Govan, *Nicholas Biddle*, p. 79; *Historical Statistics*, 3, p. 632; Rothbard, "History of Money," p. 94; Timberlake, *Monetary Policy*, pp. 29–30.

[43] William Belko, *Philip Pendleton Barbour in Jacksonian America* (Tuscaloosa: University of Alabama Press, 2016), p. 136.

[44] Ibid., pp. 134–36; Samuel Bemis, *John Quincy Adams and the Union* (Norwalk, CT: The Easton Press, 1987), p. 197; Burch, *Elites in American History*, 1, pp. 104–05, 120; Remini, *Jackson and the Bank War*, p. 34; Timberlake, *Monetary Policy*, pp. 30–33.

CHAPTER 11

ERECTING THE AMERICAN SYSTEM: SECTIONAL FISSURES

Protective Tariffs

Protective tariffs and internal improvements formed the cornerstone of the American System: they privileged industry, recruited necessary business interests, and integrated the vast empire. Henry Clay explicitly linked the policies; tariff revenue would fund public works. But the Panic of 1819 sectionalized both issues, dividing the National Republicans. They succeeded in passing the mercantilist tariffs of 1824 and 1828 by corrupting key Crawfordite Radicals and Jacksonians. But National Republicans failed to entice their opposition during internal-improvement debates, managing to only pass the 1824 General Survey Act. Despite the added difficulties, the American System lumbered onwards.

Before the panic, increased protection occurred with little sectional animosity. In 1818, at the behest of the American Society for the Encouragement of Domestic Manufactures, Congress overwhelmingly agreed to increase iron rates and make cotton rates permanent. However, as with every other issue, the panic changed the picture, crushing manufacturing enterprises and causing protectionists to long for higher tariffs. At the same time, the international crisis decreased export prices and encouraged the South to favor lower rates (in addition, southerners wanted to soothe their troubles by importing cheap manufactures).

With Monroe's support, protectionists seized the initiative. They created a flurry of new lobbying associations, spearheaded by the indefatigable protectionist Mathew Carey of Pennsylvania. In 1819, Carey, funded by wealthy manufacturers, formed the Philadelphia Society for the Promotion of National Industry and the Pennsylvania Society for the Encouragement of Domestic Manufactures. He also helped establish the Convention of the Friends of National Industry, which held a conference in New York City later in the year. The Convention boasted thirty-seven delegates from nine states, largely from New York and Pennsylvania (the South only sent tiny Delaware and Maryland).[1]

In December, protectionists sent several lobbyists to Congress, including the economist Condy Raguet of Philadelphia, at the time still a protectionist before converting to free trade, and Eleazar Lord of New York City. The House split the Committee on Commerce and Manufactures and Speaker Clay packed the new Committee on Manufactures with likeminded colleagues. He appointed to the chair Henry Baldwin of Pittsburgh, a manufacturer who owned large rolling mills. Baldwin, whose ascension marked the beginning of Pennsylvania iron's influence over tariff policy, unabashedly believed that the primary goal of tariffs should be protection, not revenue. Greed caused him to break ranks with fellow northerners on the Missouri Compromise of 1820 so the House could take up more important matters, in particular the Baldwin bill.

After the Missouri Compromise, the lower chamber debated the Baldwin bill. The proposal increased tariffs on cotton and woolen products from 25 to 33 percent and raised rates on other products, including substitutes for Pittsburgh iron and cut-glass. Lord asked Carey for new protectionist propaganda because "every new memorial does as much good as ten at the early part of the session."[2] Seven northern state legislatures urged passage. Notably, Massachusetts did not, because the Boston Associates and their Boston Manufacturing Company still preferred only the regressive minimum valuation on cotton goods, not overall protection.

Old Republican Congressmen John Randolph, Philip Barbour, and John Tyler of Virginia, along with the theorist John Taylor of Caroline, trenchantly criticized the legislation. While Clay and American System allies scorned Adam Smith, Barbour defended his free trade theories. Crucially, southern National Republicans also balked at the bill, particularly South Carolina Congressman William Lowndes. They managed to kill the proposed legislation in the Senate. The parties

---

[1] Douglas A. Irwin, *Clashing over Commerce* (Chicago: The University of Chicago Press, 2017), p. 137; Daniel Peart, *Lobbyists and the Making of US Tariff Policy* (Baltimore, MD: The Johns Hopkins University Press, 2018), pp. 28, 32–34, 44, 229; Norman Risjord, *The Old Republicans* (New York: Columbia University Press, 1965), pp. 207–08; Murray N. Rothbard, *The Panic of 1819* (Auburn, AL: Mises Institute, 2007), pp. 209–16.

[2] Peart, *Making of US Tariff Policy*, p. 46.

split in both chambers, though Federalists favored it by larger margins (Republicans voted 91-88, Federalists 21-12). The sectional schism remained far more important: the North voted 96-24 in favor, similar to 1816, while the South voted 16-76, less than half of its previous support. The first tariff battle ended as a defeat for protectionists because of the sectional rupture among National Republicans.[3]

When Speaker Clay temporarily retired to work for the SBUS, Congress hesitated to increase protection. Thanks to Crawford's Radicals, ably led by US senator Martin Van Buren, Barbour secured the speakership. He appointed anti-tariff men to the Committee on Manufactures to deliberately thwart Chairman Baldwin. Clearly, a permanent rift emerged on the tariff question. Raguet, now converted to free trade, informed David Ricardo that the country divided into two factions, one in favor of privileging manufacturers and the other for "the natural course of things."[4] Everyone knew that the conflict would reignite after the protectionist Clay returned to Congress in 1823 and regained his speakership.

In January 1824, the Committee on Manufactures, now led by John Tod of the Pennsylvania iron interests, reported on a bill similar to the earlier Baldwin proposal. Barbour once again rose up in laissez-faire opposition to attack the constitutionality of protective tariffs, arguing the Constitution only sanctioned tariffs for revenue. He demonstrated another instance of strict constructionism limiting cronyism. In response, Clay famously outlined his pro-tariff American System. In addition to acknowledging the propagandist Carey, the reactionary paid homage to one of his idols—"the master spirit of the age" Napoleon Bonaparte.[5] He knew how to build an empire, and so did Clay.[6]

Critics descended upon the Kentuckian. Congressman Churchill C. Cambreleng of New York City, president of an importing firm and Van Buren's chief House Radical, pointed out that lobbying manufacturers designed many rates. Opponents accused Clay of favoritism: the

---

[3] William Belko, *Philip Pendleton Barbour in Jacksonian America* (Tuscaloosa: University of Alabama Press, 2016), pp. 58–64; Irwin, *Clashing over Commerce*, pp. 138–39; Peart, *Making of US Tariff Policy*, pp. 34–51; Rothbard, *Panic of 1819*, pp. 216, 222–33.

[4] Joseph Dorfman, *The Economic Mind in American Civilization*, vol. 1 (New York: Viking Press, 1946), p. 389.

[5] Ibid., p. 390.

[6] Belko, *Philip Pendleton Barbour*, pp. 64–65, 107–09, 113–15; Peart, *Making of US Tariff Policy*, p. 52.

hemp tariff shielded Clay, a hemp planter, and his constituents from Russian hemp. South Carolinian Radicals particularly heaped scorn, and activists William Smith and Thomas Cooper, the aging English Jeffersonian, led the assault. Adam Smith, Ricardo, Say, and Taylor of Caroline heavily influenced Cooper, and the South Carolina professor published tracts attacking the protective tariff, consolidation, and Secretary of War John Calhoun's strident nationalism. Consequently, South Carolina turned into the most vocal free trade state.

Despite this resistance, the House narrowly passed the bill, with the North split and the South deeply opposed. In the Senate, even with Senators Nathaniel Macon and John Taylor's fierce attacks, a revised version passed, but barely, thanks to growing northern sentiment for protectionism and the new Senator Andrew Jackson, who voted on grounds of national defense and paying off the national debt.[7]

Crucially, the Crawfordite Senator Van Buren moderated. He favored low tariffs to build a new libertarian political party and recognized New York's growing free trade sentiment (from 1821 to 1831 New York City's import share of the country rose from 23 to 50 percent). But he also wanted to cater to New York textile manufacturers and wool farmers to strengthen and expand his political base. Van Buren did vote for Macon's amendment to reduce cotton bagging rates, but New York's manufacturers corrupted him into supporting the final bill, the first of two tariff votes the Radical regretted.

Clay's imperial Tariff of 1824 increased rates on a number of products, including iron and hemp. It privileged cotton and woolen product manufacturers by raising rates from 25 to 33.33 percent. Overall, the average rate on total imports increased to 47 percent, and the benefits accrued to the North at the expense of the South. However, the Boston Associates, currently shifting into woolen manufacturing, frowned at

[7] Maurice Baxter, *Henry Clay and the American System* (Lexington: The University Press of Kentucky, 1995), pp. 30–31; Michael Bordo and William Phillips, "Faithful Index to the Ambitions and Fortunes of the State," in *Economists and Higher Learning in the Nineteenth Century*, ed. William Barber (New Brunswick, NJ: Transaction Publishers, 1993), pp. 50–52, 56; Saul Cornell, *The Other Founders* (Chapel Hill: The University of North Carolina Press, 1999), pp. 291–95; George Dangerfield, *The Awakening of American Nationalism* (New York: Harper & Row, 1965), pp. 206–07; Lacy Ford, *Origins of Southern Radicalism* (New York: Oxford University Press, 1988), pp. 114–18; Peart, *Making of US Tariff Policy*, pp. 51–60; Robert Remini, *Andrew Jackson*, vol. 2 (New York: History Book Club, 1998), p. 68; Risjord, *The Old Republicans*, pp. 245–48.

the lack of a minimum valuation for woolen goods. In addition, the law raised rates on raw wool more than on woolen goods, from 15 to 30 percent. The Associates actually instructed their stool pigeon in the lower chamber, Daniel Webster, to vote against it. This could lead to only one result: another tariff bill for the woolen manufactures, to the further detriment of the American consumer and the South.[8]

After Congress passed the Tariff of 1824, several momentous changes occurred. First, John Quincy Adams controversially defeated Jackson in the presidential election after promising Clay the secretary of state position (Calhoun handily won the vice presidency). Against this third "corrupt bargain," the Radical Van Buren decided to forge his new party around the charismatic Jackson. Second, the North augmented protectionist sentiments while the South hardened resistance. Many Boston Associates now invested in manufacturing woolen goods (of course, Webster borrowed from his donors to invest in the companies). South Carolina's venom continued to grow, especially after export prices declined. Empowered Radicals convinced the state's legislature to declare protective tariffs and internal improvements unconstitutional. In Madisonian fashion, Calhoun opportunistically shifted to free trade and turned into a dedicated sectionalist, joining his supporters, particularly Senator Robert Hayne and Congressman George McDuffie. The stage was set for a climactic battle.[9]

In the fall of 1826, wealthy New England woolen manufacturers lobbied for increased protection. Recognizing the wool growers' importance, manufacturers advocated higher rates for raw wool and woolen goods, including a minimum valuation. The Boston Associates, particularly Abbott Lawrence, one of the "large-scale industrial

---

[8] Jeremy Atack and Peter Passell, *A New Economic View of American History* (New York: W.W. Norton & Company, 1994), pp. 137–38; Donald Cole, *Martin Van Buren and the American Political System* (Princeton, NJ: Princeton University Press, 1984), pp. 109–12; *Historical Statistics of the United States, Historical Statistics of the United States*, vol. 3, ed. Richard Sutch and Susan Carter (New York: Cambridge University Press, 2006), p. 510; Irwin, *Clashing over Commerce*, pp. 145–47; Peart, *Making of US Tariff Policy*, pp. 58–59, 67–68; Carl Prince and Seth Taylor, "Daniel Webster, the Boston Associates, and the U.S. Government's Role in the Industrializing Process," *Journal of the Early Republic* (Autumn 1982): 288–90; Edward Spann, *Ideals and Politics* (Albany: State University of New York Press, 1972), p. 13.

[9] Dangerfield, *Awakening of American Nationalism*, pp. 205–06; Daniel Feller, *The Public Lands in Jacksonian Politics* (Madison: The University of Wisconsin Press, 1984), p. 64; Ford, *Origins of Southern Radicalism*, pp. 114–18; *Historical Statistical*, 3, p. 188; Peart, *Making of US Tariff Policy*, p. 68; Risjord, *The Old Republicans*, p. 247.

capitalists with very deep pockets," sent lobbyists to the Committee on Manufactures.[10] The committee responded with a bill increasing rates on raw wool and added a prohibitively high minimum valuation on woolen textiles. For example, the minimum valuation assessed woolen cloth that was priced at forty-one cents at the much higher $2.50, so the 33.33 percent tariff would translate to an astounding *200 percent* rate. The proposed legislation clearly favored wool interests without any façade of national benefit, worrying Carey—some thin veneer of public interest is always required to convince the public!

In 1827, the House debated the bill. Webster, backed by the Massachusetts legislature, conducted a public relations campaign in the *National Intelligencer*. Webster's blatant flip-flopping earned the ire of the New York *Evening Post*, edited by the libertarian William Cullen Bryant. Although the House passed the measure, the Senate blocked it, thanks to Van Buren. He avoided voting to bring about a 20-20 tie, which Calhoun broke by voting nay. The entire vote split along sectional and factional lines: the South voted 9-93 and the North 117-22. The protectionist Adams supporters voted 98-21 while free trade Jacksonians stood at 28-94. Of the twenty-two northerners who sided against the bill, seventeen favored Jackson.

Ominously, the South increasingly fumed at protective tariffs. After corresponding with Van Buren, Cooper controversially questioned the "value of our union . . . [because] the monopolists are bent upon forcing the decision upon us."[11] This deeply worried Calhoun. Cooper's threat of state secession in the face of continued northern cronyism was a highly libertarian response in accordance with the Principles of 1798. South Carolina would not sit idly in the face of the protective tariff.[12]

Undeterred, protectionists redoubled their efforts. The Pennsylvania Society for the Promotion of Manufactures and the Mechanic Arts, Carey's new front, proposed a Harrisburg convention. In reality, the Pennsylvania Society did not come up with the idea; a Boston manufacturer gave it to Carey. One hundred delegates from across the

---

[10] Lawrence Peskin, *Manufacturing Revolution* (Baltimore, MD: The Johns Hopkins University Press, 2003), p. 217.

[11] Bordo and Phillips, "Faithful Index," p. 56.

[12] Belko, *Philip Pendleton Barbour*, p. 131; William Freehling, *Prelude to Civil War* (New York: Oxford University Press, 1965), pp. 130–32; Peart, *Making of US Tariff Policy*, pp. 66–75; Prince and Taylor, "Daniel Webster," pp. 290–91; Robert Remini, *Martin Van Buren and the Making of the Democratic Party* (New York: Columbia University Press, 1959), pp. 144–45; Spann, *Ideals and Politics*, pp. 21–22, 42–43.

country showed up, virtually all Adams supporters. Prominent attendees included Carey; Hezekiah Niles of the *Niles Weekly Register*; Ezekiel Webster, brother of the new senator; and Lawrence. Webster and Clay did their part by assiduously promoting the meeting. The Harrisburg Convention advocated a 50 percent rate and a minimum valuation for woolen goods as well as increases for other goods.

Notably, the arch–American System economist Friedrich List hoped the convention would "lay the axe to the root of the tree, by declaring the system of Adam Smith and Co. to be erroneous."[13] The protectionist implored "the friends of domestic industry" to establish an agency that educated the public.[14] List advocated taking over an existing organization, such as the Franklin Institute of Philadelphia or establishing a new institution of higher learning to promote the American System—with himself as a professor. The delighted Carey tried to secure List an academic job. Unfortunately for the protectionists, negotiations in the laissez-faire colleges fell through.[15]

The Harrisburg Convention worried Jacksonians because emboldened Adams supporters started attacking them for waffling on protection. While free trade in spirit, northern Jacksonians, particularly New York's Senator Van Buren and Congressman Silas Wright, still courted key protectionist areas in the North. The Adams forces hoped they could exploit this weakness. Fortunately, Jacksonians controlled Congress and could make the first move. Van Buren cleverly created a bill that appeared protectionist but actually infuriated the New England woolen manufacturers. He wanted to recreate the magic of the 1820 defeat in a twisted fashion: New England would join the South, not because of their shipping interests, but because the legislation was not protectionist enough.

In December 1827, the Jacksonian Committee on Manufactures listened to inefficient protectionists plead their case. While the bill

---

[13] Peart, *Making of US Tariff Policy*, p. 79.

[14] Joseph Dorfman, *The Economic Mind in American Civilization*, vol. 2 (New York: Viking Press, 1946), p. 581.

[15] *American Political Leaders* (Washington, DC: CQ Press, 2000), pp. 318; William Barber, "Political Economy and the Academic Setting before 1900," in *Economists and Higher Learning in the Nineteenth Century*, ed. William Barber (New Brunswick, NJ: Transaction Publishers, 1993), p. 9; Donald Cole, *Vindicating Andrew Jackson* (Lawrence: University Press of Kansas, 2009), pp. 68–70; Dorfman, *Economic Mind*, 2, pp. 513–14, 582; Irwin, *Clashing over Commerce*, p. 147; Peart, *Making of US Tariff Policy*, pp. 75–81.

reported in January 1828 increased the tariff on raw wool from 30 to 50 percent, it conspicuously kept rates on woolen goods the same. This infuriated protectionists, including Adams, Clay, Carey, and Niles. Clay complained that the bill was "framed, purposely, to create divisions among the friends of the American System, and thus to defeat the measure."[16] Maryland's Senator Samuel Smith called it a "bill of abominations."[17] During the debate, the South stayed unusually silent because they knew New England would vote against the bill and prevent its passage.

But just when the Jacksonians thought they had secured a delightful victory, catastrophe hit: nothing stopped New England woolen manufacturers from amending the bill to create a truly protectionist monster. Soon enough, Adams supporters introduced an amendment to raise rates, causing panic in the Jacksonian ranks. Shortly thereafter, the House passed the bill. In the Senate, Webster added amendments favorable to Lawrence, the oligarch who frequently gave Webster "loans of a permanent nature."[18] In May, the Boston Associate wrote that the amended bill, which included a 50 percent tariff on woolen manufactures along with a minimum valuation, was "now good enough," cheerfully noting it would "keep the South and West in debt to New England the next hundred years."[19] A Bostonian protectionist editor also wrote to Webster stating the amended bill "comes so near to the Harrisburgh Platform."[20] A Tariff of Abominations indeed!

Senator Van Buren was bested. Some historians previously argued that he always secretly wanted to pass the bill.[21] However, Daniel Peart has shown that Van Buren and his northern allies indeed desired a losing protectionist bill and convinced southerners to go along. But once New England swung in support, he privately decided to secure its passage on behalf of northern wool manufacturers. Power inexorably corrupts. It was the second vote on the tariff Van Buren

---

[16] Peart, *Making of US Tariff Policy*, p. 89.

[17] Irwin, *Clashing over Commerce*, p. 50.

[18] Philip Burch, *Elites in American History*, vol. 1 (New York: Holmes & Meier Publishers, 1981), p. 218.

[19] Prince and Taylor, "Daniel Webster," p. 290.

[20] Peart, *Making of US Tariff Policy*, pp. 94–95.

[21] Remini, "Martin Van Buren and the Tariff of Abominations," *American Historical Review* (July 1958): 903–17.

came to regret—and this one would be a very deep regret. Thanks to Van Buren, the Senate barely voted 24-22 to add the woolen provisions. If Van Buren had voted in the negative, Vice President Calhoun would have assuredly killed the measure. Shortly thereafter, the Senate narrowly passed the bill. Bryant, a die-hard Jacksonian, criticized President Adams in the *Evening Post* for signing into law a "ruinous unjust and oppressive system of monopoly."[22]

The Tariff of Abominations raised the average rate to an astounding 51 percent. The South fumed at Van Buren's treachery, and South Carolina debated its next moves. Although Jackson won the White House later in the year, the tariff actually played little role in the outcome. But to the South, the Tariff of Abominations' sectional largesse unduly punished their region. It exacerbated similar rifts emerging between the North, West, and South.[23]

A National Program for Public Works

The American System's internal improvement plank was highly sectional: Clay enlisted the West to vote for the North's protective tariffs by using tariff revenue for public works, thereby further alienating the South. In fact, because the American System also relied on revenue from high land prices, it actually injured the South and the West. The National Republicans' major federal victory, the General Survey Act of 1824, laid the groundwork for future projects. However, even though President Adams strove to build upon the law with a profligate program, he failed to convince the anti-debt Jacksonians.

At the beginning of the Monroe administration, National Republicans advocated expensive transportation projects. Unfortunately for them, strict constructionism stood in the way. In 1818, the House debated whether the Constitution allowed for such investment. Barbour, fueled by Ritchie and Roane's recent worries after *Martin v. Hunter's Lessee* (1816), launched a scathing attack on federal works, getting the House to narrowly vote against their constitutionality. In the inauguration of Clay's North-West alliance, the Mid-Atlantic and the West strongly supported federal aid. On the other hand, the lower South

---

[22] Spann, *Ideals and Politics*, p. 44.

[23] *American Political Leaders*, p. 290; *Historical Statistics of the United States*, vol. 5, ed. Richard Sutch and Susan Carter (New York: Cambridge University Press, 2006), p. 510; Irwin, *Clashing over Commerce*, pp. 147–59; Peart, *Making of US Tariff Policy*, pp. 81–98.

split (Calhoun's National Republicans favored) and New England and the Upper South dissented. Federalist New England voted along sectional lines because it did not want to lose commerce to other regions. Virginia and North Carolina, under the sway of the Old Republicans, ideologically opposed the measures.

But the National Republicans bounced back. The House Committee on Roads and Canals directed Calhoun to draft a report outlining national defense improvements. Broad constructionism and the threat of war, the twin battering rams of the statists, once again broke down the gates. The secretary of war, who had already ordered his corrupt department to embark upon lavish coastal fortifications, military academies, bureaucratic positions, and frontier explorations, agreed with relish. Calhoun's report, released in January 1819, advocated a vast military survey for federally constructed roads and canals as well as purchasing stock in various undertakings.[24]

However, the panic created a major problem. From 1815 to 1819, resuming foreign trade and imposing protective tariffs caused tax receipts to increase 56 percent. At the same time, government spending declined 34 percent, and the public debt likewise fell from $127 million to $91 million (28 percent). But from 1819 to 1821, revenue collapsed 41 percent, threatening to explode the national debt. The frugal Treasurer William Crawford called for spending cuts. Radicals concentrated their reforms on Calhoun's War Department, where spending still remained three times above prewar levels. Their investigations revealed the department's cronyism, justifying reforms in military expenditures and related bureaucracy. Congress axed Calhoun's appropriations, cutting government spending by 26 percent. Furthermore, to the horror of civil service proponents, Radicals enacted the Tenure of the Office Act, which instituted a four-year term (eligible for renewal) for presidential-class officials. This highly significant legislation embodied the principle of rotation in office.

To add insult to injury, the Radicals' elevation of Barbour to the speakership put the lid on internal improvements for the remainder of the early 1820s. Until Clay could reassume House leadership, the National Republicans would retreat to the state level and embarked

---

[24] Belko, *Philip Pendleton Barbour*, pp. 68–71; John Larson, *Internal Improvement* (Chapel Hill: The University of North Carolina Press, 2001), pp. 110–29; Robert Remini, *Andrew Jackson*, vol. 2 (New York: History Book Club, 1998), pp. 13–21, 397–99.

upon local projects. Unsurprisingly, the states created losing ventures.[25]

In the South, Federalists in Virginia created a Board of Public Works. But Republicans resisted higher taxes and the Board dispensed relatively small amounts. In North Carolina, the Federalist Archibald Douglas Murphey, a heavy investor in transportation companies, adamantly supported improvements. At the behest of Nathaniel Macon, the state blocked Murphey's proposals. The Old Republican frequently corresponded with state Senate Speaker Bartlett Yancey, an ardent National Republican who desired federal aid. In 1818, Macon wrote to Yancey, explaining that North Carolinians did not want the legislature spending their money. As for federal aid, Macon utilized Randolph's slavery scare tactic, warning, "[I]f Congress can make canals they can with more propriety emancipate."[26] Macon succeeded and the state continued to block funding. In striking contrast, South Carolina ambitiously spent $2 million on transportation. Notably, in 1827, the state chartered the South Carolina Canal and Railroad Company. It received a thirty-six-year monopoly, eminent domain rights, a $100,000 state loan, generous price regulations, and federal engineers for construction. Despite the lavish disbursement of taxpayer dollars, South Carolina's projects suffered losses and only benefited wealthy planters.[27]

In the North, New York developed the most prominent program, thanks to its steamboat monopoly and famous Erie Canal. Before the war, inventor Robert Fulton and politician Robert Livingston lobbied for an egregious thirty-year steamboat monopoly with the rights to use the legal system to seize competitors' boats. However, the company continually co-opted new competitors. This, along with recurring illegal competition, gradually weakened the monopoly. But, in 1824, the

[25] Belko, *Philip Pendleton Barbour*, pp. 71–72; *Historical Statistics, V*, pp. 80, 91; Remini, *Andrew Jackson*, 2, pp. 19–21; Risjord, *The Old Republicans*, pp. 193–96; Murray N. Rothbard, "Bureaucracy and the Civil Service in the United States," *Journal of Libertarian Studies* (Summer 1995): 32–34.

[26] Larson, *Internal Improvement*, p. 105.

[27] *American Political Leaders*, p. 330; James Broussard, *The Southern Federalists* (Baton Rouge: Louisiana State University Press, 1978), pp. 353–56; Dorfman, *Economic Mind, I*, pp. 376–77, 382; Ford, *Origins of Southern Radicalism*, pp. 15–19; Carter Goodrich, *Government Promotion of American Canals and Railroads* (New York: Columbia University Press, 1960), pp. 87–88, 102–04; Larson, *Internal Improvement*, pp. 95–105.

Marshall Court sped up the process in *Gibbons v. Ogden* on the grounds that it violated the Constitution's interstate commerce clause. While the ruling beneficially struck down a government restriction, Marshall once again fixated on transferring power from the states to the federal government. In particular, he provided legal precedent for further federal interventions justifiable by a broad construction of Congress' right to regulate interstate trade. Marshall's aggrandizement of federal power continually worried opponents of the Court.[28]

The Erie Canal was undoubtedly the state's shining star. New York had tried to secure federal funding for a canal that linked Lake Erie to the Hudson River. After Madison vetoed the Bonus Bill, the state legislature, at the behest of National Republican DeWitt Clinton, narrowly passed a law to build a state canal. The rival Van Buren and his Regency opposed the canal, but right before the 1817 gubernatorial election (which Clinton won) the Radical leader gave his support. From 1817 to 1825, the state constructed the 364-mile canal at the mammoth cost of $8.4 million, and over the next ten years the investment purportedly earned a lucrative 8 percent rate of return. The state accrued other sizable public benefits. For example, the cost of shipping a ton of wheat or flour from Buffalo to New York City plummeted from $100 to $10. Consequently, historians wax eloquently about how governments can successfully build public works.[29]

The Erie Canal did earn revenue greater than its construction costs. However, taking into consideration operating and maintenance expenses along with the opportunity cost of invested funds, the canal only covered its economic costs—hardly a monumental achievement. Furthermore, the state got greedy. In 1825, the legislature authorized surveys for seventeen proposed canals and constructed five canals over the next decade, despite predictions of excessive costs and inefficiency by the Regency politicians Silas Wright and Samuel Young. Lo and behold, the newer canals suffered losses. Soon enough, the Erie and subsidiary canals supported onerous regulations on competing

---

[28] Burton Folsom and Anna Folsom, *Uncle Sam Can't Count* (New York: HarperCollins Publishers, 2014), pp. 35–36; Brian Murphy, *Building the Empire State* (Philadelphia: University of Pennsylvania Press, 2015), pp. 110–58.

[29] Cole, *Martin Van Buren*, pp. 50, 109; Albert Fishlow, "Internal Transportation in the Nineteenth and Early Twentieth Centuries," in *The Cambridge Economic History of the United States*, vol. 2, ed. Stanley Engerman and Robert Gallman (New York: Cambridge University Press, 2000), p. 554; Folsom and Folsom, *Uncle Sam Can't Count*, pp. 57–61; Goodrich, *American Canals and Railroads*, p. 55.

railroads to stay afloat, much to the enmity of the libertarian Bryant at the *Evening Post*.[30]

Northern states that tried to mimic New York spectacularly failed, most notably Pennsylvania. In November 1824, along with Nicholas Biddle, Carey created the Pennsylvania Society for the Promotion of Internal Improvements, heartily backed by wealthy Philadelphia merchants. The American System advocate pushed for a state canal instead of the more feasible railroad. Despite political opposition from northern Pennsylvanians, who recognized such a canal benefitted only the southern environs, in February 1826 the legislature agreed to the Main Line Canal from Philadelphia to Pittsburgh. But unlike New York's flat landscape that was favorable to canal building, Pennsylvania terrain provided tough sledding: the hilly landscape required a canal high above sea level and a tunnel. While the Erie only needed eighty-four locks, the Main Line required 174. Politicians unnecessarily added to the cost, rushing construction and mandating feeder lines for their districts. Pennsylvania's wise government investors finished the Philadelphian elites' project in 1834 at a cost of a hefty $14.6 million. Its annual rate of return remained less than 2 percent, well below the opportunity cost of alternative investments. On the other hand, the privately funded canals that connected to coal interests in eastern Pennsylvania secured profitable returns for their investors.

It is clear that despite herculean efforts, state assistance in the 1820s led to an inefficient allocation of resources. The reason is crystal clear: governments cannot operate on a business basis, because they require tax revenue and lack the crucial test of profit and loss. Slowly but surely state officials recognized this.[31]

---

[30] Cole, *Martin Van Buren*, p. 142; Dorfman, *Economic Mind*, 2, pp. 522–26; Stanley Engerman and Kenneth Sokoloff, "Digging the Dirt at Public Expense," in *Corruption and Reform*, ed. Edward Glaeser and Claudia Goldin (Chicago: The University of Chicago Press, 2006), pp. 103–06; Folsom and Folsom, *Uncle Sam Can't Count*, p. 72; John Garraty, *Silas Wright* (New York: Columbia University Press, 1949), pp. 47–49; Spann, *Ideals*, pp. 126–27; Clifford Thies, "The American Railroad Network during the Early 19th Century," *Cato Journal* (Fall 2002): 236–37.

[31] Fishlow, "Internal Transportation," pp. 555–60; Folsom and Folsom, *Uncle Sam Can't Count*, pp. 59, 68–73; Thomas Govan, *Nicholas Biddle* (Chicago: The University of Chicago Press, 1959), pp. 101–03; Larson, *Internal Improvement*, pp. 80–87; George Taylor, *The Transportation Revolution* (New York: Holt, Rinehart and Winston, 1951), pp. 38–45; Thies, "American Railroad Network," pp. 238–43.

Once Clay reassumed the speakership in 1823, the National Republicans renewed their assault, devising a bill that authorized the president to institute surveys for a federal system of roads and canals. Clay shepherded the bill alongside the Tariff of 1824, aiming to bind the North and West together by blowing revenue from protectionist tariffs on internal improvements. This portended poorly for the South and debt extinguishment. Congressmen Randolph and Barbour, along with Senator Van Buren, fought Clay's machinations. Randolph invoked "the last words of Patrick Henry," declaring that the proposed law would lead to terrible extremes: interstate commerce regulation, federal control of rivers and lakes, federal labor standards, corruption, and excessive government spending.[32] Of course, hoping to rally the South and "every man who has the misfortune . . . to be born a slave-holder," Randolph warned the legislation contained the potential to "emancipate every slave in the United States."[33] But, as usual, Randolph's efforts failed and Congress passed the bill. True to Clay's plans, the Mid-Atlantic (save New York) and the West provided the margin of victory.

The law appropriated $30,000 for surveys and a Board of Engineers within the War Department, instructing engineers to devise a national program. While funding no projects, it clearly laid the necessary groundwork. Indeed, Calhoun enthusiastically dispatched army engineers before the presidential election. In December, Calhoun and the Board issued a report. The National Republican envisioned an expensive network of national transportation projects, including an interregional waterway in the Mid-Atlantic and Upper South, an extension of the National Road, a southern national road to New Orleans, and coastal canals in the East. Such imperial transportation appeared on the rise in March 1825, when Congress spent $150,000 to extend the National Road into Ohio and purchase $300,000 of Chesapeake and Delaware Canal Company stock.[34]

The new President Adams heavily supported the General Survey Act, especially with Clay as his secretary of state. His first

---

[32] David Johnson, *John Randolph of Roanoke* (Baton Rouge: Louisiana State University Press, 2012), p. 197.

[33] Larson, *Internal Improvement*, p. 143.

[34] Feller, *Public Lands*, pp. 64–66; Goodrich, *American Canals and Railroads*, p. 41; Johnson, *John Randolph*, pp. 195–98; Carl Lane, *A Nation Wholly Free* (Yardley, PA: Westholme Publishing, 2014), p. 41; Larson, *Internal Improvement*, pp. 138–66; Risjord, *The Old Republicans*, pp. 237–43.

message to Congress in December 1825 advocated an elaborate program of public works, including new roads and canals, a national university, an astronomical observatory, and a new department of the interior. He offered no cost estimates for his "unfailing streams of improvement from the Atlantic to the Pacific Ocean."[35] Adams' supporters even made Hamiltonian arguments that a national debt benefitted the public. In particular, Congressman Edward Everett of Massachusetts, a former Harvard professor who married into the wealthy family of Boston Associate Peter C. Brooks, pontificated on the benefits. In an April 1826 speech, Everett declared that wise government investment would increase economic growth and pay off the public borrowing. He failed to help his case when a month later, as chair of the House Committee on Public Buildings, he reported a bill for $25,000 in White House repairs and furnishings, including a billiard table.[36]

However, after Adams' election, the coalescing Jacksonians proved too strong. First, Jackson, an adherent of Old Republicanism, declared that public debt leads to "a moneyed aristocracy dangerous to the liberties of the country."[37] Even Vice President Calhoun, pressured by his state's Radicals, rejected Adams' program. Second, no Harrisburg Convention replica existed to corrupt Jacksonians into supporting public works. Third, the West started to sour on internal improvements, thanks to Senator Benton. After the panic, Congress eliminated the credit system, reduced the minimum land price from $2.00 to $1.25 per acre, shrank the minimum tract size from 160 to 80 acres, and cut settlers' land debts by half. Benton desired to make land even more affordable, but easterners wanted high land prices to increase revenue and stop western migration. The Missourian soon discovered the American System's true sectionalism: the tariff that subsidized northern industry hurt the South, and high land prices that helped fund public works stunted the West. Benton planned to forge a South-West alliance by getting westerners to support free trade and oppose federal transportation projects if the South voted for lower land prices. Since the Senate only narrowly defeated Benton's bill to

[35] Lane, *Nation Wholly Free*, p. 50.

[36] Burch, *Elites in American History*, 1, p. 186; Lane, *Nation Wholly Free*, pp. 47–51, 59–61; Lindsay Schakenbach, "From Discontented Bostonians to Patriotic Industrialists," *The New England Quarterly* (September 2011): 388.

[37] Remini, *Andrew Jackson*, 2, p. 33.

cut prices in 1828, a South-West alliance to eliminate northern privileges looked very possible.[38]

In the face of these Jacksonian roadblocks, Congress mustered only $2 million on the National Road, $2 million in stock subscription, and 2.5 million acres in land grants. This was hardly the expansive system of public transportation the National Republicans envisioned. Consequently, from 1821 to 1828, government expenditures increased by less than 4 percent and the public debt declined from $93 million to $58 million (38 percent).

It would only be a matter of time before the National Republicans could surmount sectionalism and dispense special-interest legislation unchecked. But the Panic of 1819 also caused an immense political uproar regarding plans to consolidate and expand the empire's domain, potentially jeopardizing the National Republicans' machinations.[39]

---

[38] Atack and Passell, *New Economic View of American History*, pp. 257–60; Feller, *Public Lands*, pp. 22–38, 66–70, 74–79, 89, 93–97; Larson, *Internal Improvement*, pp. 174–79; Remini, *Andrew Jackson*, 2, pp. 32–33, 400–01.

[39] Goodrich, *American Canals and Railroads*, p. 41; *Historical Statistics*, 5, p. 80.

CHAPTER 12

THE CULMINATION OF THE AMERICAN SYSTEM: ENLARGING THE EMPIRE

Nationalizing the West

During the Era of Corruption, the National Republicans augmented the empire by imposing new rules on western states, aggressing on Spanish lands, and forcing foreign markets to purchase American manufactures. This imperialism was the fulfillment of the American System. But reactionaries discovered that it would not come easily. After the Panic of 1819, admitting new states reignited slavery controversies, causing National Republicans to impose a divisive federal solution that strengthened slavery and weakened the rights of states— the Missouri Compromise. In addition, the successive imperialist measures—the Adams-Onís Treaty, the Monroe Doctrine, and the Panama Congress—gradually alarmed and strengthened the emerging Jacksonian reformers.

After the war, the troubling issue of slavery—the embodiment of power over liberty—split along geographical lines. Although the South contained more anti-slavery societies and free blacks than the North, slaves in the North had declined by 55 percent since 1790 while increasing 130 percent in the South. Slavery survived, not because of technological advancements related to agriculture, but because of the nationalizing Constitution and its fugitive slave clause (along with the 1793 Fugitive Slave Act) that socialized enforcement costs and made it harder for slaves to escape. State regulations buttressed the fugitive slave clause, most notably mandatory slave patrols composed of poor white men. Aside from the obvious financial penalty, many southerners, including Old Republicans, hesitated to free slaves, because they firmly believed free blacks could not peacefully coexist with whites. After prohibiting the international slave trade in 1808, their only solutions were to diffuse slaves throughout the western territories or export them

back to Africa. Unfortunately, domestic slave breeders and expansionist planters also supported these "solutions" to boost the prices of their
human property.

One cannot stress enough that northerners shared southerners'
views on race relations. The main difference was that the South's black
population averaged 37 percent, compared to the North's 2 percent.
The North's small black population made anti-slavery positions more
palatable, but the region adamantly wanted to maintain current demo-
graphics: northerners supported colonization schemes and passed
laws restricting interracial marriage, education, suffrage, immigration, and employment. Most northerners concentrated their ire not on
slavery per se but on the three-fifths clause that increased southern
representation and impeded pro-North legislation, particularly protectionist tariffs. Outside of a miniscule minority, genuine abolitionist
sentiment did not exist in the country.[1]

The grounds for a fight lay in the West, where new states could
be created. Outside of the international slave trade and the Northwest
Ordinance of 1787 that expressly prohibited slavery in the Midwest,
the legislative branch let territories autonomously decide on the slavery issue but reserved the right to regulate it. The territories could then
form states and petition Congress for acceptance into the Union. By
and large, congressmen enforced this policy and did not consciously
try to balance "free" and "slave" states. Unfortunately, Congress'
approach suffered from a fateful contradiction: it promoted liberty by
letting settlers decide territorial policy, but promoted power by sanctioning involuntary servitude.

The panic changed everything. The dramatic collapse in agricultural prices and aggravated debt burdens caused southern planters to realize that solvency required increased production from slave
labor, which reduced the region's anti-slavery sentiments. The price

---

[1] James Banner, *To the Hartford Convention* (New York: Alfred A. Knopf, 1970), pp.
105–07; George Dangerfield, *The Awakening of American Nationalism* (New York:
Harper & Row, 1965), pp. 131–32, 139–40; Joseph Dorfman, *The Economic Mind
in American Civilization*, vol. 1 (New York: Viking Press, 1946), p. 401; *Historical
Statistics of the United States, Colonial Times to 1957* (Washington, DC: 1960), pp.
11–12; Jeffrey Rogers Hummel, *Emancipating Slaves, Enslaving Free Men* (Chicago,
IL: Open Court, 2002), pp. 26–27, 37–60; Grover Moore, *The Missouri Controversy*
(Lexington: The University of Kentucky Press, 1953), pp. 25–27, 30, 236, 301–05,
321–25; Donald Ratcliffe, *The One-Party Presidential Contest* (Lawrence: University
Press of Kansas, 2015), pp. 53–54.

plunge also forced southerners to shake off their postwar protectionism. Southern sentiments collided with the North's increased affinity for high tariffs, which blamed any resistance on the three-fifths clause. It only took one policy proposal to thrust these new tensions out into the open. In February 1819, the House considered admitting Missouri, a state that autonomously decided to permit slavery. Congressman James Tallmadge of New York, once private secretary to Governor George Clinton, unexpectedly dropped a bombshell: a gradual emancipation amendment that prohibited the further introduction of slaves into Missouri and freed the children of slaves once they turned twenty-five.

While the rest of the country concentrated on the business downturn, the Tallmadge Amendment shocked every politician. Although the New Yorker wanted to reduce southern representation, he genuinely adhered to some antislavery principles. Tallmadge previously championed New York's gradual emancipation plan of 1817 and protested Illinois' state constitution because it was not antislavery enough. For Tallmadge, Missouri's small slave population warranted nipping slavery in the bud. Significantly, Tallmadge soon emphasized that he did not want the same for slave-heavy Alabama, admitted as a state in December 1819, because a large free black population could lead to a "*servile* war" that would threaten "the safety of the white population."[2] Thus, even according to this antislavery advocate, Congress could not touch slavery in the South.[3]

As George Dangerfield properly noted, the "only real accommodation" would have been to prohibit slavery in Missouri and lower tariffs, but the depression wrecked this option.[4] The Missouri controversy escalated after Maine entered the picture. In June 1819, Massachusetts let Maine secede and form an independent state but stipulated that Congress must agree by March 1820. However, southerners made it very clear that unless Congress permitted Missouri to decide its own rules regarding slavery, they would fight Maine's entry into the Union.

---

[2] Andrew Browning, *The Panic of 1819* (Columbia: University of Missouri Press, 2019), pp. 336.

[3] William Belko, *Philip Pendleton Barbour in Jacksonian America* (Tuscaloosa: University of Alabama Press, 2016), pp. 86–88; Browning, *Panic of 1819*, pp. 334–38, 348; Moore, *Missouri Controversy*, pp. 18–19, 32–33, 170–73, 320–30.

[4] Dangerfield, *Awakening of American Nationalism*, p. 104.

A compromise only emerged after northern Republicans realized that Federalists politically benefited from the gridlock. While some Federalists did harbor genuine antislavery sentiments, Martin Van Buren correctly insisted they held "rather political than philanthropical" motives.[5] Speaker Henry Clay prepared the compromise. The Kentuckian, a slave owner who wanted Missourians to choose, feared that the controversy would lead to the creation of "three distinct confederacies."[6] This secession posed a serious problem for someone who wanted to erect an imperial American System. Clay's top-down solution contained three components: Congress would make Maine a free state, Missouri a slave state, and then crucially erect a dividing line that geographically determined which new states could permit slavery. Except for Missouri, Congress forbid slavery in the land above the line (the rest of the Louisiana Purchase) and sanctioned it in the land below the line (the Arkansas Territory). In March 1820, Congress passed the compromise.[7]

With this decision, Congress essentially nationalized the West. Before, the imperial domain's western extremities maintained some semblance of decentralization, because settlers could still independently decide what territorial governments to create and on what terms they would join as states. This bore similarities with Jefferson's Empire of Liberty, though without the essential feature where settlers could create polities separate from the United States. Now, Congress decided on what terms states could join the Union. This decision temporarily saved the empire, but ominously inaugurated the debate over the extent of the Constitution's fugitive slave clause.

The Missouri Compromise directly resulted from the Louisiana Purchase. Sooner or later, expansion across the continent would stir up the slavery controversy. Of course, without the Louisiana Purchase, settlers moving west could have established their own governments separate from the United States. This would have crippled the institution of slavery due to the emergence of free polities in northern Louisiana

---

[5] Joel Silbey, *Martin Van Buren and the Emergence of American Popular Politics* (Lanham, MD: Rowman & Littlefield Publishers, 2002), p. 42.

[6] Robert Remini, *Henry Clay* (New York: W.W. Norton & Company, 1991), p. 182.

[7] Daniel Howe, *What Hath God Wrought* (New York: Oxford University Press, 2007), p. 153; Shaw Livermore, *The Twilight of Federalism* (Princeton, NJ: Princeton University Press, 1962), pp. 88–97; Moore, *Missouri Controversy*, pp. 86–103, 273–81; Andrew P. Napolitano, *Dred Scott's Revenge* (Nashville, TN: Thomas Nelson, 2009), pp. 54–57.

without any nationalizing fugitive slave clause. In fact, Clay's fear of multiple confederacies was what should have not only happened after the Missouri Crisis but also during the earlier drive for the Constitution. Instead, the desire to build a mighty empire sabotaged this natural tendency toward decentralization, ensuring slavery would grow and cause problems down the road.

Old Republicans recognized the Missouri Compromise's consolidation. They firmly believed people possessed the right to decide whether their state constitutions would allow slavery, much like they possessed the right to decide other internal regulations relating to private property. The deal smacked of the centralizing trends that had accelerated with Madison's postwar nationalism, *Martin v. Hunter's Lessee* (1816), *McCulloch v. Maryland* (1819), and the protectionist Baldwin bill of 1820. Or, in the words of William Belko, restrictions on admitting states "merely symbolized the advance of power over liberty . . . in the very same manner as . . . the American System, and nothing more."[8]

John Taylor of Caroline summed up Old Republican views best in *Construction Construed and Constitutions Vindicated* (1820): conniving speculators, bankers, and manufacturers concocted the entire controversy. "The Missouri project," wrote the Virginian, "begot the idea of using slavery as an instrument for affecting the balance of power."[9] Taylor earnestly believed that Congress' meddling in slavery destroyed federalism and created a sectional power struggle in total violation of the Tenth Amendment. According to Taylor, "Missouri has no right to compel Maine to admit of slavery, nor Maine any right to compel Missouri to prohibit it, because each state has a right to think for itself."[10] The dividing line only pitted North against South and opened the door for one group to mercilessly dominate the other.[11]

John Randolph had previously written a congressional report condemning the capital's slave trade, helped form the American Colonization Society, and privately praised an anti-slavery speech during the Missouri debates. However, he feared that the compromise would make the South more defensive of slavery and increase regional animosity. In February 1820 Randolph privately remarked that the agitators "have

---

[8] Belko, *Philip Pendleton Barbour*, p. 14. See also pp. 12, 14, 98–102.

[9] Browning, *Panic of 1819*, p. 333.

[10] Adam Tate, *Conservatism and Southern Intellectuals* (Columbia: University of Missouri Press, 2005), p. 74.

[11] Browning, *Panic of 1819*, pp. 332–33; Tate, *Southern Intellectuals*, pp. 73–75.

almost reconciled me to negro slavery. They have produced a revulsion even on my mind; what then must be the effect on those who had no scruples on the subject?"[12] Antislavery was now "put back a century, certainly a generation, by the unprincipled conduct of ambitious men."[13]

Yet as cogent as the Old Republicans' arguments sounded, they did not go far enough. Instead of attacking slavery, they openly defended it. The Missouri Compromise was crony *not* because it restricted settlers' property rights, but because it nationalized the West and protected slave owners' unjust property rights. Richard Ellis emphasizes that Old Republicans "never made the defense of slavery a central political concern" and their "arguments tended to take the form of ad hoc defensive responses."[14] However, their heightened defense of slavery after the Missouri Crisis turned into a worrisome trend.

In addition, the sting of northern insistence jolted southern nationalists, the group that Old Republicans always tried to sway. To these interventionists, slavery was less of a "necessary evil" and more of a "positive good." The Deep South, from the days of Federalist Charles Cotesworth Pinckney, held such views. Now faced with a threat, the southern National Republicans defended, and would continue to defend, the institution with vigor. Furthermore, Old Republicans started to make similar arguments. Randolph, previously reluctant about the institution, now preferred to discard the Declaration of Independence rather than slavery. Even more drastic, Nathaniel Macon and William Smith provided a positive defense. While Macon previously regretted slavery, he now declared that slaves were happy to work on the plantations and the institution was for the mutual benefit of all. Smith extolled slavery's virtues and grounded its roots in Christianity. The South Carolinian's statement was indicative of the growing sentiment in his home state, which viewed the issue with increasing anxiety because of its heavy slave population.[15]

---

[12] Norman Risjord, *Chesapeake Politics* (New York: Columbia University Press, 1978), pp. 215–16.

[13] Tate, *Southern Intellectuals*, p. 71. See also Moore, *Missouri Controversy*, pp. 96, 124–25; Nicholas Wood, "John Randolph of Roanoke and the Politics of Slavery in the Early Republic," *Virginia Magazine of History and Biography* (Summer 2012): 118–19, 122–28.

[14] Richard Ellis, *The Union at Risk* (New York: Oxford University Press, 1987), p. 193.

[15] Moore, *Missouri Controversy*, pp. 125–26, 307–08.

After the Missouri Crisis ended, the slavery controversy returned to dormancy. Old Republicans still genuinely believed in the benefits of liberty and confederation, only now with slightly more of a pro-slavery bent. Far more worrisome to them than slavery, as well as the Radicals and Jacksonians, was the emerging imperialist program—the hallmark of the National Republicans' consolidating American System.

The Birth of Imperialism

Foreign policy played a crucial, albeit neglected, role in the National Republicans' designs. Apart from pleasing expansionists, imperialistic measures in South America benefitted politically connected merchants and manufacturers in the North, particularly the Boston Associates. The central blame for their global empire, from acquiring Florida to the Monroe Doctrine and then the Panama Congress, can be laid at the doorstep of John Quincy Adams. Indeed, when it comes to international relations, this period must be understood as the Age of Adams. Only the libertarian Jacksonians stymied his grand designs.

The National Republicans split into two imperialist doctrines regarding South America. The first, expressed by Speaker Clay, called for recognition to those revolting against the Spanish. Clay worried that US manufacturers, subsidized by protective tariffs, would suffer losses from overproduction if the nation did not open up new markets. In May 1820, Clay declared that the "American System" referred to the Western Hemisphere, and "in relation to South America, the people of the United States will occupy the same position as the people of New England do the rest of the United States."[16] He envisioned a mercantilist arrangement similar to Great Britain and the colonies before the Revolutionary War, a perfect complement to his adulations of Napoleon in 1824. After providing explicit assistance to the rebels, Clay wanted Congress to increase tariffs and encourage discriminatory trade legislation in South American markets.[17]

---

[16] Randolph Campbell, "The Spanish American Aspect of Henry Clay's American System," *The Americas* (July 1967): 8.

[17] Campbell, "Clay's American System," pp. 6–7, 13–14; Dorfman, *Economic Mind*, 1, p. 390; Caitlan Fitz, *Our Sister Republics* (New York: W.W. Norton & Company, 2016), pp. 183–84; William Weeks, *John Quincy Adams and American Global Empire* (Lexington: The University Press of Kentucky, 1992), pp. 91–94; William Williams, *The Contours of American History* (Cleveland, OH: World Publishing Company, 1961), p. 221.

President Monroe and Secretary of State John Quincy Adams championed the second imperialistic program—clandestine aid. The administration supported nominal neutrality toward South America because it wanted a friendly Spain to sell Florida. In addition, the Boston Associates, such as Thomas H. Perkins, did not want to jeopardize their profitable trade with Spain, Cuba, and other loyal Caribbean colonies. At the same time, however, they secretly sold the South American rebels weapons from federal armories in New England. Furthermore, like good businessmen hedging their bets, these northern merchants sold a smaller amount of weapons and other supplies to the Spanish royalists. Monroe and Adams, under the sway of northern merchants, countenanced only this assistance, because anything public would threaten Florida negotiations.[18]

With Monroe and Adams running the executive branch, the government championed their doctrine instead of Clay's—the US kept its mind off South America so long as Florida remained in Spanish hands. Or, even in the Indians' hands—Adams wanted the US to acquire Florida at all costs. After openly defending another secret invasion of the peninsula, the secretary accomplished his coveted goal in the 1819 Adams-Onís Treaty. In the process, he secured massive subsidies for his crucial political supporters, the Boston Associates.

After the war, Adams encouraged encroaching on southwestern Indian lands. Admittedly, most natives failed to homestead the land they claimed ownership over. For example, the Cherokee and Creek hunters required two thousand acres per person for food while the average American farmer needed only two acres. Indians also failed to conserve the hunt, clinging to a mystical theory of reincarnation where Mother Nature magically regrew the dead. Understandably, as Adams remarked in 1802, "What is the right of huntsman to the forest of a thousand miles, over which he has accidentally ranged in quest of prey?"[19] Regardless, Americans aggravated relations by coercively imposing land cessions. General Andrew Jackson, now tasked with negotiations, was a perennial agitator. He genuinely cared about Indian welfare, even adopting an Indian child. But, *like virtually all other Americans*, Jackson harshly relegated the Indians to a secondary

---

[18] Fitz, *Sister Republics*, pp. 130–31, 160–68, 171, 181, 184–86, 306–07; Lindsay Regele, *Manufacturing Advantage* (Baltimore, MD: The Johns Hopkins University Press, 2019), pp. 117–23.

[19] Stanley Lebergott, *The Americans* (New York: W.W. Norton & Company, 1984), p. 18.

status: white settlers always came first. In response to frontier strife, in 1817 Jackson retaliated on the Seminoles in southern Georgia. Monroe and Secretary Calhoun gave him vague approval to pursue the Indians in Spanish Florida. Jackson seized the bait, expanding the First Seminole War by invading Spanish Florida.[20]

In Monroe's cabinet, only Adams defended the general's controversial actions. The secretary declared that Spain's lack of control over Florida's "savages" justified the invasion, which constituted "neither war against Spain nor violation of the Constitution."[21] Clearly, he wanted Jackson's bravado to demonstrate US power for Florida negotiations. Spain relented, allowing Adams and Spanish Minister Onís to sign a treaty in February 1819. After many years of chomping at the bit, the United States now controlled all of Florida. Indians in the Southwest nervously awaited their fate, and the Monroe and Adams administrations agreed to demands of Jacksonians in Georgia that they had to leave.[22]

The Treaty led to sizable benefits for the secretary's merchant allies. First, in return for ceding any claim to Texas, Spain reneged all claims to the Pacific Northwest, thereby expanding the US' domain to the West Coast. Now only vague British and Russian claims stood in the way. Boston Associates who conducted trade with China and wanted a US port on the Pacific, especially Perkins, lauded the acquisition. So did Chief Justice Marshall and SBUS President Biddle, who wanted the United States to control the continent.[23]

Second, the federal government assumed $5 million in American merchant losses against Spanish seizures of goods and ships that had occurred since the 1790s. According to Carl Prince and Seth Taylor,

---

[20] Shepard Krech, *The Ecological Indian* (New York: W.W. Norton & Company, 1999), pp. 151–71; Lebergott, *Americans*, pp. 13–18; Walter Nugent, *Habits of Empire* (New York: Vintage Books, 2009), pp. 121–23; Robert Remini, *Andrew Jackson and His Indian Wars* (New York: Penguin Books, 2001), pp. 64–69, 214–15.

[21] Robert Remini, *John Quincy Adams* (New York: Henry Holt and Company, 2002), p. 55.

[22] Nugent, *Habits of Empire*, pp. 123–27; Remini, *John Quincy Adams*, pp. 54–55, 90–100; Norman Risjord, *The Old Republicans* (New York: Columbia University Press, 1965), pp. 188–90.

[23] Thomas Govan, *Nicholas Biddle* (Chicago: The University of Chicago Press, 1959), pp. 53–56; Dangerfield, *Awakening of American Nationalism*, p. 72; Nugent, *Habits of Empire*, pp. 127, 160–63; Lindsay Schakenbach, "From Discontented Bostonians to Patriotic Industrialists," *The New England Quarterly* (September 2011): 395–96; Weeks, *American Global Empire*, pp. 51–52, 80, 178.

this bailout "marked unprecedented American underwriting of private commercial losses, losses traditionally treated as hazards of free enterprise in a world of competitive nations."[24] The recipient merchants and insurance companies based their operations in the North: New England received $1.8 million, Philadelphia $1.3 million, New York less than $1 million, Baltimore $600,000, and the South just $300,000. As expected, the Boston Associates and their affiliate Boston Marine Insurance Company and Massachusetts Fire and Marine Insurance Company led the pack, securing $1 million, far more than their rivals.

The basic reason for the Boston Associates' success was simple. First, as an eager Adams explained to Perkins, "every attention will be paid to your claim. . . . It would be peculiarly grateful to me to be instrumental in arriving at this result."[25] Second, William King—brother of arch-Federalist Rufus King, first governor of Maine, and real estate partner of senator and Boston Associate affiliate Harrison Gray Otis—sat on the three-man Spanish Claims Commission. Third, Webster, who declared to Boston Associate Peter C. Brooks that the Treaty would enrich "the Insurance Offices in Boston," filed the Associates' losses before the commission.[26]

Adams and Webster profited immensely. Perkins, who received a hefty $132,000 bailout, supported Adams in his successful 1824 presidential run. Webster received a 5 percent cut for his legal work, boasting that the merchant payout "occasioned the Treaty."[27] Historians Prince and Taylor emphasize that Webster "demonstrates his real significance in forging a Hamiltonian partnership between government and industry . . . divert[ing] public money in large sums to Associate-related coffers at a critical time in the expansion of the Bostonians' industrial empire."[28] The Adams-Onís Treaty provides a signature example of the Era of Corruption's cronyism, illustrating how businesses and politicians jointly profited at taxpayer expense.[29]

---

[24] Carl Prince and Seth Taylor, "Daniel Webster, the Boston Associates, and the U.S. Government's Role in the Industrializing Process," *Journal of the Early Republic* (Autumn 1982): 298.

[25] Schakenbach, "Discontented Bostonians," p. 392.

[26] Ibid., p. 388.

[27] Ibid., p. 390.

[28] Prince and Taylor, "Daniel Webster," p. 297.

[29] Ibid., pp. 293–98; Regele, *Manufacturing Advantage*, pp. 91–94, 98, 218–19; Schakenbach, "Discontented Bostonians," pp. 385–86, 388–95, 399.

Once Monroe and Adams acquired Florida, they swung their support to Clay's system. Unsurprisingly, the main objective of new diplomatic missions, which the secretary of state emphasized as "deserving of particular attention," was to secure favorable trade deals.[30] In Adams' words, "as navigators and manufacturers, *we* are already so far advanced in a career upon which *they* are yet to enter, that we may, for many years . . . maintain with them a commercial intercourse."[31] Many of the diplomats partnered with American businessmen, such as Boston Associate affiliate John Murray Forbes, stationed in Argentina. Consequently, the emissaries tried to secure preferential treatment instead of free trade arrangements. For example, William Tudor, a Bostonian-appointed consul to Peru, lobbied the government to only lower the tariff on cloth made by power looms, which the Boston Associates monopolized through patent laws. Rhode Island merchant Edwin T. Jenckes stationed allies in Chile so they could persuade local politicians to levy discriminatory tariffs on British products. In Mexico, Minister Joel R. Poinsett coaxed the government to grant the US most-favored-nation status.[32]

Adams and Clay's plans for quasi-colonization received a major boost in Monroe's "Doctrine" of December 1823, a response to exaggerated threats of new European interventions in South America. William Appleman Williams appropriately calls the Monroe Doctrine "the Manifesto of the American Empire," and Murray Rothbard argues it "launch[ed] the career of American imperialism in Latin America."[33] Essentially, Monroe declared that the European powers could not create new colonies in North or South America, or risk insulting the US. In return, the US would not interfere in European wars. Translation: "Europe must stay on their turf so we can take ours." This aggrandizement of the whole Western Hemisphere shocked Europeans. Monroe did not help matters by concurrently advocating higher tariffs on European products and meddling in a foreign war by praising Greek resistance against Turkey.

---

[30] Williams, *Contours of American History*, p. 217.

[31] Ibid., p. 218.

[32] Campbell, "Clay's American System," pp. 10–11; Regele, *Manufacturing Advantage*, pp. 123–29, 229.

[33] Murray N. Rothbard, "Report on George B. DeHuszar and Thomas Hulbert Stevenson, *A History of the American Republic*, 2 vols," in Rothbard, *Strictly Confidential*, ed. David Gordon (Auburn, AL: Mises Institute, 2010), p. 116, and Williams, *Contours of American History*, p. 215.

Adams played a major role in shaping the Monroe Doctrine to make sure the British stayed out of Spanish Cuba, his new conquest. Earlier in the year, he wrote to the US minister in Spain, Hugh Nelson, that "the annexation of Cuba to our federal republic will be indispensable to the continuance and integrity of the Union itself. . . . You will not conceal from the Spanish Government the repugnance of the United States to the transfer of the island of Cuba to any other power."[34] The secretary of state wanted both Spain and Great Britain to realize that Cuba was the next course in the United States' dinner.[35]

Unfortunately, one loophole could cripple Adams' doctrine: nothing prevented Mexico or Colombia from taking the island. This would remove Cuba from Spanish hands and make it harder for the US to acquire. Even worse, Cuba might independently revolt from its new master, opening the door for the British to protect their Caribbean interests. This fear, which reached a fever pitch in 1825, worried the new President Adams and Secretary of State Clay. The administration knew that invoking the Monroe Doctrine against an independent American nation was simply too aggressive, so it first tried thinly veiled threats against the US' southern neighbors.

Clay wrote to Minister Poinsett stating, that if Spain lost control of Cuba, the island "should be attached to the United States."[36] Poinsett dutifully relayed the information and astonishingly informed the British Minister to Mexico that "the United States were the head of the American powers," implying an informal confederation.[37] Adams and Clay also audaciously authorized Poinsett to purchase Texas for $1 million from Mexico, instructing him to use the insulting argument that a Texas cession would position their capital in the center of the country. Unsurprisingly, the diplomat could not make any progress on the subject. The US Ambassador in Colombia, Richard Anderson, issued a similar warning about Cuba.

---

[34] Dangerfield, *Awakening of American Nationalism*, p. 169.

[35] Ibid., pp. 161–94; Fitz, *Sister Republics*, p. 158; David Johnson, *John Randolph of Roanoke* (Baton Rouge: Louisiana State University Press, 2012), pp. 193–95; Williams, *Contours of American History*, pp. 215–18.

[36] Samuel Bemis, *John Quincy Adams and the Foundations of American Foreign Policy* (Norwalk, CT: The Easton Press, 1987), p. 539.

[37] Bemis, *John Quincy Adams*, p. 548.

Next came the Europeans. Clay wrote to James Brown, the minister to France and a family relative, that the US would never allow "any other power than Spain under any contingency whatsoever" to control Cuba.[38] Ambassador to Spain Alexander Everett, Congressman Edward Everett's brother, even ridiculously suggested to the Spanish secretary of state that the country mortgage Cuba to the tune of $15 to $20 million for US protection, a proposal that Everett confidentially believed would lead to *"the eventual acquisition of the entire sovereignty."*[39]

It turned out that Adams and Clay vastly overestimated the aggressiveness of Mexico and Colombia, who preferred to discuss Cuba at the upcoming Panama Congress. Adams and Clay leapt at the opportunity, rashly agreeing to attend before informing Congress. Besides the Cuba question, the two desperately wanted to secure approval for a US canal through the Isthmus of Panama. In December 1825, Adams sent a message to the Senate nominating two delegates, and the upper chamber debated the matter the following year.

This time, Adams and Clay overextended themselves because of the emerging Jacksonian coalition. When analyzing the congressional debates, historians unduly focus on how southern Jacksonians fretted over the new countries having freed their slaves. This was in large part due to Senator John Randolph, who seethed at Adams and Clay's recent corrupt bargain for the presidency. Although describing slavery as a "cancer" and a "disease," Randolph engaged in hyperbole, insisting that the Panama Congress would liberate Cuba, emancipate the slaves, and attack Florida to encourage domestic slave revolts.[40] Once again, Randolph was not actually worried about the threat—in the same year he privately lamented slavery and relations with the Indians. But his tactic succeeded in alarming some southern congressmen. What is usually neglected, however, is that Clay and Hezekiah Niles insisted that slave owners should actually support attendance precisely to prevent a South American takeover of Cuba. Contrary to common belief, Caitlin Fitz argues Adams "intended to *protect* slavery by sending delegates to Panama."[41]

---

[38] Dangerfield, *Awakening of American Nationalism*, p. 247.

[39] Bemis, *John Quincy Adams*, p. 542. See also pp. 154, 540, 542; Philip Burch, *Elites in American History*, vol. 1 (New York: Holmes & Meier Publishers, 1981), p. 124; Glenn Price, *Origins of the War with Mexico* (Austin: University of Texas Press, 1967), pp. 16–18; Remini, *John Quincy Adams*, p. 103.

[40] Wood, "John Randolph," p. 131.

[41] Fitz, *Sister Republics*, p. 215. See also John Belohlavek, *"Let the Eagle Soar!"* (Lincoln:

While the slavery controversy boded ominously for the future, Jeffrey Malanson stresses that it was only one of many issues the Senate debated and that "the fundamental principles of US foreign policy," particularly noninterventionism versus activism, "truly stands out as being of the greatest significance."[42] The Jacksonian critics, particularly Senator Van Buren, genuinely worried about the constitutionality of the president's actions and the precedent attendance would establish. Although many Jacksonians maintained expansionist views regarding Texas, they refused to meddle in the affairs of other countries. Even the militaristic Jackson displayed a genuine concern over entangling alliances, writing that if "we engage in confederations, or alliances with any nation, we may from that time date the down fall of our republic" because such actions could *"lead to War."*[43] Congressional Jacksonians did not hesitate to criticize the American System's "domestic policy" of "restriction and Monopoly" and its "foreign policy" of "'entangling alliances.'"[44] The direction of US foreign policy remained the primary issue of contention, and the Jacksonians wanted to take a stand.

In the end, the Jacksonians lacked the political strength to stop the mission. But the entire Panama Congress turned into a fiasco. Only a handful of countries sent delegates on time, and one US delegate arrived late while the other died en route. Although their plans failed, Adams and Clay continued to eye Cuba. In 1827, Clay sent Daniel Cook of Illinois, a lame-duck congressman crucial in securing Adams' House election, on a secret Cuba mission to report any suspicious activity. In Spain, Everett notified the authorities that if British subjects remained in Cuba, the Adams administration might *"aid the King"* by invading the island.[45] But for the time being, crucial setbacks postponed the Cuba acquisition.[46]

University of Nebraska Press, 1985), pp. 238–40; Dangerfield, *Awakening of American Nationalism*, pp. 248–53; Fitz, *Sister Republics*, pp. 214–16, 221; Jeffrey Malanson, "The Congressional Debate Over U.S. Participation in the Congress of Panama," *Diplomatic History* (November 2006): 819–21; Wood, "John Randolph," pp. 131–33.

[42] Malanson, "Congressional Debate," p. 814.

[43] Fitz, *Sister Republics*, p. 206.

[44] Campbell, "Clay's American System," p. 12.

[45] Bemis, *John Quincy Adams*, p. 543.

[46] Ibid., pp. 541–44; Dangerfield, *Awakening of American Nationalism*, p. 253; Malanson, "Congressional Debate," pp. 821–25, 834; Robert Remini, *Martin Van Buren*

Although the Jacksonians failed to stop the mission, they grew stronger by the year, causing Adams and Clay to increasingly focus on securing reelection in 1828. The crucial catalyst for the emerging reform party occurred in early 1825, when Clay helped Adams win the presidency in return for the top spot eight years down the road.

and the Making of the Democratic Party (New York: Columbia University Press, 1959), pp. 104–16.

CHAPTER 13

THE JACKSONIAN REVOLUTION AND THE DEFEAT OF THE NATIONAL REPUBLICANS

The Corrupt Bargain

By 1828, reformers created a new libertarian organization to thwart the American System juggernaut: the Democratic Party. This accomplishment can be attributed to Van Buren, who deliberately tried to return Jefferson's party to its Old Republican roots. Van Buren first attempted this feat with Crawford in 1824 before supporting the charismatic Jackson after Clay and Adams secretly exchanged favors for the presidency. This nefarious deal—the Corrupt Bargain of 1825— embodied the decade's pervasive cronyism. The Tennessean defeated Adams in the Revolution of 1828, ushering in a new reform party dedicated to attacking special privileges.

Van Buren had his flaws, but undeniably demonstrated what Murray Rothbard calls "tactical brilliance."[1] He perceptively understood the indispensable nature of political parties: without an organization favoring limited government, corruption proliferated. He first started in his home state and fought Governor DeWitt Clinton, a new affiliate of National Republicans and Federalists. Nationwide, Van Buren tried to save the Republican Party by reviving the venerable New York–Virginia axis. The Regency formed the nucleus of Crawford's Radicals, and in 1821 the New Yorker secured a Senate seat and befriended the Old Republican Randolph. The next year, Van Buren made the first of many pilgrimages to Virginia, establishing connections with Roane and Ritchie. Shortly thereafter, he strengthened his strict constructionist voting record.

Van Buren looked ahead to the upcoming presidential election in 1824, currently a dogfight between Crawford, Calhoun, Clay, Adams,

---

[1] Murray N. Rothbard, "Principle in Politics," *Inquiry* (September 1983): 35.

and Jackson. The previous three presidents had all formerly served as secretaries of states, making Adams the heir apparent. But Van Buren refused to acquiesce, rallying reformers behind Crawford. In 1823 he sojourned to Ritchie, who swung to Crawford, along with Randolph, Macon, Taylor, Jefferson, and Cooper. Van Buren continued his Virginia pilgrimages, most notably in the spring of 1824, when he met with Jefferson. Van Buren devised a simple strategy: secure victory before the election. The Crawfordite Radicals would accomplish this through the congressional caucus, the old nominating horse of the Republican Party. Aside from its thoroughly Jeffersonian heritage, Van Buren reasoned that the caucus would keep the party together and avoid an overtime House election. If the latter occurred, Van Buren feared that corrupt representatives would trade favors to elevate their preferred choice to the presidency.

Two factors complicated the picture. First, in mid-1823 Crawford suffered a debilitating stroke. Second, later in the year, Van Buren discovered that less than one-fourth of Congress, mainly Crawford supporters, consented to the caucus. The other candidates, in addition to Monroe, resisted because they knew Crawford still possessed the highest chance of winning. Even though supporters nominated Crawford, the fact that other candidates still planned to compete made it an empty nomination. Crawford's candidacy faded fast.[2]

In the presidential election of 1824, two results quickly emerged. First, Calhoun, previously dropping out of the race, easily achieved his secondary goal and secured the vice presidency. Second, no presidential candidate acquired a majority of the Electoral College. However, Jackson decisively commanded a plurality (99) over Adams (84), Crawford (41), and Clay (37). He also racked up electoral majorities in the most states (11) while Adams (7), Crawford (3), and Clay (3) lagged behind. The same held for the popular vote (143,573), with Adams (120,459), Crawford (48,334), and Clay (47,939) clearly trailing. Jackson was the man to beat.[3]

[2] Donald Cole, *Martin Van Buren and the American Political System* (Princeton, NJ: Princeton University Press, 1984), pp. 115, 125; Donald Ratcliffe, *The One-Party Presidential Contest* (Lawrence: University Press of Kansas, 2015), pp. 32–33, 81–82, 149–55; Robert Remini, *Martin Van Buren and the Making of the Democratic Party* (New York: Columbia University Press, 1959), pp. 7–29, 35–49, 59–63, 119; Norman Risjord, *The Old Republicans* (New York: Columbia University Press, 1965), pp. 230–31, 252–53.

[3] Ratcliffe, *One-Party Presidential Contest*, appendix.

Some pro-Adams historians increase the New Englander's turn-out by estimating popular vote totals in states where the legislatures chose electors, particularly New York.[4] They want to show that Adams actually secured the popular vote instead of Jackson, and therefore no corrupt bargain really occurred. This procedure compares apples to oranges. The Jacksonians deliberately chose not to campaign in New York, because the legislature picked the electors. Moreover, as these historians admit, if the state had choosen its electors via popular vote, Clinton would have entered the presidential race and significantly cut down on Adams' total. Given the election as it actually occurred, the conclusion is inescapable: Jackson received the most votes.[5]

According to the Twelfth Amendment, similar to the 1800 election, the incumbent House voted on the top three candidates, with each state delegation casting one vote for their preferred choice. Whichever candidate won the majority of states—thirteen—would be the next president. This overtime election worried Van Buren, because the chances for corruption markedly increased, though he hoped that Crawford could win as a compromise candidate if gridlock existed between Adams and Jackson supporters.

Indeed, corruption did occur, thanks to a devastated Clay, whom the overtime rules eliminated from the race. Clay's consolation prize was that as Speaker he exerted enormous power in deciding who received the honor, which meant he could wrangle a personal reward. In particular, he coveted the secretary of state position that proved such a reliable stepping stone. Clay arranged a sit-down with Adams, whom he immensely favored over Jackson and Crawford. In early 1825, Clay magnanimously asked Adams "to satisfy him with regard to some principles of great public importance [the American System], but without any personal considerations for himself."[6] Of course: two politicians who had no problem pilfering the public would now look out only for the nation's welfare. The public interest always reigns supreme! Both knew the deal: Clay would elevate Adams to the presidency while the latter appointed the Speaker to be his secretary of state, who would then become the president eight years down the road. This deal was the third corrupt bargain that rocked the nation. Adams

---

[4] Donald Ratcliffe, "Popular Preferences in the Presidential Election of 1824," *Journal of the Early Republic* (Spring 2014): 45–77.

[5] Ibid., pp. 72–73.

[6] Robert Remini, *Henry Clay* (New York: W.W. Norton & Company, 1991), p. 258.

was all the worse for it, because during the campaign, the candidates pledged they would make no secret deals, and the New Englander, along with Jackson, stated that he did not actually want the job.[7]

Adams and Clay quickly enlisted six state delegations—Kentucky, Ohio, Louisiana, Illinois, Missouri, and Maryland—necessary for victory. Jackson won the majority of the electoral votes in these states (Louisiana, Illinois, and Maryland) or finished second behind Clay in the popular vote (Kentucky, Ohio, and Missouri). In other words, the state delegations should have voted for Jackson and given him the majority necessary for victory. But this was not to be.

Clay's home state was the easiest. Although the state legislature instructed its delegation to vote for Jackson, the Speaker ordered the congressmen to vote for Adams even though the official figures showed he did not win a *single* vote in Kentucky. Clay then corrupted Ohio. He introduced a bill extending the National Road into Ohio, Indiana, Illinois, and Missouri. Shortly thereafter, Ohio declared for Adams. Thanks to Congressman Henry Gurley, a Clay supporter friendly to Adams, Clay also enlisted Louisiana.

Now Adams conjured up his magic. In Illinois, Daniel Cook served as the sole representative. Unfortunately for Jackson, Cook was friends with Adams. After some cajoling and reported bribery, he declared his vote for the New Englander. Although the furious Illinois public denied Cook's reelection bid in 1826, Adams granted his old chum a diplomatic post in Cuba. Missouri also sent only one representative, John Scott. Adams made Scott two promises: he would appoint Scott's requested publishers to print Missouri's laws and keep his brother as an Arkansas judge, even though said brother had illegally killed a colleague in a duel.

The Federalist Webster, who saw an opening in the emerging Adams-Clay alliance, also performed valuable work. He obtained assurances from Adams that Federalists would be eligible for patronage. Webster then used this pledge to convince the Maryland delegates to swing behind Adams. Crucially, Webster also solidified New York, which threatened to drop Adams down to twelve states. Although the state legislature voted for Adams, Van Buren managed to split the

[7] Ratcliffe, *One-Party Presidential Contest*, pp. 149–50; Remini, *Henry Clay*, pp. 235–58; Remini, *Making of the Democratic Party*, pp. 85–89; Robert Remini, *Andrew Jackson*, vol. 2 (New York: History Book Club, 1998), pp. 86–89; William Watkins, *Crossroads for Liberty* (Oakland, CA: The Independent Institute, 2016), pp. 251–52; Henry Watson, *Liberty and Power* (New York: The Noonday Press, 1990), pp. 81–83.

congressional delegation in the hopes of winning it for Crawford. It deadlocked, with one undecided Federalistist Stephen Van Rensselaer. If Van Rensselaer voted for Adams, the delegation would follow and give the New Englander his thirteen states. Thanks to Webster's remarks about Federalist patronage, it did.

In February, the House elected Adams president on the first ballot. Webster and Randolph, tasked with counting the votes, expressed diametrically opposed reactions. While Webster crowed, Randolph bitterly remarked: "it was impossible to win the game, gentlemen, the cards were stacked."[8] Jackson, of course, fumed: "The Judas of the West has closed the contract, and received the thirty pieces of silver. His end will be the same."[9]

Thus, Adams corruptly secured the six states necessary to win the presidency. The plurality of the people and the Electoral College chose Jackson, which put him in the strongest position to win. But without a majority of the Electoral College, the decision went to the House, where Adams and Clay thwarted the people's will. This demonstrated to the public the entrenched cronyism in Congress, signaling the need for serious reform.

The Revolution of 1828

To Van Buren, the corrupt bargain was caused by Republicans abandoning the congressional caucus. Realizing that the party was beyond repair, he created a new organization in its place. After developing this crucial political network, the Jacksonian Democrats triumphed, forever throwing the National Republicans out of power in what can be called "The Revolution of 1828." Van Buren's initial groundwork was one of the most notable accomplishments in the history of reform.

Even before Adams' first address to Congress in December 1825, the Tennessee legislature nominated Jackson for president. Van Buren realized he could forge his libertarian party around the charismatic Jackson: "If Gen Jackson & his friends will put his election

---

[8] David Johnson, *John Randolph of Roanoke* (Baton Rouge: Louisiana State University Press, 2012), p. 203.

[9] Watson, *Liberty and Power*, 82. See also Johnson, *John Randolph*, p. 203; Shaw Livermore, *The Twilight of Federalism* (Princeton, NJ: Princeton University Press, 1962), pp. 172–82; Ratcliffe, *One-Party Presidential Contest*, p. 246, appendix; Remini, *Henry Clay*, pp. 259–65; Remini, *Making of the Democratic Party*, pp. 89–92; Remini, *Andrew Jackson*, 2, pp. 89–99.

on old party grounds . . . our success when achieved will be worth something."[10] It was a perfect partnership. As Robert Remini explains, "both were committed to a states' rights philosophy and both tended to a laissez-faire notion of economic theory."[11] Van Buren built up his Old Republican credentials in the 1820s, and Jackson maintained Old Republican connections that went back to his tenure as a senator in the late 1790s. Although Jackson based his 1824 campaign largely on personality, the House debacle convinced the Tennessean of the need for serious reform. Over the next several years, he outlined a "reform retrenchment and economy" program.[12] In particular, Jackson wanted amendments to enforce strict constructionism and weaken special-interest deals in Congress; the elimination of the national debt and the Second Bank of the United States; and stringent vetoes on government spending and bureaucratic decision-making. Congressman James K. Polk and Senator Thomas Benton, among Jackson's earliest supporters, wholeheartedly agreed.[13]

In 1826, Jackson and Van Buren acquired their first ally: Vice President Calhoun, who recognized that the National Republicans had anointed Adams and Clay for the next sixteen years. Van Buren suggested to Calhoun that they bring Ritchie and his Richmond *Enquirer* on board to convince Radicals that Jackson adhered to Old Republican principles. However, Calhoun remained hostile to Ritchie, because the Virginian still appropriately considered the South Carolinian a staunch nationalist. But Van Buren pressed Calhoun until he relented. Soon Ritchie, Randolph, and Barbour joined the Jacksonians.

In January 1827, Van Buren wrote a famous letter to Ritchie outlining his grand strategy. He desired to produce a *"substantial reorganization of the old Republican Party,"* substituting *"principle* for *personal preference* as one of the leading points in the contest."[14] Van Buren recognized that "political combinations between the inhabitants of the

[10] Robert Remini, *The Election of Andrew Jackson* (New York: J.B. Lippincott Company, 1963), p. 39.

[11] Remini, *Andrew Jackson*, 2, p. 194.

[12] William Belko, *Philip Pendleton Barbour in Jacksonian America* (Tuscaloosa: University of Alabama Press, 2016), p. 140.

[13] Donald Cole, *Vindicating Andrew Jackson* (Lawrence: University Press of Kansas, 2009), p. 50; Ratcliffe, *One-Party Presidential Contest*, p. 267; Remini, *Andrew Jackson*, 2, pp. 76, 129; Risjord, *The Old Republicans*, p. 262; Charles Sellers, James K. Polk, *Jacksonian* (Princeton, NJ: Princeton University Press, 1957), pp. 105–06.

[14] Remini, *Making of the Democratic Party*, pp. 130–131.

different states are unavoidable & the most natural & beneficial to the country is that between the planters of the South [Virginia] and the plain Republicans of the North [New York]."[15] Contrary to modern perception, Van Buren did *not* try to create a pro-slavery party. Instead, he wanted to recreate the divisions between the Hamiltonian Federalists and the Jeffersonian Republicans. The new Democratic Party, according to Van Buren, must champion laissez-faire and the Spirit of 1798 against the National Republicans' American System. The old battle between liberty and power emerged once more.[16]

Meanwhile, Clay prepared for the upcoming rematch, engaging in political malfeasance and rallying the troops. First, the secretary of state dispensed federal printing contracts to favorable newspapers, particularly the *National Intelligencer*, while eschewing unreliable periodicals, such as Amos Kendall's Kentucky *Argus*. Second, he used the congressional franking privilege (free postal services) to subsidize campaign costs. Third, Clay enlisted Webster as the campaign's unofficial treasurer because of his connections with the Boston Associates. Fourth, he hit the campaign trail, preaching the American System. Or, in the words of an Adams administration newspaper, "The real question, the only question of policy and principle, that is at issue between the supporters of Mr. Adams and those of Gen. Jackson, is this: 'Shall the American System be adopted as a great leading national measure or not?'"[17]

Unfortunately for Clay, Jackson and Van Buren's coalition grew stronger by the day. In the spring of 1827, Van Buren enlisted Crawford. Later in the year, Kendall and Francis Preston Blair of Kentucky, former Clay supporters, joined Van Buren after realizing that "states rights, the Bank, [and] the power of the Judiciary . . . became the criterion to distinguish the parties."[18] Finally, Van Buren created a central committee to gather these leading politicos and then fight corruption with corruption, using the franking privilege and acquiring state-level printing contracts for Jacksonian newspapers.

---

[15] Remini, *Making of the Democratic Party*, p. 131.

[16] Belko, *Philip Pendleton Barbour*, p. 131; Cole, *Vindicating Andrew Jackson*, pp. 46–50, 71–76; Remini, *Making of the Democratic Party*, pp. 124–32; Risjord, *The Old Republicans*, pp. 262–63; Sean Wilentz, *The Rise of American Democracy* (New York: W.W. Norton, 2005), pp. 295–96, 307.

[17] Daniel Feller, *The Jacksonian Promise* (Baltimore, MD: The Johns Hopkins University Press, 1995), p. 74.

[18] Richard Ellis, *The Union at Risk* (New York: Oxford University Press, 1987), p. 14.

Over 1828, Jackson gained momentum. A favorable sign occurred in the 1826 elections, when Adams lost control of Congress, the first time ever for a sitting president. The presidential election only confirmed the bad omen. Jackson amassed 647,292 votes to Adams' 507,730, 178 Electoral College votes to the incumbent's eighty-three. Adams carried New England while the Tennessean commanded the Mid-Atlantic, the South, and the West. New York split in favor of Jackson because of the politicking of Van Buren (who successfully secured the governorship). In the legislature, Democrats comfortably controlled the House and narrowly the Senate. Clearly, the people had chosen the Jacksonians, ushering in a new era.[19]

The Revolution of 1828 ended the Era of Corruption. Thanks to Van Buren, the power-hungry Adams-Clay-Webster triumvirate could not continue their program of central banking, protective tariffs, transportation subsidies, western nationalization, and South American imperialism. Remini properly argues the election embodied

> what Kendall had called "the principles for which we are all contending." . . . They contended that . . . corruption abounds where power goes unchecked [and] demanded an administration that would restrict government power. . . . Jackson's election would not only expel a corrupt administration from office but create a new party based on mass support dedicated to the restoration of the constitutional safeguards of liberty.[20]

Now, Jackson, Van Buren, and their libertarians needed to figure out how to avoid the pitfalls of Jefferson's Republican Party and successfully remove special privileges.

---

[19] Donald Cole, *A Jackson Man* (Baton Rouge: Louisiana State University Press, 2004), pp. 95–97; Cole, *Vindicating Andrew Jackson*, pp. 59–71, 76, 183–86, 193–94; Ellis, *Union at Risk*, pp. 14–15; *Historical Statistics of the United States, Historical Statistics of the United States*, vol. 5, ed. Richard Sutch and Susan Carter (New York: Cambridge University Press, 2006), p. 200; Remini, *Election of Andrew Jackson*, pp. 84–85, 126–31.

[20] Remini, *Andrew Jackson*, 2, p. 129.

PART V

THE FAILED JACKSONIAN REVOLUTION, 1829–1849

CHAPTER 14

DISMANTLING THE AMERICAN SYSTEM: DECENTRALIZING MONEY

Reforming the Executive

Admirably, the virtually uninterrupted Democratic reign of Andrew Jackson, Martin Van Buren, John Tyler, and James K. Polk severely weakened cronyism, though moderations occurred. The Jacksonians succeeded where the Jeffersonians failed because of greater tenacity, refusing to work with the opposition, the increased influence of free market thought, and tacit cooperation with free market British politicians. Crucially, they triumphed with the executive branch, morphing the office from a corrupt shield into an anti-crony sword. First, Jacksonians transformed the presidential veto and exercised greater use of rotation. Then, they achieved a quasi-free market in money by vetoing the Second Bank of the United States' recharter, instituting the Independent Treasury, and adopting quasi-free banking on the state level. But in doing so, Democrats helped turn the executive into a leader with enormous authority and control.

Originally, the Federalists envisioned Congress spearheading special-interest legislation. The president played the defense: similar to colonial governors, he could use the veto to protect cronyism if Congress succumbed to the people. Altogether, the six presidents from Washington to John Quincy Adams exercised the veto only ten times over forty years, mostly for minor legislative matters or to encourage a strengthening of proposed special privileges. By contrast, Democrats envisioned the veto as an offensive reform and an expression of the people's will: true reform required a democratically elected executive, because corruption proliferated in Congress. Only the executive, not the legislature, could lead the charge against cronyism. Amos Kendall and Francis Preston Blair, editors of the new administration newspaper the *Washington Globe*, emphatically championed this perspective.

Over the next twenty years, the Jacksonians utilized the veto twenty-six times, largely on important bills.[1]

Jackson's veto found a firm advocate in Philip Barbour, who proclaimed the executive had a constitutional duty to actively dissent from legislation. He was one of the many strict constructionists who saw the veto strategy as a savior from Congress' inexorable subsidies and regulations. Barbour moved beyond Jefferson, who famously told a hesitant Washington to defer to Congress on Hamilton's Bank. While Barbour recognized the problem of executive usurpation, he believed that Jackson represented the people and was "placed at the helm" to bring the "vessel of State" back "into the right course."[2] William Belko is surely correct that many Old Republicans, previously viewing "executive presence [as] the bane of liberty and the manifestation of corruption," now "turned to [it] to rescue the republic."[3]

In stark contrast, Adams, Clay, and Webster vehemently attacked Jacksonian vetoes, soon naming their new party in reference to the English Whigs that fought monarchical tyranny in the eighteenth century. They even advocated a constitutional amendment to weaken the veto. In reality, the Whig Party was only against a commander vetoing monetary intervention, protective tariffs, and subsidies. These reactionaries eagerly looked forward to a strong president when they controlled the White House.

The Jacksonians undoubtedly played with fire. Although Democrats increased the veto power to whittle down cronyism, they increased the power of the *federal* president, corrupting the office. One man now wielded two-thirds the legislative influence of Congress, providing a heady wine to its wielder. The president's augmented veto power made him very important, *almost* an emperor, opening the door for enormous influence in legislative matters. This no doubt fit in with one of Jackson's greatest flaws, his penchant for militarism.[4]

---

[1] Stephen Campbell, *The Bank War and the Partisan Press* (Lawrence: University Press of Kansas, 2019), p. 39; *Historical Statistics of the United States, Historical Statistics of the United States*, vol. 5, ed. Richard Sutch and Susan Carter (New York: Cambridge University Press, 2006), p. 197; Gerard Magliocca, "Veto!," *Nebraska Law Review* (1999): 213–26; Leonard White, *The Jacksonians* (New York: Macmillan, 1954), pp. 28–29.

[2] William Belko, *Philip Pendleton Barbour in Jacksonian America* (Tuscaloosa: University of Alabama Press, 2016), p. 157.

[3] Ibid., pp. 160–61.

[4] Robert Kelley, *The Transatlantic Persuasion* (New York: Alfred A. Knopf, 1969), p.

Jackson and his successors also revolutionized the executive through widespread rotation of bureaucrats. Many historians argue that this "spoils system" bred corruption more than the previous quasi-civil service.[5] This perspective results from the unrealistic assumption that bureaucrats promote the public interest. In reality, rotation is only *visibly* more corrupt; but it actually decreases cronyism. It admittedly empowers the president and incentivizes him to replace officials according to political preferences, but does not inherently lead to a more bloated and unaccountable bureaucracy.

While Jefferson removed some Federalists early on, little rotation occurred in subsequent administrations. By the Era of Corruption, Washington had turned into a swamp, and many officials viewed their sinecures as property rights they could bequeath to their sons. In fact, due to seemingly impenetrable tenure, politicians could only reward campaign supporters by creating new jobs. This encouraged a steady increase in the number of government officials and bureaucrats. The National Republicans' civil service profited from their offices by embezzling funds and supported the American System to increase demand for their posts. No wonder Murray Rothbard describes civil service as leading to a "permanent and self-conscious . . . caste, set aside from, and in fundamental opposition to, the mass of the citizenry."[6]

This protected bureaucracy deeply worried Jackson, who declared "rotation in office . . . will perpetuate our liberty."[7] In his first address to Congress, the president attacked the corrupt bureaucracy for enjoying "office and power" to the detriment of the public, making government "an engine for the support of the few at the expense of the many," something at variance with strict constructionism and the Spirit of 1798.[8] To destroy "office as property," Jackson endorsed the dead-letter 1820 Tenure of the Office Act, which instituted terms for upper-level bureaucrats.[9] He also gave special instructions to his new fourth auditor of the treasury, Kendall, to trim the bloated payroll.

251; Magliocca, "Veto," p. 255; Robert Remini, *Andrew Jackson*, vol. 3 (New York: History Book Club, 1998), pp. 136–37; White, *Jacksonians*, pp. 27–30, 46–47.

[5] Jay Cost, *A Republic No More* (New York: Encounter Books, 2015), pp. 62–82.

[6] Murray N. Rothbard, "Bureaucracy and the Civil Service in the United States," *Journal of Libertarian Studies* (Summer 1995): 23.

[7] Robert Remini, *Andrew Jackson*, 2 (New York: History Book Club, 1998), p. 190.

[8] Rothbard, "Bureaucracy," p. 35.

[9] Robert Remini, *The Legacy of Andrew Jackson* (Baton Rouge: Louisiana State University Press, 1988), p. 31.

Against furious Whigs who defended the entrenched bureaucracy, Jackson practiced considerable rotation. While the presidents from Washington to John Quincy Adams removed 213 presidential class officials, Jackson fired 252 appointees. Jackson's dismissals led to a removal rate of 41 percent, a noticeable improvement over Jefferson's 25 percent. Although Jackson's removal rate for all federal employees totaled less than 20 percent, it significantly surpassed that of previous administrations.[10]

Jackson experienced less success with his replacements. Although Whigs charged Jackson with employing mere commoners, his appointees were just as qualified as their predecessors, but that did not make them less corrupt. Friendship and political support clouded the president's judgment, most notably with Samuel Swartwout, Jackson's customs collector for New York ports. Swartwout, whom Van Buren strenuously opposed, embezzled $1.2 million over the years, a major embarrassment that mortified Jackson. The president also appointed men to his executive cabinet based on personal loyalty rather than ideology. Similarly to Jefferson's cabinet, most were moderates. However, in complete contrast to Jefferson, Jackson generally eschewed their advice, instead relying on an informal "Kitchen" cabinet composed of Van Buren, Kendall, Blair, Benton, Polk, and others.[11] This was a notable improvement, for it allowed Jackson's libertarian advisors to influence policy.[12]

To attack the American System and its special privileges, Jacksonians transformed the executive branch. However, by empowering the president they risked a major corruption of the office. There is no greater example of the Jacksonians' use of the executive than their most important struggle: eliminating the SBUS and creating the Independent Treasury.

---

[10] Donald Cole, *A Jackson Man* (Baton Rouge: Louisiana State University Press, 2004), pp. 123–31, 139; Remini, *Andrew Jackson*, 2, pp. 183–91; David Rosenbloom, *Federal Service and the Constitution* (Washington, DC: Georgetown University Press, 2014), pp. 43–49.

[11] Arthur M. Schlesinger Jr., *The Age of Jackson* (Boston, MA: Little, Brown and Company, 1945), p. 67.

[12] Donald Cole, *Martin Van Buren and the American Political System* (Princeton, NJ: Princeton University Press, 1984), pp. 192–93; Bray Hammond, *Banks and Politics in America* (Princeton, NJ: Princeton University Press, 1957), pp. 329–40; Remini, *Andrew Jackson*, 2, pp. 186, 194–99; Remini, *Legacy of Andrew Jackson*, pp. 31–32; Schlesinger, *Age of Jackson*, pp. 59–73.

The War against Central Banking

The Democrats launched total war against monetary interventionism. The Invisible Hand Jacksonians wanted to institute hard money and cripple fractional reserve banking, arguing that government privileges supported the institutions and that credit expansion caused the Panic of 1819. The Jacksonians increased executive power to first fight the Second Bank of the United States, climaxing with Jackson's veto against recharter. Unfortunately, they then postponed their Independent Treasury, moderating instead with a system of politically connected state banks.

Many historians argue that Jackson's war resulted from a clash between assertive personalities, insisting that Jackson only wanted to change Nicholas Biddle's SBUS or replace it with his own bank.[13] In reality, the president fought all fractional reserve banking. Constitutionally, Jackson disagreed with *McCulloch v. Maryland*, insisted paper-issuing banks violated the Constitution, and interpreted the coinage clause to sanction a purely specie currency. Economically, the president listened to American hard money economists and the like-minded British Currency School, a group that wanted to limit credit expansion. Since these theorists explained that corporate bank charters bred inefficiency and caused business cycles, the president attacked the SBUS' restrictionist charter, monopoly on federal deposits, and immunity from state taxes. Furthermore, Jackson vented at the monster's corruption of politicians, businesses, and newspapers. He sincerely wanted to weaken the government-bank partnership, a fundamental alliance in the powerful empire.

Historians' confusion results from two factors. First, while scheming behind the scenes with his Kitchen Cabinet, the president used his actual cabinet to communicate with Biddle. Jackson, experienced in war, sent confusing signals to "keep his political opponents off-balance," a tactic they belatedly recognized.[14] Second, and more importantly, the president struggled with the SBUS' replacement, not understanding how to achieve monetary laissez-faire. The Independent Treasury was an evolving concept that at times bordered on a central bank, and Jacksonian economists did not grasp free-banking

---

[13] Larry Schweikart, "Jacksonian Ideology, Currency Control and Central Banking," *The Historian* (November 1988): 78–102.

[14] Paul Kahan, *The Bank War* (Yardley, PA: Westholme Publishing, 2016), p. 70.

theories until the mid- to-late 1830s. This problem also affected the British Currency School, and to a greater extent.[15]

In early 1829, economists William Gouge and Condy Raguet fired the opening shot in the bank war, castigating the banking system as the "foundation of *artificial* inequality of wealth, and thereby, of *artificial* inequality of power."[16] After Van Buren's anti-SBUS meeting, Kendall exhorted the president to strongly denounce the Bank in his December message. Consequently, Jackson declared that the institution was "well questioned by a large portion of our fellow citizens."[17] This disturbed Biddle, who thought that he previously obtained assurances about the charter's renewal. Indeed, the swipe bushwhacked other American System proponents, particularly Clay, Webster, and Niles.

Biddle countered with propaganda and bribes. First, he communicated with Senator Samuel Smith and Congressman George McDuffie, pro-SBUS chairs of influential committees, and sent them pro-central banking information. Second, Biddle enlisted the help of *American Quarterly Review*, an academic journal owned by Robert Walsh, a recipient of SBUS loans. Third, the central banker corrupted newspapers. Most prominently, Biddle flipped the Jacksonian James Webb, editor of the *Courier and Enquirer*, for a $15,000 loan. By July 1832, the SBUS had spent between $50,000 and $100,000 for pro-Bank material, lent $100,000 to newspapers, and loaned congressmen from $100,000 to $200,000. Biddle would not give up easily.[18]

However, Jackson continued the assault. In 1830, he proposed a rudimentary Independent Treasury, "a bank . . . without power to make loans or purchase property . . . [and] though issuing no paper,

[15] Campbell, *Bank War*, pp. 64–65, 95; Cole, *Jackson Man*, pp. 157, 166, 168; Jeffrey Rogers Hummel, "The Jacksonians, Banking, and Economic Theory," *Journal of Libertarian Studies* (Summer 1978): 151–65; Kahan, *Bank War*, pp. 67–70, 88–90; Murray N. Rothbard, *An Austrian Perspective of Economic Thought*, vol. 2, *Classical Economics* (Auburn, AL: Mises Institute, 2006), pp. 211–16, 234–35, 246; Schlesinger, *Age of Jackson*, pp. 77, 227.

[16] Schlesinger, *Age of Jackson*, p. 79.

[17] Campbell, *Bank War*, p. 50.

[18] Ibid., pp. 11, 50–52, 68, 82–83; Cole, *Jackson Man*, p. 138; Joseph Dorfman, *The Economic Mind in American Civilization*, vol. 2 (New York: Viking Press, 1946), p. 604; Hammond, *Banks and Politics*, p. 371; Kahan, *Bank War*, pp. 37–38, 93; Scott Nelson, *A Nation of Deadbeats* (New York: Alfred A. Knopf, 2012), pp. 109–10; Schlesinger, *Age of Jackson*, pp. 81, 92.

would check the issues of the State banks by taking their notes in deposit and for exchange only so long as they continue to be redeemed with specie."[19] He continued to feed misleading information through his official cabinet, causing Biddle to realize "the kitchen would predominate over the Parlor."[20] In the Senate, Thomas Benton blasted the institution as a privileged monopoly unbecoming of a "confederacy of States."[21] Webster, a longtime beneficiary of Biddle's slush fund, called a vote to end discussion. Disastrously for the Whigs, the measure only passed by a narrow margin.

At the same time, Jackson's new Treasurer, Louis McLane, whose family owned SBUS stock, desperately tried to sway the president. Van Buren had previously warned Jackson about McLane. Despite this, Jackson's 1831 address eschewed Kendall's attacks, and the secretary's separate report caused a violent response from John Randolph and the Van Burenite Churchill Cambreleng. But Jackson quickly reassured his Kitchen Cabinet, professing that the independent McLane did not speak for him.[22]

As 1832 dawned, Biddle's supporters advised pushing for early recharter, a prospect that delighted the presidential candidate Clay. The Kentuckian adamantly supported Biddle; his running mate was John Sergeant, a former SBUS shareholder, director, and lawyer. Clay's rationale was simple: if Jackson vetoed an early recharter, he would lose reelection, and if he meekly signed the bill, he would still lose reelection. Biddle attacked, pressing for an early recharter and instructing state banks to support the decision. In a legislature where many politicians previously worked for the SBUS, no one doubted the outcome. Most notably, the new Whig Congressman John Quincy Adams defended the Bank. The recharter passed in July by comfortable bipartisan majorities, but not the two-thirds necessary to override a veto. It all came down to Jackson. Biddle expected approval, triumphantly appearing before Congress.

However, the president secretly tasked Kendall with the veto message for the "corrupting monster."[23] Arthur Schlesinger is surely

---

[19] Kahan, *Bank War*, pp. 81–82.

[20] Cole, *Jackson Man*, p. 158.

[21] Remini, *Andrew Jackson*, 2 , p. 303.

[22] Philip Burch, *Elites in American History*, vol. 1 (New York: Holmes & Meier Publishers, 1981), p. 139; Remini, *Andrew Jackson*, 2, pp. 303–04, 335, 337–40.

[23] Campbell, *Bank War*, p. 77.

correct when he describes Jackson's response as a "thunderclap over the nation," and Blair did not exaggerate by comparing it to the Declaration of Independence.[24] Without a doubt, Jackson's veto was the greatest presidential stand against cronyism. Constitutionally, the veto questioned *McCulloch v. Maryland* and blasted broad constructionist arguments regarding the coinage clause. Economically, it attacked the SBUS' monopoly, special privileges, and corrupting influence. In particular, Jackson emphasized that when the "rich and the powerful" scheme to devise "artificial distinctions, to grant titles, gratuities, and exclusive privileges," the public has "a right to complain of the injustice."[25] As Donald Cole explains, "the veto is an attack on government privilege, not, as some have suggested, on capitalism."[26] Nor did it criticize class warfare between the rich and poor; the veto attacked *caste* warfare between the subsidized political elites and the public at large. Heroically, Jackson would not, like Washington and Jefferson, defer. The veto was Jackson's crowning victory and embodied the anti-American System thrust of his movement.[27]

Unsurprisingly, the stunned Biddle described Jackson's decision as "anarchy."[28] Since Jackson declared that the veto expressed the people's will, the upcoming election served as a referendum. Although Biddle invested mightily in Clay's campaign, Kendall and Blair delivered Jackson and his vice presidential nominee, Van Buren, a smashing victory. It was official: Jackson had finished central banking. After the election, Van Buren wrote to Jackson and stated, "The idea of the establishment of *any bank in any of the States*, is, I take it, entirely done away with by the veto."[29] When the *Globe* reaffirmed the party's hostility, pro-central bank Democrats joined the Whig Party.[30]

---

[24] Schlesinger, *Age of Jackson*, p. 90.

[25] Kahan, *Bank War*, p. 105.

[26] Cole, *Jackson Man*, p. 169.

[27] Steven Calabresi and Larissa Leibowitz, "Monopolies and the Constitution," *Harvard Journal of Law & Public Policy* (Summer 2013): 1026–28; Campbell, *Bank War*, pp. 77–80; Cole, *Jackson Man*, pp. 165–71; John McFaul, *The Politics of Jacksonian Finance* (New York: Cornell University Press, 1972), pp. 17–28; Schlesinger, *Age of Jackson*, pp. 86–90; David Schwartz, "Coin, Currency, and Constitution," *Michigan Law Review* (2020): 1019.

[28] Remini, *Andrew Jackson*, 2, p. 369.

[29] McFaul, *Politics of Jacksonian Finance*, p. 51.

[30] Campbell, *Bank War*, pp. 87–91, 106–07; Kahan, *Bank War*, pp. 108–11; McFaul, *Politics of Jacksonian Finance*, pp. 51–55.

Despite the triumph, the veto only prevented the SBUS' recharter in 1836. Or, as Jackson wrote to Congressman Polk, "the hydra of corruption is only *scotched, not dead.*"[31] Democrats needed to go for the jugular. Unfortunately, political gridlock forced them to moderate and pass measures that just chipped away at the SBUS. Even worse, to accomplish these reforms they corruptly partnered with partisan banks and enacted new monetary interventions.

In 1833, Gouge published *A Short History of Paper Money and Banking*. This free market treatise contained ideological ammunition for the next offensive, earning the praise of Democrats and Currency School reformers. Gouge argued that fractional reserve banking was fraudulent and caused credit-induced business cycles. Government privileges that encourage inflation included monopolistic corporate charters with limited liability, sanctioning specie suspensions, and accepting bank notes for tax payments. According to Joseph Dorfman, Gouge believed "banking, like all other businesses, should be free," achievable by gradually restricting bank notes (building on an Adam Smith proposal), ending bank charters, eliminating limited liability, and establishing 100 percent reserves.[32] Most importantly, building on Jefferson and Randolph, Gouge devised the Independent Treasury: prohibit the government from subsidizing banks by depositing federal monies in them or accepting their notes in payment. Implementation of this specie program would disconnect the federal government from banks, crippling the American System and the empire it strengthened. Gouge's proposals achieved the Jacksonians' hard money sanctioned by a strict construction of the coinage clause.[33]

Unfortunately, Jackson did not adopt Gougian policies. In particular, only states could enact most of his bank reforms and the Independent Treasury faced an uphill battle in Congress. Furthermore, Biddle committed to causing short-term economic havoc. To stymie

---

[31] Campbell, *Bank War*, p. 94.

[32] Joseph Dorfman, "William M. Gouge and the Formation of Orthodox American Monetary Policy," in *William Gouge, A Short History of Paper Money and Banking* (Auburn, AL: Mises Institute, 2007), p. 17.

[33] Paul Conkin, *Prophets of Prosperity* (Bloomington: Indiana University Press, 1980), pp. 207–15; Dorfman, "William M. Gouge," pp. 5, 9–10, 13–21; Susan Hoffman, *Politics and Banking* (Baltimore, MD: The John Hopkins University Press, 2001), pp. 61–65; Schlesinger, *Age of Jackson*, pp. 117–19, 123, 127–28, 227–28, 314–17; Larry Schweikart, *Banking in the American South from the Age of Jackson to Reconstruction* (Baton Rouge: Louisiana State University Press, 1987), p. 17.

Biddle and avoid a legislative quagmire, in his December 1832 address Jackson advocated a Kendall proposal: sever the SBUS partnership by selling government shares and order the Treasurer to shift the $10 million of federal deposits into various state banks. Jackson's make-shift solution undeniably weakened what Kendall called the SBUS' "concentrated power," but it also subsidized certain banks by giving them federal deposits and Treasury protection.[34] The new partnership had a similar, albeit much more limited, corrupting influence on fed-eral officials: it still incentivized politicians and bureaucrats to patron-ize banks for political and financial support. Even Kendall's report on the selection of banks preferred those "politically friendly."[35]

Jackson's program caused immense controversy, and in early 1833 the House voted against Polk's resolution to sell the government's shares. Furthermore, Treasurer McLane fought deposit removal. But this did not deter Jackson. In May, while Congress recessed until December, he rotated his cabinet and appointed William J. Duane as Treasurer. But when Duane refused the orders, Jackson rotated him out with Maryland's Roger Taney, the current attorney general who also served in the Kitchen Cabinet. Taney shifted deposits into seven "pet" banks, five of which maintained friendly relations with the administration, and soon increased the number to twenty-two. When Congress convened, it furiously criticized Jackson's maneuvers, call-ing them executive aggrandizement. Famously, Senator John Tyler of Virginia caustically broke with the administration.[36]

Thus, Jacksonian reform tripped upon the pet bank moderation, and soon the president himself criticized it as an inefficient solution. Democratic bureaucrats and politicians eagerly abused the program, illegally borrowing from pet banks and shifting federal deposits to their favored institutions. Even Kendall succumbed: he borrowed $10,000 from the pet Girard Bank of Philadelphia for land specu-lation. Some individuals floated independent treasury proposals in 1834, including one by Raguet, but they went nowhere in Congress.

---

[34] Cole, *Jackson Man*, p. 188.

[35] Ibid., 184.

[36] Burch, *Elites in American History*, 1, pp. 284–85; Cole, *Jackson Man*, pp. 173, 177–80, 187–90; Kahan, *Bank War*, pp. 119–20; Remini, *Andrew Jackson*, 3, pp. 105–07; Nor-man Risjord, *The Old Republicans* (New York: Columbia University Press, 1965), p. 277; Richard Timberlake, *Monetary Policy in the United States* (Chicago: The Univer-sity of Chicago Press, 1993), pp. 43–46, 67.

When Gouge started working for the Treasury Department, the new Secretary Levi Woodbury asked him to outline his independent treasury. Unfortunately, Woodbury, corrupted by the pet banks that coveted their deposit subsidies, put Gouge's measure aside. After encouragement from Kendall, Gouge drafted another independent treasury plan, but it failed to gain traction.[37]

In the meantime, Jacksonian reformers tried to restrict what the administration's *Globe* called the "frauds of paper money."[38] Congress devalued the dollar in terms of gold, legalized foreign specie, and established new mints. Significantly, it passed the 1836 Deposit Act, increasing the pet banks to ninety-one and requiring them to honor redemption, restrict note issuance, and accept fewer notes in payments. However, the act also included the distribution of the budget surplus stored at the pet banks to the state legislatures. Although Jackson had previously supported distribution, by 1836 he recognized that the subsidy increased centralization and dependency on Congress. Reluctantly signing the bill, the president countered with the Specie Circular, an executive order requiring the Treasury to accept only specie for public land payments. Jackson reasoned that increased use of specie would drain the deposit subsidy and surplus from the pet banks.

These reforms showed some growing Jacksonian pitfalls. First, Democrats accomplished their goals through presidential edicts, rotation, and discretionary Treasury action, worrying libertarians. Second, Jacksonians increased regulatory control over the pet banks. This "exercise of governmental power," John McFaul explains, "was incompatible with the Jacksonian ideology of laissez faire."[39] The Democrats did destroy the SBUS, forcing it to secure a Pennsylvania charter in 1836, but the executive now partnered with select state banks. To make matters worse, the states continued their banking partnerships. In Whig fashion, Democrats in the state legislatures doled out special privileges through new corporate charters and other cushy regulations.[40]

---

[37] Campbell, *Bank War*, pp. 122–27; Cole, *Jackson Man*, p. 196; Dorfman, *Economic Mind*, 2, pp. 611–12; Dorfman, "William M. Gouge," pp. 21–22; Kahan, *Bank War*, pp. 120–27; McFaul, *Jacksonian Finance*, pp. 126–27.

[38] McFaul, *Politics of Jacksonian Finance*, p. 74.

[39] Ibid., pp. 80–81.

[40] Remini, *Andrew Jackson*, 3, pp. 321–29; Murray N. Rothbard, "The History of Money and Banking Before the Twentieth Century," in *A History of Money and Banking in the United States*, ed. Joseph T. Salerno (Auburn, AL: Mises Institute, 2002), pp. 93, 104–07.

Most notably, when Van Buren briefly served as New York's governor in 1829, he insisted on reforming the corrupt banking system. Unfortunately, Van Buren settled on an insurance program, forcing banks to pay into a government-backed fund that would reimburse noteholders of failed banks. In addition to maintaining charters, the Safety Fund Act increased risk taking. Soon enough, Democratic Governor William Marcy and others defended New York's regional monopolies. This moderation earned the criticism of the Gougians William Cullen Bryant and William Leggett at the *Evening Post*. Notably, the two classical liberals supported genuine free banking, recognizing that the adverse clearing mechanism limited credit expansion while intervention encouraged it. This significantly advanced laissez-faire economic thought.[41]

In Virginia, anti-bank Democrats, led by Thomas Ritchie, blocked proposals to increase charters while fighting for reserve requirements and note restrictions. They correctly viewed banks as sources of corruption, but incorrectly pushed for restricting their number, which caused the monopoly problems they wanted to avoid. In the West, fluid party lines led to outright bank cronyism. Michigan Democrats chartered their own banks and subsidized them with state deposits, particularly the Michigan State Bank. In Mississippi, they actually invested massive government funds into newly chartered banks, especially the Planters' Bank and the Union Bank, by issuing bonds that creditors could redeem if the banks failed.[42]

---

[41] Howard Bodenhorn, *State Banking in Early America* (New York: Oxford University Press, 2003), pp. 157–82; Howard Bodenhorn, "Bank Chartering and Political Corruption in Antebellum New York," in *Corruption and Reform*, ed. Edward Glaeser and Claudia Goldin (Chicago: University of Chicago Press, 2006), pp. 236–43; McFaul, *Politics of Jacksonian Finance*, pp. 89, 102–06; Fritiz Redlich, *The Molding of American Banking* (New York: Johnson Reprint Corporation, 1968), p. 189; Edward Spann, *Ideals and Politics* (Albany: State University of New York Press, 1972), pp. 56–63, 70–72, 97, 100–01; Lawrence White, "William Leggett," *History of Political Economy* (June 1986): 313–17.

[42] Ronald Formisano, *The Birth of Mass Political Parties* (Princeton, NJ: Princeton University Press, 1971), pp. 41–42; McFaul, *Politics of Jacksonian Finance*, pp. 93–101; Schweikart, "Jacksonian Ideology," pp. 93–94; William Shade, *Banks or No Banks* (Detroit, MI: Wayne State University Press, 1972), pp. 20–39; James Sharp, *The Jacksonians versus the Banks* (New York: Columbia University Press, 1970), pp. 56, 63.

Clearly, the determined Jacksonians used the executive branch to apply their free market theories, but they did not come close to finishing monetary intervention on the federal and state level. Democrats required a new shock to reenergize their reform movement.

The Separation of Bank and State

Once Jackson left office, the Panic of 1837 ended the preceding economic boom and totally revitalized monetary reform, symbolized by Van Buren's Independent Treasury. Although the Whigs repealed it in 1841, President Tyler vetoed new central bank bills, and President Polk reinstituted the Independent Treasury in 1846. In the state realm, Democrats pushed for genuine free banking laws, restrictions on chartered banks, and even eliminating banks altogether, meeting varying degrees of success.

Historians frequently argue that Jackson's quasi-deregulation through deposit removal caused hasty credit expansion, while the Deposit Act and Specie Circular encouraged credit contraction and the Panic of 1837.[43] Actually, Jackson's policies played ancillary roles at best. Undoubtedly, inflation and price increases occurred after the veto. However, from 1829 to 1832, the money supply drastically augmented from $105 million to $150 million (43 percent, or 13 percent per year). The reason was simple: the SBUS, far from restraining banks, increased its own credit expansion by 52 percent and made loans to banks. After the veto, inflation accelerated to 84 percent (16 percent per year), pushing up prices by 20 percent (5 percent per year) from 1832 to 1836. But this was caused by a massive 135 percent increase in specie reserves from politically unstable China and Mexico. Likewise, the proximate reason for the 1837 panic was the Bank of England raising interest rates to protect specie holdings. The Deposit Act and Specie Circular undoubtedly put pressure on state banks, but historians exaggerate their effects relative to the Bank of England's actions.[44]

When New York City banks suspended specie payments in May 1837, other banks followed suit, ushering in a panic. A year later, banks resumed specie payments and recklessly inflated to reignite the boom.

---

[43] Hammond, *Banks and Politics*, pp. 451–67.

[44] *Historical Statistics*, 3, p. 181; Peter Temin, *The Jacksonian Economy* (New York: W.W. Norton & Co., 1969), pp. 71, 120–47; Timberlake, *Monetary Policy*, pp. 30, 51–64; Rothbard, "History of Money," pp. 95–100; Robert Whaples, "Were Andrew Jackson's Policies 'Good for the Economy'?" *The Independent Review* (Spring 2014): 550–51.

But the fundamentals remained the same, and to arrest a specie out-flow, the Bank of England contracted credit again in 1839, resulting in another US bank crisis and suspension of specie payments. Overall, between 1836 and 1842, the money supply collapsed from $276 million to $158 million, or by 43 percent (9 percent per year). The number of banks similarly dropped, and intense deflation caused a 28 percent plummet in prices.

Although contemporaries perceived the period as a time of economic depression, they once again mistook nominal changes for declines in real output. From 1832 to 1836, industrial production and real GDP increased by 28 and 14 percent (6.3 percent and 3.3 percent per year). But from 1836 to 1837, industrial production only declined by 1 percent and real GDP actually rose by 1 percent. Far more importantly, from 1837 to 1842, they still grew by 20.1 percent and 13 percent, respectively (3.7 percent and 2.5 percent per year). Positive growth rates only declining from their abnormally high levels hardly constitutes a severe economic crisis. Population did continue to grow at relatively the same rate, so real GDP per capita declined by a minor 0.3 percent per year, but it had risen during the boom by only 0.3 percent each year. Clearly, despite the 1838 inflation, the federal government's laissez-faire policy allowed for a healthy reallocation of resources.[45]

Van Buren triumphed in 1836, but the panic came as a rude shock. The hard-money Jacksonians fumed at the pet banks suspending specie payments. In July 1837, Jackson indignantly advocated "separat[ing] the government from all banks" and "receiv[ing] and disburs[ing] the revenue in nothing but gold and silver coin."[46] After additional counsel, Van Buren decided that he would establish the long-awaited Independent Treasury. The panic had a similar jolting effect on the British Currency School, and Parliament created committees to investigate monetary reform.

In a special congressional session in September, Van Buren preached a hands-off approach, articulating the Gougian business

---

[45] Joseph Davis, "An Annual Index of U.S. Industrial Production," *Quarterly Journal of Economics* (November 2004): 1189; *Historical Statistics*, 3, pp. 181–82; Jeffrey Rogers Hummel, "Martin Van Buren," in *Reassessing the Presidency*, ed. John V. Denson (Auburn, AL: Mises Institute, 2001), pp. 189–93; Louis Johnston and Samuel Williamson, "What Was the U.S. GDP Then?" *Measuringworth.com*; Rothbard, "History of Money," pp. 99–104; Temin, *Jacksonian Economy*, pp. 71, 113, 152, 159.

[46] Hammond, *Banks and Politics*, p. 491.

cycle and shrewdly recognizing that Great Britain experienced a similar downturn despite the Bank of England. Most importantly, the president introduced the Independent Treasury, which would ideally end all banking privileges. The concept thrilled hard money Democrats, particularly Kendall, Bryant, Leggett, and Benton. However, moderate Democrats sided with the Whigs, who adamantly fought the measure. Despite such moderation, the hard money contingent refused to buckle. For example, Preston King of New York "damn[ed] the idea of compromise. . . . Van Buren's message is a banner in the sky—Stand to its doctrines."[47] Similarly, the president's young advisor and disciple of Adam Smith, Samuel J. Tilden, sprang into action. He wrote a highly libertarian and economically sophisticated tract on the Independent Treasury, attacking Whig statism and pinpointing credit expansion as the cause of business cycles. Gouge and Raguet praised Tilden's writing, and Jacksonians shipped it to the Currency School reformers.

The hard-money strategy paid off when banks suspended specie payments in 1839. As a result of yet another banking embarrassment, the moderate Democrats acquiesced. Van Buren signed the Independent Treasury bill on July 4, 1840, symbolizing its connection to Jefferson's Declaration of Independence. The legislation was a major victory for liberty against power and for decentralization against empire, because no longer could the Treasury subsidize any bank with deposits and accept their notes in tax payments. Instead, the federal government separated itself from the banks—a relinquishment of its own economic control—and decided to only accept payments in specie, storing these funds in its own vaults.[48]

Tragically, Van Buren lost reelection, thanks to the New Yorker Thurlow Weed. He cunningly realized that Whigs could only win with a flashy campaign full of slogans, symbols, razzle dazzle, and songs. Weed convinced the Whigs to nominate William Henry Harrison of Ohio, a former general and land speculator. He then created a massive campaign movement that fabricated Harrison's background, appealed to the common man, and exaggerated the downturn's severity. Although Van Buren racked up an impressive four hundred thousand more votes

---

[47] Schlesinger, *Age of Jackson*, p. 258.

[48] Cole, *Jackson Man*, p. 228; Hummel, "Martin Van Buren," pp. 178–86; Kelley, *Transatlantic Persuasion*, pp. 246–49, 256–59; Rothbard, *Austrian Perspective on the History of Economic Thought*, 2, pp. 238–48; Schlesinger, *Age of Jackson*, pp. 234–36, 265.

than in 1836, Harrison and his southern vote magnet, John Tyler, crushed the incumbent.

Harrison portended crucial repairs to the American System. The Boston Associates lobbied for his nomination, and Abbott Lawrence even gave the president a $5,000 "loan" after his inauguration. Clay partisans filled the cabinet, and Webster served as secretary of state. The president, a previous appointee to the SBUS' Cincinnati board, even contemplated making Biddle his Treasurer, but then settled on Thomas Ewing, a lawyer close to Lawrence. With the agreeable executive branch, Senator Clay planned to charter another central bank. But, in an odd fluke, Harrison died, elevating Tyler to the presidency. Whigs feared a catastrophe because the states' rights Tyler only left the Democratic Party in opposition to Jackson strengthening the executive.[49]

Harrison's death did not deter Clay. The legislature repealed the Independent Treasury and created a new central bank; the bill landed on Tyler's lap in August 1841. Unfortunately for reform, the president signed the bill repealing Van Buren's system, associating it with executive power, but partially redeemed himself by vetoing the bank bill on constitutional grounds. When Congress passed another bank bill in September, Tyler responded in the same manner. This caused the Whig cabinet, save Webster, to resign in protest. With Tyler's unfortunate repeal of the Independent Treasury, Congress returned to the pet bank system. New pet banks acquired government deposits, most notably Corcoran & Riggs in Washington DC, headed by W. W. Corcoran. Thanks to Democratic Senator Robert J. Walker of Mississippi, affiliated with Corcoran, the bank secured depository status and turned into a leading holder of government funds. Corcoran and his institution would exercise an unusually large political influence in the future.[50]

---

[49] Burch, *Elites in American History*, 1, pp. 179–82, 218; Thomas Govan, *Nicholas Biddle* (Chicago: The University of Chicago Press, 1959), p. 388; Hummel, "Martin Van Buren," p. 199; Henry Watson, *Liberty and Power* (New York: The Noonday Press, 1990), pp. 213–26.

[50] Henry Cohen, *Business and Politics in America from the Age of Jackson to the Civil War* (Westport, CT: Greenwood Publishing, 1971), pp. 18–29; Dan Monroe, *The Republican Vision of John Tyler* (College Station: Texas A&M University Press, 2003), pp. 83–110, 117–19; Robert Remini, *Henry Clay* (New York: W.W. Norton & Company, 1991), pp. 586–97; Timberlake, *Monetary Policy*, pp. 69–72.

In 1844, Polk secured the Democratic nomination and defeated Clay. A die-hard Jacksonian, Polk wanted to restore the Independent Treasury. Notably, the president emphasized that the greater demand for specie in government transactions would cause banks to hold higher reserve ratios, thereby restricting credit expansion. However, against Jackson's wishes, Polk chose Walker as his Treasurer. It looked as if the pet system would continue after Walker made Corcoran & Riggs the only depository in Washington, DC, and Corcoran started to advise the president on investment matters. Fortunately, Polk and Walker disappointed the banker. In 1846, the two pressured wavering Democratic senators to vote for reestablishing the "constitutional currency."[51] Thanks to this executive influence, Congress reestablished the Independent Treasury by a party vote.[52]

After a long struggle, thanks to free market economics and sixteen years of executive intervention through vetoes, appointments, orders, and influence in Congress, Democrats finally severed the connection between the federal government and the banks. The Independent Treasury mirrored a similar (though less effective) law that the Currency School secured for Britain in 1844: Peel's Act. Prime Minister Robert Peel, whom Van Buren long admired, sponsored the law with the assistance of Manchester classical liberals such as the ardent free trader Richard Cobden.[53]

The Jacksonians were not content to rest: Democratic governors implemented hard money policies in the states, because "the increased use of specie was seen as a laissez-faire reform device that would add a kind of automatic balance to the banking system."[54] Two different strands of laissez faire motivated them. The first echoed older economists who advocated prohibiting notes or note-issuing banks altogether. The second used modern free-banking theories to argue that

[51] Charles Sellers, *James K. Polk, Continentalist* (Princeton, NJ: Princeton University Press, 1966), p. 345.

[52] Cohen, *Business and Politics*, pp. 28–36; Sellers, *James K. Polk, Continentalist*, pp. 344–45, 469–70; James Shenton, *Robert John Walker* (New York: Columbia University Press, 1961), pp. 87–89.

[53] Avner Cohen, "Cobden's Stance on the Currency and the Political Forces behind the Approval of the Bank Charter Act of 1844," *European Journal of the History of Economic Thought* (Summer 1998): 253–54, 261–62; Kelley, *Transatlantic Persuasion*, pp. 189, 247–49; Rothbard, *Austrian Perspective on the History of Economic Thought*, 2, pp. 248–59.

[54] Sharp, *Jacksonians versus the Banks*, p. 323.

open competition curbed inflation. The second strand was clearly superior, building on recent economic thought and eliminating intervention. Ultimately, free market Democrats achieved mixed success. First, moderate Democrats and Whigs blocked hard money proposals in favor of a "free banking" that tied note issuance to government debt. Second, with the exception of New York, the older version of laissez-faire influenced most reformers. New York, Virginia, Michigan, and Mississippi provide canonical examples.

In New York, after the moderate Democratic legislature legalized specie suspension in May 1837, radical Democrats denounced suspension and criticized "*all* special legislation whereby privileges are granted to the few and withheld from the many."[55] Exacerbating the party rift, Governor Marcy criticized the proposed Independent Treasury. In the face of this party split, the Whigs won the fall 1837 elections and seized the legislature. Congressman Cambreleng wrote to Van Buren professing that the party was now ripe for purification.

A fantastic cure emerged from Samuel Young, a student of the Currency School. The Democrat advocated for a free banking law in New York that abolished charters and required owners to only pledge some property and capital. He argued that note competition, not a bond-backing provision requiring banks to insure their notes' value with government bonds, promoted sound money. Unfortunately, the Whig legislature in 1838 passed a general incorporation law that included a bond-backing requirement. Moreover, the state would continue to accept bank notes in payments. A $100,000 capitalization requirement restricted banking to wealthy investors while the bond-backing feature tied note issuance to government debt, incentivizing banks to purchase state securities. Unsurprisingly, free bankers Bryant and Leggett attacked the law and only reluctantly supported it as a first step toward monetary laissez-faire. Major Wilson astutely remarks that the legislation "was a Whig coup" because they opportunistically exploited the Democrats' anti-monopoly spirit.[56]

---

[55] Ibid., p. 301.

[56] Major Wilson, *The Presidency of Martin Van Buren* (Lawrence: University Press of Kansas, 1984), p. 120. See also Lee Benson, *The Concept of Jacksonian Democracy* (Princeton, NJ: Princeton University Press, 1961), pp. 68–69, 97–104; Redlich, *Molding of American Banking*, pp. 189–90, 196–204; Rothbard, *Austrian Perspective on the History of Economic Thought*, 2, pp. 198, 235–36, 242; Rothbard, "History of Money," pp. 112–14; Sharp, *Jacksonians versus the Banks*, pp. 300–04; Spann, *Ideals and Politics*, pp. 102–05; Wilson, *Presidency of Van Buren*, pp. 118–20.

Leggett suffered an untimely death in 1839, but libertarian Democrats continued the struggle. By this time, Bryant and Leggett's disciples were known as "Barnburners," willing to burn down their political offices (the "barn"). Moderates, such as Marcy, were "Hunkers," because after winning the election they "hunkered" in office and refused to enact reforms that could jeopardize their positions. In 1844, Barnburner Silas Wright defeated the Whig Millard Fillmore for the governorship. The following year, Wright supported Barnburner efforts for a New York constitutional convention in 1846 and criticized the free banking law because it incentivized banks to favor a large public debt. At the convention, Barnburners did not eliminate the bond-backing regulation, instead weakening the state's ability to borrow. In addition, they forbade the legislature from sanctioning suspensions of specie payments or "granting any special charter for banking purposes."[57] It is clear from these proposals that New York Democrats supported free banking and tried to restrict bank cronyism by keeping entry open. No wonder Arthur Ekirch wrote that the new constitution "embodied the laissez-faire position better than any document in the state's history."[58]

In Virginia, during the panic, banks suspended specie payments and the Whigs seized the legislature. Hugh Garland decided that it was time for Democrats "to divorce [banks] entirely from all connection with the Government, State and Federal—to tear asunder that unnatural connection which has been injurious and corrupting."[59] Edmund Ruffin, who founded the Association for Promoting Currency and Banking Reform, sounded the charge of John Taylor by declaring that "the paper banking system is essentially and necessarily fraudulent."[60] Hard money forces focused on higher reserve ratios and specie payment, but soft money Democrats and Whigs blocked their efforts. When the Whig legislature let banks suspend convertibility again in 1839, Thomas Ritchie's *Enquirer* demanded "the specie standard—*a*

---

[57] L. Gunn, *The Decline of Authority* (Ithaca, NY: Cornell University Press, 1988), p. 186.

[58] Arthur Ekirch, "Democracy and Laissez Faire," *Journal of Libertarian Studies* (Fall 1977): 322. See also p. 322; John Garraty, *Silas Wright* (New York: Columbia University Press, 1949), pp. 309–32, 353–55; Gunn, *Decline of Authority*, pp. 186–87; Spann, *Ideals and Politics*, pp. 122, 124, 128.

[59] Sharp, *Jacksonians versus the Banks*, p. 226.

[60] Ibid., p. 261.

radical reform, or total extermination of our present paper system."[61]
Unfortunately, banks controlled the Virginia legislature: fifty members owed a combined $111,000. Only after fierce Democrat insistence did the legislature make banks resume specie payment by November 1842. The struggle continued at the 1850 constitutional convention, where Democrats unsuccessfully pushed for a New York–style ban on suspensions of specie payments. Afterwards, against Democrat resistance, Whigs passed their version of bond-backed free banking.[62]

By 1836, many Michigan Democrats had grown uneasy at the party's connection with state-sponsored banks, particularly the Michigan State Bank. Consequently, the *Free Press* followed New York's debates and reprinted free-banking articles. On the other hand, the Whig *Daily Advertiser* remained silent and supported a continuation of the existing system. In 1837, before the panic, Democrats passed a free banking law. Unfortunately, shortly thereafter the legislature sanctioned a suspension of convertibility, encouraging new banks to issue irredeemable notes. Failing to recognize that suspending specie payments, not free banking, caused the problem, the state repealed the law in early 1839. Matters drastically changed in the fall, when banks once again suspended specie payments and the Whigs seized control of the government. This time, the Democrats' Michigan State Bank failed, and the end of its corruption "allowed [Democrats] to be consistently antibank."[63] When the Whigs passed a Currency Bill sanctioning the previous suspension of specie payments in exchange for internal improvement loans to the state, hard money Democrats violently protested.

In 1841, Democrat John Barry captured the governorship on an anti-bank and government retrenchment platform. He made the legislature pass laws requiring redemption as a test of solvency, abolishing banks' corporate rights, repealing the charters of institutions that suspended specie payments, and prohibiting municipalities from issuing currency. Soon enough, the editor of the *Free Press* declared, "Our government is based upon equal rights—banks upon fraud and

---

[61] Ibid., p. 242.

[62] William Shade, *Democratizing the Old Dominion* (Charlottesville: University Press of Virginia, 1996), pp. 95–96, 170, 275–76, 281–82; Sharp, *Jacksonians versus the Banks*, pp. 227–46, 261; Schweikart, *Banking in the American South*, pp. 34–37, 120–27; John Wallis, "Constitutions, Corporations, and Corruption," *The Journal of Economic History* (March 2005): 219.

[63] Shade, *Banks or No Banks*, p. 89.

corruption. . . . and in justice to equal rights let us have no banks."[64] At the 1850 constitutional convention, Democrats successfully prohibited special bank charters and a year later the legislature blocked a Whig free banking law. Barry, back in the governor's saddle, distrusted free banking because bond-backing requirements perpetuated the public debt, or what he called "the evidence of public misfortunes."[65] Michigan only enacted a free banking law in 1857.[66]

Democrat hostility to banking was extremely harsh in Mississippi, whose chartered banks, particularly the state-owned Union Bank and Planters' Bank, suspended convertibility during the panic. The new hard money governor, Democrat Alexander G. McNutt, wanted the legislature to rescind the charters of suspending banks, recognizing that the public valued a bank note based on "its convertibility into specie."[67] By 1840, after failing to accomplish this goal, McNutt advocated closing insolvent banks and repudiating government debt invested in the Union Bank. McNutt would not countenance raising taxes to benefit the stockholders and directors who borrowed heavily and mismanaged the institutions. Furthermore, he recognized the difference between a private debt and a government bond that required coercive taxes. Whigs and soft money Democrats fought repudiation, because they wanted the state's credit to finance public works. After Democrats won the 1841 elections, they repudiated the Union Bank bonds, helping to sever Mississippi's government-bank alliance.

Unfortunately, after McNutt left the governorship, the Union Bank's debtors—particularly the large planters and land speculators who mismanaged the institution—seized control of the anti-bank movement, led by associates of Senator Walker: John F. H. Claiborne and William Gwin (the latter owed $311,000 to the Union Bank). In 1842, Parmenas Briscoe introduced a bill, allowing bank debtors to escape their obligations (Briscoe owed the banks $30,000). This split the Mississippi Democrats because many recognized that repudiating voluntary contracts violates property rights, which the Whigs opposed. Despite the opposition, large debtors controlling the movement secured

---

[64] Ibid., p. 124.

[65] Ibid., p. 146.

[66] Formisano, *Birth of Mass Political Parties*, pp. 38–42; Shade, *Banks or No Banks*, pp. 36–39, 50–57, 62–70, 88–100, 110–20, 146–48, 150, 173, 190–94; Sharp, *Jacksonians versus the Banks*, pp. 198–99, 203–04, 207.

[67] Sharp, *Jacksonians versus the Banks*, p. 64.

the Briscoe Bill in 1846. Banking controversies died thereafter, because banking disappeared, and Mississippi never hosted a constitutional convention.[68]

Thanks to their executive reforms, the Jacksonians succeeded in crippling the American System's monetary cronyism. They destroyed the SBUS, separated the federal government from banking, and made serious in-roads toward removing banking privileges on the state level. The party expected to reap similar rewards when they attacked internal improvements and protective tariffs, two other planks of the American System.

---

[68] Ibid., pp. 61–88; Schweikart, *Banking in the American South*, pp. 24–27, 175–82; John Wallis, Richard Sylla, and Arthur Grinath, "Sovereign Debt and Repudiation, *NBER Working Paper Series* (September 2004): 12–15.

CHAPTER 15

DISMANTLING THE AMERICAN SYSTEM: A LAISSEZ-FAIRE ECONOMY

The Struggle for Free Trade

To weaken the American Empire, Democrats drastically reduced protective tariffs and public works subsidies, most notably with the Walker Tariff, the Maysville veto, and states' general incorporation laws. They achieved resounding success because of South Carolina's nullification movement, laissez-faire British reformers, and the growth of free market economics. Once again, Jacksonians relied on an empowered executive branch to weaken special-interest legislation, particularly Jackson's Force Bill, Tyler's tariff vetoes, and Jackson and Polk's infrastructure vetoes.

The tariff war began with the Nullification Crisis, when South Carolina threatened nullification and secession. In the late 1820s, at risk of losing his home state to Radicals Thomas Cooper and William Smith, Vice President John Calhoun secretly drafted the *Exposition and Protest*. In essence, this influential pamphlet articulated Calhoun's rendition of nullification: if a state legislature considered a federal law unconstitutional, it could vote for a convention to consider nullifying the law. If the convention voted to nullify the law, the state would not have to obey or enforce the law unless the Constitution was amended, at which point the nullifying state would have to obey the law or secede. To Calhoun, the *Exposition* allowed South Carolina to block protective tariffs and Cooper's call for secession.[1]

Importantly, the *Exposition* was far less radical than Jefferson's Kentucky Resolutions or the neo-Antifederalist thought of Cooper and John Taylor of Caroline. First, Calhoun previously supported big

---

[1] William Watkins, *Reclaiming the American Revolution* (Oakland, CA: The Independent Institute, 2004), pp. 99–104.

government and never sincerely adhered to strict constructionism. Second, Calhoun grounded the *Exposition* in *The Federalist Papers*. This starkly contrasted with the 1820s writings of Cooper and Taylor, works heavily influenced by Robert Yates' *Secret Proceedings* (1821) and its bitter criticisms of Madison, the Constitutional Convention, and *The Federalist Papers*. Third, Calhoun essentially nationalized Jefferson's theory by granting that states no longer possessed the right to nullify a law if overruled by a constitutional amendment. Lastly, Calhoun advocated nullification as a substitute for, not a complement to, secession: he still wanted the presidency. Consequently, Calhoun's nullification is closer to the Federalist opportunism of the Jeffersonian era than Antifederalist ideology. No wonder Democrats, especially Randolph, Macon, Barbour, Tyler, Crawford, and Smith, reacted negatively. These compact theory adherents believed that the best way to combat protective tariffs was through the electoral process or secession. Old Republicans' suspicions only heightened when their nemesis Calhoun publicly supported nullification in 1831. Furthermore, Jefferson and Taylor could no longer mediate, leaving the elderly Madison, the author of the less radical Virginia Resolutions, to characteristically take the nationalist high road and denounce the doctrine.[2]

But the *Exposition* appealed to the South Carolina public, groaning under unjust taxation. Party loyalties experienced a confusing realignment: Calhoun's former big-government supporters, such as Congressman George McDuffie and Senator Robert Hayne, rapidly turned into Nullifiers while the earlier Radicals, such as Smith, became Unionists. For his part, Cooper turned into a Nullifier who still advocated secession, though he remained out of the spotlight after making inflammatory comments about religion. In the face of such chaotic developments, Jacksonians correctly perceived that opportunistic politicians led the Nullifiers, but erred by assuming that the Antifederalist tradition rejected nullification and that the doctrine was

---

[2] William Belko, *Philip Pendleton Barbour in Jacksonian America* (Tuscaloosa: University of Alabama Press, 2016), p. 172; Saul Cornell, *The Other Founders* (Chapel Hill: The University of North Carolina Press, 1999), pp. 289, 294–98; Richard Ellis, *The Union at Risk* (New York: Oxford University Press, 1987), pp. 8–12, 134; Ivan Jankovic, *American Counter-Revolution in Favor of Liberty* (Switzerland: Palgrave Macmillan, 2019), pp. 266–69; Dan Monroe, *The Republican Vision of John Tyler* (College Station: Texas A&M University Press, 2003), p. 49; Norman Risjord, *The Old Republicans* (New York: Columbia University Press, 1965), pp. 272–76.

unpopular. Quite the contrary: nullification was a true reform tool and the South Carolina public demanded an immediate move to free trade. It is for this reason, William Bolt writes, that "nullification had begun as a grassroots movement."[3] It firmly continued the classical liberal tradition of resistance to cronyism.[4]

In 1829, Democrats vacillated over tariff reductions, because they had committed to paying down the national debt, refusing to default or repudiate. Therefore, in his December message, Jackson recommended lowering tariffs only on miscellaneous goods. Fortunately, in the same month, Condy Raguet published *The Banner of the Constitution*, a journal defending Adam Smith and Jean-Baptiste Say against Mathew Carey and Hezekiah Niles. In the first issue, Raguet, who sympathized with the Nullifiers, sounded the charge for liberty to attack monopolistic tariffs. When Bryant's *Evening Post* called for a free trade convention, Raguet set arrangements for September 1831.

William Belko shows that the Philadelphia Free Trade Convention scintillatingly understood the eternal battle between liberty and power. Prominent delegates included President Barbour; Gallatin; Secretary Raguet; William Smith; and Clement C. Biddle, the editor of Say's work. The convention drafted the free trade *Address to the People of the United States* and *Memorial to Congress*. The latter, written by Gallatin, insisted that once Congress paid off the national debt, it should lower tariffs to a uniform rate between 20 and 25 percent. With this "first movement of the Free Trade *Army*," Raguet proudly noted that "decisive action [now] must be fought" in Congress.[5]

---

[3] William Bolt, *Tariff Wars and the Politics of Jacksonian America* (Nashville, TN: Vanderbilt University Press, 2017), p. 118.

[4] Michael Bordo and William Phillips, "Faithful Index to the Ambitions and Fortunes of the State," in *Economists and Higher Learning in the Nineteenth Century*, ed. William Barber (New Brunswick, NJ: Transaction Publishers, 1993), pp. 56–58; Ellis, *Union at Risk*, p. 50; Lacy Ford, *Origins of Southern Radicalism* (New York: Oxford University Press, 1988), pp. 126–34, 149.

[5] Daniel Peart, *Lobbyists and the Making of US Tariff Policy* (Baltimore, MD: The Johns Hopkins University Press, 2018), p. 105. See also William Belko, *The Triumph of the Antebellum Free Trade Movement* (Gainesville: University Press of Florida, 2012), pp. 9–12, 18–22, 30–45, 61–63, 106, 110–34, 158–59, 163, 169; Ellis, *Union at Risk*, pp. 21, 34–36; Douglas A. Irwin, *Clashing over Commerce* (Chicago: The University of Chicago Press, 2017), pp. 167–69; Peart, *Making of US Tariff Policy*, pp. 101–02.

Protectionists defended their fortress. First, Carey organized a larger convention and criticized the *Address* under the appropriate pseudonym "Hamilton."[6] Second, Senator Clay concocted a "compromise" that lowered rates on goods only produced abroad to postpone debt extinguishment, thereby prolonging high rates on goods produced domestically. Third, lobbyists Carey, Niles, Harrison Gray Otis, and Boston Associate Abbott Lawrence bombarded the legislature. Against this, Democrats only achieved the Compromise Tariff of July 1832, with sectional opposition concentrated among southern Democrats, frustrated that tariffs remained too high, and northern Whigs, upset Congress had cut tariffs at all. The average rate had previously declined from 51 to 39 percent, and the new tariff would lower it to 29 percent. However, while abolishing the regressive minimum valuation for woolens, it maintained the cotton minimum and 50 percent rates for cotton, woolen, and iron goods. After so much effort, the free traders failed to achieve their goals.[7]

Fortunately, South Carolinians renewed the siege. In August, one Nullifier confessed how difficult it was "to hold the people back" and "keep the war dogs chained."[8] In the 1832 elections, Nullifiers crushed the Unionists and, in a special session, the new legislature voted for a state convention. William Harper, a delegate to the Philadelphia Free Trade Convention, drafted the Ordinance of Nullification. This document declared the Tariffs of 1828 and 1832 "null, void, and no law," effective February 1833.[9] If Congress attempted coercion, South Carolina would secede. Similar to earlier suggestions of Congressman McDuffie, the convention demanded a uniform tariff of 12 percent to eliminate any preferential rates. The rest of the pieces fell into place: Hayne replaced James Hamilton as governor and the lame duck Calhoun, who had long grown distant from Jackson, resigned the vice presidency to take Hayne's senate seat.

All eyes turned to Jackson. In his December message, the president firmly rejected protective tariffs now that the extinguishment of the national debt was imminent. Unfortunately, he also sent the

---

[6] Belko, *Antebellum Free Trade Movement*, p. 75.

[7] Bolt, *Tariff Wars*, pp. 109–16; *Historical Statistics of the United States, V*, ed. Richard Sutch and Susan Carter (New York: Cambridge University Press, 2006), p. 510; Irwin, *Clashing over Commerce*, pp. 169–72; Peart, *Making of US Tariff Policy*, pp. 104–15, 119; Watkins, *American Revolution*, p. 107.

[8] Bolt, *Tariff Wars*, p. 116.

[9] Watkins, *Reclaiming the American Revolution*, p. 109.

Nullification Proclamation, adamantly declaring nullification and secession unconstitutional. The executive made it clear he would march troops into South Carolina and hang the traitors, particularly Calhoun. If the nullification convention provided an example of anti-crony reform, the Proclamation contained all the makings of executive abuse because the emperor demanded a brutal suppression of resistance.[10]

Fortunately, the Kitchen Cabinet, disapproving of nullification and Jackson's proclamation, wanted to settle the crisis through tariff reductions. In the lame-duck Congress, New York's Gulian C. Verplanck reported a tariff bill which Cambreleng, Polk, and Wright heartily supported. By drastically reducing rates to 20 percent within two years and removing the cotton minimum, Ritchie believed Verplanck's bill would "pour oil on the stormy waves" of South Carolinian discontent.[11] Unfortunately, though the president supported it, Jackson focused on acquiring legislative support for his Force Bill, which provided congressional authorization to suppress Nullifier resistance. Second, Senator Calhoun hated Van Buren and wanted to deprive New Yorkers of a resolution to the crisis. Third, and most importantly, protectionists vehemently attacked it. Clay astutely realized that if Congress failed to pass a new tariff, the incoming Jacksonian Congress would pass such legislation, and one even more free trade than Verplanck's. To stop free trade tariffs, Clay proposed a compromise that slowly lowered rates to 20 percent over *ten* years. Reinforcing his counterattack, Clay introduced a separate bill that distributed revenue to the states to prolong protection.

To resolve the Nullification Crisis, Congress passed Clay's tariff, the Force Bill, and distribution by early March. To get the president's signature on the tariff, Congress overwhelmingly passed the Force Bill, though John Tyler cast the lone vote against it in the upper chamber. The House passed the tariff with strong Democratic support and heavy Whig resistance. Clearly, as Thomas E. Woods Jr. notes, the crisis demonstrates "the value of nullification," for South Carolinians secured lower rates and the reassembled convention the rescinded the

[10] Bolt, *Tariff Wars*, p. 120; Ellis, *Union at Risk*, pp. 46–50, 81–88; Irwin, *Clashing over Commerce*, pp. 173–75; Peart, *Making of US Tariff Policy*, pp. 117–18; Watkins, *Reclaiming the American Revolution*, pp. 109–14.

[11] Bolt, *Tariff Wars*, p. 129.

Ordinance.[12] Admittedly, Jackson diverted crucial firepower to his draconian Force Bill and belatedly recognized that the new tariff only moderately decreased rates. However, the president partially redeemed himself by vetoing Clay's distribution bill and did nothing when the South Carolina convention nullified the Force Bill. Therefore, despite the complications, William Cullen Bryant applauded the Compromise Tariff of 1833, declaring the triumph of liberty over power.[13]

Some historians have argued that protecting slavery was the secret motivation behind the nullification movement.[14] South Carolinians feared that if Congress could successfully impose protective tariffs, it could also pass laws restricting slavery. There is no question that South Carolina overwhelmingly supported slavery. However, the South Carolina Nullifiers, and the South overall, focused on protective tariffs. "The slavery issue," William Belko properly notes, "had absolutely no relevance, nor was it even a remote consideration, at the Philadelphia convention or in the months following as the tariff issue fought its way to conclusion in 1833."[15]

During Jackson's second term, the Compromise Tariff remained inviolate and created burgeoning Treasury surpluses, allowing senators Clay and Calhoun to push for distribution in the 1836 Deposit Act. Early next year, Cambreleng and Wright unsuccessfully tried to lower tariffs further. When the Panic of 1837 drained federal revenue, Van Buren maintained the compromise's planned reductions but ended distribution. By January 1840, the compromise had instituted a 40 percent reduction in the excess of all rates over 20 percent. After the protectionist Harrison achieved victory in 1840, chances for a renewal of monopolistic privileges dramatically grew. The Whigs planned to justify tariff hikes by increasing spending through distribution of land revenue to the states, but John Tyler's ascension complicated their

---

[12] Thomas Woods, *Nullification* (Washington, DC: Regnery, 2010), p. 77.

[13] Bolt, *Tariff Wars*, pp. 128–38; Donald Cole, *Martin Van Buren and the American Political System* (Princeton, NJ: Princeton University Press, 1984), pp. 240–43; Ellis, *Union at Risk*, p. 181; Daniel Feller, *The Public Lands in Jacksonian Politics* (Madison: The University of Wisconsin Press, 1984), pp. 164–65; Irwin, *Clashing over Commerce*, pp. 177–81; Peart, *Making of US Tariff Policy*, pp. 118–35; Robert Remini, *Andrew Jackson*, vol. 3 (New York: History Book Club, 1998), pp. 40–42; Edward Spann, *Ideals and Politics* (Albany: State University of New York Press, 1972), pp. 53; Watkins, *Reclaiming the American Revolution*, pp. 114–16.

[14] William Freehling, *Prelude to Civil War* (New York: Oxford University Press, 1965).

[15] Belko, *Antebellum Free Trade Movement*, p. 162. See also Ford, *Origins of Southern Radicalism*, pp. 121–25, 137; Remini, *Andrew Jackson*, 3, pp. 14–16, 34, 42–44.

plans. In 1841, to appease the Whigs, Tyler disastrously signed a bill that raised some rates to 20 percent as well as the Distribution Act for land revenue. He at least stipulated the suspension of distribution if tariff rates exceeded 20 percent.

Congress scheduled the compromise's final cuts for July 1842, but this would not stop Clay's Whigs from jacking up rates that year. After lobbyists descended upon the capital and pro-tariff forces sent petitions (including one from the upcoming-and-coming Whig lawyer Abraham Lincoln of Illinois), New York's Millard Fillmore, chair of the House Ways and Means Committee, reported on the "Great Tariff" and the "Little Tariff" in June. Both repealed Tyler's stipulation regarding distribution, and the former raised rates to protectionist levels while the latter delayed the Compromise Tariff's final cuts. Whigs passed both bills against solid Democrat resistance, but Tyler responded with vetoes. The Whigs then decided to pass the Great Tariff's protection and distribution provisions separately to appease Tyler and weaken Democrat opposition. The tariff bill squeaked through both chambers by the barest of majorities, 104-103 in the House and 24-23 in the Senate, with Whigs overwhelmingly in favor and Democrats heavily against. Although Democrats constituted virtually all northern opposition (the region favored the tariff by 108-33), enough northern Democrats, including Senator Wright, broke ranks because the tariff raised revenue for the government and no longer included distribution. Although Tyler let his guard down when he signed the tariff bill, he at least vetoed distribution.

The Tariff of 1842 raised the average rate from 20 to 30 percent, but this is misleading because the new law reduced rates on many miscellaneous items while drastically raising rates on woolen, cotton, and iron products. It included an especially egregious 160 percent rate on iron, and several owners of copper rolling mills personally visited Fillmore to ensure similar privileges for themselves. Thanks to a 70 percent tariff on textiles, the Boston Associates soon boasted annual profits of 19 percent.[16]

---

[16] Bolt, *Tariff Wars*, pp. 142–61, 176; Feller, *Public Lands*, pp. 175–83; *Historical Statistics*, 5, p. 510; Jeffrey Rogers Hummel, "Martin Van Buren," in *Reassessing the Presidency*, ed. John V. Denson (Auburn, AL: Mises Institute, 2001), pp. 179–80; Irwin, *Clashing over Commerce*, pp. 181–84; Peart, *Making of US Tariff Policy*, pp. 135–45, 210–11; Lindsay Regele, *Manufacturing Advantage* (Baltimore, MD: The Johns Hopkins University Press, 2019), p. 144.

The outlook for free trade improved after Democrats captured the presidency. Polk achieved substantial reductions with the 1846 Walker Tariff, named after Treasurer Robert J. Walker, who declined to attend the Philadelphia Free Trade Convention. Only a parallel push for free trade in Great Britain made this reform possible. David Ricardo had previously complained about the Corn Laws, which erected protective tariffs on foreign grains to benefit British landlords. Now, free traders Richard Cobden and John Bright traveled across Great Britain to preach laissez-faire, establishing the Anti–Corn Law League in 1839. Both British and American free traders realized they had to jointly destroy protectionists' greatest argument: the need to retaliate against countries that legislated high rates. This concern featured prominently in midwestern tariff debates, which only supported free trade if farmers could profitably sell agricultural products across the Atlantic.[17]

The president trumpeted free trade in his December 1845 message, castigating the crony Tariff of 1842 for providing monopolistic privileges at the expense of the poor, who disproportionately suffered the burden of higher rates. The anti–Corn Law Parliament even reprinted Walker's 1845 tariff report for distribution. This earned the Treasurer the epithet of "Sir Robert" by the Whig Horace Greeley of the *New-York Tribune*, a reference to Prime Minister Robert Peel.[18] In January 1846, Polk wrote to his ambassador to Great Britain, emphasizing the importance of repealing the Corn Laws. In February, the Treasurer submitted his own bill to the House Ways and Means Committee, leading to criticism of executive usurpation. Walker's tariff drastically reduced protection on cotton, woolens, and iron. Once Peel and Cobden achieved victory in May, the House started debates.

As expected, protectionists, particularly the Boston Associates, vigorously defended their restrictions. But Walker and Polk exerted pressure over House Democrats, who narrowly passed the bill (114-95) against adamant Whig opposition. The administration experienced greater difficulty in the upper chamber, where the forces of power and liberty were evenly matched. Webster, the unflagging protection-

[17] Peart, *Making of US Tariff Policy*, pp. 145–47; Jim Powell, *The Triumph of Liberty* (New York: The Free Press, 2000), pp. 123–30; Murray N. Rothbard, *An Austrian Perspective on the History of Economic Thought*, vol. 2, *Classical Economics* (Auburn, AL: Mises Institute, 2006), pp. 97, 447–48.

[18] James Shenton, *Robert John Walker* (New York: Columbia University Press, 1961), p. 76.

ist who returned to the Senate after the Boston Associates and other manufacturers paid him a hefty $37,000, led the Whigs. He developed a simple strategy: add amendments to force the bill back into the House and then try to split the free traders. The situation turned dire when William Haywood from North Carolina declared his opposition and resigned. Democrats no longer had enough strength to pass the bill. Fortunately, Polk personally enlisted Whig Senator Spencer Jarnagin of Tennessee, who agreed to vote only if the vice president, Pennsylvania's George Dallas, cast a tie-breaking vote to move it out of committee while Jarnagin abstained. Dallas felt enormous pressure: he hailed from a protectionist state and was the son of former Treasurer Alexander J. Dallas, the man responsible for the Tariff of 1816. Heroically, the vice president did not succumb to corruption, interpreting the 1844 election as a mandate for lower tariffs. Consequently, the Senate narrowly passed the tariff, 28-27.[19]

The Walker Tariff made free trade a national policy for the democracy: with the repeal of the Corn Laws, midwestern senators gave their support. The new law slashed the average rate to 24 percent in 1847, which gradually moved toward 20 percent in the 1850s. No wonder, then, the *Cincinnati Enquirer* boasted in August 1846: "The simultaneous triumph of free trade in the United States and Great Britain, whose citizens and subjects comprehend one-sixth of the human race, is the greatest event of our age."[20]

Thanks to South Carolinians utilizing nullification and the growth of free trade economics in the United States and Great Britain, the Jacksonian executive triumphed against the American System's protectionism. With free trade achieved, the Democrats moved on to the vexing question of government-supported internal improvements.

A Decentralized Program for Public Works

The Jacksonian goal to institute frugality and whittle away charter regulations faced an uphill battle. They recognized that spending

---

[19] William Belko, "'A Tax on the Many, to Enrich a Few'," *Journal of the History of Economic Thought* (June 2015): 281–82; Bolt, *Tariff Wars*, pp. 174–86; Irwin, *Clashing over Commerce*, pp. 185–92; Peart, *Making of US Tariff Policy*, pp. 147–67, 211; Charles Sellers, *James K. Polk, Continentalist* (Princeton, NJ: Princeton University Press, 1966), pp. 447–67; Shenton, *Robert John Walker*, pp. 49, 75–85.

[20] Bolt, *Tariff Wars*, p. 185. See also *Historical Statistics*, 5, pp. 510–11; Irwin, *Clashing over Commerce*, pp. 192–93.

taxpayer funds and chartering monopolies easily corrupts politicians into supporting various interventions for electoral success. Remarkably, the determined laissez-faire Democrats used strict constructionism and executive vetoes to cut spending, pay off the public debt, strike down monopolies in the courts, and pass state-level general incorporation laws. They only failed to reduce western land prices, a goal many Jacksonians linked to axing internal improvements.

Jackson obsessed over the national debt and corporate monopolies. The president and his intellectual supporters recognized that deficit-financed internal improvements and government ownership in private corporations encouraged waste and logrolling, burdened taxpayers, and incentivized the public to support a centralized empire instead of a confederation. They also understood that government special privileges through corporate charters and other restrictions elevated one group above the rest and led to higher prices and reduced production. The Jacksonian solution was to downsize the federal and state governments, privatize transportation networks, and enact general incorporation laws that abolished the restrictive charter system.[21]

In his 1829 December message, Jackson criticized government-subsidized local internal improvements and related stock purchases. Once Congress paid off the debt, distribution of the surplus (sanctioned by a constitutional amendment) would allow states to build their own infrastructure projects. Senator Benton, desiring to cripple the American System, embraced the message. In early 1830, the Missourian again proposed his South-West alliance: if the South favored reducing land prices from the current $1.25 minimum per acre, the West would renounce internal improvements (which Benton desired for his region) and support lower tariffs (the overriding goal of southerners). Unfortunately, Benton's proposal floundered because southeastern Democrats, such as Senators John Tyler and William Smith, believed that lower land prices would decrease revenue and postpone debt payment. After Benton once again failed to reduce land prices, he and other western Democrats returned to supporting public works.[22]

---

[21] Anthony Comegna, "'The Dupes of Hope Forever'," Doctoral dissertation in history, University of Pittsburgh (2016), pp. 29–30, 35–36; Ellis, *Union at Risk*, pp. 19–25; Spann, *Ideals and Politics*, pp. 67–72, 128; Lawrence White, "William Leggett," *History of Political Economy* (June 1986): 311–13.

[22] Ellis, *Union at Risk*, pp. 20–24; Feller, *Public Lands*, pp. 111–36.

Without the congressional strength to tackle expenditures, the burden fell on the president. He needed to act soon: while Barbour's explication of the Invisible Hand in early 1830 convinced the House to defeat a proposed national road from New York to Louisiana, enough Democrats voted with Whigs to authorize new internal improvement surveys; a lighthouse and coastal improvements bill; a $200,000 appropriation for the National Road; and government ownership in the Louisville and Portland Canal, the Washington Turnpike, and the Maysville Road. Clay especially desired the latter appropriation ($150,000), because the road ran entirely through Kentucky and his home town of Lexington, crucial largesse for the upcoming 1832 election.

Van Buren advised the president that the recent appropriations would strengthen the Whigs, promote consolidation, and postpone debt extinguishment. Jackson wholeheartedly agreed and vetoed the Maysville Road bill in May. Written with the assistance of Van Buren and Polk, the veto message openly defended "the construction of the Constitution set up in 1798," arguing that local projects and stock purchases incentivized logrolling and wasteful expenditures.[23] Astutely, the veto emphasized the hidden costs of such projects, rather than their inflated benefits, to help the public recognize their inefficient nature. Shortly thereafter, Jackson vetoed the other legislation except the survey and National Road appropriation bills, because he believed the Constitution warranted them. However, the president advocated an amendment to distinguish between local and national projects and pushed for state control of the National Road. Clay and other Whigs charged Jackson with executive usurpation, but Barbour defended the president. Notably, Thomas Ritchie praised the Maysville veto for "arresting those . . . local appropriations . . . which were wasting the public funds and bribing members of Congress out of their Constitutional principles."[24]

From 1828 to 1831, Democrats trimmed federal spending by 7 percent, and with high tariffs, the public debt shriveled from $58 million to $7 million by 1832 (88 percent). Clay, recognizing debt extinguishment would allow lower tariffs, schemed to increase spending by

---

[23] Paul Kahan, *The Bank War* (Yardley, PA: Westholme Publishing, 2016), pp. 77–78.

[24] Risjord, *The Old Republicans*, p. 271. See also Belko, *Philip Pendleton Barbour*, pp. 151–58; Feller, *Public Lands*, pp. 136–42; Carl Lane, *A Nation Wholly Free* (Yardley, PA: Westholme Publishing, 2014), pp. 79–85; Robert Remini, *Andrew Jackson*, vol. 2 (New York: History Book Club, 1998), pp. 248–56.

distributing land revenue to the states. When Clay secured distribution in March 1833, Jackson vetoed it on constitutional grounds and advocated lower western land prices to help the West. Unfortunately, after Congress paid off the debt in 1835 and included distribution in the 1836 Deposit Act, Jackson decided not to use the veto message he had prepared. Instead, the president signed the bill with "repugnance of feeling, and a recoil of judgement," because he did not want to ruin his vice president's election chances.[25] The Washington *Globe* was on the mark when it criticized distribution as "corrupting largesses."[26] The *Globe* properly noted that the solution to the surplus was Benton's South-West alliance, which Jackson himself advocated in 1833: "[R]educe the taxes; reduce the price of the public lands to actual settlers; let each and all be reduced so as to keep the revenue within the expenses of the Government."[27]

Overall, Jackson's administration maintained a mixed record of frugality. After falling until 1831, federal expenditures, including on transportation, increased 15 percent until 1835 and then by a massive 76 percent from 1835 to 1836. In total, from 1828 to 1836 spending increased by 88 percent. Compared to Adams' single-term transportation expenditures of $6.2 million, the two-term Jackson administration spent $16.1 million (roughly a one-third increase per term). The president failed to hold the line for several reasons. First, election years, particularly 1836, corrupted the president into not vetoing spending bills. Second, though Democrats cut all stock subscriptions and heavily reduced canal expenditures, they worked with Whigs to spend tremendously on lighthouses, rivers, and harbors. Congress attached these appropriations to general spending bills, making them difficult for Jackson to detect. Third, some of the increase was a nominal illusion because of exogenous price increases, which caused higher nominal expenditures. Fourth, in 1836, military spending surged during the Second Seminole War. If the Democrats wanted to achieve true reform regarding internal improvements and overall spending, they would need to practice greater fiscal discipline.[28]

---

[25] Feller, *Public Lands*, p. 183.

[26] Remini, *Andrew Jackson*, 3, p. 326.

[27] Ibid., p. 326.

[28] Ellis, *Union at Risk*, pp. 24–25; Feller, *Public Lands*, pp. 162–71, 180–83; *Historical Statistics*, V, pp. 80, 91; John Larson, *Internal Improvement* (Chapel Hill: The University of North Carolina Press, 2001), pp. 188, 190–91; Remini, *Andrew Jackson*, 3, pp. 318–26.

Fortunately, the Jackson administration experienced genuine success in attacking corporate privilege. After Chief Justice Marshall died in 1835, the president changed the dispensation of the Federalist court by appointing Roger Taney to Chief Justice and Barbour to associate justice (another vacancy existed). Both men opposed the American System's special privileges, which they expressed in the spectacularly anti-crony *Charles River Bridge v. Warren Bridge* (1837).

In 1785, Massachusetts chartered the Charles River Bridge (CRB) for forty years, and soon extended it to seventy years. Free of competition, the CRB earned monopoly profits from tolls. But in 1828, the legislature chartered the Warren Bridge, threatening the CRB. In Federalist fashion, the CRB sued the Warren Bridge on grounds that the new charter violated the contract clause, arguing that Massachusetts had granted an irrevocable monopoly charter. In February 1837, Taney delivered the majority decision: the CRB only possessed the right to build a bridge, not the right to exclude all future competitors.

The ruling significantly weakened corporate cronyism: chartered companies did not possess an inherent monopoly. Although the ruling displayed similarities with *Gibbons v. Ogden* (1824), a major difference existed. While Marshall weakened a state's right to charter a monopoly by strengthening the interstate commerce clause, Taney defended a state's right to charter new competition. In other words, Taney struck down a monopoly *and* strengthened states' rights. Furthermore, Taney's decision led to state-level rulings against cronyism. For example, in *Mohawk Bridge v. Utica and Schenectady Railroad* (1837), a New York court declared that a bridge's charter did not prohibit competition from a ferry, and in *Tuckahoe Canal v. Tuckahoe and James River Railroad* (1840), the Supreme Court of Appeals of Virginia ruled that a canal's charter did not prevent railroad competition.[29]

Despite these legal victories, the assault on government spending and privileges was nowhere near finished, especially at the state level. Between 1830 and 1839, Democrats and Whigs funneled vast

---

[29] Belko, *Philip Pendleton Barbour*, pp. 180–81, 186–87; Philip Burch, *Elites in American History*, vol. 1 (New York: Holmes & Meier Publishers, 1981), pp. 158, 166, 173; Steven Calabresi and Larissa Leibowitz, "Monopolies and the Constitution," *Harvard Journal of Law & Public Policy* (Summer 2013): 1019–23; Arthur M. Schlesinger Jr., *The Age of Jackson* (Boston, MA: Little, Brown, 1945), pp. 324–26.

sums into newly chartered canals and railroads, ballooning state debts from \$26 million to \$170 million. Unsurprisingly, the governments inefficiently allocated scarce resources and the panic added insult to injury, resulting in complete catastrophes.

New York, Michigan, and Indiana provide standard examples. After the Whig William Seward secured the governorship in 1838, New York hoped to recreate the Erie Canal's magic, lavishly expanding the state's transportation. While Whigs justified the appropriations according to "political prudence," the branch canals unexpectedly cost \$9.4 million and earned losses.[30] In 1837, Michigan spent \$5 million on public works. Every project succumbed to inefficiency and waste, particularly the Michigan Southern Railroad. For this undertaking, the state awarded construction contracts to the politically connected Cole & Clark, which charged three to four times the market price for supplies. Even worse, constructors used faulty strap-iron rails and improperly installed spikes. When Michigan sold the railroad in 1846, it recovered only \$500,000 out of its \$1.2 million investment. Reckless Indiana passed the Mammoth Internal Improvement Act in 1836, \$10 million legislation George Taylor describes as "a maximum of incompetence, political logrolling, and large-scale peculation."[31] By 1841, Whigs admitted that the state had only finished three hundred miles out of a thirteen hundred mile system, which required an astounding \$12 million more, an onerous burden for Indiana's already belt-busting \$15 million of debt.[32]

These and other states could only pay their soaring obligations through punitive taxes. But newly elected Democrats refused to consent, opting for default and repudiation. They understood that unlike a voluntary loan, government borrowing ultimately relies on coercive taxes and is therefore an illegitimate transaction. Dishonoring government obligations only violates *unjust* private property. Of course,

---

[30] Lee Benson, *The Concept of Jacksonian Democracy* (Princeton, NJ: Princeton University Press, 1961), p. 105.

[31] George Taylor, *The Transportation Revolution* (New York: Holt, Rinehart and Winston, 1951), p. 47.

[32] Arthur Ekirch, "Democracy and Laissez Faire," *Journal of Libertarian Studies* (Fall 1977): 321; Burton Folsom and Anita Folsom, *Uncle Sam Can't Count* (New York: HarperCollins Publishers, 2014), pp. 61–67, 70; Larson, *Internal Improvement*, pp. 208–14; Reginald McGrane, *Foreign Bondholders and American State Debts* (New York: Macmillan, 1935), pp. 6–7; John Wallis, Richard Sylla, and Arthur Grinath, "Sovereign Debt and Repudiation, *NBER Working Paper Series* (September 2004): 17.

the Whigs would not countenance an abrogation of any government contract. But, recognizing the unpopularity of taxes, in classic Hamiltonian fashion they pushed to have the federal government assume the obligations—make the taxpayers of other states pay! Fortunately, the Van Buren and Tyler administrations held the line and Congress assumed no state debts. Instead, from 1836 to 1845, they slashed spending by 26 percent. Unfortunately, plummeting tax revenue caused the national debt to increase from $0 in 1835 to $16 million in 1845. However, the public debt had actually risen to $33 million in 1843, so by 1845 the debt was once again on a downward trajectory. Therefore, it is clear that by the beginning of Polk's term the Jacksonian Democrats had committed to achieving true fiscal reform: paying off the national debt *and* cutting expenditures.[33]

This stern discipline left states to their own measures. Some, such as Michigan and Indiana, defaulted, while others, such as Mississippi, repudiated their debt obligations. More importantly, Democrats in various states held constitutional conventions from the mid-1840s to the early 1850s. They pushed for anti-crony reforms at these highly libertarian events. First, Jacksonians severely restricted the states' ability to borrow and invest in corporations. This led to beneficial results: over the next several decades, states that defaulted and adopted restrictions experienced smaller increases in indebtedness than other states. Second, Democrats secured general incorporation laws that removed the old charter system, significantly weakening corrupt government-business partnerships. For this reason, Steven Calabresi and Larissa Leibowitz justly note that "general incorporation laws were at the core of *laissez faire* and of Jacksonian thought."[34] Unfortunately, some loopholes existed, such as special incorporation for eminent domain and land grants. These exceptions aside, the constitutional conventions victoriously attacked cronyism.[35]

---

[33] *Historical Statistics*, 5, p. 80; McGrane, *Bondholders, Debts*, pp. 26–28, 35–40, 46–48; Murray N. Rothbard, "The History of Money and Banking Before the Twentieth Century," in *A History of Money and Banking in the United States*, ed. Joseph T. Salerno (Auburn, AL: Mises Institute, 2002), pp. 101–03.

[34] Calabresi and Leibowitz, "Monopolies and the Constitution," p. 1072.

[35] Folsom and Folsom, *Uncle Sam Can't Count*, p. 71; Jeffrey Rogers Hummel, "The Consequences of a United States Default or Repudiation," in *Economic and Political Change after Crisis*, ed. Stephen Balch and Benjamin Powell (London: Routledge, 2016), pp. 115–16; John Wallis, "Constitutions, Corporations, and Corruption," *The Journal of Economic History* (March 2005): 216–19, 231–35, 242–45.

Polk planned to continue the tradition of weakening the American System. He long favored "a plain economical Government," insisting on frugality for public works when he served as governor of Tennessee from 1839 to 1841.[36] Furthermore, he supported lower land prices for western settlers. The new president worried about the Memphis Convention of November 1845, a gathering of southern and western states that advocated federal support for internal improvements. Calhoun presided as the convention's president, and his good friend James Gadsden, president of the South Carolina Railroad Company, helped organize the event. Calhoun reconciled his lifelong enthusiasm for internal improvements with his recently acquired strict constructionism on the grounds of defense, interstate commerce, and distribution. His stance, though popular in the West, cost him dearly in the South, including in his home state.[37]

Congress felt the convention's pressure. In 1846, western Democrats introduced a bill appropriating $1.5 million for local rivers and harbors. Proponents, such as John Wentworth, wanted Congress to embark upon a vast array of improvements. The initiation of "as many projects as possible," explains Charles Sellers, would force "later Congresses to complete them in order to prevent the earlier appropriations from going to waste."[38] Translation: the cost of the new projects would be far higher than $1.5 million. It was a classic illustration of politicians concealing, or at best postponing, the actual cost of proposals to better facilitate their passage. Future taxpayers, never current voters, must always foot the bill. Party lines in the upper chamber once again displayed a clear division on the contentious issue: Whigs favored the measure 21-3, while Democrats split 13-13. At the same time, Democrats in both chambers pushed for bills lowering the price of western lands from the stubbornly high $1.25 an acre.

Polk could have secured Senator Benton's original South-West alliance of cheap land, low tariffs, and no internal improvements, a dream even the Missourian had unfortunately given up on. This

---

[36] Charles Sellers, *James K. Polk, Jacksonian* (Princeton, NJ: Princeton University Press, 1957), p. 152.

[37] Norman Graebner, *Empire on the Pacific* (New York: The Ronald Press Company, 1955), p. 96; John Niven, *John C. Calhoun and the Price of Union* (Baton Rouge: Louisiana State University Press, 1988), pp. 293–95; Sellers, *James K. Polk, Continentalist*, pp. 318, 329, 346; Sellers, *James K. Polk, Jacksonian*, pp. 344–48, 362–63, 439.

[38] Sellers, *James K. Polk, Continentalist*, p. 453.

required Polk vetoing the Rivers and Harbors Bill and making sure Congress actually lowered the price of western lands. Instead, Polk rightfully vetoed the Rivers and Harbors bill but disastrously allowed southern Democrats to kill the land bill. This quite naturally frustrated western Democrats, though many admirably maintained party principles and refused to override Polk's Rivers and Harbors veto. Even with this flaw, Polk's admirable veto demonstrated his devotion to strict constructionism and weakening the American System.[39]

The president's decision regarding internal improvements was one of the last anti-crony victories achieved by the Jackson–Van Buren–Tyler–Polk quadrumvirate. Unlike the Jeffersonian Republicans, the Jacksonian Democrats' determination, radical economic theories, and cooperation with British reformers prevented power from corrupting them to patronize Whig constituencies and expand their electoral base. The Jacksonians refused to moderate and actually practiced what they preached: free market economics. It is for this reason that Robert Kelley justly notes that by Polk's veto,

> The Manchester Radicals in Britain and the American Democrats had the substance of their dream: . . . a community whose basic economic nature was shaped by the ideas of the Scotsman Adam Smith . . . Mercantilism in its traditional form seemed to have met its demise. Tariffs were low in order to encourage international trade and subject all producers to competition; a reasonably complete separation between government and business had been achieved; and "sound money" principles to keep prices low and damp down boom and bust oscillations were being observed.[40]

In a similar vein, Edward Spann accurately writes that "liberals found 1846 a banner year."[41]

But no victory is perfect. To achieve their goal, Jacksonians empowered the executive branch. Democrats relied on vetoes, presidential rotation, and executive influence over the lawmaking process.

---

[39] Sellers, *Polk, Continentalist*, pp. 320, 452–53, 471–74; Silbey, *Shrine*, pp. 44–48, 71–72, 76, 84.

[40] Robert Kelley, *The Cultural Pattern in American Politics* (New York: University Press of America, 1979), p. 158.

[41] Spann, *Ideals and Politics*, p. 130.

CHAPTER 16

RESURRECTING THE AMERICAN SYSTEM: THE GROWTH OF IMPERIALISM

Removing the Indians

The Jacksonians succeeded in eliminating Clay's American System—save for the imperialist plank that empowered the empire through aggressive acquisition of territory and international commerce. Similar to the Jeffersonian Republicans' corruption by the Louisiana Purchase, land did the reform coalition in. Although Jackson aggressed on frontier Indians, he and Van Buren pursued a peaceful foreign policy in the 1830s. However, the growing temptation of Texas annexation and the related issue of slavery in the West split the two men apart. Even worse, the lure of California's coveted western ports pushed Polk to clandestinely maneuver the country into a war of conquest. During the mid-1840s, the party rapidly embraced the debt and land speculators, internationalist merchants, privilege-seeking bankers, and other groups they once criticized. Executive authority primarily facilitated the aggrandizement—a clear sign that power corrupted the Jacksonians into using the presidency to pursue coercive empire building.

Historians increasingly demonize Jackson for enacting "ethnic cleansing," ranking his Indian removal program as one of the era's most momentous laws.[1] They ignore the insights of Robert Remini and Sean Wilentz, who emphasize that the truth is far more complicated.[2] First, Jackson genuinely cared about the Indians' welfare, albeit in a highly flawed manner: condescendingly, impatiently, and coercively. To the president, the savages could either obtain second-class status

---

[1] Daniel Howe, *What Hath God Wrought* (New York: Oxford University Press, 2007), p. 423.

[2] Robert Remini, *Andrew Jackson and His Indian Wars* (New York: Penguin Books, 2001), pp. 277–81; Sean Wilentz, *The Rise of American Democracy* (New York: W.W. Norton & Co., 2005), pp. 324–26.

in civilized society or peacefully maintain their lifestyle by moving to the West. Jackson was actually somewhat unique, since very few Democrats and Whigs cared about the Indians' plight, and those who did usually hailed from states with no Indian populations. Second, most Americans did not view Indian relations as very significant, weighing banking, tariffs, internal improvements, land prices, foreign policy, and even slavery as far more important. Americans had engaged in heavy-handed Indian relations since the colonial era and saw it as a fact of life.

To Americans in 1829, the basic problem remained: Indian hunters claimed ownership of land beyond those that they farmed, particularly in the Southwest and Florida. This directly conflicted with the heavy influx of westward settlers. As Robert Whaples explains, "Indians' claims to vast tracts of forested lands made no sense to all [the] European Americans who saw it sitting idle."[3] Jackson shared these concerns and insisted the Indians either had to assimilate into society—and remain subordinate because they were not white—or relocate to the West, where they could continue their nomad existence.

Consequently, Jackson's December 1829 message to Congress proposed a new "voluntary" program: Indians could agree to the government's offers to purchase their land (at a price US officials dictated) and remove to an area west of the Mississippi River (modern-day Oklahoma) or civilize and obey state laws. Jackson knew that settlers would continue to encroach on the lands the Indians claimed, especially given Georgians' recent discovery of gold. "It seems to me visionary," Jackson wrote, echoing Adams, "to suppose that . . . claims can be allowed on tracts of country on which [Indians] have neither dwelt nor made improvements, merely because they have seen them from the mountains or passed them in the chase."[4]

The Democrats obediently reported on a removal bill in the Senate in February 1830. Whig Senator Theodore Frelinghuysen of New Jersey, a religious man who genuinely cared about the welfare and rights of the Indians—albeit those in other states, because New Jersey had previously removed its Indians—criticized the bill for imposing removal on a reluctant people and attacked the executive for interfering in the legislative process. Democrats John Forsyth of Georgia

---

[3] Robert Whaples, "Were Andrew Jackson's Policies 'Good for the Economy'?" *The Independent Review* (Spring 2014): 547.

[4] Richard Ellis, *The Union at Risk* (New York: Oxford University Press, 1987), p. 27.

and Robert Adams of Mississippi shot back, accusing northerners of hypocrisy for denying to southerners what they had previously carried out in their own region. Whigs tried to make political capital out of the situation: most notably, the anti-Indian Clay opportunistically opposed removal in the 1832 election. After heated partisan debate, the Senate passed the bill by a party vote (28-19) and the House followed by a narrow 102-97, thanks to Jackson's personal exhortations with congressmen—clear executive influence. In both votes, New England sided against and the South for, while the Mid-Atlantic and the Midwest split. Although the bill's passage was controversial, the removal issue died down over time and "most Americans accepted what had happened."[5]

The Indian Removal Act provided executive authority to relocate the Indians and transfer their eastern land claims to a western reserve, with $500,000 appropriated for all necessary expenses. This absurdly low number highlights the eternal truth that politicians will always try to conceal the expense of proposed legislation—the taxpayer must never know the full cost! Far more worrisome was that such a massive government undertaking, inherently hobbled by inefficiency and corruption, could lead to only one result—a crony redistribution of resources from Indians to politically connected insiders. As Robert Remini explains,

> The President's noble desire to give the Indians a free choice between staying and removing, one devoid of coercion, was disregarded by land-greedy state and federal officials, who practiced fraud and deception to enrich themselves and their friends at the expense of the native tribes.[6]

A blatant example of corrupt profiteering occurred with Mississippi's Choctaws. Thanks to bribes, corrupt Indians chiefs signed the Treaty of Dancing Rabbit Creek in September 1830, ceding ten million

---

[5] Remini, *Jackson and His Indian Wars*, p. 238. See also Ellis, *Union at Risk*, pp. 27–28; Walter Nugent, *Habits of Empire* (New York: Vintage Books 2009), pp. 225, 339; Remini, *Jackson and His Indian Wars*, pp. 222–38, 262; Wilentz, *Rise of American Democracy*, pp. 326, 867.

[6] Remini, *Jackson and His Indian Wars*, pp. 237. See also Ellis, *Union at Risk*, p. 28; Nugent, *Habits of Empire*, pp. 225, 339; Remini, *Jackson and His Indian Wars*, pp. 222–38; Wilentz, *Rise of American Democracy*, p. 326.

acres their people claimed. Enter the young Robert J. Walker and William Gwin, who organized a land speculation syndicate to corner one
million acres up for sale in October 1833. Thanks to the work of the
local land office register Samuel Gwin (William's brother), the group
snatched up seven hundred thousand acres and resold most of it.
Walker kept fifty thousand acres for himself and others, and the state
representatives of the settlers graciously elected the aspiring politician
to the US Senate. Fittingly, he became chair of the Senate Committee
on Public Lands. To compound the punishment, Gwin, with the help
of W. W. Corcoran of Corcoran & Riggs, performed legal services for
dispossessed Indians at the hefty fee of $56,000. Walker's involvement
with Indian land speculation sullied his image in the eyes of Jackson,
who actually advised Polk not to appoint him as Treasurer after he
assumed the presidency.[7]

Other Indian tribes resisted the government's program, but the
end result still occurred. By far, the Cherokee had civilized the most
out of the southwestern Indian tribes, farming, wearing Western cloth-
ing, adopting a written language and constitution, developing schools,
and establishing a newspaper. Significantly, some farmers also used
slaves. Cherokees even pursued legal avenues in the courts, but the
Supreme Court could not save them from Georgia. More to the point,
Jackson and his supporters used the information they had available
to demonstrate that the Cherokees still inefficiently used the land and
had failed to modernize enough for the president. When a delegation
pleaded their case in 1835, the president bluntly told them that "a large
portion of your people have acquired little or no property in the soil
itself. . . . How, under these circumstances, can you live in the country
you now occupy?"[8] The Cherokees finally "agreed" to leave, and the
Senate ratified the treaty in 1836. Congress gave the Cherokees two
years to vacate. When their leader, John Ross, foolishly instructed his
people to stay put and wait for a miracle, the result could only mean
trouble: in 1838, the Van Buren administration forcibly drove them

---

[7] Henry Cohen, *Business and Politics in America from the Age of Jackson to the Civil
War* (Westport, CT: Greenwood Publishing Corporation, 1971), pp. 26–27, 31, 119;
H. Jordan, "A Politician of Expansion," *Mississippi Valley Historical Review* (December 1932): 363–65; Glenn Price, *Origins of the War with Mexico* (Austin: University
of Texas Press, 1967), p. 84; Remini, *Jackson and His Indian Wars*, p. 249; James
Shenton, *Robert John Walker* (New York: Columbia University Press, 1961), pp. 13–
16, 25, 33, 63, 67, 71.

[8] Remini, *Jackson and His Indian Wars*, p. 266.

out. Bad weather and government inefficiency led to numerous deaths, an unmitigated disaster.

The Florida Seminoles refused to abide by the treaties they signed, and when the US government sent soldiers to evict them, a bitter guerrilla conflict erupted—the Second Seminole War. The Department of War's budget ballooned 111 percent from 1835 to 1836. By the time Jackson left the presidency, the government had spent $10 million on the conflict and each month after required another $460,000. The war only ended in 1842 under General Zachary Taylor. Whigs proved no more generous to the Indians than the Democrats, and this attitude continued in the decades ahead.

In total, the Jackson administration signed roughly seventy Indian treaties and obtained one hundred million acres in return for $68 million and thirty-two million acres west of the Mississippi River. The one hundred million acres was more than twice what Indians had ceded in the prior eight years. If the public had known of the astronomical $68 million cost instead of the stated $500,000, Congress assuredly would have been unable to pass the original law. Despite Jackson's intentions, the entire process aggravated relations among Indians and settlers, led to rapacious land speculation, and caused costly wars. What had occurred within the United States did not bode well for adjacent countries the Jacksonians covetously eyed.[9]

The Texas Question

Similar to the Louisiana Purchase, Texas annexation drastically increased the United States' size and thereby exploded the American Empire's power. Several interests supported annexation. First, debt holders wanted Congress to bail out the Texas government. Second, land speculators desired a US monopoly over cotton. Lastly, slave owners wanted to make it harder for fugitive slaves to escape. Furthermore, annexation and the related issue of slavery's expansion caused Van Buren and Benton to momentously split from Jackson and Polk,

---

[9] *Historical Statistics of the United States*, vol. 5, ed. Richard Sutch and Susan Carter (New York: Cambridge University Press, 2006), p. 91; Jeffrey Rogers Hummel, "Martin Van Buren," in *Reassessing the Presidency*, ed. John V. Denson (Auburn, AL: Mises Institute, 2001), p. 194; Remini, *Jackson and His Indian Wars*, pp. 238, 250–77; Whaples, "Andrew Jackson's Policies," p. 547; David Wishart, "Evidence of Surplus Production in the Cherokee Nation Prior to Removal," *Journal of Economic History* (March 1995): 137.

corrupting the libertarian Democratic Party into increasingly bellicose and expansionist policies.

Despite the Missouri Compromise, by the early 1830s, slavery had returned to the political realm. The British abolitionist movement and the 1833 gradual compensated emancipation in the West Indies caused this momentous return. Most notably, Massachusetts' William Lloyd Garrison founded *The Liberator* newspaper in 1831 and helped organize the American Anti-Slavery Society in 1833. Garrison declared slavery a moral sin, urging immediate abolition without any compensation to the owners whatsoever. He astutely recognized that the Constitution protected slavery through its crony fugitive slave and three-fifths representation clauses. As a result, he advocated northern secession to induce a massive hemorrhaging of southern slaves and peacefully end the practice. Garrison and William Cullen Bryant informally worked with followers of the British abolitionist Richard Cobden, emphasizing the similarities between free trade and free men as well as protectionism and slavery. The activities of the libertarian Garrison shook up the nation.[10]

It is extremely important to understand that the abolitionist movement was still a very small, albeit extremely vocal, minority. Yankees, descendants of the New England Puritans, filled the abolitionists' ranks. These pietists wanted to stamp out sin, which also included restricting Catholic immigration, suspending Sunday mail delivery, prohibiting alcohol, and controlling schools. Most northerners did not share the Yankee's abolitionist sentiments or care about the plight of blacks, and the French traveler Alexis de Tocqueville actually remarked that northern prejudice was stronger than southern. To the extent the average northerner fought slavery, he fought its westward extension to prevent the three-fifths clause from taking effect and to stop black slaves from competing with white yeomen. Northerners did not want to interfere with slavery in the southern states or increase their small black population, because freed slaves would compete with white workers and lead to an integrated society. Instead, they embraced colonizing the freed slaves.

Equally crucial, the South rapidly changed its sentiments. The death in 1833 of John Randolph, who manumitted his slaves in his will,

---

[10] Jeffrey Rogers Hummel, *Emancipating Slaves, Enslaving Free Men* (Chicago, IL: Open Court, 2002), pp. 20–22; Marc-William Palen, "Free-Trade Ideology and Transatlantic Abolitionism," *Journal of the History of Economic Thought* (June 2015): 294–97.

symbolically marked the end of an era. Paranoid southerners increasingly worried that a small group of vocal abolitionists threatened their property: the "slavery scare" that Antifederalists and Old Republicans had conjured up in years past to discourage federal aggrandizement now seemed like a frightening possibility. As a result, the region suffocated antislavery sentiments, tightened slavery regulations, and transitioned from the "necessary evil" regret to the "positive good" argument. In March 1833, the *Richmond Whig* wrote that the anti-slavery agitators were doing more to "alienate the south from their northern brethren, than the tariff or any or all political causes, that we complain about."[11] The South viewed slavery as an issue separate from tariffs, but still one that could cause a massive problem. Soon enough, the philosophy of South Carolina's Calhoun, who proclaimed that the "great institution" of slavery provided "the most safe and stable basis for free institutions in the world," dominated southern sentiments.[12]

Even with changing regional views, to most Americans, the important political issues concerned the American System. The average politician believed slavery agitation by Yankee abolitionists and southern sectionalists could wreck the Whig and Democratic Parties, making it harder to achieve their goals. Consequently, Democrats and Whigs minimized debate. Some vocal holdouts in Massachusetts existed, such as John Quincy Adams, who adopted anti-slavery principles after his humiliating 1828 defeat. But Adams' actions starkly contrasted with those of the Boston Associates, particularly Abbott Lawrence and their political lackey Webster. The abolitionist emphasis on slavery and calls for secession horrified these men, because their large textile companies depended on cheap slave cotton.[13]

---

[11] Ellis, *Union at Risk*, p. 191.

[12] Hummel, *Emancipating Slaves*, pp. 22–23. See also Ellis, *Union at Risk*, pp. 191–93; Thomas Hietala, *Manifest Design* (New York: Cornell University Press, 2003), p. 30; Hummel, *Emancipating Slaves*, pp. 22, 26; Robert Kelley, *The Cultural Pattern in American Politics* (New York: University Press of America, 1979), pp. 160–81; Phil Magness, "The American System and the Political Economy of Black Colonization," *Journal of the History of Economic Thought* (June 2015): 187–94; Murray N. Rothbard, "Report on George B. DeHuszar and Thomas Hulbert Stevenson, *A History of the American Republic*, 2 vols," in Rothbard, *Strictly Confidential*, ed. David Gordon (Auburn, AL: Mises Institute, 2010), p. 122; Nicholas Wood, "John Randolph of Roanoke and the Politics of Slavery in the Early Republic," *Virginia Magazine of History and Biography* (Summer 2012): 133–34.

[13] Kinley Brauer, *Cotton versus Conscience* (Lexington: The University of Kentucky Press, 1967), pp. 23–24; Hummel, *Emancipating Slaves*, pp. 81–82; Thomas O'Connor, *Lords*

The Democrats led the suppression of slavery debates, because they controlled Congress and wanted to dismantle the American System. In August 1835, the American Anti-Slavery Society flooded the postal system with abolitionist literature. The Charleston postmaster censored the mail, and Postmaster General Amos Kendall allowed this illegal censorship of free speech. Later that year, Jackson, an ardent slave owner, requested that Congress prohibit the distribution of such publications. When the House narrowly refused, Kendall continued to allow subordinates to decide on the delivery of antislavery literature. However, Congress did subsequently institute a "gag rule" tabling various anti-slavery petitions.[14] Kendall's decision earned the ire of William Leggett, who criticized him for privileging slave owners and restricting free speech. The Washington *Globe* promptly attacked Leggett and Democrats cast the libertarian out of the party. The experience turned Leggett into a dedicated opponent of slavery and an advocate of northern secession. In addition, Vice President Van Buren and Senator Benton uneasily watched the unfolding proslavery policies. Although they ultimately agreed with the decisions, their acquiescence would not last forever.[15]

The massive elephant in the room, Texas, threatened to amplify the slavery question and destroy the Jacksonians' classical liberal foreign policy. Americans increasingly brought their slaves to settle in Texas, and annexing the region threatened to resurrect the western slavery controversy and potentially spark war with Mexico. In 1829, when Jackson authorized Van Buren to purchase the region for up to $5 million, Van Buren delayed. By the mid-1830s, Jackson had cooled on the question, realizing that amplifying Texas could sabotage Van Buren's election and their goal to end the American System. In fact, when Texas seceded from Mexico in 1835, Jackson astutely turned down their pleas for aid. This continued after Texas became an independent republic in 1836 and declared ownership down to the Rio

---

of The Loom (New York: Charles Scribner's Sons, 1968), pp. 46–47, 51–52, 56–59; Robert Remini, *The Legacy of Andrew Jackson* (Baton Rouge: Louisiana State University Press, 1988), pp. 83–111.

[14] Donald Cole, *Martin Van Buren and the American Political System* (Princeton, NJ: Princeton University Press, 1984), p. 272.

[15] William Chambers, *Old Bullion Benton* (New York: Russell & Russell, 1956), pp. 213–14; Cole, *Martin Van Buren*, pp. 269–72, 281; Anthony Comegna, "'The Dupes of Hope Forever,'" Doctoral dissertation in history, University of Pittsburgh, (2016), pp. 39–41; Hummel, *Emancipating Slaves*, p. 26.

Grande River, land Texans never homesteaded. Jackson would only recognize the young republic if Congress requested it, instead preferring that Mexico or a European power do it first. Unfortunately, despite efforts by Congressman Churchill Cambreleng and Senator Silas Wright, in March 1837, Congress passed resolutions favoring recognition and Jackson appointed a representative to the country.[16]

Fortunately, the noninterventionist President Van Buren rebuffed Texas President Sam Houston's annexation pleas, insisting that the Constitution did not authorize the acquisition of independent countries. Van Buren might have been able hold the line in the early 1840s if he had won reelection. Instead, Tyler wanted to achieve presidential glory by acquiring Texas. After the Whigs resigned from the cabinet en masse, save for Secretary of State Webster, Tyler surrounded himself with a pro-annexation group of advisors. They included Virginia judge Nathaniel Beverly Tucker, his new Secretary of the Navy Abel Upshur of Virginia (who eventually became secretary of state), Massachusetts' Congressman Caleb Cushing (whom Tyler unsuccessfully tried to appoint treasury secretary three times), and Virginia congressmen Henry Wise and Thomas Gilmer (who later served as secretary of the Navy). Like other annexationists, these advisors had a vested interest in the question.[17]

The holders of Texas debt formed the first pro-annexation group. During its war for independence, Texas sold bonds at highly depreciated rates. In the early 1840s, the debt sold for less than 10 percent of its face value, standing at $10 million. Speculators, most prominently Nicholas Biddle, who bought debt for himself and the Bank of the United States of Pennsylvania, hoped for a Hamiltonian bailout. Admittedly, financial distress after the Panic of 1837 forced the Whig to sell much of his personal holdings, but he still vigorously pushed for annexation to benefit his former central bank (after the institution failed in 1841, its creditors owned the Texas debt). Other prominent speculators included James Hamilton, a former governor of South Carolina; John Slidell, a Louisiana congressman; William S. Wetmore,

[16] John Belohlavek, *"Let the Eagle Soar!"* (Lincoln: University of Nebraska Press, 1985), pp. 113–17, 124–26, 218–23, 230–31, 233–37; Cole, *Martin Van Buren*, pp. 197–98, 201–03, 317–19; Nugent, *Habits of Empire*, pp. 137–54.

[17] John Belohlavek, *Broken Glass* (Kent: The Kent State University Press, 2005), pp. 84–86, 192; Philip Burch, *Elites in American History*, vol. 1 (New York: Holmes & Meier Publishers, 1981), pp. 183–84, 219–20, 299, 303; Hietala, *Manifest Design*, p. 59; Hummel, "Martin Van Buren," pp. 174–76; Nugent, *Habits of Empire*, p. 154.

a New York merchant involved in the China trade; Samuel Swartwout, Jackson's corrupt collector at the New York ports; and Tyler advisors Gilmer and Tucker, the latter of whom candidly admitted that "his own large interests" influenced his view on Texas.[18] These men were not fringe lobbyists.[19]

Land speculators also pushed for annexation. If the independent Texas joined the Union, the decrease in international cotton competition would increase land values. Biddle, who acquired large Texas landholdings, also led these lobbyists. He ardently wanted the United States to control the Atlantic, Pacific, Caribbean, Gulf of Mexico, and Isthmus of Panama. After annexation, Tyler candidly credited Biddle's "bright and accomplished mind" with emphasizing the "value of the virtual monopoly of the cotton plant."[20] Other important land speculators included Gilmer, Tucker, and Senator Walker, who acquired large Texas landholdings from his brother. In the early 1840s, financial difficulties forced Walker to sell his investments, but he successfully convinced his two close friends Gwin and John F. H. Claiborne to purchase six hundred thousand acres. Like Biddle, Walker stressed that an independent Texas would turn into "a great rival in the cotton markets of the world," a threat that had to be stopped.[21]

Lastly, the slave interests desired Texas. Southerners feared that an independent Texas would be susceptible to British abolitionism, leading to a significant drain of escaping southwestern slaves. In reality, southerners widely overestimated the extent of British antislavery designs, but that did not stop paranoid southerners from wanting to acquire the region to strengthen the Constitution's fugitive slave protection. Prominent southern politicians, most of whom owned slaves, raised the slavery argument. Jackson, firmly on the annexationist side

---

[18] Joseph Dorfman, *The Economic Mind in American Civilization,* vol. 2 (New York: Viking Press, 1946), p. 915.

[19] Cohen, *Business and Politics,* pp. 128–29; Thomas Govan, *Nicholas Biddle* (Chicago: The University of Chicago Press, 1959), pp. 353–54, 396, 409–11; Holman Hamilton, "Texas Bonds and Northern Profits," *The Mississippi Valley Historical Review* (March 1957): 582–83, 586–87; Charles Sellers, *James K. Polk, Continentalist* (Princeton, NJ: Princeton University Press, 1966), pp. 171–72; Elgin Williams, *The Animating Pursuits of Speculation* (New York: Columbia University Press, 1949), pp. 33, 100–01, 119, 139, 141, 171, 208.

[20] Williams, *Pursuits of Speculation,* p. 159.

[21] Hietala, *Manifest Design,* p. 66. See also Burch, *Elites in American History,* 1, pp. 190, 193, 220, 222–24; Govan, *Nicholas Biddle,* pp. 353, 409–10; Shenton, *Robert John Walker,* pp. 12–13, 22, 32–34; Williams, *Pursuits of Speculation,* p. 108.

in the mid-1840s, noted that a free Texas would make "slaves in the great valley of the Mississippi worth nothing, because they would all run over to Texas."[22] Tyler, Upshur, Gilmer, and Walker agreed. Above all, pro-slavery clamor came from Calhoun, who became Tyler's secretary of state in March 1844. In a letter to the British ambassador to the United States, Calhoun described slavery as a "wise and humane" institution and annexation as "the most effectual, if not the only, means of guarding against" British abolitionism.[23] Calhoun's remarks served as a veritable bomb scare that brought the slavery issue to the forefront of American politics.[24]

Matters rapidly reached a fever pitch in 1844, when Calhoun presented an annexation treaty that included debt assumption. Opponents knew it would lead to war because Mexico held a better claim to the Rio Grande lands. Clay announced opposition to immediate annexation to prevent hostilities with Mexico. However, after securing the Whig nomination, he weakened his stance because of campaign manager Leslie Combs, a significant owner of Texas debt. At the same time, Van Buren, the presumptive Democratic nominee, announced his opposition. Heroically, the New Yorker refused to give into "the lust of power, with fraud and violence in the train, [which] has led other and differently constituted governments to aggression and conquest."[25] Van Buren's supporters, particularly Wright, Tilden, and Francis Preston Blair, knew they witnessed his finest hour. Surprisingly, Benton, formerly a staunch annexationist, agreed with Van Buren, because proponents of "Texas scrip and land speculation" had joined forces with southern sectionalists.[26] Disastrously, the pro-annexation Jackson and Polk split with Benton and Van Buren, depriving the latter of the nomination.

In the Senate, Benton unleashed what William Chambers described as "a pyrotechnic attack."[27] He thundered that the administration, in agreeing with Texas' land claims, attempted to seize "two

---

[22] Hietala, *Manifest Design*, p. 24.

[23] Matthew Karp, *This Vast Southern Empire* (Cambridge, MA: Harvard University Press, 2016), pp. 94–95.

[24] Hietala, *Manifest Design*, pp. 18, 22–24; Karp, *Vast Southern Empire*, pp. 83–95.

[25] Hummel, "Martin Van Buren," pp. 173–74.

[26] Chambers, *Old Bullion Benton*, p. 271.

[27] Ibid., p. 275.

thousand miles of a neighbor's dominion."[28] The "ratification of the treaty," he roared, would lead to "war between the United States and Mexico."[29] This war would be "unjust in itself—upon a peaceable neighbor—in violation of treaties and of pledged neutrality—unconstitutionally made."[30] The Missourian also declared that while he supported slavery, he opposed the institution's *"extension* into regions where it was never known."[31] After fierce debate, the Senate flatly refused annexation. Whigs overwhelmingly opposed while Democrats split, with Benton and Wright in the minority. Subsequently, Benton proposed his own annexation treaty, dividing Texas into half free and half slave and authorizing the president to negotiate with Mexico over the boundary, but the Senate failed to act.

When Polk won the presidential election, annexation appeared increasingly likely. The emboldened Tyler and Calhoun treated Polk's victory as a mandate and decided to secure annexation through a joint congressional resolution, spearheaded by Illinois' Representative Stephen Douglas and Senator Walker. Barnburner Democrat Congressman George Rathbun sarcastically remarked how "surprising" is was that Secretary Calhoun, the supposed "standard-bearer of strict construction," supported this approach.[32] When the Senate narrowly voted 27-25 for the resolution in February 1845, Benton supported annexation after obtaining assurances that Tyler would not act and Polk would cautiously press for boundary negotiations. Unfortunately, Tyler wanted the credit and quickly sent over Andrew Jackson Donelson, nephew of the former president, to initiate annexation. Polk happily agreed, sending Archibald Yell and Charles Wickliffe to assist, providing them secret executive funds to speed up arrangements. Even worse, the new president, eyeing California, started to position troops in the Southwest to provoke a war between Texas and Mexico. Benton bitterly criticized Tyler and Polk's treacherous lies.

Although debt speculators did not secure assumption under the second annexation movement, their goal seemed far more achievable now that the Union included Texas. Consequently, in the ensuing years, new speculators gobbled up the debt, including the prominent

---

[28] Ibid.

[29] Ibid.

[30] Ibid.

[31] Ibid., p. 276.

[32] Karp, *Vast Southern Empire*, p. 98.

bankers and financial houses Jay Cooke, W. W. Corcoran, and Drexel & Co. However, annexation benefited the other interests immediately: Texas land values soared, and in July 1845 British officials in the new state noted that slave prices "have risen in value at least 30 per Cent."[33] The United States moved closer to a cotton monopoly and strengthened slavery protections.[34]

To his credit, Polk still wanted to dismantle the American System, diligently securing the Independent Treasury, the Walker Tariff, and anti-internal improvements victories. But, thanks to Texas annexation, he also aggressively provoked Mexican hostilities. As far as the president was concerned, the imperial executive could secure additional—and far larger—land holdings than Texas.

Western Ports on the Pacific Coast

In the 1840s, Democrats abandoned their peace and noninterventionism, siding with northern merchants to build an international empire. Equipped with the Monroe Doctrine, they intervened in the Gulf of Mexico, the Caribbean, Hawaii, and China. Furthermore, Jacksonians strategized how to aggressively take Oregon from Great Britain and California from Mexico. While expansionists settled for less than the whole loaf in the Pacific Northwest, Polk used Texas annexation to singlehandedly provoke a war of plunder by moving troops into Mexican territory. In doing so, he transformed the presidency into an emperorship.

In 1845, the newspaper editor John O'Sullivan used the term "manifest destiny" to describe the seemingly inexorable control of North America by the United States.[35] Initially, the Van Burenite envisioned this being accomplished through the peaceful settlement of homesteading pioneers would form autonomous governments that would then petition for annexation. In addition, O'Sullivan supported general incorporation laws for private transportation networks across the country. O'Sullivan's libertarian program for expansion bore clear

[33] Karp, *Vast Southern Empire*, p. 109.

[34] Chambers, *Old Bullion Benton*, pp. 271–91; Cohen, *Business and Politics*, pp. 129–31; Cole, *Martin Van Buren*, pp. 393–94; Hietala, *Manifest Design*, pp. 47–49, 224; Karp, *Vast Southern Empire*, pp. 106–09; Robert Remini, *Andrew Jackson*, vol. 2 (New York: History Book Club, 1998), pp. 5–6; Wilentz, *Rise of American Democracy*, p. 595; Williams, *Pursuits of Speculation*, pp. 139, 165–83.

[35] Hietala, *Manifest Design*, p. 255.

similarities with Thomas Jefferson's Empire of Liberty and should have formed the basis for the Democrats' expansionism. But, once again, it was just too much land. The power of such a vast territory quickly tempted O'Sullivan, and only a year later he jettisoned peaceful gradualism and swung to rapid aggression. O'Sullivan was merely keeping up with the main currents driving US expansion: top-down aggression by political and business elites to secure lucrative ports on the Pacific coast, or what Norman Graebner calls "ocean frontage" for an "Asiatic mercantile empire."[36]

Commerce with China, particularly in textile goods, grew tremendously in the 1830s. This caused merchants and manufacturers, especially the Boston Associates, to lobby for three privileges. First, they wanted a stronger navy that could protect American commerce abroad. Second, they advocated "assertive" diplomacy (i.e., negotiations backed by the intimidating US Navy) in Asia to forcibly open markets and establish US dominance. Third, they wanted ports on the West Coast, particularly in the Oregon Country (near modern-day Seattle) and California's San Francisco and San Diego Bays. These goals would increase the political and economic strength of the American Empire and allow it to exert a domineering imperialism over the world.

Northern businessmen were not the only factions looking to benefit from a strong navy. With the new pro-slavery South, many southerners supported a strong navy in the Caribbean to sooth exaggerated fears of creeping British abolitionism. This stood in sharp contrast to years past, when Macon and Randolph vigorously fought naval appropriations. As a sign of how the times had changed, the New Orleans *Commercial Bulletin* now believed that the "meddling spirit of Great Britain" over slavery violated the Monroe Doctrine.[37] The South particularly fretted that the potential abolition of Cuban slavery could lead to US abolition. An additional motivation was that many prominent southerners, such as Calhoun and Whig congressional naval advocate Thomas Butler King of Georgia, had close relatives involved

---

[36] Norman Graebner, *Empire on the Pacific* (New York: The Ronald Press Company, 1955), pp. 26–27. See also Yonatan Eyal, *The Young America Movement and the Transformation of the Democratic Party* (New York: Cambridge University Press, 2007), pp. 73–75, 129–30; Hietala, *Manifest Design*, p. 255; Kelley, *Cultural Pattern in American Politics*, pp. 181–82.

[37] Karp, *Vast Southern Empire*, p. 67.

in Cuba businesses. As a result of the South's prodding, the US fortified slavery on the island by informally allying with Spain and dispatching US warships to Havana.[38]

The navy sympathetically listened to businessmen's demands. In the 1830s, a new crop of officers—Matthew C. Perry, Matthew F. Maury, Alexander Slidell Mackenzie, and Robert Stockton—wanted the government to mimic Great Britain and play what John Schroeder describes as "an active and integral role in the extension of the nation's overseas commercial empire."[39] Indicative statements of the new dispensation come from Mackenzie. In 1837, he trumpeted that the navy should "follow the adventurous trader, in his path of peril, to every sea with cruisers ready to spread over him the protecting flag of the republic!"[40] Translation: strong arm other nations in to trade agreements and offload the mercantile business' market risk onto the US taxpayer. But unfortunately for Mackenzie, the US only possessed the eighth-ranked navy, and increasing naval expenditures did not interest Van Buren.

Matters changed with Tyler and Secretary of the Navy Abel Upshur. "A commerce such as ours," Upshur opined, "*demands* the protection of an adequate naval force."[41] Upshur recruited a crucial ally in one of Tyler's associates, Massachusetts Whig Congressman Caleb Cushing. He was the son of John N. Cushing, a wealthy merchant in the Pacific Northwest and China trade. Furthermore, Caleb's cousin was John Perkins Cushing, a China merchant and textile manufacturer whose uncle was Thomas H. Perkins, a major behind-the-scenes Boston Associate in the Era of Corruption's foreign policy. Clearly, the Cushing family supported a strong navy.[42]

With Cushing's backing, in 1841, Upshur advocated that Congress increase naval expenditures by 50 percent, establish a naval base in the independent Hawaii, create a naval academy, and reorganize the Department of the Navy. The Whig Congress agreed with

---

[38] Ibid., pp. 40, 59–68; Lindsay Regele, *Manufacturing Advantage* (Baltimore, MD: The Johns Hopkins University Press, 2019), p. 140; John Schroeder, *Shaping a Maritime Empire* (Westport, CT: Greenwood Press, 1985), pp. 8, 59.

[39] Schroeder, *Shaping a Maritime Empire*, p. 42.

[40] Ibid., p. 43.

[41] Hietala, *Manifest Design*, p. 57.

[42] Belohlavek, *Broken Glass*, p. 154; Burch, *Elites in American History*, 1, pp. 184, 203, 219–20; Regele, *Manufacturing Advantage*, pp. 141–42; Schroeder, *Shaping a Maritime Empire*, pp. 42–43.

most of Upshur's demands, increasing naval expenditures by 40 percent from 1841 to 1842, along with centralizing control in the secretary. The $8.4 million for the Navy Department in 1842 was its largest peacetime appropriation up to that time, consuming 33 percent of the federal budget. When it came to achieving their goals, the New England merchants were right on schedule. They moved to their second goal: strong-armed Asian diplomacy. In particular, merchants no longer wanted to assume the market risks of the China trade they had conducted since the 1780s. Influential northeastern businessmen, particularly Thomas H. Perkins, Gideon Nye, and Asa Whitney, had already initiated lobbying efforts in the late 1830s.[43]

In December 1842, Tyler urged Congress to appoint a China diplomat to secure trade advantages. He and Cushing also stressed the importance of the rest stop, Hawaii, extending the Monroe Doctrine to the independent country. In early 1843, Adams steered a $40,000 appropriation for a Chinese mission through the House. Adams, an old friend of Thomas H. Perkins, was so bellicose toward China that he supported Britain's war against the decaying Asian empire because it opened up trade opportunities. In the Senate, Benton fought the measure even though his state benefited from the China trade, recognizing that the appropriation was excessive and the treaty superfluous. "Forty thousand dollars," Benton grumbled, "to enable one of our citizens to get to Peking, and to bump his head nineteen times on the ground, to get the privilege of standing up in the presence of his majesty of the celestial empire."[44] But the Senate passed the appropriation. Webster appointed Cushing as the emissary (Cushing had loaned Webster considerable amounts of money over the years) and his oldest son, Fletcher Webster, as his assistant.

Cushing and Congress worried about the influence of Britain over China. Their fears should have been allayed when they found out that the British in 1843 had negotiated a Chinese treaty that granted favored nation status to all foreign merchants. Cushing, however, had travelled a long way (he arrived in February 1844) and wanted his glory. When Chinese officials declined Cushing, he sent the navy

[43] Belohlavek, *Broken Glass*, p. 151; Hietala, *Manifest Design*, pp. 57–58; *Historical Statistics*, 5, pp. 91, 200; Karp, *Vast Southern Empire*, pp. 32–49; Schroeder, *Shaping a Maritime Empire*, pp. 59–66; William Williams, *The Contours of American History* (Cleveland, OH: World Publishing Company, 1961), p. 272.

[44] Belohlavek, *Broken Glass*, p. 153.

to deliver his "courtesy call."[45] The Chinese understood the subtle but forceful threat and signed the Treaty of Wanghia, ratified by the Senate in early 1845. The treaty formalized trade relations with China but also implicitly established the US as the dominant negotiator, providing the opening wedge to future interventions on behalf of American business. When debating the treaty, Benton considered Cushing a belligerent whose "revolting" conduct "attracted the general reprobation of the country."[46]

The third and most challenging goal for the mercantile and manufacturing community was securing western ports, either in the Pacific Northwest or more preferably San Francisco. Matters grew complicated when national attention shifted to Texas and Polk secured the presidency. First, the Boston Associates maintained few business connections in Texas and believed the acquisition would make it harder to obtain San Francisco from Mexico. In fact, Webster believed that San Francisco was "twenty times as valuable" as Texas and resigned his position in 1843 over the growing controversy (he was soon succeeded by the pro-Texas Upshur).[47] Second, though expansionist Democrats wanted Pacific commerce, their bellicosity worried Whig businessmen, who wanted to first try peaceful purchase before resorting to "other" options. As John Cushing stated in 1846, the US must obtain San Francisco "by purchase or some other way" (the only alternative to peaceful resolution is violent conflict).[48] Consequently, Whigs played the role of the Federalist opposition party and fought everything Polk did. Despite these difficulties, the northeastern business community still managed to exert considerable influence over the administration's policies.[49]

Oregon, jointly occupied by the British and Americans since the 1820s, was the first target. Americans had only settled up to the Columbia River, significantly below the lucrative Strait of Juan de Fuca and the Puget Sound. To make matters worse, many reasoned that Oregon

---

[45] Ibid., 165.

[46] Belohlavek, *Broken Glass*, p. 183. See also pp. 151–67, 183; Samuel Bemis, *John Quincy Adams and the Union* (Norwalk, CT: The Easton Press, 1987), pp. 484–85; Burch, *Elites in American History*, 1, p. 228; Hietala, *Manifest Design*, pp. 59–61.

[47] Graebner, *Empire on the Pacific*, p. 99.

[48] Belohlavek, *Broken Glass*, p. 417.

[49] Burch, *Elites in American History*, 1, p. 183; Graebner, *Empire on the Pacific*, pp. 39, 71; Hietala, *Manifest Design*, pp. 73–74, 80–81; Michael Holt, *The Rise and Fall of the American Whig Party* (New York: Oxford University Press, 1999), pp. 232–33.

would form its own independent government and compete with the United States in the Pacific trade. Consequently, the mercantile community wanted Congress to secure the Strait and solidify their control. Since the late 1830s, John Cushing continually advocated to his son the need for a government settlement on the Columbia River, which Caleb relayed to Congress. In early 1845, Boston Associate William Sturgis emphasized the commercial importance of the Strait of Juan de Fuca, and only a couple of months later Polk received documents written by Asa Whitney, who warned how an independent Oregon could turn into "our most dangerous and successful rivals in the commerce of the world."[50]

Although Polk privately recognized Oregon's "fine harbors," in his inaugural address the president sided with the grandiose expansionism of western Democrats, who ridiculously demanded Oregon all the way up to Russian Alaska, land the British clearly controlled.[51] Furthermore, in his December 1845 address to Congress, Polk championed the Monroe Doctrine. This earned him the support of the Whig Congressman Adams as well as Democratic Congressman Stephen Douglas and Michigan's Senator Lewis Cass. However, Polk's position worried northeastern merchants because they only wanted the Strait, not war with Great Britain. Pro-slavery southerners satisfied with Texas, such as Senator Calhoun, also feared confrontation with abolitionist Great Britain. Senator Benton, one notable Democrat who broke sectional ranks, wrote to Van Buren stressing peace while criticizing the western Democrats' demands. Debate continued until mid-1846, even after the United States declared war on Mexico. Polk, realizing the dangers of a two-front war, agreed to a British compromise that ceded land up to the Strait. Thus, the United States risked hostile confrontation to build a northwestern port even with no American settlements above the Columbia River. Walter Nugent appropriately comments on the entire affair: "The Americans no doubt did get more than they deserved, if 'deserved' is a function not only of discovery but of settlement."[52]

---

[50] David Pletcher, *The Diplomacy of Annexation* (Columbia: University of Missouri Press, 1973), p. 224.

[51] Graebner, *Empire on the Pacific*, p. 105.

[52] Nugent, *Habits of Empire*, p. 182. See also Belohlavek, *Broken Glass*, pp. 93–95; Bemis, *Adams and the Union*, pp. 488–92; Chambers, *Old Bullion Benton*, pp. 294–300; Graebner, *Empire on the Pacific*, pp. 25, 126–28; Karp, *Vast Southern Empire*, pp. 105–06; Nugent, *Habits of Empire*, pp. 161, 178–86, 193; Pletcher, *Diplomacy of Annexation*, p. 224.

Oregon controversies aside, the main course for commercial interests was always California, particularly San Francisco. San Diego constituted an important but secondary attraction for merchants. Mexico nominally possessed the huge swath of land encompassed by California and New Mexico (the modern Southwest), where few Mexican or American settlers existed. The proper procedure, then, was O'Sullivan's process of Americans migrating into the region, homesteading the land, and then forming their own governments that seceded from Mexico and petitioned for annexation. This is what Texas did, save for its egregious land grabbing down to the Rio Grande. But the United States discarded this reasonable option in favor of immediate control through coerced purchase or a covert war.

Democrats originally tried to acquire California when they annexed Texas, planning to provoke a war between Texas and Mexico and then annex after the war. Duff Green, an executive agent of Tyler, formulated this plan. In late 1844, Green proposed to Texas officials that they charter the Del Norte Company to conquer California and New Mexico with an army of sixty thousand Indians, led by Green himself. Green naturally wanted some attractive land grants as compensation. But the Texas government shot down Green's absurd proposal. Although Green received no official backing for his plan, it clearly fit in with the Polk administration's desires, which later appointed him during the Mexican War.

The Polk administration renewed efforts after Texas annexation. In April 1845, Secretary of the Navy George Bancroft of Massachusetts dispatched Commodore Robert F. Stockton to southern Texas. Stockton, a wealthy businessman from New Jersey, espoused extremely nationalist views. The Polk administration secretly instructed Stockton to finance an army and incite a war on the border. Clearly, the strong Jacksonian executive had corrupted Polk into implicitly sanctioning an outrageously unconstitutional proposal. However, the president's plan fell through, and Texas annexation brought no immediate war.[53]

---

[53] R. Brockmann, *Commodore Robert F. Stockton* (Amherst, NY: Cambria Press, 2009), pp. 149–54; Burch, *Elites in American History*, 1, pp. 191–92; Hietala, *Manifest Design*, pp. 44–46, 146, 154; Karp, *Vast Southern Empire*, pp. 107–08; Nugent, *Habits of Empire*, pp. 189–91; Price, *War with Mexico*, pp. 43–48, 51, 65, 122–23.

Polk was undeterred: he wanted California for its proximity to China, and he would get it one way or another. He was particularly fearful that the British were scheming to acquire the region (they did not). Consequently, in the fall of 1845, Polk invoked the Monroe Doctrine. He appointed Thomas Larkin, a wealthy New England merchant who traded along the California coast, a secret executive agent to keep an eye on developments, emphasizing "the interests of our commerce and our whale fisheries on the Pacific ocean."[54] He also sent John Slidell to Mexico City to purchase California for up to $25 million. Implicit force backed Slidell's efforts, because Polk concurrently ordered General Zachary Taylor to southern Texas. When Mexico rebuffed Slidell, Polk tightened the noose. He ordered Taylor into the "disputed territory" near the Rio Grande, which was really Mexican land. In other words, Polk invaded Mexico and waited for the enemy to fire the first shot. In March 1846, the president informed Congress that he had stationed two-thirds of the army along the southwestern frontier.

Polk's plan worked: Mexico attacked Taylor in April. The president met with Benton, still a fellow Jacksonian, the next month. The senator told the president he would vote for defense appropriations but not "aggressive war on Mexico" and that Texas had never owned the land Polk sent Taylor's men into.[55] Unfortunately, the president did not care, requesting Congress declare war (for a conflict he had already started) and provide fifty thousand volunteers and $10 million. The emperor declared that he wanted the legislature to "place at the discretion of the Executive the means of prosecuting the war with vigor."[56] To bulldoze over the opposition, Polk's loyal followers limited congressional debate and attached the war declaration to troop appropriations. This ensured that anyone who opposed the war unpatriotically opposed the soldiers on the frontier, hamstringing Benton and other anti-war congressmen. The House limited debate to just two hours and overwhelmingly passed the bill. The Senate quickly followed and only two Whigs dissented. When Polk signed the law, he officially commenced the Mexican War.[57]

---

[54] Graebner, *Empire on the Pacific*, p. 119.

[55] Chambers, *Old Bullion Benton*, p. 306.

[56] Karp, *Vast Southern Empire*, p. 110.

[57] Chambers, *Old Bullion Benton*, pp. 306–08; Graebner, *Empire on the Pacific*, pp. 8, 118–20; Hietala, *Manifest Design*, pp. 84–86; Karp, *Vast Southern Empire*, pp. 107–12; Nugent, *Habits of Empire*, pp. 194–200.

It is clear that presidential power caused the war. Polk sent sitting ducks into Mexican territory to draw enemy fire. The Constitution admittedly gave the president control of the army, but Polk could only justify what he did with an extremely broad interpretation of presidential authority that relied on zero sanction from Congress. The Jacksonian executive, strengthened by vetoes and other actions that dismantled the American System, corrupted its wielders into a war of naked aggression. The president had become an emperor.

With any war comes an increase in government intervention, which opens the door for special-interest wheeling and dealing. Bankers, merchants, promoters of transcontinental internal improvements, and land speculators now plotted their next moves.

The Mexican War

Similarly to the War of 1812, the Mexican War destroyed reform. Admittedly, the Republicans had turned into a party of power long before the conflict, but their war swept away most remaining pockets of dissent. The Mexican War's effects occurred far more suddenly, but the consequences remained the same: the Democrats completely lost their drive to create a limited confederation. The Jacksonians engaged in military maneuvers for merchants, established corrupt alliances with bankers, increased the public debt, and embraced transcontinental internal improvements and new programs for land speculators. The entire enterprise was truly a gigantic catastrophe, and once again, liberty lost and power won.

Polk undisputedly initiated a war of conquest and ruthlessly achieved his goal. The ramshackle Mexican government stood no chance of preventing the United States from capturing strategic ports and large swaths of territory. Furthermore, the conflict was undeniably what Whig Congressman Alexander H. Stephens of Georgia called an "Executive war," and what others labelled "Mr. Polk's War."[58] Polk dragged the nation into the confrontation and, along with his cabinet, commanded the planning. The strict constructionist Polk, corrupted by the Jacksonian presidency, justified his control by arguing that congressmen were only pliant tools for the executive, who was elected by the overall public. Unlike past presidents, Polk defended absolute executive secrecy in foreign policy and actually tried to set

---

[58] Graebner, *Empire on the Pacific*, p. 151 and Wilentz, *Rise of American Democracy*, p. 582.

up a clandestine Mexican coup d'état without any congressional authorization. Clearly, he envisioned himself an emperor conducting the war effort.[59]

From the beginning, the Polk administration focused on the ultimate prize: California's ports. The administration initially wanted only San Francisco and Monterey, but prominent merchants soon persuaded it to secure the rest. In June 1846, Secretary Bancroft wrote to Samuel Hooper, the merchant son-in-law of the Boston Associate William Sturgis, hoping that the navy had seized northern California, "never to be given up."[60] The acquisition pleased Hooper, but he urged Bancroft to also take the southern ports down to San Diego. Only in this way, Hooper noted, would the United States control the California coast's lucrative trade. Bancroft dutifully relayed the orders, and by July Commodores John Sloat and Stockton had seized California's ports. Although the administration kept up the charade of temporary occupation, Sloat told his men that "it is not only our duty to take California, but to preserve it afterwards as a part of the United States."[61] In his December 1847 message, Polk triumphantly proclaimed that California would "shelter . . . merchant vessels employed in the Pacific ocean, [facilitating] . . . an extensive and profitable commerce with China."[62]

In fact, by January of that year the army had conquered California and New Mexico, moving into Mexico proper. The administration hoped for a lightning-strike victory, but Mexican guerrillas resisted. This only emboldened Polk and his cabinet to demand more land and drive deeper into enemy territory. By September, the army had moved into Mexico City. Treasurer Walker championed the All Mexico annexation movement, but most Democrat expansionists balked at such a massive acquisition—at least until enough Americans settled in the region—and the president settled for the Treaty of Guadalupe Hidalgo in early 1848, which "only" ceded California and New Mexico.

But even this was not enough. In spring 1848, Polk flirted with invading the Yucatán Peninsula and even offered Spain an astronomical

---

[59] Hietala, *Manifest Design*, pp. 208, 223; Holt, *Rise and Fall of the American Whig Party*, p. 160; Karp, *Vast Southern Empire*, pp. 112–16;

[60] Graebner, *Empire on the Pacific*, p. 157.

[61] Ibid., p. 158.

[62] Ibid., p. 225. See also pp. 155–58, 224–26; Nugent, *Habits of Empire*, p. 203; Sellers, *James K. Polk, Continentalist*, pp. 422–24.

$100 million for Cuba (recall that Polk previously valued California at $25 million). Senator Henry Foote of Mississippi argued for both acquisitions in the name of "complete control of the Gulf of Mexico, and of all the commerce that floats over its surface . . . [and] the rich monopoly of the East India trade."[63] Unfortunately for Polk and Foote, the upper chamber provided too much resistance to enter the conflict. Spain also flatly refused the paternalistic and domineering offer to purchase Cuba.

These setbacks aside, the president still acquired a considerable amount of land. Including Texas annexation, Oregon, and land taken from Mexico, Polk's acquisitions totaled approximately 800 million acres, more than the Louisiana Purchase's 500 million. The American Empire now had enough territory to dominate surrounding nations and control world trade. No wonder, then, that in 1850 Caleb Cushing, a staunch supporter of the war, declared land "the footstool of our power" and "the throne of our empire."[64] However, the additions required a new nationalizing American System to bind the extremities, providing opportunities for special privileges and redistribution.[65]

First, and most importantly, the military conquests required money. From 1845 to 1848 increases in the military caused government spending to explode by 98 percent, completely wrecking the Jacksonian drive to control expenditures. Commodore Stockton tossed rational cost-benefit analysis to the winds when he declared that it did not matter "if the war were prolonged for fifty years, and cost money enough to demand from us each year half of all that we possess."[66] However, Walker knew that financial difficulties could torpedo the war effort and settled on a simple method of finance: Mexico will pay. Walker proposed that the military seize needed supplies and levy "onerous" and "burdensome" tariffs on Mexican ports.[67] The administration instructed Congress about how the war's yoke must be saddled "upon our enemies, the people of Mexico, and not upon ourselves."[68] But Mexico imported little during the conflict, and Secretary of War William

---

[63] Hietala, *Manifest Design*, p. 248.

[64] Belohlavek, *Broken Glass*, p. 81.

[65] Ibid., pp. 192–93; Hietala, *Manifest Design*, pp. 2, 117–18, 157–59, 211–12, 247–48; Nugent, *Habits of Empire*, pp. 202–04, 210–17.

[66] Brockmann, *Robert F. Stockton*, p. 255.

[67] Price, *War with Mexico*, p. 11.

[68] Ibid., p. 11.

Marcy estimated that captured property totaled less than $4 million (military expenditures for 1847 alone totaled $46 million). These setbacks forced the Treasurer to borrow: the public debt ballooned from $16 million in 1845 to $47 million in 1848 (a 194 percent increase), a serious setback for the Jacksonian economic program. In doing so, Walker greased the wheels for his banker friend W. W. Corcoran of Corcoran & Riggs.

The banking house of Corcoran & Riggs, a previous holder of government deposits during the pet banking system, fought against reinstituting the Independent Treasury. Corcoran previously accrued valuable political capital by befriending Walker and Polk (as well as Walker's nephew James Knox Walker), serving as the president's investment advisor, lending money to his brother William H. Polk, wining and dining leading politicians, and even financing White House refurbishments. Corcoran saw the Mexican War as his opportunity, and earlier predicted that if hostilities broke out his "field for making money will be greatly enlarged."[69] When Walker needed to borrow, Corcoran helped him sell debt. The banker underwrote $15 million of an $18 million loan in 1847 and then another $14 million of a $16 million loan in 1848. From selling both loans, Corcoran personally collected $755,000 in profit, an enormous increase compared to the meager $15,000 he previously earned. After the war, Corcoran served as the Democratic Party's preeminent banker and lobbyist, working behind the scenes for speculators (particularly the holders of Texas debt). Samuel Swartwout referred to him as "the American Rothschild."[70] Corcoran's cozy relationship sabotaged the party's previous victories against the crony banking-government partnership.[71]

Wartime finance aside, a crucial issue emerged over the conquests. Previously, the Louisiana Purchase required internal improvements to keep the environs around the Mississippi River linked with the East. Now, with the coveted western ports on the Pacific Coast, expansionists argued for transcontinental internal improvements. Of

---

[69] Cohen, *Business and Politics*, p. 40.

[70] Williams, *Pursuits of Speculation*, p. 25.

[71] Stuart Brandes, *Warhogs* (Lexington: The University Press of Kentucky, 1997), pp. 65–66; Burch, *Elites in American History*, 1, p. 223; Cohen, *Business and Politics*, pp. 32, 39–62, 96; Janet Coryell, "W.W. Corcoran," in *Encyclopedia of American Business History and Biography*, ed. Larry Schweikart (New York: Facts on File, 1990), p. 148; *Historical*, 5, pp. 80, 91; Shenton, *Robert John Walker*, pp. 94–98.

course, gradual settlement and annexation would have ensured O'Sullivan's solution of private companies performing the job, but violent and swift conquest prodded the Democratic Party into railroad and steamship subsidies.

These schemes even appeared before the war in late 1845: Stephen Douglas advocated land grants to build a railroad from Chicago to San Francisco while James Gadsden at the Memphis Convention urged subsidizing a southern railroad across Texas. In essence, these men wanted Congress to hand them unappropriated land they could construct a railroad on as well as sell at artificially high prices to settlers. The most vigorous proponent of such cronyism was China merchant Asa Whitney, who lobbied Congress to get western land grants for a railroad from Lake Michigan to Oregon.

In 1846, Democrat Senator Sidney Breese of Illinois, chair of the Committee on Public Lands, presented Whitney's petition to the upper chamber. Based on the advice of explorer John C. Fremont, Whitney asked for a land grant sixty miles wide and twenty-four hundred miles long (roughly ninety million acres) to finance the $50 million construction cost. During the war, the merchant pled to Walker that the United States could "for[ce] tribute" and "dictate to all the world."[72] Unfortunately for Whitney, the Mexican War depleted the Treasury's funds and Walker prioritized a railroad through Central America. His proposal also got short shrift in the Senate. Benton, perpetually torn on internal improvements, sided against his son-in-law Fremont, blasting the land grant proposal as "one of the most absurd and ridiculous that could be presented to Congress."[73] But the damage was done, and in the ensuing years, Democrats across the country, not just in the West, supported mass subsidization of railroads to facilitate transportation to the Pacific.[74]

To make matters worse, during the war, Congress sympathetically listened to other proposals for transcontinental internal improvements, particularly steamship subsidies, justifiable on grounds of military necessity. Edward K. Collins wanted government appropriations for his steamships to compete with the British steamships in the Atlantic. Corcoran served as his preeminent lobbyist, and in 1847 and 1848

---

[72] Hietala, *Manifest Design*, p. 200.

[73] Ibid., p. 202.

[74] Graebner, *Empire on the Pacific*, pp. 95–96; Hietala, *Manifest Design*, pp. 91–92, 196–202.

Collins secured a ten-year contract for $385,000 in annual assistance to his New York & Liverpool United States Mail Steamship Company. Prominent stockowners included Corcoran & Riggs and Texas debt speculator William S. Wetmore. Congress also doled out $500,000 in annual assistance to the US Mail Steamship Company and the Pacific Mail Steamship Company to connect the coasts via a railroad through Panama. Congress' actions once again showed that it could not pick winners and losers: the subsidized companies, numb to cost cutting, built expensive and inefficient ships that languished against the private lines of Cornelius Vanderbilt.[75]

Democrats also wanted to secure the western domain by handing it to speculators. In particular, Walker advocated for a new Department of the Interior to administer the booty. The recent discovery of gold in California only magnified the rewards from the new conquests. The Treasurer stressed that new "valuable mineral lands" will increase "the business of the Land Office."[76] In early 1849, Congress responded accordingly and established the new executive department. Furthermore, the legislature equipped a new Commission on Mexican Claims with $3.25 million to handle American claims against Mexico lost during the war. Soon, speculators swooped in and purchased land titles at depreciated rates, hoping to wrangle a bailout. One such speculator and claims agent, Corcoran, proudly admitted that without his lobbying efforts the act "would not have been passed."[77] Indeed, Corcoran relished his newfound prestige and looked forward to similar dominance in the 1850s.[78]

The Mexican War delivered a fatal blow to the Jacksonians. Conquests in the name of imperial commerce blew up the debt and corrupted the Polk administration and the Democratic Party toward banking privileges and transcontinental public works. Before, libertarian Democrats fought statist Whigs, steadily weakening the American System. No more. To add insult to injury, the spoils of war—those massive acquisitions of western territory—dramatically amplified the slavery controversy that had emerged during Texas annexation. Missouri

---

[75] Cohen, *Business and Politics*, pp. 109–13; Burton Folsom and Anita Folsom, *Uncle Sam Can't Count* (New York: HarperCollins Publishers, 2014), pp. 39–50.

[76] Shenton, *Robert John Walker*, p. 120.

[77] Cohen, *Business and Politics*, p. 123.

[78] Ibid., pp. 123–27; Holman Hamilton, *Prologue to Conflict* (Lexington: The University Press of Kentucky, 1964), p. 1; Shenton, *Robert John Walker*, pp. 120–22.

was one thing, and Texas another, but potentially spreading slavery to the Pacific increased sectional tensions like never before.

The Deathknell of Reform

Polk and his cabinet were not motivated to invade Mexico to spread slavery; the Pacific ports always reigned supreme. Even Senator Calhoun remained hesitantly sympathetic to the conflict and absented himself from the initial war declaration, worrying that conquering Mexico would hurt slavery. But this did not stop antislavery activists from insisting on the conflict's pro-slavery cause, such as Congressman Adams, who voted against the war. Critics of slavery formed the significant opposition, albeit a minority: for the most part, Democrats and Whigs supported the war effort and partisan Whigs concentrated their ire upon the Democrats' management.

Opponents of slavery decided to make an early stand. In August 1846, Democratic Congressmen Preston King of New York, a Barnburner, and David Wilmot of Pennsylvania, a Van Burenite sympathizer, attempted to add to a war appropriations bill a proviso forbidding slavery in any territory acquired from Mexico. The Wilmot Proviso set out to accomplish what the Tallmadge Amendment tried to do for the Louisiana Purchase: stop the spread of slavery. But the ever-present desire for a strong and vast empire, and the immense privileges it could grant, led to the defeat of the proviso.

Despite this setback, a revolution in the Democratic Party was in the making. After the moderate Hunker Democrats seized control of the New York party and the nationwide organization rallied behind the expansionist and slavery advocate Lewis Cass of Michigan for the presidency, Barnburners allied with other opponents of slavery and formed the Free Soil Party to oppose the spread of slavery in the West. The party chose none other than Van Buren as its presidential candidate. The Free Soilers remained optimistic, but in 1848, Van Buren failed to carry a single state, amassing only 10 percent of the popular vote against Cass and the victorious Whig candidate, General Zachary Taylor of Virginia.[79]

---

[79] Burch, *Elites in American History*, 1, p. 194; Cole, *Martin Van Buren*, pp. 409–18; Jonathan Earle, *Jacksonian Antislavery and the Politics of Free Soil* (Chapel Hill: The University of North Carolina Press, 2004), pp. 68–75; Karp, *Vast Southern Empire*, pp. 111–21; Wilentz, *Rise of American Democracy*, p. 582.

Van Buren described his decision as "an exceedingly unpleasant but unavoidable sacrifice."[80] Surely the New Yorker did not exaggerate: by leading the Free Soil ticket, he broke with the Democratic Party, the network of anti-crony activists he worked so hard to forge. Put more forcefully, "this tragic split in the Democratic Party," explains Murray Rothbard, cost the organization "its libertarian conscience and drive."[81] The party fell under the sway of aggressive southern expansionists who wanted to continue extending the American Empire into the West and the Caribbean, fortified by a vast system of internal improvements. This certainly could not muster any real anti-crony resistance to the equally pro-slavery Whigs, who also wanted to strengthen the American Empire through protective tariffs and their own transportation projects. No significant laissez-faire party remained, only two groups in favor of special privileges.

The Mexican War, the emergence of the slavery controversy, and Van Buren's Free Soil candidacy led to the ideological disintegration of the Democratic Party and the collapse of reform. Jackson's party remained, but it lost all motivation to weaken the central government, destroy the American System, and stop the American Empire dead in its tracks. The reason for the failed Jacksonian Revolution, as with the ratification of the US Constitution and failed Jeffersonian Revolution, was simple: "[P]ower tends to corrupt and absolute power corrupts absolutely."[82]

---

[80] Cole, *Martin Van Buren*, p. 418.

[81] Rothbard, "Report on George B. DeHuszar," p. 126.

[82] John Acton, *Essays on Freedom and Power* (New York: A Meridian Book, 1955), p. 335.

BIBLIOGRAPHY

Acton, John. *Essays on Freedom and Power.* New York: A Meridian Book, 1955.

Adams, Donald. *Finance and Enterprise in Early America.* Philadelphia: University of Pennsylvania Press, 1978.

American Political Leaders. Washington, D.C.: CQ Press, 2000.

Appleby, Joyce. *Capitalism and a New Social Order.* New York: New York University Press, 1984.

Atack, Jeremy, and Peter Passell. *A New Economic View of American History.* New York: W.W. Norton & Company, 1994.

Bailyn, Bernard. *The Ideological Origins of the American Revolution.* Cambridge, MA: Harvard University Press, 2017.

Banner, James. *To the Hartford Convention.* New York: Alfred A. Knopf, 1970.

Barber, William. "Political Economy and the Academic Setting before 1900." In *Economists and Higher Learning in the Nineteenth Century,* ed. William Barber. New Brunswick, NJ: Transaction Publishers, 1993.

Baxter, Maurice. *Henry Clay and the American System.* Lexington: The University Press of Kentucky, 1995.

Beeman, Richard. *The Old Dominion and the New Nation.* Lexington: The University Press of Kentucky, 1972.

Belko, William. "'A Tax on the Many, to Enrich a Few'." *Journal of the History of Economic Thought.* June 2015.

——. *Philip Pendleton Barbour in Jacksonian America.* Tuscaloosa: University of Alabama Press, 2016.

——. *The Triumph of the Antebellum Free Trade Movement.* Gainesville: University Press of Florida, 2012.

Bellow, Adam. *In Praise of Nepotism.* New York: Doubleday, 2003.

Belohlavek, John. *"Let the Eagle Soar!".* Lincoln: University of Nebraska Press, 1985.

——. *Broken Glass.* Kent: The Kent State University Press, 2005.

Bemis, Samuel. *Jay's Treaty*. New York: Macmillan Company, 1923.

——. *John Quincy Adams and the Foundations of American Foreign Policy*. Norwalk, CT: The Easton Press, 1987.

——. *John Quincy Adams and the Union*. Norwalk, CT: The Easton Press, 1987.

Benson, Lee. *The Concept of Jacksonian Democracy*. Princeton, NJ: Princeton University Press, 1961.

Bilder, Mary. *Madison's Hand*. Cambridge, MA: Harvard University Press, 2015.

Bodenhorn, Howard. "Bank Chartering and Political Corruption in Antebellum New York." In *Corruption and Reform*, ed. Edward Glaeser and Claudia Goldin. Chicago: University of Chicago Press, 2006.

——. *State Banking in Early America*. New York: Oxford University Press, 2003.

Bolt, William. *Tariff Wars and the Politics of Jacksonian America*. Nashville, TN: Vanderbilt University Press, 2017.

Bordewich, Fergus. *The First Congress*. New York: Simon & Schuster, 2016.

Bordo, Michael, and William Phillips. "Faithful Index to the Ambitions and Fortunes of the State." In *Economists and Higher Learning in the Nineteenth Century*, ed. William Barber. New Brunswick, NJ: Transaction Publishers, 1993.

Boyd, Julian. *Number 7*. Princeton, NJ: Princeton University Press, 1964.

Brandes, Stuart. *Warhogs*. Lexington: The University Press of Kentucky, 1997.

Brant, Irving. *James Madison, Father of the Constitution*. New York: The Bobbs-Merrill Company, 1950.

——. *James Madison, Secretary of State*. New York: Bobbs-Merrill Co., 1953.

——. *James Madison, The Nationalist*. New York: Bobbs-Merrill Company, 1948.

——. *James Madison, The President*. New York: Bobbs-Merrill Company, 1956.

Brauer, Kinley. *Cotton versus Conscience*. Lexington: The University of Kentucky Press, 1967.

Breckinridge, S. "Monetary Power and the Constitutional Convention." In *Government's Money Monopoly*, by Henry Holzer. New York: Books in Focus, 1981.

Brockmann, R. *Commodore Robert F. Stockton*. Amherst, NY: Cambria Press, 2009.

Broussard, James. *The Southern Federalists*. Baton Rouge: Louisiana State University Press, 1978.

Brown, Roger. *The Republic in Peril*. New York: Columbia University Press, 1964.

Browning, Andrew. *The Panic of 1819*. Columbia: University of Missouri Press, 2019.

Buchanan, James, and Gordon Tullock. *The Calculus of Consent*. Ann Arbor: The University of Michigan Press, 1962.

Burch, Philip. *Elites in American History*, Volume 1. New York: Holmes & Meier Publishers, Inc., 1981.

Calabresi, Steven, and Larissa Leibowitz. "Monopolies and the Constitution." *Harvard Journal of Law & Public Policy*. Summer 2013.

Campbell, Randolph. "The Spanish American Aspect of Henry Clay's American System." *The Americas*. July 1967.

Campbell, Stephen. *The Bank War and the Partisan Press*. Lawrence: University Press of Kansas, 2019.

Carson, David. "Blank Paper of the Constitution." *Historian*. March 1992.

Cassell, Frank. *Merchant Congressman in the Young Republic*. Madison: The University of Wisconsin Press, 1971.

Chambers, William. *Old Bullion Benton*. New York: Russell & Russell, 1956.

Cohen, Henry. *Business and Politics in America from the Age of Jackson to the Civil War*. Westport, CT: Greenwood Publishing Corporation, 1971.

Cohen, Avner. "Cobden's Stance on the Currency and the Political Forces behind the Approval of the Bank Charter Act of 1844." *European Journal of the History of Economic Thought*. Summer 1998.

Cole, Donald. *A Jackson Man*. Baton Rouge: Louisiana State University Press, 2004.

——. *Martin Van Buren and the American Political System*. Princeton, NJ: Princeton University Press, 1984.

——. *Vindicating Andrew Jackson*. Lawrence: University Press of Kansas, 2009.

Coleman, Aaron. "'A Second Bounaparty?'." *Journal of the Early Republic*. Summer 2008.

Comegna, Anthony. "'The Dupes of Hope Forever'." Doctoral dissertation in history, University of Pittsburgh, 2016.

Conkin, Paul. *Prophets of Prosperity*. Bloomington: Indiana University Press, 1980.

Cornell, Saul. *The Other Founders*. Chapel Hill: The University of North Carolina Press, 1999.

Cost, Jay. *A Republic No More*. New York: Encounter Books, 2015.

Coryell, Janet. "W.W. Corcoran." In *Encyclopedia of American Business History and Biography*, ed. Larry Schweikart. New York: Facts on File, Inc., 1990.

Cunningham, Noble. *The Jeffersonian Republicans*. Chapel Hill: The University of North Carolina Press, 1957.

——. *The Jeffersonian Republicans in Power*. Chapel Hill: The University of North Carolina Press, 1963.

Curott, Nicholas, and Tyler Watts. "A Monetary Explanation for the Recession of 1797." *Eastern Economic Journal*. June 2018.

Dangerfield, George. *The Awakening of American Nationalism*. New York: Harper & Row, 1965.

Dauer, Manning. *The Adams Federalists*. Baltimore, MD: The John Hopkins Press, 1953.

Davis, Joseph. "An Annual Index of U.S. Industrial Production." *Quarterly Journal of Economics*. November 2004.

——. "An Improved Annual Chronology of U.S. Business Cycles since the 1790s." *Journal of Economic History*. March 2006.

De Mesquita, Bruce, and Alastair Smith. *The Spoils of War*. New York: Public Affairs, 2016.

DeConde, Alexander. *This Affair of Louisiana*. New York: Charles Scribner's Sons, 1976.

Devanny, John. "A Loathing of Public Debt, Taxes, and Excises." *Virginia Magazine of History and Biography*. Winter 2001.

Dilorenzo, Thomas J. *Hamilton's Curse*. New York: Three Rivers Press, 2008.

——. *How Capitalism Saved America*. New York: Crown Forum, 2004.

——. "Yankee Confederates." In *Secession, State and Liberty*, ed. David Gordon. New Brunswick, NJ: Transaction Publishers, 1998.

Dorfman, Joseph. *The Economic Mind in American Civilization*, Volume 1. New York: The Viking Press, 1946.

——. *The Economic Mind in American Civilization*, Volume 2. New York: The Viking Press, 1946.

——. "William M. Gouge and the Formation of Orthodox American Monetary Policy." In William Gouge, *A Short History of Paper Money and Banking*. Auburn, AL: Mises Institute, 2007.

Earle, Jonathan. *Jacksonian Antislavery and the Politics of Free Soil*. Chapel Hill: The University of North Carolina Press, 2004.

Edling, Max, and Mark Kaplanoff. "Alexander Hamilton's Fiscal Reform." *William and Mary Quarterly*. October 2004.

Einhorn, Robin. "Patrick Henry's Case Against the Constitution." *Journal of the Early Republic*. Winter 2002.

Ekirch, Arthur. "Democracy and Laissez Faire." *Journal of Libertarian Studies*. Fall 1977.

Ellis, Richard. *The Jeffersonian Crisis*. New York: Oxford University Press, 1971.

——. *The Union at Risk*. New York: Oxford University Press, 1987.

Engerman, Stanley, and Kenneth Sokoloff. "Digging the Dirt at Public Expense." In *Corruption and Reform*, ed. Edward Glaeser and Claudia Goldin. Chicago: The University of Chicago Press, 2006.

Eyal, Yonatan. *The Young America Movement and the Transformation of the Democratic Party*. New York: Cambridge University Press, 2007.

Farrand, Max. *The Records of the Federal Convention of 1787*. New Haven, CT: Yale University Press, 1911.

Feller, Daniel. *The Jacksonian Promise*. Baltimore, MD: The Johns Hopkins University Press, 1995.

——. *The Public Lands in Jacksonian Politics*. Madison: The University of Wisconsin Press, 1984.

Ferguson, E. James. *The Power of the Purse*. Chapel Hill: The University of North Carolina Press, 1961.

Fishlow, Albert. "Internal Transportation in the Nineteenth and Early Twentieth Centuries." In *The Cambridge Economic History of the United States*,

Volume 2, ed. Stanley Engerman and Robert Gallman. New York: Cambridge University Press, 2000.

Fitz, Caitlan. *Our Sister Republics*. New York: W.W. Norton & Company, 2016.

Folsom, Burton. *Empire Builders*. Traverse City, MI: Rhodes & Easton, 1998.

Folsom, Burton, and Anita Folsom. *Uncle Sam Can't Count*. New York: HarperCollins Publishers, 2014.

Ford, Lacy. *Origins of Southern Radicalism*. New York: Oxford University Press, 1988.

Formisano, Ronald. *The Birth of Mass Political Parties*. Princeton, NJ: Princeton University Press, 1971.

Freehling, William. *Prelude to Civil War*. New York: Oxford University Press, 1965.

Garraty, John. *Silas Wright*. New York: Columbia University Press, 1949.

Goodman, Paul. *The Democratic-Republicans of Massachusetts*. Cambridge, MA: Harvard University Press, 1964.

Goodrich, Carter. *Government Promotion of American Canals and Railroads*. New York: Columbia University Press, 1960.

Gordon, David. "George Washington." In *Reassessing the Presidency*, ed. John V. Denson. Auburn, AL: Mises Institute, 2001.

Gouge, William. *A Short History of Paper Money and Banking*. Auburn, AL: Mises Institute, 2007.

Govan, Thomas. *Nicholas Biddle*. Chicago: The University of Chicago Press, 1959.

Graebner, Norman. *Empire on the Pacific*. New York: The Ronald Press Company, 1955.

Grubb, Farley. "Creating the U.S. Dollar Currency Union." *American Economic Review*. December 2003.

Gunn, L. *The Decline of Authority*. Ithaca, NY: Cornell University Press, 1988.

Gutzman, Kevin. *Virginia's American Revolution*. Lanham, MD: Lexington Books, 2007.

Haeger, John. *John Jacob Astor*. Detroit, MI: Wayne State University Press, 1991.

Hamilton, Holman. *Prologue to Conflict*. Lexington: The University Press of Kentucky, 1964.

——. "Texas Bonds and Northern Profits." *The Mississippi Valley Historical Review*. March 1957.

Hamlin, Talbot. *Benjamin Henry Latrobe*. New York: Oxford University Press, 1955.

Hammond, Bray. *Banks and Politics in America*. Princeton, NJ: Princeton University Press, 1957.

Hamowy, Ronald. "Foreword." In *The English Libertarian Heritage*, ed. David Jacobson. San Francisco: Fox & Wilkes, 1994.

Harrison, Joseph. "'Sic Et Non'." *Journal of the Early Republic*. Winter 1987.

Herndon, G. "George Mathews." *The Virginia Magazine of History and Biography*. July 1969.

Hickey, Donald. *The War of 1812*. Chicago: University of Illinois Press, 2012.

Hietala, Thomas. *Manifest Design*. New York: Cornell University Press, 2003.

Higgs, Robert. "Not Merely Perfidious but Ungrateful." *The Independent Review*. Fall 2005.

Historical Statistics of the United States, Colonial Times to 1957. Washington D.C., 1960.

Historical Statistics of the United States, Millennial Edition, Volume 3, ed. Richard Sutch and Susan Carter. New York: Cambridge University Press, 2006.

Historical Statistics of the United States, Volume 5, ed. Richard Sutch and Susan Carter. New York: Cambridge University Press, 2006.

History of Congress. June–July 1812.

Hoffmann, Susan. *Politics and Banking*. Baltimore, MD: The John Hopkins University Press, 2001.

Holdsworth, John. *The First Bank of the United States*. Washington, DC: Government Printing Office, 1910.

Holt, Michael. *The Rise and Fall of the American Whig Party*. New York: Oxford University Press, 1999.

Horsman, Reginald. "On To Canada." *Michigan Historical Review*. Fall 1987.

——. "The Dimensions of an 'Empire for Liberty'." *Journal of the Early Republic.* Spring 1989.

Howe, Daniel. *What Hath God Wrought.* New York: Oxford University Press, 2007.

Hummel, Jeffrey Rogers. "Benefits of the American Revolution." *The Library of Economics and Liberty.* July 2018.

——. *Emancipating Slaves, Enslaving Free Men.* Chicago, IL: Open Court, 2002.

——. "Martin Van Buren." In *Reassessing the Presidency*, ed. John V. Denson. Auburn, AL: Mises Institute, 2001.

——. "Mises, the Regression Theorem, and Free Banking." *Liberty Matters.* January 2014.

——. "The American Militia and the Origin of Conscription." *Journal of Libertarian Studies.* Fall 2001.

——. "The Consequences of a United States Default or Repudiation." In *Economic and Political Change after Crisis*, ed. Stephen Balch and Benjamin Powell. London: Routledge, 2016.

——. "The Jacksonians, Banking, and Economic Theory." *Journal of Libertarian Studies.* Summer 1978.

Hyland, William. *George Mason.* Washington, DC: Regnery History, 2019.

Irwin, Douglas A. *Clashing over Commerce.* Chicago: The University of Chicago Press, 2017.

Jankovic, Ivan. *The American Counter-Revolution in Favor of Liberty.* Switzerland: Palgrave Macmillan, 2019.

Jensen, Merrill. *The Articles of Confederation.* Madison: The University of Wisconsin Press, 1940.

——. *The New Nation.* New York: Alfred A. Knopf, 1950.

Johnson, David. *John Randolph of Roanoke.* Baton Rouge: Louisiana State University Press, 2012.

Johnson, Calvin. "The Dubious Enumerated Power Doctrine." *Constitutional Commentary.* 2005.

——. "The Panda's Thumb." *William and Mary Bill of Rights Journal.* October 2004.

Johnston, Louis, and Samuel Williamson. "What Was the U.S. GDP Then?" *Measuringworth.com.*

Jordan. H. "A Politician of Expansion." *Mississippi Valley Historical Review.* December 1932.

Kahan, Paul. *The Bank War.* Yardley, PA: Westholme Publishing, 2016.

Kaminski, John. *George Clinton.* Madison, WI: Madison House Publishers, 1993.

Karp, Matthew. *This Vast Southern Empire.* Cambridge, MA: Harvard University Press, 2016.

Kauffman, Bill. *Forgotten Founder, Drunken Prophet.* Wilmington, DE: ISI Books, 2008.

Kelley, Robert. *The Cultural Pattern in American Politics.* New York: University Press of America, 1979.

——. *The Transatlantic Persuasion.* New York: Alfred A. Knopf, 1969.

Klarman, Michael. *The Framers' Coup.* New York: Oxford University Press, 2016.

Daniel Klein. "The Voluntary Provision of Public Goods?." *Economic Inquiry.* October 1990.

Klein, Daniel, and John Majewski. "Economy, Community, and Law." *Law & Society Review.* Fall 1992.

——. "Turnpikes and Toll Roads in Nineteenth-Century America." *EH.Net Encyclopedia*, ed. Robert Whaples. February 2008.

Kidd, Thomas. *Patrick Henry.* New York: Basic Books, 2011.

Kirk, Russell. *John Randolph of Roanoke.* Indianapolis, IN: Liberty Fund, 1997.

Kohn, Richard. *Eagle and Sword.* New York: The Free Press, 1975.

Krech, Shepard. *The Ecological Indian.* New York: W.W. Norton & Company, 1999.

Kukla, Jon. *A Wilderness so Immense.* New York: Alfred A. Knopf, 2003.

——. *Patrick Henry.* New York: Simon & Schuster, 2017.

Kulikoff, Allan. "Such Things Ought Not to Be." In *The World of the Revolutionary American Republic,* ed. Andrew Shankman. New York: Routledge, 2014.

Lane, Carl. *A Nation Wholly Free.* Yardley, PA: Westholme Publishing, 2014.

Larson, John. *Internal Improvement.* Chapel Hill: The University of North Carolina Press, 2001.

Lebergott, Stanley. "Changes in Unemployment." In *The Reinterpretation of American Economic History,* ed. Robert Fogel and Stanley Engerman. New York: Harper & Row, 1971.

——. *The Americans.* New York: W.W. Norton & Company, 1984.

Lindert, Peter, and Jeffrey Williamson. "American Incomes Before and After the Revolution." *Journal of Economic History.* September 2013.

Livermore, Shaw. *The Twilight of Federalism.* Princeton, NJ: Princeton University Press, 1962.

Lowenstein, Roger. *America's Bank.* New York: Penguin Press, 2015.

McClanahan, Brion. *How Alexander Hamilton Screwed Up America.* Washington, DC: Regnery History, 2017.

McCoy, Drew. *The Elusive Republic.* Chapel Hill: The University of North Carolina Press, 1980.

McCraw, Thomas. *The Founders and Finance.* Cambridge, MA: The Belknap Press of Harvard University Press, 2012.

McDonald, Forrest. *We The People.* Chicago: The University of Chicago Press, 1958.

McFaul, John. *The Politics of Jacksonian Finance.* New York: Cornell University Press, 1972.

McGrane, Reginald. *Foreign Bondholders and American State Debts.* New York: Macmillan, 1935.

Maass. Richard. "'Difficult to Relinquish Territory Which Had Been Conquered'." *Diplomatic History.* January 2015.

Magliocca. Gerard. "Veto!." *Nebraska Law Review.* 1999.

Magness. Phil. "The American System and the Political Economy of Black Colonization." *Journal of the History of Economic Thought.* June 2015.

Maier, Pauline. *Ratification.* New York: Simon & Schuster Paperbacks, 2010.

Main, Jackson. *The Anti-federalists.* Chapel Hill: The University of North Carolina Press, 2004.

Malanson, Jeffrey. "The Congressional Debate Over U.S. Participation in the Congress of Panama." *Diplomatic History.* November 2006.

Malone, Dumas. *Jefferson and the Ordeal of Liberty.* Boston: Little, Brown and Co., 1962.

——. *Jefferson and the Rights of Man*. Boston: Little, Brown and Co., 1951.

——. *Jefferson the President, First Term*. Boston, MA: Little, Brown and Co., 1970.

——. *Jefferson the President, Second Term*. Boston MA: Little, Brown and Co., 1974.

——. *Jefferson the Virginian*. Boston: Little, Brown and Co., 1948.

Marina, William. "The American Revolution and the Minority Myth." *Modern Age*. Summer 1976.

May, Gregory. *Jefferson's Treasure*. Washington, D.C.: Regnery History, 2018.

Mayer, Henry. *A Son of Thunder*. New York: Grove Press, 1991.

Miller, John. *Alexander Hamilton and the Growth of the New Nation*. New York: Harper & Row, 1959.

——. *The Federalist Era*. New York: Harper & Brothers, 1960.

Monroe, Dan. *The Republican Vision of John Tyler*. College Station: Texas A&M University Press, 2003.

Moore, Grover. *The Missouri Controversy*. Lexington: The University of Kentucky Press, 1953.

Moss, David. *Democracy*. Cambridge, MA: The Belknap Press of Harvard University Press, 2017.

Murphy, Brian. *Building the Empire State*. Philadelphia: University of Pennsylvania Press, 2015.

Napolitano, Andrew P. *Dred Scott's Revenge*. Nashville, TN: Thomas Nelson, 2009.

Natelson, Robert. "Paper Money and the Original Understanding of the Coinage Clause." *Harvard Journal of Law and Public Policy*. Summer 2008.

Nelson, Scott. *A Nation of Deadbeats*. New York: Alfred A. Knopf, 2012.

Nelson, John. *Liberty and Property*. Baltimore, MD: The John Hopkins University Press, 1987.

Nettels, Curtis. *The Emergence of a National Economy*. New York: Holt, Rinehart and Winston, 1962.

Niven, John. *John C. Calhoun and the Price of Union*. Baton Rouge: Louisiana State University Press, 1988.

Nock, Albert Jay *Our Enemy, The State.* Auburn, AL: Mises Institute, 2010.

Nugent, Walter. *Habits of Empire.* New York: Vintage Books, 2009.

O'Connor, Thomas. *Lords of The Loom.* New York: Charles Scribner's Sons, 1968.

Palen, Marc-William. "Free-Trade Ideology and Transatlantic Abolitionism." *Journal of the History of Economic Thought.* June 2015.

Palmer, R.R., and Joel Colton. *A History of the Modern World.* New York: McGraw-Hill, 1995.

Pancake, John. *Samuel Smith and the Politics of Business.* Tuscaloosa: University of Alabama Press, 1972.

Peart, Daniel. *Lobbyists and the Making of US Tariff Policy.* Baltimore, MD: The Johns Hopkins University Press, 2018.

Peskin, Lawrence. *Manufacturing Revolution.* Baltimore, MD: The John Hopkins University Press, 2003.

Philbin, James. "The Political Economy of the Antifederalists." *Journal of Libertarian Studies.* Fall 1994.

Pletcher, David. *The Diplomacy of Annexation.* Columbia: University of Missouri Press, 1973.

Powell, Jim. *The Triumph of Liberty.* New York: The Free Press, 2000.

Pratt, Julius. *Expansionists of 1812.* New York: The Macmillan Company, 1925.

Price, Glenn. *Origins of the War with Mexico.* Austin: University of Texas Press, 1967.

Prince, Carl, and Seth Taylor. "Daniel Webster, the Boston Associates, and the U.S. Government's Role in the Industrializing Process." *Journal of the Early Republic.* Autumn 1982.

Quinn, Sarah. *American Bonds.* Princeton, NJ: Princeton University Press, 2019.

Ratcliffe, Donald. "Popular Preferences in the Presidential Election of 1824." *Journal of the Early Republic.* Spring 2014.

——. *The One-Party Presidential Contest.* Lawrence: University Press of Kansas, 2015.

Redlich, Fritiz. *The Molding of American Banking.* New York: Johnson Reprint Corporation, 1968.

Regele, Lindsay. *Manufacturing Advantage*. Baltimore, MD: The Johns Hopkins University Press, 2019.

Remini, Robert. *Andrew Jackson*, Volume 2. New York: History Book Club, 1998.

——. *Andrew Jackson*, Volume 3. New York: History Book Club, 1998.

——. *Andrew Jackson and His Indian Wars*. New York: Penguin Books, 2001.

——. *Andrew Jackson and the Bank War*. New York: W.W. Norton & Company, 1967.

——. *Daniel Webster*. New York: W.W. Norton & Company, 1997.

——. *Henry Clay*. New York: W.W. Norton & Company, 1991.

——. *John Quincy Adams*. New York: Henry Holt and Company, 2002.

——. *Martin Van Buren and the Making of the Democratic Party*. New York: Columbia University Press, 1959.

——. "Martin Van Buren and the Tariff of Abominations." *American Historical Review*. July 1958.

——. *The Election of Andrew Jackson*. New York: J.B. Lippincott Company, 1963.

——. *The Legacy of Andrew Jackson*. Baton Rouge: Louisiana State University Press, 1988.

Risjord, Norman. *Chesapeake Politics*. New York: Columbia University Press, 1978.

——. *The Old Republicans*. New York: Columbia University Press, 1965.

Roll, Charles. "We, Some of the People." *Journal of American History*. June 1969.

Rosenbloom, David. *Federal Service and the Constitution*. Washington, D.C.: Georgetown University Press, 2014.

Rothbard, Murray N. "America's Two Just Wars." In *The Costs of War*, ed. John V. Denson. New Brunswick, NJ: Transaction Publishers, 1999.

——. *An Austrian Perspective on the History of Economic Thought*, Volume 1, *Economic Thought Before Adam Smith*. Auburn, AL: Mises Institute, 2006.

——. *An Austrian Perspective on the History of Economic Thought*, Volume 2, *Classical Economics*. Auburn, AL: Mises Institute, 2006.

——. "Bureaucracy and the Civil Service in the United States." *Journal of Libertarian Studies*. Summer 1995.

——. *Conceived in Liberty,* Volumes 1–4. Auburn, AL: Mises Institute, 2019.

——. *Conceived in Liberty,* Volume 5, *The New Republic, 1784–1791*, ed. Patrick Newman. Auburn AL, Mises Institute, 2019.

——. "Mercantilism." In *Economic Controversies*. Auburn, AL: Mises Institute, 2011.

——. "Principle in Politics." *Inquiry*. September 1983.

——. "Report on George B. DeHuszar and Thomas Hulbert Stevenson, *A History of the American Republic,* 2 vols." In Murray Rothbard, *Strictly Confidential*, ed. David Gordon. Auburn, AL: Mises Institute, 2010.

——. "The History of Money and Banking Before the Twentieth Century." In Murray Rothbard, *A History of Money and Banking in the United States*, ed. Joseph Salerno. Auburn, AL: Mises Institute, 2002.

——. *The Mystery of Banking*. Auburn, AL: Mises Institute, 2008.

——. *The Panic of 1819*. Auburn, AL: Mises Institute, 2007.

Rousseau, Peter. and Richard Sylla. "Emerging Financial Markets and Early US Growth." *Explorations in Economic History*. January 2005.

Rutland, Robert. *The Birth of the Bill of Rights*. London: Collier-Macmillan, 1962.

Sakolski, Aaron. *The Great American Land Bubble*. New York: Harper & Brothers Publishers, 1932.

Salerno, Joseph T.. "Introduction." In Murray Rothbard, *A History of Money and Banking in the United States*, ed. Joseph Salerno. Auburn, AL: Mises Institute, 2002.

——. "The Neglect of the French Liberal School in Anglo-American Economics." *Review of Austrian Economics*. December 1988.

Schakenbach, Lindsay. "From Discontented Bostonians to Patriotic Industrialists." *The New England Quarterly*. September 2011.

Schlesinger, Arthur M., Jr. *The Age of Jackson*. Boston, MA: Little, Brown and Company, 1945.

Schroeder, John. *Shaping a Maritime Empire*. Westport, CT: Greenwood Press, 1985.

Schwartz, Anna. "The Beginning of Competitive Banking in Philadelphia." In Anna Schwartz, *Money in Historical Perspective*. Chicago: The University of Chicago Press, 1987.

Schwartz, David. "Coin, Currency, and Constitution." *Michigan Law Review*. 2020.

Schweikart, Larry. *Banking in the American South from the Age of Jackson to Reconstruction*. Baton Rouge: Louisiana State University Press, 1987.

——. "Jacksonian Ideology, Currency Control and Central Banking." *The Historian*. November 1988.

Sellers, Charles. *James K. Polk, Continentalist*. Princeton, NJ: Princeton University Press, 1966.

——. *James K. Polk, Jacksonian*. Princeton, NJ: Princeton University Press, 1957.

Shade, William. *Banks or No Banks*. Detroit, MI: Wayne State University Press, 1972.

——. *Democratizing the Old Dominion*. Charlottesville: University Press of Virginia, 1996.

Shankman, Andrew. "'A New Thing on Earth'." *Journal of the Early Republic*. Autumn 2003.

——. *Crucible of American Democracy*. Lawrence: University Press of Kansas, 2004.

Sharp, James. *The Jacksonians versus the Banks*. New York: Columbia University Press, 1970.

Shenton, James. *Robert John Walker*. New York: Columbia University Press, 1961.

Silbey, Joel. *Martin Van Buren and the Emergence of American Popular Politics*. Lanham, MD: Rowman & Littlefield Publishers, 2002.

——. *The Shrine of Party*. Pittsburgh, PA: University of Pittsburgh Press, 1967.

Silverstone, Scott. *Divided Union*. Ithaca, NY: Cornell University Press, 2004.

Siry, Steven. *DeWitt Clinton and the American Political Economy*. New York: Peter Lang, 1990.

Sisson, Daniel. *The American Revolution of 1800*. New York, Alfred A. Knopf, 1974.

Slaughter, Thomas. *The Whiskey Rebellion*. New York: Oxford University Press, 1986.

Sloan, Herbert. *Principle and Interest*. New York: Oxford University Press, 1995.

Spann, Edward. *Ideals and Politics*. Albany: State University of New York Press, 1972.

Stagg, J. "Between Black Rock and a Hard Place." *Journal of the Early Republic*. Autumn 1999.

——. *Mr. Madison's War*. Princeton, NJ: Princeton University Press, 1983.

Stromberg, Joseph R. "Country Ideology, Republicanism, and Libertarianism." *Journal of Libertarian Studies*. Winter 1982.

——. "Mercenaries, Guerrillas, Militias, and the Defense of Minimal States and Free Societies." In *The Myth of National Defense*, ed. Hans-Hermann Hoppe. Auburn, AL: Mises Institute, 2003.

Sylla, Richard. "The Transition to a Monetary Union in the United States." *Financial History Review*. April 2006.

Sylla, Richard, Robert Wright, and David Cowen. "Alexander Hamilton, Central Banker." *Business History Review*. Spring 2009.

Tate, Adam. *Conservatism and Southern Intellectuals*. Columbia: University of Missouri Press, 2005.

Taylor, George. *The Transportation Revolution*. New York: Holt, Rinehart and Winston, 1951.

Temin, Peter. *The Jacksonian Economy*. New York: W.W. Norton & Co., 1969.

Terrell, Timothy. "The Economics of Destutt de Tracy." In Destutt de Tracy, *A Treatise on Political Economy*, ed. Thomas Jefferson. Auburn, AL: Mises Institute, 2009.

Thies, Clifford. "The American Railroad Network during the Early 19th Century." *Cato Journal*. Fall 2002.

Timberlake, Richard. *Gold, Greenbacks, and the Constitution*. Berryville, VA: The George Edward Durell Foundation, 1991.

——. *Monetary Policy in the United States*. Chicago: The University of Chicago Press, 1993.

Tolles, Frederick. *George Logan of Philadelphia*. New York: Oxford University Press, 1953.

Trask, H. Arthur Scott. "Thomas Jefferson." In *Reassessing the Presidency*, ed. John V. Denson. Auburn, AL: Mises Institute, 2001.

Tucker, Glenn. *Dawn Like Thunder*. New York: Bobbs-Merrill Company, 1963.

Tucker, Robert, and David Hendrickson, *Empire of Liberty*. New York: Oxford University Press, 1990.

Unger, Harlow Giles, *Lion of Liberty: Patrick Henry and the Call to a New Nation*. Cambridge, MA: Da Capo Press, 2010.

Van Cleve, George. *We Have Not a Government*. Chicago: The University of Chicago Press, 2017.

Wallis, John. "Constitutions, Corporations, and Corruption." *The Journal of Economic History*. March 2005.

Wallis, John, Richard Sylla, and Arthur Grinath. "Sovereign Debt and Repudiation." *NBER Working Paper Series*. September 2004.

Watkins, William. *Crossroads for Liberty*. Oakland, CA: The Independent Institute, 2016.

——. *Reclaiming the American Revolution*. Oakland, CA: The Independent Institute, 2004.

Watner, Carl. "Libertarians and Indians." *Journal of Libertarian Studies*. Spring 1983.

Watson, Henry. *Liberty and Power*. New York: The Noonday Press, 1990.

Weeks, William. *John Quincy Adams and American Global Empire*. Lexington: The University Press of Kentucky, 1992.

Whaples, Robert. "Were Andrew Jackson's Policies 'Good for the Economy'?" *The Independent Review*. Spring 2014.

White, Lawrence, and George Selgin. "Laissez-Faire Monetary Thought in Jacksonian America." In *Perspectives on the History of Economic Thought*, ed. Donald Moggridge. Aldershot, UK: Edward Elgar, 1990.

White, Lawrence. "William Leggett." *History of Political Economy*. June 1986.

White, Leonard. *The Federalists*. New York: The Macmillan Company, 1948.

——. *The Jacksonians*. New York: The Macmillan Company, 1954.

——. *The Jeffersonians*. New York: The Macmillan Company, 1951.

Wilentz, Sean. *No Property in Man*. Cambridge, MA: Harvard University Press, 2018.

———. *The Rise of American Democracy*. New York: W.W. Norton & Co., 2005.

Williams, Elgin. *The Animating Pursuits of Speculation*. New York: Columbia University Press, 1949.

Williams, William. *The Contours of American History*. Cleveland, OH: World Publishing Company, 1961.

Wilson, Major. *The Presidency of Martin Van Buren*. Lawrence: University Press of Kansas, 1984.

Wishart. David. "Evidence of Surplus Production in the Cherokee Nation Prior to Removal." *Journal of Economic History*. March 1995.

Wood, Gordon. *Empire of Liberty*. New York: Oxford University Press, 2009.

———. *The Creation of the American Republic*. Chapel Hill: The University of North Carolina Press, 1998.

Wood, Nicholas. "John Randolph of Roanoke and the Politics of Slavery in the Early Republic." *Virginia Magazine of History and Biography*. Summer 2012.

Woods, Thomas E, Jr. *Nullification*. Washington, D.C.: Regnery, 2010.

Wright, Robert. *One Nation Under Debt*. New York: McGraw Hill, 2008.

———. "Rise of the Corporation Nation." In *Founding Choices,* eds. Douglas Irwin and Richard Sylla. Chicago: The University of Chicago Press, 2011.

Young, Alfred. *The Democratic Republicans of New York*. Chapel Hill: The University of North Carolina Press, 1967.

Zornow, William. "New York Tariff Policies." *New York History*. January 1956.

INDEX OF SUBJECTS

(compiled by Patrick Newman)

INDEX OF NAMES

(compiled by Patrick Newman)

THE MISES INSTITUTE, founded in 1982, is a teaching and research center for the study of Austrian economics, libertarian and classical liberal political theory, and peaceful international relations. In support of the school of thought represented by Ludwig von Mises, Murray N. Rothbard, Henry Hazlitt, and F.A. Hayek, we publish books and journals, sponsor student and professional conferences, and provide online education. Mises.org is a vast resource of free material for anyone in the world interested in these ideas. For we seek a radical shift in the intellectual climate, away from statism and toward a private property order.

For more information, see mises.org, write us at contact@mises.org, or phone us at 1.800.OF.MISES.

To become a Member, visit mises.org/membership

Mises Institute
518 West Magnolia Avenue
Auburn, Alabama 36832
mises.org

Made in the USA
Monee, IL
19 November 2021